# Lecture Notes in Computer Science 4391

*Commenced Publication in 1973*
Founding and Former Series Editors:
Gerhard Goos, Juris Hartmanis, and Jan van Leeuwen

## Editorial Board

T0223137

Yannis Stylianou   Marcos Faundez-Zanuy
Anna Esposito (Eds.)

# Progress
# in Nonlinear
# Speech Processing

 Springer

Volume Editors

Yannis Stylianou
University of Crete
Computer Science Department
Heraklion, Crete, Greece, 71409
E-mail: yannis@csd.uoc.gr

Marcos Faundez-Zanuy
Escola Universitària Politècnica de Mataró
Barcelona, Spain
E-mail: faundez@eupmt.es

Anna Esposito
Seconda Università di Napoli
Dipartimento di Psicologia
Via Vivaldi 43, 81100 Caserta, Italy
E-mail: iiass.annaesp@tin.it

Library of Congress Control Number: 2007922930

CR Subject Classification (1998): H.5.2, H.5, I.2.6-7, I.4-5, I.2.10, F.4.3

LNCS Sublibrary: SL 6 – Image Processing, Computer Vision, Pattern Recognition, and Graphics

ISSN        0302-9743
ISBN-10     3-540-71503-7 Springer Berlin Heidelberg New York
ISBN-13     978-3-540-71503-0 Springer Berlin Heidelberg New York

Springer is a part of Springer Science+Business Media

springer.com

© Springer-Verlag Berlin Heidelberg 2007
Printed in Germany

Typesetting: Camera-ready by author, data conversion by Scientific Publishing Services, Chennai, India
Printed on acid-free paper    SPIN: 12038923    06/3142    5 4 3 2 1 0

# Preface

The last meeting of the Management Committee of the COST Action 277: "Nonlinear Speech Processing" was held in Heraklion, Crete, Greece, September 20–23, 2005 during the Workshop on Nonlinear Speech Processing (WNSP). This was the last event of COST Action 277. The Action started in 2001. During the workshop, members of the Management Committee and invited speakers presented overviews of their work during these four years (2001–2005) of research combining linear and nonlinear approaches for processing the speech signal. In this book, 13 contributions summarize part of this (mainly) European effort in this field. The aim of this book is to provide an additional and/or an alternative way to the traditional approach of linear speech processing to be used by researchers working in the domain. For all the chapters presented here, except Chaps. 4, 5, and 12, there is audiovisual material available at http://www.ics.forth.gr/wnsp05/index.html, where corresponding lectures and Power Point presentations are available by the authors.

The contributions cover the following areas:

1. Speech analysis for speech synthesis, speech recognition, speech–non-speech discrimination and voice quality assessment
2. Speaker recognition/verification from a natural or modified speech signal
3. Speech recognition
4. Speech enhancement
5. Emotional state detection

## Speech Analysis

Although in many speech applications the estimation of the glottal waveform is very useful, the estimation of this signal is not always robust and accurate. Given a speech signal, the glottal waveform may be estimated through inverse filtering. For certain speech processing areas like the analysis of pathologic voices, where voice quality issues are closely related to the vocal folds activity, an accurate inverse filtering is highly desired. The chapter by Jacqueline Walker and Peter Murphy provides and extensive review on the estimation and analysis of the glottal waveform. The presentation starts with analog inverse filtering approaches and extends to approaches based on nonlinear least squares estimation methods.

Analysis of speech signals provides many features for efficient voice quality assessment. Peter Murphy presents a tool based on the rahmonic analysis of speech for detecting irregularities in synthetic and natural human voice signals. The cepstrum is decomposed into two areas; the low quefrency and the high quefrency. The first rahmonic in the high-quefrency region provides information about the periodicity of a signal. In this chapter, a new measure taking into account all rahmonics in the cepstrum is proposed, and results using synthetic and real speech data are presented providing therefore an additional measure to the usual harmonic-to-noise ratio-related measures for voice quality assessment.

A new tool for spectral analysis of speech signals referred to as chirp group delay is presented by Baris Bozkurt, Thierry Dutoit and Laurent Couvreur. With this tool a certain number of group delay functions are computed in the z-plane on circles different from the usual unit circle. Two important applications of this tool are presented by the authors; formant tracking and a new set of features for the automatic speech recognition task.

Two applications of the so-called neurocomputational speech and sounds processing are presented in the chapter prepared by Jean Rouat, Stéphane Loiselle and Ramin Pichevar. There is evidence that for both the visual and auditory systems the sequence order of firing is crucial to perform recognition tasks (rank order coding). In the first application a speech recognition system based on rank order coding is presented and it is compared against a conventional HMM-based recognizer. In the second application the acoustical source separation is addressed where simultaneous auditory images are combined with a network of oscillatory spiking neurons to segregate and bind auditory objects.

In the chapter presented by Maria Markaki, Michael Wohlmayer and Yannis Stylianou a speech–non-speech classifier is developed based on modulation spectrograms. The information bottleneck method is used for extracting relevant speech modulation frequencies across time and frequency dimensions creating therefore a set of characteristic modulation spectra for each type of sound. An efficient and simple classifier based on the similarity of a sound to these characteristic modulation spectra is presented.

The chapter by Yannis Pantazis and Yannis Stylianou deals with the automatic detection of audible discontinuities in concatenative speech synthesis. Both linear and nonlinear features are extracted at the boundaries of connected speech segments and a list of distances is evaluated. For the evaluation purposes, results from a subjective test for the same task have been taken into account. Among the most promising features for this task are the amplitude and frequency modulations occuring in the spectra of the continuous speech when two perceptually incompatible speech segments are joined. The Fisher linear discriminator seems to perform a high detection score.

## Speaker Recognition/Verification

A review and perspectives on voice disguise and its automatic detection are given in the chapter prepared by Patrick Perrot, Guido Aversano and Gérard Chollet. A list of ways for modifying the quality of voice is presented along with the different techniques proposed in the literature. A very difficult topic is that of automatic detection of disguised voice. The authors describe a list of main indicators that can be used for this task.

Bouchra Abboud, Hervé Bredin, Guido Aversano, and Gérard Chollet present an overview on audio-visual identity verification tasks. Face and voice transformation techniques are reviewed for the face, speaker and talking face verification.

It is shown that rather a limited amount of information can be modified for troubling state-of-the-art audiovisual identity verification systems. An explicit talking face modeling is then proposed to overcome the weak points of these systems.

State-of-the-art systems and challenges in the text-independent speaker verification task are presented in the chapter prepared by Dijana Petrovska-Delacrétaz, Asma El Hannani and Gérard Chollet. Speakers' variability and variabilities on the transmission channel are discussed along with the possible choices of speech parameterization and speaker models. The use of speech recognition for the speaker verification task is also discussed, showing that a development of new services based on speaker and speech recognition is possible.

Marcos Faundez-Zanuy and Mohamed Chetouani present an overview of nonlinear predictive models and their application in speaker recognition. Challenges and possibilities in extracting nonlinear features towards this task are provided along with the various strategies that one can follow for using these nonlinear features. Both nonparametric (e.g., codebook based) and parametric approaches (e.g., Volterra series) are described. A nonlinear extension of the well-known linear prediction theory is provided, referred to as neural predictive coding.

## Speech Recognition

Although hidden markov models dominate the speech recognition area, the support vector machine(SVM) is a powerful tool in machine learning and the chapter by R.Solera-Ureña, J.Padrell-Sendra, D. Martín-Iglesias, A. Gallardo-Antolín, C.Peláez-Moreno and F.Díaz-de-María is an overview of the application of SVMs for automatic speech recognition, for isolated word recognition and for continuous speech recognition and connected digit recognition.

## Speech Enhancement

Considering single and multichannel-based solutions for the speech enhancement task, A. Hussain, M. Chetouani, S. Squartini, A. Bastari and F. Piazza present an overview of the noise reduction approaches focusing on the additive independent noise case. The non-Gaussian properties of the involved signals and the lack of linearity in the related processes provide a motivation for the development of nonlinear algorithms for the speech enhancement task. A very useful table summarizing the advantages and drawbacks of the currently proposed nonlinear techniques is presented at the end of the chapter.

## Emotional State Detection

The use of visual and auditory information for predicting the emotional state of humans is discussed in the chapter by Anna Esposito. Results from subjective tests using a single channel (audio or visual) and combined channels (using both visual and auditory information) are provided. Based on these results, auditory channels outperform visual channels of information in predicting the emotional state of a human being. An information theoretic model is then proposed to support these results.

The editors are grateful to the colleagues who contributed to this book, and to the reviewers for their willingness to review the chapter and provide useful feedback to the authors. We would like also to thank the COST office that provided financial support for the organization of the WNSP in Crete, the University of Crete and the Institute of Computer Science at FORTH for technically supporting the event. Especially, we would like to thank Theodosia Bitzou for designing the logo of the meeting and the folder given to the participants, and Manolis Zouraris, Andreas Holzapfel and Giorgos Kafentzis for organizing the audio-visual material. Finally, we would like to thank Springer, and particularly Alfred Hofmann and Ursula Barth for their help in publishing this post-conference book.

January 2007                                                    Yannis Stylianou
                                                         Marcos Faundez-Zanuy
                                                                Anna Esposito

# Organization

WNSP 2005 was organized by the department of Computer Science, Univeristy of Crete, the Institute of Computer Science of the Foundation for Research and Technology Hellas (FORTH), and the COST (European Cooperation in the field of Scientific and Technical Research) office.

## Scientific Committee

| | |
|---|---|
| Gérard Chollet | ENST Paris, France |
| Thierry Dutoit | FPMS, Mons, Belgium |
| Anna Esposito | 2nd University of Napoli, Italy |
| Marcos Faundez-Zanuy | EUPMT, Barcelona, Spain |
| Eric Keller | University of Lausanne, Switzerland |
| Gernot Kubin | TUG, Graz, Austria |
| Petros Maragos | NTUA, Athens, Greece |
| Jean Schoentgen | University Libre Bruxelles, Belgium |
| Yannis Stylianou | University of Crete, Greece |

## Program Committee

| | |
|---|---|
| Conference Chair | Yannis Stylianou (University of Crete, Greece) |
| Organizing Chair | Yannis Agiomyrgiannakis (University of Crete, Greece) |
| Audio-Video Material | Manolis Zouraris (University of Crete, Greece) |
| Local Arrangements | Maria Markaki (University of Crete, Greece) |

## Sponsoring Institutions

COST Office, Brussels, Belgium
University of Crete, Heraklion, Crete, Greece
Institute of Computer Science, FORTH, Heraklion, Crete, Greece

# Table of Contents

## Progress in Nonlinear Speech Processing

# A Review of Glottal Waveform Analysis

Jacqueline Walker and Peter Murphy

Department of Electronic and Computer Engineering,
University of Limerick,
Limerick, Ireland
jacqueline.walker@ul.ie,peter.murphy@ul.ie

## 1  Introduction

Glottal inverse filtering is of potential use in a wide range of speech processing applications. As the process of voice production is, to a first order approximation, a source-filter process, then obtaining source and filter components provides for a flexible representation of the speech signal for use in processing applications. In certain applications the desire for accurate inverse filtering is more immediately obvious, e.g., in the assessment of laryngeal aspects of voice quality and for correlations between acoustics and vocal fold dynamics, the resonances of the vocal tract should firstly be removed. Similarly, for assessment of vocal performance, trained singers may wish to obtain quantitative data or feedback regarding their voice at the level of the larynx.

In applications where the extracted glottal signal is not of primary interest in itself the goal of accurate glottal inverse filtering remains important. In a number of speech processing applications a flexible representation of the speech signal, e.g., harmonics plus noise modelling (HNM) [74] or sinusoidal modelling [65], is required to allow for efficient modification of the signal for speech enhancement, voice conversion or speech synthesis. In connected speech it is the glottal source (including the fundamental frequency) that changes under a time-varying vocal tract and hence an optimum representation should track glottal and filter changes. Another potential application of glottal inverse filtering is speech coding, either in a representation similar to HNM, for example (but incorporating a glottal source), or as in [3], [11], [19] applying coding strategies termed glottal excited linear prediction (GELP) which use glottal flow waveforms to replace the residual or random waveforms used in existing code excited linear prediction (CELP) codecs. In the studies cited the perceptual quality of the GELP codecs is similar to that of CELP.

The speaker identification characteristics of glottal parameters have also recently undergone preliminary investigation [64] (note this is quite different from investigating the speaker identification characteristics of the linear prediction residual signal). Identification accuracy up to approximately 70% is reported using glottal parameters alone. Future studies employing explicit combinations of glottal and filter components may provide much higher identification rates. In addition, the more that is understood regarding glottal changes in connected speech

Y. Stylianou, M. Faundez-Zanuy, A. Esposito (Eds.): WNSP 2005, LNCS 4391, pp. 1–21, 2007.

the better this knowledge can be used for speaker identification (or conversely it may lead to improved glottal de-emphasis strategies for speech recognition).

Due to non-availability of a standard, automatic GIF algorithm for use on connected speech (perhaps due to a lack of knowledge of the overall voice production process), representation and processing of the speech signal has generally side stepped the issue of accurate glottal inverse filtering and pragmatic alternatives have been implemented. However these alternatives come at a cost, which can necessitate the recording of considerably more data than would be required if the dynamics of voice production were better understood and the appropriate parameters could be extracted. For example, in existing methods for pitch modification of voiced speech, the glottal parameters are not manipulated explicitly, e.g., in the sinusoidal model a deconvolution is performed to extract the filter and residual error signal. The linear prediction residual signal (or the corresponding harmonic structure in the spectrum) is then altered to implement the desired pitch modification. This zero-order deconvolution ensures that the formant frequencies remain unaltered during the modification process, giving rise to a shape-invariant pitch modification. However, examining this from a voice production viewpoint reveals two important consequences of this approach: to a first approximation, the glottal closed phase changes and eventually overlaps as the fundamental frequency (f0) increases and if the glottal periods are scaled the spectral tilt will change [38]. The former may explain the hoarseness reported in [65] after 20% modification. The solution to this problem has been to record more data over a greater range of f0 and always modify within this limit. Integrating better production knowledge into the system would facilitate modification strategies over a broader range without recourse to such an extensive data set. In what follows, we review the state of the art in glottal inverse filtering and present a discussion of some of the important issues which have not always been at the forefront of consideration by investigators. After first establishing a framework for glottal waveform inverse filtering, the range of approaches taken by different investigators is reviewed. The discussion begins with analog inverse filtering using electrical networks [53] and extends to the most recent approaches which use nonlinear least squares estimation [64]. A brief review of the earliest approaches shows that most of the basic characteristics of the glottal waveform and its spectrum were established very early. There was also interest in developing specialist equipment which could aid recovery of the waveform. With the introduction of the technique of linear prediction and the steady improvement of computing power, digital signal processing techniques came to dominate. Although parametric modelling approaches have been very successful, alternatives to second-order statistics have not been used extensively and have not, so far, proved very productive. As the glottal waveform is a low frequency signal, recording conditions and phase response play a very important role in its reconstruction. However, sufficient attention has not always been paid to these issues. Finally, the question of identifying a good result in the reproduction of such an elusive signal is discussed.

## 2    A Framework for Glottal Waveform Inverse Filtering

Linear prediction is a very powerful modelling technique which may be applied to time series data. In particular, the all-pole model is extensively used. In this model, as shown in (1), the signal is represented as a linear combination of past values of the signal plus some input [47]:

$$s_n = \sum_{k=1}^{p} a_k s_{n-k} + Ap(n) \ . \tag{1}$$

where $A$ is a gain factor applied to the input $p(n)$. In the frequency domain, this model represents an all-pole filter applied to the input:

$$V(z) = \frac{A}{1 + \sum_{k=1}^{p} a_k z^{-k}} \ . \tag{2}$$

As is well known, using the method of least squares, this model has been successfully applied to a wide range of signals: deterministic, random, stationary and non-stationary, including speech, where the method has been applied assuming local stationarity. The linear prediction approach has been dominant in speech due to its advantages:

1. Mathematical tractability of the error measure (least squares) used.
2. Favorable computational characteristics of the resulting formulations.
3. Wide applicability to a range of signal types.
4. Generation of a whitening filter which admits of two distinct and useful standard input types.
5. Stability of the model.
6. Spectral estimation properties.

Applied to the acoustic wave signal, linear prediction is used to produce an all-pole model of the system filter, $V(z)$, which turns out to be a model of the vocal tract and its resonances or formants. As noted above, the assumed input to such a model is either an impulse or white noise, both of which turn out to suit speech very well. White noise is a suitable model for the input to the vocal tract filter in unvoiced speech and an impulse (made periodic or pseudo-periodic by application in successive pitch periods) is a suitable model for the periodic excitation in voiced speech. In the simplest model of voiced speech, shown in Fig. 1, the input is the flow of air provided by the periodic opening and closing of the glottis, represented here by a periodic impulse train $p(n)$. The vocal tract acts as a linear filter, $v(n)$, resonating at specific frequencies known as formants. Speech, $s(n)$, is produced following radiation at the lips represented by a simple differentiation, $r(n)$.

### 2.1    Closed Phase Inverse Filtering

In linear prediction, the input is assumed unknown: the most information we can recover about the input is a prediction of its equivalent energy [47]. As

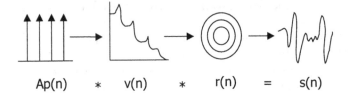

Ap(n)     *     v(n)     *     r(n)     =     s(n)

(a) In the time domain

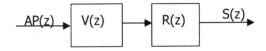

(b) In the Z-domain

**Fig. 1.** Simplest model of voiced speech

a consequence of the least squares modelling approach, two models fit the assumptions of linear prediction: the input impulse and white noise. Both of these inputs have a flat spectrum. In other words, the inverse filter which results from the process is a whitening filter and what remains following inverse filtering is the modelling error or residual. The simplest glottal pulse model is the periodic impulse train [21] as used in the LPC vocoder [78]. However, speech synthesizers and very low bit rate speech coders using only periodic impulses and white noise as excitations have been found to be poor at producing natural sounding speech. To improve speech quality, it has been found useful to code the residual, for example using vector quantized codebooks, in speech coding techniques such as CELP [68], since to the extent that the residual differs from a purely random signal in practice, it retains information about the speech including the glottal waveform.

The linear speech production model can be extended as shown in Fig. 2 so that it includes two linearly separable filters [21]. The glottal excitation, $p\,(n)$ does not represent a physical signal but is simply the mathematical input to a filter which will generate the glottal flow waveform, $g\,(n)$. In this model, lip radiation is represented by a simple differencing filter:

$$R(z) = 1 - z^{-1} \ . \tag{3}$$

and glottal inverse filtering requires solving the equation:

$$P(z)\,G(z) = \frac{S(z)}{AV(z)\,R(z)} \ . \tag{4}$$

To remove the radiation term, define the differentiated glottal flow waveform as the effective driving function:

$$Q(z) = P(z)\,G(z)\,R(z) \ . \tag{5}$$

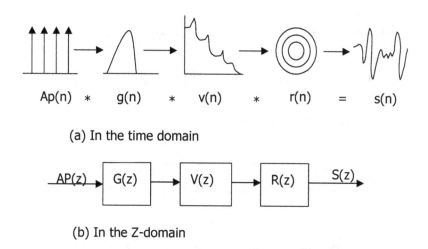

$$Ap(n) \quad * \quad g(n) \quad * \quad v(n) \quad * \quad r(n) \quad = \quad s(n)$$

(a) In the time domain

$$AP(z) \rightarrow \boxed{G(z)} \rightarrow \boxed{V(z)} \rightarrow \boxed{R(z)} \xrightarrow{S(z)}$$

(b) In the Z-domain

**Fig. 2.** The linear speech model with linearly separable source model

as shown in part (a) of Fig. 3. Now, as shown in part (b) of Fig. 3, inverse filtering simplifies to:

$$Q\left(z\right) = \frac{S\left(z\right)}{AV\left(z\right)} \ . \tag{6}$$

To solve for both $Q(z)$ and $V(z)$ is a blind deconvolution problem. However, during each period of voiced speech the glottis closes, $g(n) = 0$, providing an impulse to the vocal tract. While the glottis is closed, the speech waveform must be simply a decaying oscillation which is only a function of the vocal tract and its resonances or formants [81] i.e. it represents the impulse response of the vocal tract. Solving for the system during this closed phase should exactly capture the vocal tract filter, $V(z)$, which may then be used to inverse filter and recover $Q(z)$. $G\left(z\right)$ may then be reconstructed by integration (equivalently by inverse filtering by $\frac{1}{R(z)}$). This approach is known as closed phase inverse filtering and is the basis of most approaches to recovering the glottal flow waveform.

**Early Analog Inverse Filtering.** According to [81], in analog inverse filtering, a "physically meaningful mathematical basis for glottal inverse filtering has not been explicitly applied." (p. 350), rather the glottal closed region was estimated and parameters were adjusted until a smooth enough glottal waveform emerged. This description is perhaps a bit unfair as the first inverse vocal tract filters were analog networks as in [53] which had to be built from discrete components and required laborious tuning. Because of these difficulties, in [53] only the first two formants were considered and removed, which led to considerable ripple in the closed phase of the recovered glottal waveforms. Nevertheless the recovered glottal waveforms were quite recognizable. A ripple on the glottal waveform corresponding to the first formant was also noted a sign of inaccurate first formant

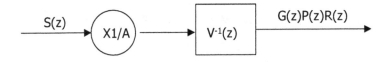

$$Ap(n) \quad * \quad g(n) \quad * \quad r(n) \quad = \quad q(n)$$

(a) In the time domain

S(z) → ⟨X1/A⟩ → [V⁻¹(z)] → G(z)P(z)R(z)

(b) Applied to inverse filtering in the Z-domain

**Fig. 3.** The effective driving function

estimation and a capacitor in the inverse filter network could be adjusted until the ripple disappeared. As well as attempting to recover the glottal waveform in the time domain, it could be modelled in the frequency domain. In [49], a digital computer was used to perform a pitch synchronous analysis using successive approximations to find the poles and zeros present in the speech spectrum. With the assumption of complete glottal closure, there will be discontinuous first derivatives at the endpoints of the open phase of the glottal waveform, 0 and $T_c$, and a smooth glottal waveform open phase (i.e. the second derivative exists and is bounded), it is then shown that the glottal waveform can be modelled by a set of approximately equally spaced zeros $\sigma + j\omega$ where:

$$\sigma = \ln(\frac{-g\prime(T_c-)}{g\prime(0+)}) \tag{7}$$

$$\omega = \frac{\pi}{T_c}(1 \pm 2n) \tag{8}$$

Thus, the vocal tract is modelled by poles and the glottal waveform by zeros. Despite its simplicity, this approach to finding a model of the glottal waveform has not often been pursued since. Most pole-zero modelling techniques are applied to find vocal tract zeros, especially those occurring in nasal or consonant sounds. Furthermore, it is often pointed out that it is not possible to unambiguously determine whether zeros 'belong' to the glottal waveform or the vocal tract. However, there are exceptions [48].

Glottal waveform identification and inverse filtering with the aim of developing a suitable glottal waveform analog to be used in speech synthesis was first attempted in [66]. In this work, inverse filtering was performed pitch synchronously over the whole pitch period. A variety of waveforms ranging from simple shapes such as a triangle and a trapezoid through to piecewise sinusoids which more closely matched the inverse filtered glottal waveform shape were used to synthesize speech which was assessed for naturalness in listening tests. It was found that the shapes which produced the most natural sounding speech had a spectral decay of 12 dB/octave: consistent with continuous functions with discontinuous first and higher order derivatives, as postulated by [49].

**Approaches Requiring Special Equipment.** The Rothenberg mask was introduced to overcome some of the perceived difficulties with inverse filtering, in particular: susceptibility to low frequency ambient noise, the difficulty of amplitude calibration and the inability to recover the correct DC offset level [67]. The mask is a specially vented pneumotachograph mask which permits direct measurement of the oral volume velocity and so, by eliminating the lip radiation component, removes the pole at DC in the inverse filter. According to [67], knowledge of the glottal waveform down to DC allows for periods of glottal closure to be identified absolutely, rather than by the relative flatness of the wave. The main disadvantage of the mask is its limited frequency response which extends to only 1 kHz and limits its ability to reasonably resolve glottal waveforms to those with a fundamental frequency of at most about 200 Hz [67]. While not limiting its applicability entirely to the speech of adult males, this does make its range "somewhat inadequate for most female speakers and for children." ([67], p. 1637). However, the Rothenberg mask has been applied to study glottal waveforms in female speakers [33]. While useful for precise laboratory-based studies, inverse filtering using the Rothenberg mask is obviously not suited to many other applications such as speech coding and speaker identification as it requires special equipment, trained operators and takes some time to apply.

A second equipment based approach was introduced by Sondhi [70] who pointed out that speaking into a reflectionless, rigid-walled tube can cancel out the vocal tract contribution allowing the investigator simply to record the glottal waveform directly by a microphone inserted into the wall of the tube. Here, the equipment is relatively cheap and easy to construct and, as for the Rothenberg mask, provides some built-in protection against low frequency ambient noise. A number of subsequent investigations have employed this technique [56], [57], [71]. Compared with the waveforms recovered using the Rothenberg mask, the waveforms recovered using the Sondhi tube have a certain peakiness. A detailed study of the frequency response of the tube set-up in [56] showed that while the tube was effective down to frequencies of 90 Hz, it had a resonance at 50 Hz and the low frequency response (below 50 Hz) had 'additional factors' (quite what these were is not made fully clear, but it could have been simply noise) which were removed by high pass filtering by the microphone and pre-amplifier (at 20 Hz and 30 Hz respectively). Compensation for the resulting high pass characteristic of the overall system removed peakiness from the glottal waveforms. As Sondhi also applied high pass filtering with a cut-off of 20 Hz and did not compensate for it, this could be the cause of the observed peaky shape of the recovered waveforms. Another possible source of distortion is the acoustic load or impedance provided by the tube which could have been too high [32]. Mask (or tube) loading can cause attenuation of and, more importantly, shifts in the formants [67].

**Approaches Requiring a Second Channel.** The main difficulty in closed phase inverse filtering is to identify precisely the instants of glottal closure and opening. For example, in [81], the closed phase is identified as that part of the waveform for which the normalized total squared error is below some threshold. As it is more forceful, glottal closure may be identified more easily than glottal opening, which is more gradual [81]. Due to these difficulties, some investigators have made use of the electroglottography (EGG) signal to locate the instants of glottal closure and opening [17], [43],[44],[51],[79]. In particular, it is claimed that use of the EGG can better identify the closed phase in cases when the duration of the closed phase is very short as in higher fundamental frequency speech (females, children) or breathy speech [79]. As with the methods requiring special equipment, two-channel methods are not useful for more portable applications or those requiring minimal operator intervention. However, precisely because they can identify the glottal closure more accurately, results obtained using the EGG can potentially serve as 'benchmarks' by which other approaches working with the acoustic pressure wave alone can be evaluated. The same is clearly true of the equipment-based approaches as long as the characteristics of the equipment being used are recognized and appropriately compensated for.

## 2.2   Pole-Zero Modeling Approaches

A more complete model for speech is as an ARMA (autoregressive moving average) process with both poles and zeros:

$$s\left(n\right) = \sum_{i=1}^{L} b_i s_{n-i} + \sum_{j=1}^{M} a_j g_{n-j} + g(n) \ . \tag{9}$$

Such a model allows for more realistic modeling of speech sounds apart from vowels, particularly nasals, fricatives and stop consonants [58]. However, estimating the parameters of a pole-zero model is a nonlinear estimation problem [47]. There are many different approaches to the estimation of a pole-zero model for speech ranging from inverse LPC [47], iterative pre-filtering [72], [73], SEARMA (simultaneous estimation of ARMA parameters) [58], weighted recursive least squares (WRLS) [29], [54], [55], weighted least squares lattice [45], WRLS with variable forgetting factor (WRLS-VFF) [18]. These methods can give very good results but are computationally more intensive. They have the advantage that they can easily be extended to track the time-varying characteristics of speech [18],[54],[77], but the limited amount of data can lead to problems with convergence. Parametric techniques also have stability problems when the model order is not estimated correctly [58].

The periodic nature of voiced speech is a difficulty [55] which may be dealt with by incorporating simultaneous estimation of the input [54], [55]. If the input is assumed to be either a pseudo-periodic pulse train or white noise, the pole-zero model obtained will include the lip radiation, the vocal tract filter and the glottal waveform and there is no obvious way to separate the poles and zeros which model these different features [54].

ARMA modeling approaches have been used to perform closed phase glottal pulse inverse filtering [77] giving advantages over frame-based techniques such as linear prediction by eliminating the influence of the pitch, leading to better accuracy of parameter estimation and better spectral matching [77]. In [46],[77], WRLS-VFF is used to perform closed phase glottal pulse inverse filtering and the variable forgetting factor is used to predict the presence or absence of the glottal closed phase which then allows for a more accurate estimate of the formants and anti-formants. The main drawbacks of the approach [77] are computational complexity and the difficulty of obtaining good a priori information on model order and model type i.e. the relative number of poles and zeros.

**Model Based Approaches.** As seen above, it is possible to develop time-varying pole-zero models of speech, but, if the input is modelled as a pulse train or white noise, it is not possible unambiguously to determine which poles and zeros model the glottal source excitation. Only by a combination of adaptive ARMA modelling and inverse filtering such as in [77] is it then possible to recover the glottal waveform. An extension of pole-zero modelling to include a model of the glottal source excitation can overcome the drawbacks of inverse filtering and produces a parametric model of the glottal waveform. In [43], the glottal source is modelled using the LF model [27] and the vocal tract is modelled as two distinct filters, one for the open phase, one for the closed phase [63]. Glottal closure is identified using the EGG. In [30,31] the LF model is also used in adaptively and jointly estimating the vocal tract filter and glottal source using Kalman filtering. To provide robust initial values for the joint estimation process, the problem is first solved in terms of the Rosenberg model [66]. One of the main drawbacks of model-based approaches is the number of parameters which need to be estimated for each period of the signal [43] especially when the amount of data is small e.g. for short pitch periods in higher voices. To deal with this problem, inverse filtering may be used to remove higher formants and the estimates can be improved by using ensemble averaging of successive pitch periods.

Modeling techniques need not involve the use of standard glottal source models. Fitting polynomials to the glottal wave shape is a more flexible approach which can place fewer constraints on the result. In [51], the differentiated glottal waveform is modelled using polynomials (a linear model) where the timing of the glottis opening and closing is the parameter which varies. Initial values for the glottal source endpoints plus the pitch period endpoints are found using the EGG. The vocal tract filter coefficients and the glottal source endpoints are then jointly estimated across the whole pitch period. This approach is an alternative to closed phase inverse filtering in the sense that even closed phase inverse filtering contains an implied model of the glottal pulse [51], i.e. the assumption of zero airflow through the glottis for the segment of speech from which the inverse filter coefficients are estimated. An alternative is to attempt to optimize the inverse filter with respect to a glottal waveform model for the whole pitch period [51]. Interestingly in this approach, the result is the appearance of ripple in the source-corrected inverse filter during the closed phase of the glottal source even for synthesized speech with zero excitation during the glottal phase, (note that the speech was synthesized using the Ishizaka-Flanagan model [37]). Thus, this ripple must be an analysis artefact due to the inability of the model to account for it [51]. Improvements to the model are presented in [52],[76] and the sixth-order Milenkovic model is used in GELP [19].

In terms of the potential applications of glottal inverse filtering, the main difficulty with the use of glottal source models in glottal waveform estimation arises from the influence the models may have on the ultimate shape of the result. This is a particular problem with pathological voices. The glottal waveforms of these voices may diverge quite a lot from the idealized glottal models. As a result, trying to recover such a waveform using an idealized source model as a template may give less than ideal results. A model-based approach which partially avoids this problem is described in [64] where nonlinear least squares estimation is used to fit the LF model to a glottal derivative waveform extracted by closed phase filtering (where the closed phase is identified by the absence of formant modulation). This model-fitted glottal derivative waveform is the coarse structure. The fine structure of the waveform is then obtained by subtraction from the inverse filtered waveform. In this way, individual characteristics useful for speaker identification may be isolated. This approach also shows promise for isolating the characteristics of vocal pathologies.

### 2.3   Adaptive Inverse Filtering Approaches

For successful glottal waveform inverse filtering, an accurate vocal tract filter must first be acquired. In closed phase inverse filtering, the vocal tract filter impulse response is obtained free of the influence of the glottal waveform input. The influence of the glottal waveform can also be removed in the frequency domain. In the iterative adaptive inverse filtering method (IAIF-method) [5], a 2 pole model of the glottal waveform based on the characteristic 12dB/octave tilt in the spectral envelope [26] is used to remove the influence of the glottal waveform from the speech signal. The resulting vocal tract filter estimate is applied to the original speech signal to obtain a better estimate of the glottal waveform. The procedure is then repeated using a higher order parametric model of the glottal waveform. As the method removes the influence of the glottal waveform from the speech before estimating the vocal tract filter, it does not take a closed phase approach but utilises the whole pitch period. A flow diagram of the IAIF-method is shown in Fig. 4.

The method relies on linear prediction and is vulnerable to the deficiencies of that technique such as incorrect formant estimation due to the underlying harmonic structure in speech [47]. In particular, the technique performs less well for higher fundamental frequency voices [6]. To remove the influence of the pitch period, the iterative adaptive procedure may be applied pitch synchronously [7] as shown in Fig. 5.

Comparing the results of the IAIF method with closed phase inverse filtering show that the IAIF approach seems to produce waveforms which have a shorter and rounder closed phase. In [7] comparisons are made between original and estimated waveforms for synthetic speech sounds. It is interesting to note that pitch synchronous IAIF produces a closed phase ripple in these experiments (when there was none in the original synthetic source waveform).

In [8] discrete all-pole modelling was used to avoid the bias given toward harmonic frequencies in the model representation. An alternative iterative approach is presented in [2]. The method de-emphasises the low frequency glottal information using high-pass filtering prior to analysis. In addition to minimising the influence of the glottal source, an expanded analysis region is provided in the form of a pseudo-closed phase. The technique then derives an optimum vocal tract filter function through applying the properties of minimum phase systems.

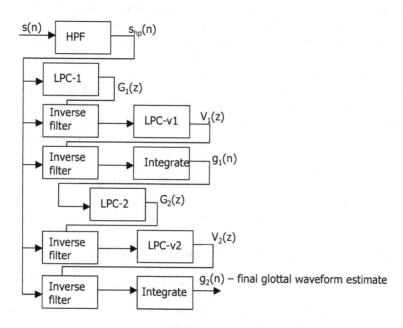

**Fig. 4.** The iterative adaptive inverse filtering method

**Other Iterative Approaches.** In [48] another iterative approach to glottal waveform estimation is developed. It is based on iterative inverse filtering (ITIF) [41], a technique for simultaneously estimating the poles and zeroes of an ARMA model based on the assumption that the input has a flat spectrum. In [48], the ITIF is used to find the poles and zeroes of a filter which will generate the

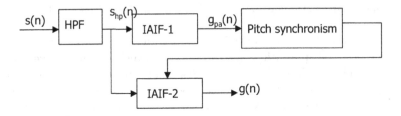

**Fig. 5.** The pitch synchronous iterative adaptive inverse filtering method

glottal waveform given an impulse train input. Doubly differentiating the speech production model gives:

$$(1 - z^{-1})S(z) = AV(z)(1 - z^{-1})Q(z) \tag{10}$$

where the doubly differentiated glottal waveform $Q(z)(1 - z^{-1})$, is just a periodic impulse train and so the estimation error may be approximated as the linear prediction residual. The inverse filter $I(z) = \frac{1}{V(z)}$ is determined using the covariance method and used to inverse filter the pre-emphasized speech. The residual is then integrated twice to yield the signal which has a spectrum which is an approximation of the glottal waveform amplitude spectrum [48] and from which a pole-zero glottal filter model may be determined using ITIF. The glottal filter may be used to generate an estimate of the glottal waveform when an input of a periodic impulse train is applied in the reverse time direction. The glottal waveforms so obtained typically have a negative-going closed phase, even when synthetic glottal waveforms with closed phase equal to zero are recovered. Typically, the models used in the glottal filter in this work have 14 zeros and 2 poles. However, it has been suggested [49], that the glottal waveform can be modelled purely by equally spaced zeros. Interestingly, in [48], an improved result is found when an all-zero filter is developed, where as many as 26 zeros may be required.

### 2.4   Higher Order Statistics and Cepstral Approaches

These approaches exploit the additional properties of new statistical techniques. For example, higher order statistics such as the bispectrum (third-order spectrum) are theoretically immune to Gaussian noise (in practice there is always some noise because of fixed length data records) [50], [59]. The bispectrum also contains system phase information and many bispectrum-based blind deconvolution algorithms have been developed to recover any type of system including non-minimum phase systems for a non-Gaussian white input. By assuming the pseudo-periodic pulse train as input (non-Gaussian white noise) the periodic aspect of the speech is assumed to be accounted for, but this is not necessarily the case. The main drawback with bispectral and other higher order statistics approaches is that they require greater amounts of data to reduce the variance in the spectral estimates [35]. As a result, multiple pitch periods are required which would necessarily be pitch asynchronous. This problem may be overcome by using the Fourier series and thus performing a pitch synchronous analysis [34]. It has been demonstrated that the higher order statistics approach can recover a system filter for speech, particularly for speech sounds such as nasals [34]. Such a filter may be non-minimum phase and when its inverse is used to filter the speech signal will return a residual which is much closer to a pure pseudo-periodic pulse train than inverse filters produced by other methods [14], [34]. In [14], the speech input estimate generated by this approach is used in a second step of ARMA parameter estimation by an input-output system identification method.

The properties of the cepstrum have also been exploited in speech processing. Transformed into the cepstral domain, the convolution of input pulse train and vocal tract filter becomes an addition of disjoint elements, allowing the separation of the filter from the harmonic component [61]. Cepstral techniques also have some limitations including the requirement for phase unwrapping and the fact that the technique cannot be used (although it often is) when there are zeros on the unit circle. In [42], various ARMA parameter estimation approaches are applied to the vocal tract impulse response recovered from the cepstral analysis of the speech signal [60].

There are a few examples of direct glottal waveform recovery using higher order spectral or cepstral techniques. In [80], ARMA modelling of the linear bispectrum [25] was applied to speech for joint estimation of the vocal tract model and the glottal volume velocity waveform using higher-order spectral factorization [75] with limited success. Direct estimation from the complex cepstrum was used in [4] based on the assumption that the glottal volume velocity waveform may be modelled as a maximum phase system. As the complex cepstrum separates into causal and acausal parts corresponding to the minimum and maximum phase parts of the system model this then permits a straightforward separation of the glottal waveform.

## 3   Effect of Recording Conditions

With a fundamental frequency varying in the range 80–250 Hz the glottal waveform is a low-frequency signal and so the low-frequency response, including the phase response, of the recording equipment used is an important factor in glottal pulse identification. However, many authors do not report in detail on this. In [81], the following potential problems are identified: ambient noise, low-frequency bias due to breath burst on the microphone, equipment and tape distortion of the signal and improper A/D conversion (p. 355). The problem of ambient noise can be overcome by ensuring suitable recording conditions. Use of special equipment [67], [70] can also minimize the noise problem, but is not always possible, or may not be relevant to the method under investigation. Paradoxically, the problem of the low-frequency bias producing a trend in the final recovered waveform can occur when a high quality microphone and amplifier with a flat frequency response down to 20 Hz are used. It can be overcome by high pass filtering with a cut-off frequency no greater than half the fundamental frequency [81] or by cancelling out the microphone transfer function [51], [79].

Phase distortion was a problem with analog tape recording [12], [36] and is illustrated as a characteristic 'humped' appearance, although doubtless there are other causes as such waveforms are still being recovered [43]. For example, phase distortion can result from HOS and cepstral approaches when phase errors occur due to the need for phase unwrapping [80]. However, more modern recording techniques especially involving the use of personal computer (PC) sound cards can also introduce phase distortion at low frequencies which will impact on the glottal waveform reconstruction. This is clearly demonstrated by experiments conducted by [1] where synthetic glottal waveforms created using the LF model were recorded through a PC sound card (Audigy2 SoundBlaster) resulting in the characteristic humped appearance. The effect was noticeable up to 320 Hz, but was especially pronounced at the lowest fundamental frequency (80 Hz). In all cases, the flat closed phase was entirely lost. The correction technique proposed is to model the frequency response of the recording system using a test signal made of a sum of sinusoids and thus to develop a compensating filter [1].

Few researchers take the care shown in [79] who plots an example of a glottal waveform with a widely varying baseline due to the influence of low-frequency noise picked up by a high-quality microphone such as a Brüel & Kjær 4134 [6], [79]. To overcome this problem, it is common to high-pass filter the speech [6], [42], [81] but according to [79] this is not sufficient as it removes the flat part of the closed phase and causes an undershoot at glottal closure: a better approach is to compensate by following the high pass filter by a low pass filter. According to [81], a pole may arise at zero frequency due to a non-zero mean in the typically short duration closed phase analysis window. It appears that in [81] such a pole is removed from the inverse filter if it arises (and not by linear phase high pass filtering as suggested by [79]), whereas in [79] the resulting bias is removed by polynomial fitting to 'specific points of known closed phase' (presumably the flattest points). An alternative approach is to take advantage of specialized equipment such as the Rothenberg mask [67] to allow for greater detail of measurement of the speech signal at low frequencies. The characteristics of the mask may then be removed by filtering during analysis [51].

Most experimenters who have reported on recording conditions have used condenser type microphones [6], [79], [81] with the exception of [51] who claims that these microphones are prone to phase distortion around the formant frequencies. However, available documentary information on microphone characteristics [13], the weight of successful inverse filtering results using condenser microphone recordings and direct comparison of results with different microphone types [15], [64] seem to contradict this claim. Depending on the application, it will not always be possible to apply such stringent recording conditions. For example, Plumpe et al. [64] test a glottal flow based speaker identification on samples from the TIMIT and NTIMIT databases. The TIMIT database is recorded with a high-quality (Sennheiser) microphone in a quiet room while the NTIMIT database represents speech of telephone-channel quality. Here it is in fact the cheaper microphone which is suspected of causing phase distortion which shows up in the estimated glottal flow derivatives. In other cases, the recording conditions may not be under the control of the investigator who may be using commercially provided data sources such as [16].

## 4   Evaluation of Results

One of the primary difficulties in glottal pulse identification is in the evaluation of the resulting glottal flow waveforms. How do we know we have the 'right answer'? How do we even know what the 'right answer' looks like? There are several approaches which can be taken. One approach is to verify the algorithm which is being used for the glottal flow waveform recovery. Algorithms can be verified by applying the algorithm to a simulated system which may be synthesized speech but need not be [41], [42]. In the case of synthesized speech, the system will be a known all-pole vocal tract model and the input will be a model for a glottal flow waveform. The success of the algorithm can be judged by quantifying the error between the known input waveform and the version recovered by the algorithm. This approach is most often used as a first step in evaluating an algorithm [6], [7], [48], [77], [80] and can only reveal the success of the algorithm in inverse filtering a purely linear time-invariant system. Synthesized speech can also be provided to the algorithm using a more sophisticated articulatory model [37] which allows for source-tract interaction [51].

Once an algorithm has been verified and is being used for inverse filtering real speech samples, there are two possible approaches to evaluating the results. One is to compare the waveforms obtained with those obtained by other (usually earlier) approaches. As, typically, the aim of this is to establish that the new approach is superior, the objectivity of this approach is doubtful. This approach can be made most objective when methods are compared using synthetic speech and results can be compared with the original source, as in [7]. However, the objectivity of this approach may also be suspect because the criteria used in the comparison are often both subjective and qualitative as for example in [77] where visual inspection seems to be the main criterion: "The WRLS-VFF method appears to agree with the expected characteristics for the glottal excitation source such as a flat closed region and a sharp slope at closure better than the other two methods." (p. 392) Other examples of such comparisons are in [24] and [43]. In many papers no comparisons are made, a stance which is not wholly unjustified because there is not a great deal of data available to say which are the correct glottal flow waveforms.

On the other hand, using two different methods to extract the glottal flow could be an effective way to confirm the appearance of the waveform as correct. The rationale behind this is that if two (or more) different approaches garner the same result then it has a greater chance of being 'really there'. If one of the methods, at least for experimental work, utilizes additional help such as the EGG to accurately identify glottal closure, then that would provide additional confirmation. This approach was taken in [43] but the results, albeit similar for two approaches, are most reminiscent of a type of waveform labelled as exhibiting phase distortion in

[81]. The same could be said about many of the results offered in [24] and [80], where low-frequency (baseline) drift is also in evidence. Once again, if new techniques for glottal inverse filtering produce waveforms which 'look like' the other waveforms which have been produced before, then they are evaluated as better than those which do not: examples of the latter include [4], [22].

Improved guidelines for assessing glottal waveform estimates can come from experiments with physiologically based articulatory synthesis methods. Glottal inverse filtering can be applied to speech produced with such models where the models are manipulated to produce various effects. The types of glottal waveforms recovered can then be assessed in the light of the perturbations introduced. An interesting example of what is possible with this idea is shown by [20] where various degrees and types of air leakage are shown to correlate with varying amounts of open and closed phase ripple in the derivative glottal flow and the glottal flow itself.

An alternative approach is to apply some objective mathematical criterion. In [23], it is shown how the evolution of the phase-plane plot of $g(t)$ versus $\frac{dg(t)}{dt}$ to a single closed loop indicates that a periodic solution has been produced and all resonances have been removed since resonances will appear as self-intersecting loops on the phase-plane plot.

## 4.1 Separability of Tract and Source

Glottal source models based on the linearly separable speech production model [27], [39], [40], [66], and derived from these early studies are still very successfully used in speech coding and speech synthesis [21]. Most of these models, while not as simple as the periodic impulse train, are relatively simple to generate, while the more complex models such as the LF model [27] produce the best results and have the added advantage of being a model of the derivative glottal flow and so automatically include lip radiation [21]. The method cannot be used where the actual speech production does not fit the model, for example in higher pitched voices (females, children) where the glottis does not close completely.

According to [44], the vocal tract filter is separable from the source only if the source itself is correctly defined. It has been shown that source-tract interaction can affect the glottal waveform [44] including the appearance of a first formant ripple on the waveform. There are effectively two ways of achieving this separation [9]: either assume the source is independent and have a time-varying vocal tract filter which will have different formants and bandwidths in closed and open phases or define the source as derived from the closed phase vocal tract as the true source and assume the vocal tract filter is time-invariant. Using the second solution, the variation in the formant frequency and bandwidth has to go somewhere and it ends up as a ripple on the open phase part of the glottal volume velocity (see for example Fig. 5c in [81]). Thus, strictly speaking, due to source-tract interaction, linear prediction analysis applied to a whole pitch period will contain slight formant frequency and bandwidth errors [44]. Also, according to this definition, a 'true' glottal volume velocity waveform can only be obtained by inverse filtering by a closed phase method and it should have the ripple (more visible on the differentiated waveform) and a flat closed phase.

However, a common result in inverse filtering is a ripple in the closed phase of the glottal volume velocity waveform. In [79] this occurs in hoarse or breathy speech and is assumed to show that there is air flow during the glottal closed phase. In [79] it is shown through experiments that this small amount of air flow does not significantly alter the inverse filter coefficients (filter pole positions change by $< 4\%$) and that true non-zero air flow can be captured in this way. However, the non-zero air flow and resultant source-tract interaction may still mean that the 'true' glottal volume velocity waveform is not exactly realized [79]. A similar effect is observed when attempting to recover source waveforms from nasal sounds. Here the strong vocal tract zeros mean that the inverse filter is inaccurate and so a strong formant ripple appears in the closed phase [79].

Most recently, a sliding window approach to closed phase inverse filtering has been attempted [21], [24]. Originally this approach required manual intervention to choose the best glottal waveform estimates from those obtained in periods of glottal closure in the speech waveform which were also identified by the operator [21]. Again, this is a very subjective procedure. Such an approach may be automated by using the maxiumum amplitude negative peaks in the linear prediction residual to estimate the glottal closure, but this is nothing new [81]. The best glottal waveform estimates are also chosen automatically by choosing the smoothest estimates [24]. The results obtained by this method were verified by comparing with waveforms obtained using the EGG to detect glottal closure.

## 5   Conclusion

Although convincing results for glottal waveform characteristics are reported in the literature from time to time, a standard fully automatic inverse filtering algorithm is not yet available. An extensive review of the literature has established that the salient features of the glottal waveform were established fairly early on, as was the technique of choice which continues to be closed phase inverse filtering. This technique has been successful because it allows the adoption of the linear time-invariant model for both determining the filter in the source-filter speech model and then for applying it as an inverse filter to recover the source. Despite concern about features of recovered waveforms which may be due to inaccuracies and oversimplifications in this model, alternative approaches have met with limited success. ARMA modelling has limitations due to the insufficiency of data and the 'magic bullet' promise of alternative statistical techniques such as the cepstrum and higher order statistics has not delivered. Low frequency phase response and low frequency noise have been shown to be important issues for glottal waveform recovery (at least in some contexts such as vocal pathology, experimental studies on voice production and benchmark generation) which have not always received due attention by researchers. However, nonlinear approaches (with the exception of the statistical techniques mentioned already) are only just beginning to be explored.

# References

1. Akande, O., O.: Speech analysis techniques for glottal source and noise estimation in voice signals. Ph. D. Thesis, University of Limerick (2004)
2. Akande, O. and Murphy, P. J.: Estimation of the vocal tract transfer function for voiced speech with application to glottal wave analysis. Speech Communication, **46** (2005) 15–36
3. Akande, O., Murphy, P. J.: Improved speech analysis for glottal excited linear predictive speech coding. Proc. Irish Signals and Systems Conference. (2004) 101–106
4. Alkhairy, A.: An algorithm for glottal volume velocity estimation. Proc. IEEE Int. Conf. Acoustics, Speech and Signal Processing. **1** (1999) 233–236
5. Alku, P., Vilkman, E., Laine, U. K.,: Analysis of glottal waveform in different phonation types using the new IAIF-method. Proc. 12th Int. Congress Phonetic Sciences, **4** (1991) 362–365
6. Alku, P.: An automatic method to estimate the time-based parameters of the glottal pulseform. Proc. IEEE Int. Conf. Acoustics, Speech and Signal Processing. **2** (1992) 29–32
7. Alku, P.: Glottal wave analysis with pitch synchronous iterative adaptive inverse filtering. Speech Communication. **11** (1992) 109–118
8. Alku, P., Vilkman, E.: Estimation of the glottal pulseform based on Discrete All-Pole modeling. Proc. Int. Conf. on Spoken Language Processing. (1994) 1619-1622
9. Ananthapadmanabha, T. V., Fant, G.: Calculation of true glottal flow and its components. STL-QPR. (1985) 1–30
10. Atal, B. S., Hanauer, S. L.: Speech analysis and synthesis by linear prediction of the speech wave. J. Acoust. Soc. Amer. **50** (1971) 637–655
11. Bergstrom, A., Hedelin, P.: Codebook driven glottal pulse analysis. Proc. IEEE Int. Conf. Acoustics, Speech and Signal Processing. **1** (1989) 53–56
12. Berouti, M., Childers, D., Paige, A.: Correction of tape recorder distortion. Proc. IEEE Int. Conf. Acoustics, Speech and Signal Processing. **2** (1977) 397–400
13. Brüel & Kjær: Measurement Microphones. 2nd ed. (1994)
14. Chen, W.-T., Chi, C.-Y.: Deconvolution and vocal-tract parameter estimation of speech signals by higher-order statistics based inverse filters. Proc. IEEE Workshop on HOS. (1993) 51–55
15. Childers, D. G.: Glottal source modeling for voice conversion. Speech Communication. **16** (1995) 127–138
16. Childers, D. G.: Speech processing and synthesis toolboxes. Wiley: New York (2000)
17. Childers, D. G., Chieteuk, A.: Modeling the glottal volume-velocity waveform for three voice types. J. Acoust. Soc. Amer. **97** (1995) 505–519
18. Childers, D. G., Principe, J. C., Ting, Y. T. Adaptive WRLS-VFF for Speech Analysis. IEEE Trans. Speech and Audio Proc. **3** (1995) 209–213
19. Childers, D. G., Hu, H. T.: Speech synthesis by glottal excited linear prediction. J. Acoust. Soc. Amer. **96** (1994) 2026-2036
20. Cranen, B., Schroeter, J.: Physiologically motivated modelling of the voice source in articulatory analysis/synthesis. Speech Communication. **19** (1996) 1–19
21. Cummings, K. E., Clements, M. A.: Glottal Models for Digital Speech Processing: A Historical Survey and New Results. Digital Signal Processing. **5** (1995) 21–42
22. Deng, H., Beddoes, M. P., Ward, R. K., Hodgson, M.: Estimating the Glottal Waveform and the Vocal-Tract Filter from a Vowel Sound Signal. Proc. IEEE Pacific Rim Conf. Communications, Computers and Signal Processing. **1** (2003) 297–300

23. Edwards, J. A., Angus, J. A. S.: Using phase-plane plots to assess glottal inverse filtering. Electronics Letters **32** (1996) 192–193

24. Elliot, M., Clements, M.: Algorithm for automatic glottal waveform estimation without the reliance on precise glottal closure information. Proc. IEEE Int. Conf. Acoustics, Speech and Signal Processing. **1** (2004) 101–104

25. Erdem, A. T., Tekalp, A. M.: Linear Bispectrum of Signals and Identification of Nonminimum Phase FIR Systems Driven by Colored Input. IEEE Trans. Signal Processing. **40** (1992) 1469–1479

26. Fant, G. C. M.: Acoustic Theory of Speech Production. (1970) The Hague, The Netherlands: Mouton

27. Fant, G., Liljencrants, J., Lin, Q.: A four-parameter model of glottal flow. STL-QPR. (1985) 1–14

28. Fant, G., Lin, Q., Gobl, C.: Notes on glottal flow interaction. STL-QPR. (1985) 21–45

29. A recursive maximum likelihood algorithm for ARMA spectral estimation. IEEE Trans. Inform. Theory **28** (1982) 639–646

30. Fu, Q., Murphy, P.: Adapive Inverse filtering for High Accuracty Estimation of the Glottal Source. Proc. NoLisp'03. (2003)

31. Fu, Q., Murphy, P. J.: Robust glottal source estimation based on joint source-filter model optimization. IEEE Trans. Audio, Speech Lang. Proc., **14** (2006) 492–501

32. Hillman, R. E., Weinberg, B.: A new procedure for venting a reflectionless tube. J. Acoust. Soc. Amer. **69** (1981) 1449–1451

33. Holmberg, E. R., Hillman, R. E., Perkell, J. S.: Glottal airflow and transglottal air pressure measurements for male and female speakers in soft, normal and loud voice. J. Acoust. Soc. Amer. **84** (1988) 511–529

34. Hinich, M. J., Shichor, E.: Bispectral Analysis of Speech. Proc. 17th Convention of Electrical and Electronic Engineers in Israel. (1991) 357–360

35. Hinich, M. J., Wolinsky, M. A.: A test for aliasing using bispectral components. J. Am. Stat. Assoc. **83** (1988) 499-502

36. Holmes, J. N.: Low-frequency phase distortion of speech recordings. J. Acoust. Soc. Amer. **58** (1975) 747–749

37. Ishizaka, K., Flanagan, J. L.: Synthesis of voiced sounds from a two mass model of the vocal cords. Bell Syst. Tech. J. **51** (1972) 1233–1268

38. Jiang, Y., Murphy, P. J.: Production based pitch modification of voiced speech. Proc. ICSLP, (2002) 2073–2076

39. Klatt, D.: Software for a cascade/parallel formant synthesizer. J. Acoust. Soc. Amer. **67** (1980) 971–994

40. Klatt, D., Klatt, L.: Analysis, synthesis, and perception of voice quality variations among female and male talkers. J. Acoust. Soc. Amer. **87** (1990) 820–857

41. Konvalinka, I. S., Mataušek, M. R.: Simultaneous estimation of poles and zeros in speech analysis and ITIT-iterative inverse filtering algorithm. IEEE Trans. Acoust., Speech, Signal Proc. **27** (1979) 485–492

42. Kopec, G. E., Oppenheim, A. V., Tribolet, J. M.: Speech Analysis by Homomorphic Prediction IEEE Trans.Acoust., Speech, Signal Proc. **25** (1977) 40–49

43. Krishnamurthy, A. K.: Glottal Source Estimation using a Sum-of-Exponentials Model. IEEE Trans. Signal Processing. **40** (1992) 682–686

44. Krishnamurthy, A. K., Childers, D. G.: Two-channel speech analysis. IEEE Trans. Acoust., Speech, Signal Proc. **34** (1986) 730–743

45. Lee, D. T. L., Morf, M., Friedlander, B.: Recursive least squares ladder estimation algorithms. IEEE Trans. Acoust., Speech, Signal Processing. **29** (1981) 627–641

46. Lee, K., Park, K.: Glottal Inverse Filtering (GIF) using Closed Phase WRLS-VFF-VT Algorithm. Proc. IEEE Region 10 Conference. **1** (1999) 646–649
47. Makhoul, J.: Linear Prediction: A Tutorial Review. Proc. IEEE. **63** (1975) 561–580
48. Mataušek, M. R., Batalov, V. S.: A new approach to the determination of the glottal waveform. IEEE Trans. Acoust., Speech, Signal Proc. **28** (1980) 616–622
49. Mathews, M. V., Miller, J. E., David, Jr., E. E.: Pitch synchronous analysis of voiced sounds. J. Acoust. Soc. Amer. **33** (1961) 179–186
50. Mendel, J. M.: Tutorial on Higher-Order Statistics (Spectra) in Signal Processing and System Theory: Theoretical Results and Some Applications. Proc. IEEE. **79** (1991) 278–305
51. Milenkovic, P.: Glottal Inverse Filtering by Joint Estimation of an AR System with a Linear Input Model. IEEE Trans. Acoust., Speech, Signal Proc. **34** (1986) 28–42
52. Milenkovic, P. H.: Voice source model for continuous control of pitch period. J. Acoust. Soc. Amer. **93** (1993) 1087-1096
53. Miller, R. L.: Nature of the Vocal Cord Wave. J. Acoust. Soc. Amer. **31** (1959) 667-677
54. Miyanaga, Y., Miki, M., Nagai, N.: Adaptive Identification of a Time-Varying ARMA Speech Model. IEEE Trans. Acoust., Speech, Signal Proc. **34** (1986) 423–433
55. Miyanaga, Y., Miki, N., Nagai, N., Hatori, K.: A Speech Analysis Algorithm which eliminates the Influence of Pitch using the Model Reference Adaptive System. IEEE Trans. Acoust., Speech, Signal Proc. **30** (1982) 88–96
56. Monsen, R. B., Engebretson, A. M.: Study of variations in the male and female glottal wave. J. Acoust. Soc. Amer. **62** (1977) 981–993
57. Monsen, R. B., Engebretson, A. M., Vemula, N. R.: Indirect assessment of the contribution of subglottal air pressure and vocal-fold tension to changes of fundamental frequency in English. J. Acoust. Soc. Amer. **64** (1978) 65–80
58. Morikawa, H., Fujisaki, H.: Adaptive Analysis of Speech based on a Pole-Zero Representation. IEEE Trans. Acoust., Speech, Signal Proc. **30** (1982) 77–87
59. Nikias, C. L., Raghuveer, M. R.: Bispectrum Estimation:A Digital Signal Processing Framework. Proc. IEEE. **75** (1987) 869–891
60. Oppenheim, A. V.: A speech analysis-synthesis system based on homomorphic filtering. J. Acoust., Soc. Amer. **45** (1969) 458–465
61. Oppenheim, A. V., Schafer, R. W.: Discrete-Time Signal Processing. Englewood Cliffs:London Prentice-Hall (1989)
62. Pan, R., Nikias, C. L.: The complex cepstrum of higher order cumulants and non-minimum phase system identification. IEEE Trans. Acoust., Speech, Signal Proc. **36** (1988) 186–205
63. Parthasarathy, S., Tufts, D. W.: Excitation-Synchronous Modeling of Voiced Speech. IEEE Trans. Acoust., Speech, Signal Proc. **35** (1987) 1241–1249
64. Plumpe, M. D., Quatieri, T. F., Reynolds, D. A.: Modeling of the Glottal Flow Derivative Waveform with Application to Speaker Identification. IEEE Trans. Speech and Audio Proc. **7** (1999) 569–586
65. Quatieri, T. F., McAulay, R. J.: Shape invariant time-scale and pitch modification of speech. IEEE Trans. Signal Process., **40** (1992) 497–510
66. Rosenberg, A.: Effect of the glottal pulse shape on the quality of natural vowels. J. Acoust. Soc. Amer. **49** (1971) 583–590
67. Rothenberg, M.: A new inverse-filtering technique for deriving the glottal air flow waveform. J. Acoust. Soc. Amer. **53** (1973) 1632–1645

68. Schroeder, M. R., Atal, B. S.: Code-excited linear prediction (CELP): High quality speech at very low bit rates. Proc. IEEE Int. Conf. Acoustics, Speech and Signal Processing. **10** (1985) 937–940
69. Shanks, J. L.: Recursion filters for digital processing. Geophysics. **32** (1967) 33–51
70. Sondhi, M. M.: Measurement of the glottal waveform. J. Acoust. Soc. Amer. **57** (1975) 228–232
71. Sondhi, M. M., Resnik, J. R.: The inverse problem for the vocal tract: Numerical methods, acoustical experiments, and speech synthesis. J. Acoust. Soc. Amer. **73** (1983) 985–1002
72. Steiglitz, K.: On the simultaneous estimation of poles and zeros in speech analysis. IEEE Trans. Acoust., Speech, Signal Proc. **25** (1977) 194–202
73. Steiglitz, K., McBride, L. E.: A technique for the identifcation of linear systems. IEEE Trans. Automat. Contr., **10** (1965) 461–464
74. Stylianou, Y.: Applying the harmonic plus noise model in concatenative speech synthesis. IEEE Trans. Speech Audio Process., **9**(2001) 21–29
75. Tekalp, A. M., Erdem, A. T.: Higher-Order Spectrum Factorization in One and Two Dimensions with Applications in Signal Modeling and Nonminimum Phase System Identification. IEEE Trans. Acoust., Speech, Signal Proc. **37** (1989) 1537–1549
76. Thomson, M. M.: A new method for determining the vocal tract transfer function and its excitation from voiced speech. Proc. IEEE Int. Conf. Acoustics, Speech and Signal Processing. **2** (1992) 23–26
77. Ting, Y., T., Childers, D. G.: Speech Analysis using the Weighted Recursive Least Squares Algorithm with a Variable Forgetting Factor. Proc. IEEE Int. Conf. Acoustics, Speech and Signal Processing. **1** (1990) 389–392
78. Tremain, T. E.: The government standard linear predictive coding algorithm: LPC-10. Speech Technol. 1982 40–49
79. Veeneman, D. E., BeMent, S. L.: Automatic Glottal Inverse Filtering from Speech and Electroglottographic Signals. IEEE Trans. Acoust., Speech, Signal Proc. **33** (1985) 369–377
80. Walker, J.: Application of the bispectrum to glottal pulse analysis. Proc. NoLisp'03. (2003)
81. Wong, D. Y., Markel, J. D., Gray, A. H.: Least squares glottal inverse filtering from the acoustic speech waveform. IEEE Trans. Acoust., Speech, Signal Proc. **27** (1979) 350–355

# Rahmonic Analysis of Signal Regularity in Synthesized and Human Voice

Peter J. Murphy

Department of Electronic and Computer Engineering
University of Limerick, Limerick, Ireland
`Peter.Murphy@ul.ie`

**Abstract.** Aperiodicity in sustained phonations can result from temporal, amplitude and waveshape perturbations, aspiration noise, nonlinear phenomena and
non-stationarity of the vocal tract. General measures of the periodicity of the
signal are of interest in quantifying voice quality and in the assessment of
pathological voice. Cepstral techniques have been employed to supply an index
of the degree of signal regularity. Two distinct regions of the cepstrum, low and
high quefrency, have been used in assessing the regularity of the voice signal.
In the high quefrency region the first rahmonic has been employed to provide
an indication of the periodicity of the signal. In the present work, one such
method (cepstral peak prominence, CPP) is assessed with synthesis data (six
levels of random jitter, cyclic jitter, shimmer and additive noise). In addition a
new measure, employing all rahmonics in the cepstrum, is tested against the
same set of synthesis data. Both measures are then examined using a group of
patient (13) and normal (12) data sets. The assessment suggests that rahmonic
peaks incorporate an extra dimension, beyond harmonics-to-noise ratio measures, that is useful for voice quality classification.

## 1 Introduction

Aperiodicity of the voice signal can result from jitter, shimmer, aspiration noise,
nonlinear phenomena, inter-period glottal waveshape differences, non-stationarity of
the vocal tract or some combination of these attributes. An index for representing the
degree of aperiodicity of the voice signal is useful for non-invasive analysis of voice
disorders. A popular measurement for extracting this information is the harmonics-to-
noise ratio (HNR); it provides an indication of the overall periodicity of the voice
signal. Specifically, it quantifies the ratio between the periodic and aperiodic components in the signal. A reliable method for estimating the degree of abnormality in the
acoustic waveform of the human voice is important for effective evaluation and management of voice pathology.

A number of temporal and spectral based methods have been employed for HNR
estimation. However, pitch synchronous time-domain methods for HNR estimation
are problematic because of the difficulty in estimating the fundamental period for
voiced speech (especially for pathological conditions), while frequency-domain
methods encounter the problem of estimating the noise level at harmonic locations.
Cepstral techniques have been introduced to supply noise estimates at all frequency
locations in the spectrum and/or to avoid the need for accurate fundamental frequency

Y. Stylianou, M. Faundez-Zanuy, A. Esposito (Eds.): WNSP 2005, LNCS 4391, pp. 22–40, 2007.
© Springer-Verlag Berlin Heidelberg 2007

(f0) or harmonic estimation. These methods have employed the use of either the low quefrency cepstral coefficients or the rahmonic amplitude corresponding to the fundamental frequency.

In this chapter, two existing low quefrency cepstral-based noise estimation techniques [1-2] are briefly reviewed. It is shown that the techniques can provide a traditional HNR measure though they appear to have originally been developed to supply an average of the dB HNRs calculated over specific frequency bands. In the high quefrencies, the cepstrum is comprised of prominent peaks termed rahmonics, spaced at the fundamental period and it's multiples. The first rahmonic amplitude has been employed to assess voice quality [3] and pathological voice [4]. A specific measure of the first rahmonic energy, termed cepstral peak prominence (CPP) has been used on real speech by a number of investigators [3-5]. Presently it is tested on synthesis data. In addition, a more recent method [6] employing all rahmonics in the cepstrum is tested against the same synthesis data. The performance of both measures in terms of separating a set of patient and normal data is also assessed.

## 2   Existing Methods for Quantifying Irregularity in the Voice Signal

In recent decades research has aimed at developing objective measures for quantifying the noise level in voiced speech. Objective and quantitative evaluation of signal-to-noise levels is now possible through estimation of the harmonics-to-noise ratio (HNR). This quantity (HNR) is a function of the additive noise and other factors such as jitter and shimmer, which are responsible for the aperiodic component in voiced speech. In addition to aperiodic components in pathological voice the waveform may, in theory at least, be different from 'normal' yet consistent from period to period. This type of waveshape difference would not show up in a traditional HNR estimate. Hence methods that go beyond the traditional HNR description are also of interest. The many methods that have been proposed for HNR estimation can be broadly classified as (a) time domain, (b) frequency domain and (c) quefrency domain techniques. Time domain techniques are described in [7-13]. Frequency domain methods include the work of [14-24] while cepstral-based techniques include [1-6].

### 2.1   Time-Domain Methods

Representative time domain HNR estimation techniques are reported in, for example, [7] and [8]. In general, these methods calculate the harmonics-to-noise ratio by first computing the average waveform of a single period of speech through calculating the mean of successive periods. The noise energy is then calculated as the mean squared difference between the average waveform and the individual periods. The ratio of the energy of the average waveform to the average variance gives the HNR (Eq.1). Though very simple and less computationally intensive as compared to frequency and cepstral based approaches, time domain HNR estimation requires accurate estimation of the beginning and end of individual periods in the underlying speech waveform. This requires the use of complex signal processing algorithms. Moreover, the pitch boundaries are very sensitive to phase distortion, hence a high quality recording device with good amplitude and phase response is required for collecting the speech data.

$$HNR = 10 \log_{10} \left( \frac{M \sum_{n=0}^{T} s_{avg}^2(n)}{\sum_{n=0}^{T} \sum_{i=1}^{M} (s_i(n) - s_{avg}(n))^2} \right) \tag{1}$$

M is the total number of fundamental periods, i is the $i^{th}$ fundamental period (of length T) and $s_{avg}(n)$ is the waveform averaged over M fundamental periods at each point 'n' in the cycle.

## 2.2 Frequency-Domain Methods

Frequency domain approaches to HNR estimation may overcome, to a certain degree, the necessity for accurate fundamental period estimation. The periodic component is approximated by extracting from the spectrum the summed energy at harmonic locations. The noise energy is estimated by summing the between-harmonic estimates. The noise at harmonic locations is typically estimated as the average of the noise estimates either side of the harmonic locations (c.f. [16]). The final harmonics-to-noise ratio is expressed in dBs. A further advantage of HNR estimation in the frequency domain is the ability to estimate HNR over a desired frequency band.

The HNR is computed as

$$HNR = 10 \log 10 \left\{ \frac{\sum_{i}^{N/2} |S_i|^2}{\sum_{i=1}^{N/2} |N_i|^2} \right\} \tag{2}$$

where $|S_i|$ represents harmonic amplitudes, and $|N_i|$ is the noise estimate.

## 2.3 Cepstrum-Based Methods

Before examining the cepstral-based voice irregularity indices a brief introduction to the cepstrum of voiced speech is provided.

### 2.3.1 Cepstral Analysis of Voiced Speech

An initial description of cepstral processing of speech is given in [25]. Cepstrum analysis belongs to the class of homomorphic filtering developed as a general method of separating signals, which have been non-additively combined. It has been used in general speech analysis for pitch [25] and vocal-tract transfer function [26] estimation. A brief review of Noll's interpretation [25] is given. The cepstrum is defined as the square of the Fourier transform of the power spectrum of the speech signal.

Voiced speech, s(t) is considered as a periodic source component, e(t) convolved by the impulse response of the vocal tract, v(t).

$$s(t)=e(t)*v(t) \tag{3}$$

Taking the Fourier transform magnitude gives

$$|S(f)|=|E(f)\times V(f)| \tag{4}$$

Taking the logarithm changes the multiplicative components into additive components.

$$\log|S(f)|=\log|E(f)|+\log|V(f)| \tag{5}$$

It is noted (Fig.1(a)) that the vocal tract contributes a slow variation, while the periodicity of the source manifests itself as a fast variation in the log spectrum. Taking the Fourier transform of the logarithmic power spectrum yields a prominent peak corresponding to the high frequency source component and a broader peak corresponding to the low frequency formant structure. To distinguish between the frequency components in a temporal waveform and the frequency in the log spectrum the term quefrency is used to describe the log spectrum "frequency", while the first prominent cepstral peak is termed the first rahmonic (Fig.1(b)). In present day processing the inverse Fourier transform of the log magnitude spectrum is generally taken to represent the cepstrum of voiced speech. The *real cepstrum* is defined as the inverse Fourier transform of the log of the magnitude spectrum:

$$\hat{C}(t) = \int_{-\infty}^{\infty} \log |S(f)| e^{j2\pi f t} \, df . \tag{6}$$

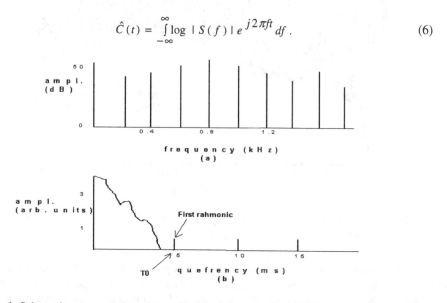

**Fig. 1.** Schematic representation of (a) a Fourier spectrum of a periodic speech waveform, and (b) its corresponding cepstrum with rahmonics spaced at integer multiples of T0, the fundamental period

### 2.3.2  Cepstrum-Based Estimation of Voice Signal Irregularities

Two distinct regions of the cepstrum have been used for assessing the regularity of the voice signal. A low quefrency technique for estimating the HNR in voiced speech was introduced in [1]. The potential advantage of the approach lies in the fact that it supplies a noise estimate at all frequencies in the spectrum. The cepstrum is applied to a segment of voiced speech and the Fourier transform of the liftered cepstral coefficients approximates a noise baseline from which the harmonics-to-noise ratio is estimated. The ratio (expressed in dB) of the energy of the original speech spectrum at harmonic locations to the energy of the Fourier transformed liftered noise baseline is taken as the HNR estimate. The basic procedure presented in [1] is as follows; the cepstrum is produced for a windowed segment of voiced speech, the rahmonics are zeroed and the resulting liftered cepstrum is Fourier transformed to provide a noise spectrum. After performing a baseline correction procedure on this spectrum (the original noise estimate is high), the summed energy of the modified noise spectrum (in dB) is subtracted from the summed energy of the original harmonic spectrum (in dB) in order to provide the harmonics-to-noise ratio estimate.

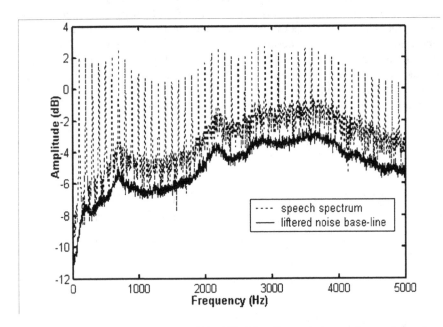

**Fig. 2.** HNR estimation using de Krom [1] cepstral baseline technique using a window length of 1024 sample points

A modification to the de Krom technique [1] is presented in [2]. Problems with the baseline fitting procedure are highlighted and a way to avoid these problems by calculating the energy and noise estimates at harmonic locations only is proposed. In addition, rather than comb-liftering the rahmonics, the cepstrum is low-passed filtered to provide a smoother baseline (Fig.3).

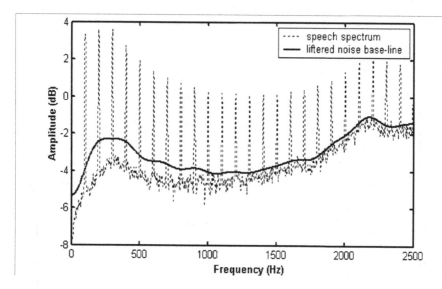

**Fig. 3.** HNR estimation (Qi and Hillman [2]) cepstral baseline technique (window length 3200 points)

In a recent study [28] the basis behind, and the accuracies of the cepstral-based HNR estimation techniques in [1] and [2] were evaluated and a new cepstral-based HNR method was proposed and tested. HNR is overestimated in [1] while [2] gives underestimates due to underestimating and overestimating the noise baseline respectively (as is evident in Fig.2 and Fig.3).

A new technique described in [27] employed a harmonic pre-emphasis to overcome the problem of baseline fitting to the noise floor (Fig.4). The noise baseline (which is equivalent to a traditional vocal tract transfer function estimate via the cepstrum) is influenced by the glottal source excited vocal tract and by the noise excited vocal tract. The liftered spectral baseline does not rest on the actual noise level but interpolates the harmonic and between harmonic estimates and, hence, resides somewhere between the noise and harmonic levels. As the window length increases, the contribution of harmonic frequencies to the cepstral baseline estimate decreases. However, the glottal source still provides a bias in the estimate. To remove the influence of the source, pre-emphasis is applied to the harmonics for the voiced speech signals (i.e. noiseless signals). Noise-free harmonics are approximated through periodogram averaging [28].

A pre-emphasis filter,

$$h(z) = 1 - 0.97 \, z^{-1} \tag{7}$$

is applied to these estimates in the frequency domain by multiplying each harmonic value by the appropriate pre-emphasis factor.

In the review [27] of the methods described in [1] and [2] the measures described are understood to be taken in order to estimate HNR but it appears that what the authors may have intended was not in fact HNR estimation in the traditional sense but

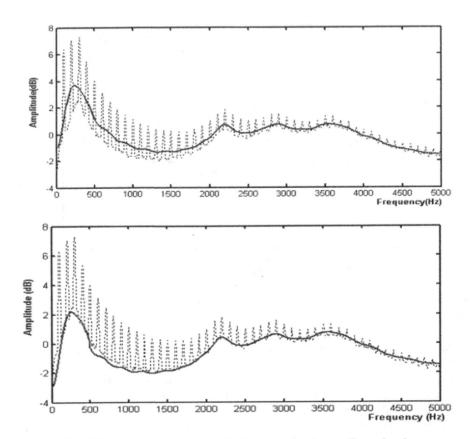

**Fig. 4.** Harmonic pre-emphasis method of cepstral noise-baseline estimation

an average of the HNRs in dB at each harmonic location which is quite different. This interpretation has a close relationship to the index extracted from the high quefrencies as will be shown.

Cepstral estimation of irregularity in voice signals has also focussed on the high quefrency region of the cepstrum [3, 29-31]. In particular the amplitude of the first rahmonic is used for voice quality assessment. In [29], the height of the first cepstral peak (first rahmonic) is used as an indicator of periodicity and the location of this peak on the quefrency axis determines the pitch period. Objective assessment is reported through using the method and a call for further studies is made. The height of the first cepstral peak is also estimated in [3], using a normalisation procedure, in which pitch tracking errors were not checked for, and the resulting index is found to be a strong predictor (correlation coefficient 0.84) of breathiness. In [4] it is reported that the main cepstral peak integrates both high frequency noise and aperiodicity aspects of pathological voice and hence the measure shows promise for quantifying improvements in voice quality following phonosurgery. The measure is found to be a superior indicator of voice quality when compared against other acoustic indices. CPP has been used by a number of researchers and the measure is shown to provide a stronger correlate of voice quality/dysphonia than other acoustic measures tested (c.f. [3, 5, 32]). However, to-date, CPP has not been tested with synthesis data. The CPP measure is implemented in the present study and tested on synthesis data. Hillenbrand's normalisation scheme and band-limited analysis [3] is also investigated. In addition, a new method employing all rahmonics is proposed and tested.

The rahmonic amplitude provides information regarding the richness of the harmonic structure (expressed in dB) in the spectrum of voiced speech. As such the measure provides an indication of the average (over the spectrum) of the HNRs (in dB) at specific harmonic/between-harmonic locations. It appears that the authors of the papers in [1] and [2] may also be extracting an average of the HNRs in dB at each harmonic location. Hence the acoustic indices extracted from the low- and high-quefrencies appear to be closely related.

Investigations described in [1] and [2] use synthesized speech samples to simulate various amounts of jitter and additive noise conditions in a manner similar to the files produced here. In [1] de Krom points out the absence of a database of pathological voice samples from which researchers might investigate new analysis techniques and citing the dangers of using pathological voice samples with vague assessments suggested the use of synthetic signals as an objective, quantifiable alternative. This is the procedure followed in the present study. In addition, the methods (cepstral peak prominence and sum of rahmonic amplitudes) are then tested for their ability to discriminate between a group of thirteen patients with various voice disorders and twelve normal speakers.

## 3  Method

A one second sample of voiced speech is used and the following two methodological procedures are followed:

Cepstral Peak Prominence (CPP)

1. A Hamming window of 52 ms is applied and hopped 50% to the end of the data record.
2. The logarithmic amplitude spectrum is calculated at each window position.
3. The cepstrum is estimated at each window position.
4. A regression line is fitted to the cepstrum and the height of the first rahmonic peak above the regression line is taken as the estimate of CPP (Fig.5).
5. An average of the estimates produced in 4 is taken across the data record to provide CPP.

Sum of Rahmonic Amplitudes (SRA)

1. A 2048-point Hamming window is applied to the data (sampling frequency = 10 kHz).
2. FFT is taken and magnitude spectrum produced.
3. Window is successively hopped by 50% to the end of the data record and magnitude spectra are produced for each windowed segment.
4. Magnitude spectra are averaged and the logarithm is taken.

5. The cepstrum is produced for this averaged spectrum (now in logarithmic scale).
6. Rahmonic peaks are located (e.g. for a 110 Hz signal: 11×9.1ms up to 1024 points (one-sided), Fig.6, for human speech peaks are sought at quefrency locations corresponding to the fundamental period and its multiples).
7. Sum each rahmonic in order to directly obtain the SRA index.

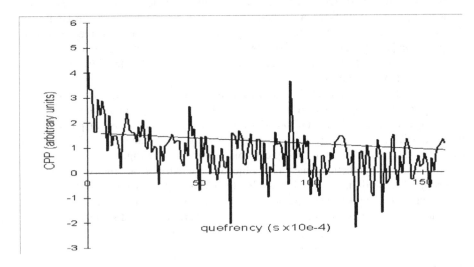

**Fig. 5.** Estimation of cepstral peak prominence (CPP). Distance from regression line to prominent peak indicated CPP.

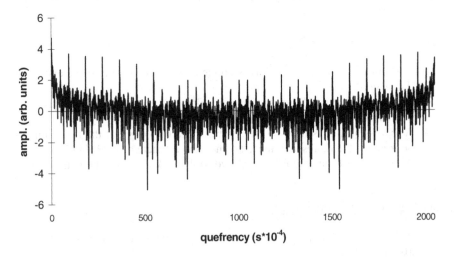

**Fig. 6.** Estimation of sum of rahmonic amplitudes (SRA). Rahmonic peaks are located and summed (one sided cepstrum up to 1024 points) to produce SRA.

# 4 Analysis

## 4.1 Synthesis Speech Signals

A sequence of glottal pulses (type C) [33] was used as input into a delay line digital filter, where the filter coefficients were obtained based on area function data for the vowel /AH/ and a reflection coefficient at the lip end of 0.71 [34]. Radiation at the lips was modelled by the first order difference equation $R(z) = (1-z^{-1})$. The sampling frequency for the synthesis was 10 kHz.

Aperiodicity was introduced into the waveform by altering the impulse train or the glottal input directly for a 110 Hz waveform. Random shimmer was introduced by adding a random variable gain factor (of a given std. dev. ranging form 1 to 32 %) to the amplitude of the pitch period impulse train prior to convolution with the glottal pulse. Jitter was introduced through scaling of the glottal periods. Two variations of jitter were implemented, cyclic jitter (1 to 6 %) and random jitter (std. dev. 1 to 6 %); for the former, alternate periods are equal while in the latter the variation is random. Random additive noise was introduced by multiplying the glottal pulse by a random noise generator arranged to give signal dependent additive noise of a user specified variance (std. dev. 1 to 32 %). Further files were also created for three levels of additive noise for signals beginning at 80 Hz and increasing in six, approximately equi-spaced steps of 60 Hz up to 350 Hz.

## 4.2 Human Speech Signals

Recordings were made of the participants phonating the sustained vowel /AH/ and uttering the phonetically balanced sentence "Joe took father's shoe bench out" at their comfortable pitch and loudness level. All recordings were made using a Tandberg audio recorder (AT 771, Audio Tutor Educational, Japan) prior to the participants (thirteen in all) undergoing laryngovideostroboscopic (LVS, Endo-Stroboskop, Atmos, Germany) evaluation at the outpatient's ENT clinic in Beaumont Hospital, Dublin.

Along with the results of the stroboscopic examination, full medical details regarding the vocal pathology were taken for each patient as well as any further diagnostic comments at the time of assessment. The audio (and video) data from the stroboscopic evaluation were recorded using SONY SVHS (E-180, France) cassettes. Twelve normals were subsequently recorded under the same conditions. All recordings were low-passed filtered at 4 kHz and digitized at a sampling rate of 10 kHz into a data acquisition expansion card (Integrated Measurement Systems, PCL-814, Southampton, UK) with 14-bit resolution and stored for subsequent analysis.

## 4.3 Analysis Procedure

Points (1) to (7) in the second list under Method provide the outline of the SRA algorithm used for analysis. Another program implements Hillenbrand's normalisation scheme (CCP, first list under Method). Band-pass and high-pass versions (of CPP) using a 250th order, finite impulse response filter, are also coded. In the SRA analysis, a window length of 2048 points is used.

# 5  Results

## 5.1  Synthesis Data

In order to test the analysis techniques in a systematic manner they are firstly applied to the synthetically generated voice signals. The methods are tested with six levels of noise, jitter (both random and cyclic) and shimmer for signals at 110 Hz. The methods are also tested with three different noise levels for six different fundamental frequencies ranging from 80 Hz to 350 Hz and therefore covering the extremes of the expected vocal pitch range in modal register.

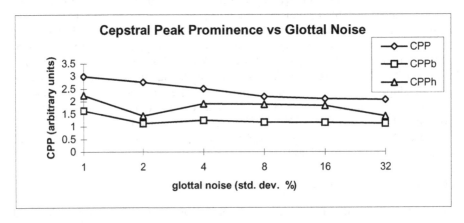

**Fig. 7.** Cepstral Peak Prominence (CPP) and filtered versions (CPPb, cepstrum applied to bandpassed (2.5-3.5 kHz) filtered speech) (CCPh, cepstrum applied to high-passed (2.5 kHz) filtered speech) vs glottal noise (110 Hz signal)

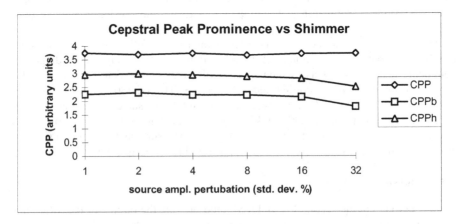

**Fig. 8.** Cepstral Peak Prominence (CPP) and filtered versions (CPPb, cepstrum applied to bandpassed (2.5-3.5 kHz) filtered speech) (CCPh, cepstrum applied to high-passed (2.5 kHz) filtered speech) vs shimmer (110 Hz signal)

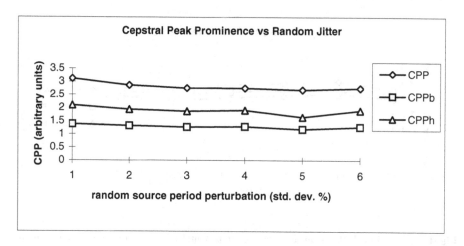

**Fig. 9.** Cepstral Peak Prominence (CPP) and filtered versions (CPPb, cepstrum applied to band-passed (2.5-3.5 kHz) filtered speech) (CCPh, cepstrum applied to high-passed (2.5 kHz) filtered speech) vs random jitter (110 Hz signal)

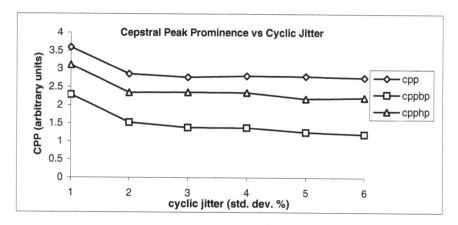

**Fig. 10.** Cepstral Peak Prominence (CPP) and filtered versions (CPPb, cepstrum applied to band-passed (2.5-3.5 kHz) filtered speech) (CCPh, cepstrum applied to high-passed (2.5 kHz) filtered speech) vs cyclic jitter (110 Hz signal)

The response of CPP to the aperiodicity measures is shown in Fig.7-Fig.10. Fig.8 and Fig.10 indicate that CPP is somewhat insensitive to cyclic jitter (2%-6%) and random shimmer. In consideration of the spectral characteristics of each of these sources of perturbation, with cyclic jitter containing sub-harmonics and shimmer resulting in a HNR that is equal at all frequencies, strong harmonic structure remains throughout the spectrum in each case. For shimmer, the increased height of the valleys between harmonic locations is seen to have a relatively small effect on the CPP calculation. The CPP measure is more responsive to additive noise (Fig.7). The

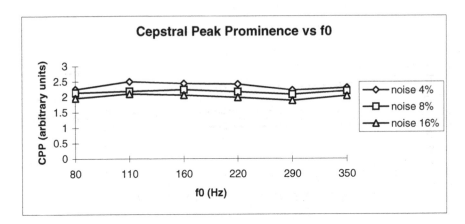

**Fig. 11.** Cepstral Peak Prominence (CPP) vs fundamental frequency for three levels of glottal noise

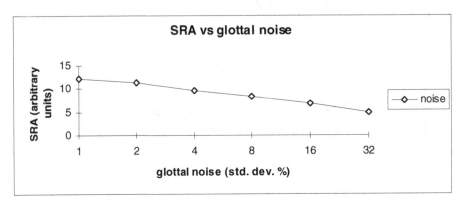

**Fig. 12.** Sum of rahmonic amplitudes (SRA) vs glottal noise for 110 Hz signal (vowel /AH/)

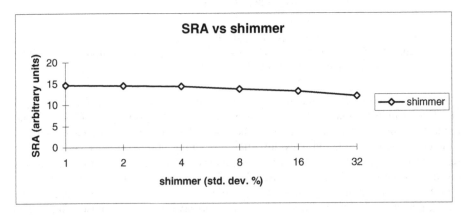

**Fig. 13.** Sum of rahmonic amplitudes (SRA) vs shimmer for 110 Hz signal (vowel /AH/)

corresponding spectrum for speech signals containing additive noise shows early harmonic structure that quickly deteriorates with increasing frequency. CPP decreases slightly as random jitter increases (Fig.9). Band-pass or high-pass filtering does not provide any new information and occasionally the results are less sensitive or less reliable (Fig.7 and Fig.9). CPP is somewhat invariant across f0, representing increased noise levels with decreased CPP values (Fig.11).

Sum of rahmonic amplitudes (SRA) is tested against the same synthesis data (six levels of additive noise, shimmer, random jitter and cyclic jitter).

The response of SRA to the aperiodicity measures is shown in Fig.12-Fig.14. The measure is similar in response to cyclic jitter and shimmer i.e. it is relatively (compared to noise and random jitter) less sensate to these measures. The SRA measure is more responsive to additive noise and random jitter (Fig.7 and Fig.9). SRA is not invariant across f0, however it represents increased noise levels with decreased SRA values (Fig.15).

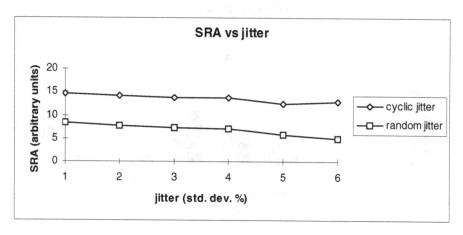

**Fig. 14.** Sum of rahmonic amplitudes (SRA) vs jitter for 110 Hz signal (vowel /AH/)

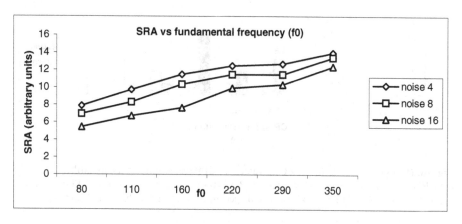

**Fig. 15.** Sum of rahmonic amplitudes (SRA) vs fundamental frequency for three levels of glottal noise (vowel /AH/)

## 5.2  Human Voice Signals

Both CPP (including filtered versions) and SRA are evaluated against the patient (13)/normal (12) data sets. All data were rated by two speech and language therapists (individually) based on a modified GRBAS scale. Two of the normals

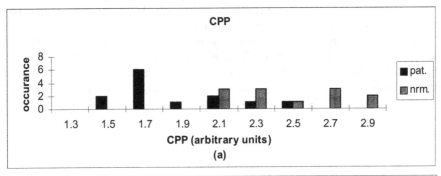

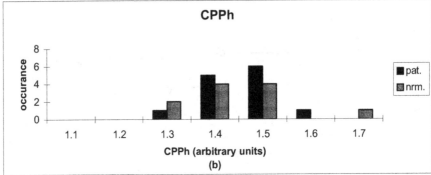

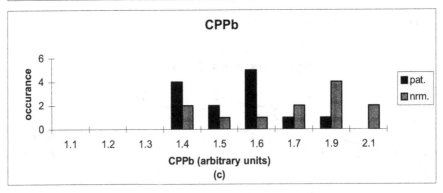

**Fig. 16.** Histogram of the estimated CPP values (a) CPP (cepstrum applied to unfiltered speech) (b) CPPh (cepstrum applied to high-passed (2.5 kHz) filtered speech) and (c) CPPb (cepstrum applied to band-passed (2.5-3.5 kHz) filtered speech) for normal and disordered corpus

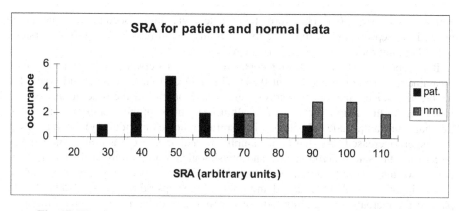

**Fig. 17.** Histogram of the estimated SRA values for normal and disordered corpus

were considered to have very mild symptoms of dysphonia (equivalent to a grade one on the GRBAS scale [35]). All patient voices were rated as dysphonic (with two rated mild (equivalent to a grade of 1-2 on the GRBAS scale)).

## 6  Discussion

The CPP and SRA measures in general decrease as noise or perturbation increases. CPP and SRA decrease more noticeably for noise and random jitter than for shimmer and cyclic jitter. This is explainable through considering the spectral consequences of these underlying aperiodicities. Signals containing shimmer and cyclic jitter retain strong harmonic structure in the spectrum whereas the higher harmonics are reduced when random noise or random jitter is present. However, the response of CPP and SRA to the aperiodicities is not exactly the same.

CPP appears less sensitive than SRA.

CPP differs from SRA in four distinct ways:

1. The window lengths differ.
2. Only the first rahmonic is used in the CPP evaluation.
3. The CPP results from a normalization procedure that involved taking a logarithm of the cepstral amplitudes and a noise floor.
4. In calculating CPP an average of logarithmic values is taken.

Therefore, the apparent reduced sensitivity produced using CPP may be conjectured to be due to any one of these four variations. However, it is hypothesized that with a window length of 52 ms, that harmonic structure should be present in the signal. Further, it is expected that the height of all rahmonics will vary in a similar fashion to that of the first rahmonic only. The reduced sensitivity therefore, is conjectured to be due to the fact that the normalization involves taking dB values of the first cepstral rahmonic, which has previously been stated to be representative of the mean of dB ratios (that the amplitude of the first rahmonic represents a mean of dB HNRs - at each harmonic/between harmonic location - in the log spectrum has been formally validated recently [36]). Therefore, taking the logarithm a second time has compressed the cepstral index, reducing its sensitivity. Band-pass and high-pass versions of CPP did not reflect the aperiodicity increases.

It is reported [3] that a strong correlation existed between CPP and perceived breathiness (correlation coefficient 0.84). The reduced rahmonic amplitude recorded for breathy voices may not be entirely due to aperiodicity of the time domain waveform. One of the main indicators of breathiness reported in the literature is increased first harmonic amplitude [13] along with aspiration noise (aperiodicity). Each acoustic parameter (increased first harmonic amplitude and increased aspiration noise) has direct (and the same) aerodynamic and physiological correlations in the form of increased volume velocity and more abducted vocal folds respectively. Therefore, in the case of breathy signals the reduced amplitude of the cepstral peak may also be due, in part, to the increase in the amplitude of the first harmonic. To understand this, it is observed that periodicity in the frequency domain is offset by this increase in amplitude of the first harmonic, leading to a less obvious 'separation of the log'. It is noted that periodicity in one domain does not necessarily indicate periodicity in another. On the contrary, a sharp peak in one domain corresponds to a more broadened (sinusoidal) event in the other domain (in fact, this is the reverse of the cepstrum). Therefore, perfect periodicity (sinusoid) can exist in the time-domain and yet no cepstral peak is found at the expected quefrency location.

In summary, SRA provides dependable estimates of noise levels and it is also affected by jitter. The CPP measure also reflects the deterioration in harmonic structure quite well but the trend is less reliable. The filtered versions are unsuccessful in following the trends of increased aperiodicity/reduced magnitude of acoustic index. All methods were applied to the patient data in an attempt to separate the patients from the normals (Fig.16 and Fig.17). The CPP method shows good ability in differentiating between the patient/normal data sets with it's filtered versions showing no discriminatory ability. However, SRA gives the best overall discrimination, being highly significant at the 5 % level (one tailed, equal variance, two sample mean, student's t-test).

## 7  Conclusion

Two high–quefrency acoustic indices, cepstral peak prominence (CPP) and sum of rahmonic amplitudes (SRA) have been implemented and evaluated using synthesized data and a set of patient and normal productions of the vowel /AH/. The reduction in the ability to 'separate the log' when signals become more dominantly sinusoidal (i.e. reduced richness of harmonics) has been proposed as a contributory factor for the success of rahmonic amplitude(s) in differentiating between patient and normal data sets and for the high correlation with perceived breathiness ratings. In this sense the high quefrency cepstral measures may comprise an extra dimension not captured in a traditional HNR estimate. SRA has been shown to be a potentially useful indicator of vocal pathology, reflecting additive noise levels and discriminating between a set of 13 patients with varying vocal pathologies and a group of 12 'normals' with statistical significance. CPP is shown to be relatively f0-independent, however the index appears to be compressed when compared against SRA. Band-passing the original time-domain signals prior to extracting the cepstral coefficients results in less useful acoustic indices of voice quality. Future work will examine the benefit of normalisation in CPP and will explore, in a quantitative fashion, the relationship between, noise and perturbation levels, and the measures CPP, first rahmonic amplitude and SRA. In addition, aperiodicities due to waveshape change, asymmetry or nonlinearities in vocal fold dynamics and non-stationarity of the vocal tract need to be examined.

## Acknowledgements

Partial support for this work is provided through an Enterprise Ireland Research Innovation Fund 2002/RIF/037 and a Health Research Board Grant 01/1995. The author wishes to thank Professor Michael Walsh and Dr. Michael Colreavy, ENT, Beaumont Hospital, Dublin for examination of voice patients and Dr. Kevin McGuigan, Royal College of Surgeons in Ireland, Dublin and Yvonne Fitzmaurice, Antonio Hussey and Jenny Robertson, SLT, Beaumont Hospital, Dublin for participating in this work and/or performing perceptual ratings of the voice recordings.

## References

1. de Krom, G.: A cepstrum based technique for determining a harmonics-to-noise ratio in speech signals. J. Speech Hear Res. **36** (1993) 254-266
2. Qi, Y. and Hillman, R.E.: Temporal and spectral estimations of harmonics-to-noise ratio in human voice signals. J. Acoust. Soc. Am. **102(1)** (1997) 537-543
3. Hillenbrand, J., Cleveland, R.A. and Erickson, R.L.: Acoustic correlates of breathy vocal quality. J. Speech and Hear. Res. **37** (1994) 769-777
4. Dejonckere, P. and Wieneke, G.H.: Spectral, cepstral and aperiodicity characteristics of pathological voice before and after phonosurgical treatment. Clinical Linguistics and Phonetics **8(2)** (1994) 161-169
5. Herman-Ackah, Y., Michael, D.D. and Goding, Jr., G.S.: The relationship between cepstral peak prominence and selected parameters of dysphonia. J. Voice. **16(1)** (2002) 20-27
6. Murphy, P.J.: A cepstrum-based harmonics-to-noise ratio in voice signals. Proceedings International Conference on Spoken Language Processing, Beijing, China (2000) 672-675
7. Yumoto, E., Gould, W. J., and Baer, T.: Harmonics-to-noise ratio as an index of the degree of hoarseness. J. Acoust. Soc. Am. **71** (1982) 1544–1549
8. Kasuya, Y.: An adaptive comb filtering method as applied to acoustic analysis of pathological voice. Proceedings IEEE ICASSP, Tokyo (1986) 669–672
9. Kasuya, H., and Ando, Y. Analysis, synthesis and perception of breathy voice. In: Gauffin, J., Hammarberg, B. (eds.): Vocal Fold Physiology: Acoustic, Perceptual and Physiologic Aspects of Voice Mechanisms, Singular Publishing Group, San Diego (1991) 251-258
10. Imaizumi, S.: Acoustic measurement of pathological voice qualities for medical purposes. Proceedings IEEE ICASSP, Tokyo (1986) 677–680
11. Klatt, D., Klatt, L.: Analysis, synthesis, and perception of voice quality variations among female and male talkers. J. Acoust. Soc. Amer., **87** (1991) 820-857
12. Qi, Y.: Time normalization in voice analysis. J. Acoust. Soc. Am. **92** (1992) 1569–1576.
13. Ladefoged, P., and Antonanzas-Barroso, N.: Computer measures of breathy voice quality. UCLA Working Papers in Phonetics **61** (1985) 79–86
14. Kitajima, K.: Quantitative evaluation of the noise level in the pathologic voice, Folia Phoniatr. **3** (1981) 145-148

15. Klingholtz, M., and Martin, F.: Quantitative spectral evaluation of shimmer and jitter, J. Speech Hear. Res. **28** (1985) 169–174
16. Kasuya, H., Ogawa, S., Mashima, K., and Ebihara, S.: Normalized noise energy as an acoustic measure to evaluate pathologic voice, J. Acoust. Soc. Am. **80** (1986) 1329–1334
17. Kasuya, H., and Endo, Y.: Acoustic analysis, conversion, and synthesis of the pathological voice. In: Fujimura, O., Hirano, M. (eds.): Vocal Fold Physiology: Voice Quality Control, Singular Publishing Group, San Diego, (1995) 305–320
18. Kojima, H., Gould, W. J., Lambiase, A., and Isshiki, N.: Computer analysis of hoarseness, Acta Oto-Laryngol. **89** (1980) 547–554
19. Muta, H., Baer, T., Wagatsuma, K., Muraoka, T., and Fukuda, H.: A pitch synchronous analysis of hoarseness in running speech. J. Acoust. Soc. Am. **84** (1988) 12292–1301
20. Hiraoka, N., Kitazoe, Y., Ueta, H., Tanaka, S., and Tanabe, M.: Harmonic intensity analysis of normal and hoarse voices, J. Acoust. Soc. Am. **76** (1984) 1648–1651
21. Qi, Y., Weinberg, B., Bi, N., and Hess, W. J.: Minimizing the effect of period determination on the computation of amplitude perturbation in voice, J. Acoust. Soc. Am. **97** (1995) 2525–2532
22. Michaelis, D., Gramss, T., and Strube, H. W.: Glottal to noise excitation ratio-a new measure for describing pathological voices, Acust. Acta Acust. **83** (1997) 700–706
23. Murphy, P.J.: Perturbation-free measurement of the harmonics-to-noise ratio in speech signals using pitch-synchronous harmonic analysis, J. Acoust. Soc. Am. **105(5)** (1999) 2866:2881
24. Manfredi, C., Iadanza, E., Dori, F. and Dubini, S.: Hoarse voice denoising for real-time DSP implementation: continuous speech assessment. Models and analysis of vocal emissions for biomedical applications:3rd International workshop, Firenze, Italy (2003)
25. Noll, AM.: Cepstrum pitch determination. J. Acoust. Soc. Am. **41** (1967) 293-309
26. Schafer, RW. and Rabiner, LR.: System for automatic formant analysis of voiced speech, J. Acoust. Soc. Am. **47** (1970) 634-648
27. Murphy, P.J. and Akande, O.: Cepstrum-based harmonics-to-noise ratio measurement in voiced speech. In: Chollet, G., Esposito, A., Faundez-Zanuy, M., Marinaro, M. (eds.): Nonlinear Speech Modeling and Applications. Lecture notes in Artificial Intelligence, Vol. 3445. Springer Verlag, Berlin Heidelberg New York (2005) 119-218.
28. Murphy, P.J.: Averaged modified periodogram analysis of aperiodic voice signals. Proceedings Irish Signals and Systems Conference, Dublin (2000) 266-271
29. Koike, Y.: Cepstrum analysis of pathological voices. J. Phonetics **14** (1986) 501-507
30. Koike, Y. and Kohda, J.: The effect of vocal fold surgery on the speech cepstrum. In: Gaufin, J., Hammarberg, B. (eds.): Vocal fold physiology: Acoustic, perceptual and physiologic aspects of voice mechanisms. Singular, San Diego (1991) 259-264
31. Yegnanarayana, B., d'Alessandro, C. and Darsinos, V.: An iterative algorithm for decomposition of speech signals into periodic and aperiodic components. IEEE Trans. Speech and Audio Processing **6(1)** (1998) 1-11.
32. Awan, S. and Roy, N.: Toward the development of an objective index of dysphonia severity: A four-factor acoustic model. Clinical Linguistics and Phonetics **20(1)** (2005) 35-49
33. Rosenberg, A.: Effect of glottal pulse shape on the quality of natural vowels. J. Acoust. Soc. Am. **49** (1971) 583-590
34. Rabiner, L. and Schafer, R.: Digital processing of speech signals. Prentice Hall, Englewood Cliffs, NJ (1978)
35. Isshiki, N., Takeuchi, Y.: Factor analysis of hoarseness. Studia Phonologica **5** (1970) 37-44
36. Murphy, P.: On first rahmonic amplitude in the analysis of synthesized aperiodic voice signals. J. Acoust. Soc. Am. **120(5)** (2006) 2896-2907

# Spectral Analysis of Speech Signals Using Chirp Group Delay

Baris Bozkurt, Thierry Dutoit, and Laurent Couvreur

TCTS Lab., Faculté Polytechnique De Mons, Initialis Scientific Parc, B-7000
Mons/Belgium
barisbozkurt@iyte.edu.tr, Laurent.Couvreur@fpms.ac.be,
Thierry.Dutoit@fpms.ac.be

**Abstract.** This study presents chirp group delay processing techniques for spectral analysis of speech signals. It is known that group delay processing is potentially very useful for spectral analysis of speech signals. However, it is also well known that group delay processing is difficult due to large spikes that mask the formant structure. In this chapter, we first discuss the sources of spikes on group delay functions, namely the zeros closely located to the unit circle. We then propose processing of chirp group delay functions, *i.e.* group delay functions computed on a circle other than the unit circle in $z$-plane. Chirp group delay functions can be guaranteed to be spike-free if zero locations can be controlled. The technique we use here for that is to compute the zero-phased version of the signal for which the zeros appear very close (or on) the unit circle. The final representation obtained is named as the chirp group delay of zero-phased version of a signal (CGDZP). We demonstrate use of CGDZP in two applications: formant tracking and feature extraction for automatic speech recognition (ASR). We show that high quality formant tracking can be performed by simply picking peaks on CGDZP and CGDZP is potentially useful for improving ASR performance.

**Keywords:** Phase processing, chirp group delay, group delay, zzt, ASR feature extraction.

## 1 Introduction

Magnitude spectrum has been the preferred part of Fourier Transform (FT) spectrum in most of the speech processing methods although it carries only part of the available information. One of the main reasons for this is the difficulties involved in phase processing. In speech processing research, phase processing is often cited as very difficult. Especially when linear models are used in analysis of speech signals, the phase components is to a great extend left remained in the residual, the component left over from linear modeling.

By its nature, the phase spectrum is in a wrapped form and the negative first derivative of its unwrapped version, the so-called group delay function is generally preferred since it is easier to study and process. It has been shown by Yegnanarayana and Murthy that group delay functions are potentially very useful for spectral analysis since vocal tract resonance peaks appear with higher resolution than in the magnitude

Y. Stylianou, M. Faundez-Zanuy, A. Esposito (Eds.): WNSP 2005, LNCS 4391, pp. 41–57, 2007.
© Springer-Verlag Berlin Heidelberg 2007

spectrum [1], [2], [3]. However they also report that group delay functions suffer from having many spikes and direct processing of group delay spectra is very difficult. In various papers, they have presented ways to indirectly compute smoothed group delay functions using cepstral transformations and smoothing.

This paper describes a similar approach but uses a new technique and a new representation to perform spectral processing using group delay functions. Our previous studies [4] showed that for most speech frames, a 'cloud' of zeros/roots of polynomials computed as the $z$-tranform of the speech samples is located around the unit circle, resulting in many spikes in the group delay function. One way to overcome this problem is to control/modify the location of the zeros/roots and also to use an analysis circle other than the unit circle for group delay computation, $i.e.$ to compute chirp group delay (CGD) functions instead. We show in two applications that chirp group delay processing is potentially very useful for spectral analysis of speech signals.

In Section 2, we start by explaining the difficulties in group delay processing and the methods proposed in literature to tackle those problems. In Section 3, we present our alternative: chirp group delay of zero-phase version of signals. Section 4 and 5 are dedicated to applications in formant tracking and feature estimation for automatic speech recognition (ASR), respectively. In Section 6, we present our conclusions.

## 2   Difficulties in Group Delay Analysis and Proposed Solutions

### 2.1   Difficulties in Group Delay Analysis

For a short-term discrete-time signal $\{x(n)\}$, $n=0,1,...,N-1$, the group delay function (GDF) is defined as the negative first-order derivative of the discrete-time Fourier transform phase function $\theta(\omega)$,

$$GDF(\omega) = \frac{-d\theta(\omega)}{d\omega} \tag{1}$$

with $\theta(\omega) = arg(X(\omega))$ and $X(\omega)$ being the Fourier transform of $\{x(n)\}$. Equation (1) can also be expressed as:

$$GDF(\omega) = \frac{X_R(\omega)Y_R(\omega) + X_I(\omega)Y_I(\omega)}{|X(\omega)|^2} \tag{2}$$

where $Y(\omega)$ is defined as the Fourier transform of $\{nx(n)\}$ [5]. The notations $R$ and $I$ refer to real and imaginary parts, respectively. The advantage of this representation is that explicit phase unwrapping operation, which is generally a problematic task, is not necessary in order to compute the group delay function.

Group delay analysis is known to be difficult because many large spikes are often present [6]. This is simply explained by noting that the term $|X(\omega)|^2$ in Equation (2) can get very small at frequencies where there exist one or more zeros of the $z$-transform of the signal $x(n)$ very close to the unit circle [7].

This can also be explained geometrically. For a given short-term discrete-time signal $x(n)$, the $z$-transform polynomial $X(z)$ can be expressed using an all-zero/root representation as:

$$X(z) = \sum_{n=0}^{N-1} x(n)z^{-n} = x(0)z^{-N+1} \prod_{m=1}^{N-1} (z - Z_m) \qquad (3)$$

where $Z_m$ are the zeros/roots of the $z$-transform polynomial[1] $X(z)$. The Fourier transform, which is simply the $z$-transform computed on the unit circle, can be expressed as:

$$X(\omega) = x(0)\left(e^{j\omega}\right)^{(-N+1)} \prod_{m=1}^{N-1} (e^{j\omega} - Z_m) \qquad (4)$$

provided that $x(0)$ is non-zero. Each factor in Equation (4) corresponds to a vector starting at $Z_m$ and ending at $e^{j\omega}$ in the $z$-plane. In practice, the Fourier transform is evaluated at frequencies regularly spaced along the unit circle, the so-called frequency bins. As illustrated in Fig. 1, the vector $e^{j\omega} - Z_m$ changes drastically its orientation when going from a frequency bin to the next one around the root $Z_m$. The change increases as the root gets closer to the unit circle. Hence the group delay function, $i.e.$ the rate of change in the phase spectrum, is very high at frequency bins close to a root/zero of the $z$-transform polynomial. It becomes ill-defined when the zero/root coincides with a frequency bin. This results in spikes in the group delay function that get larger as the roots come closer to the unit circle.

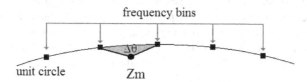

**Fig. 1.** Geometric interpretation for spikes in the group delay function of a signal at frequency locations on the unit

Due to the strong link between the position of zeros of the $z$-transform (ZZT) and spikes on the group delay functions, a study of the ZZT patterns obtained from the $z$-transform of short-term discrete-time speech signals would be very valuable. Such a study, however, would require the analytical computation of root locations of high order polynomials, which is impossible. The problem becomes even more complicated due to windowing in time domain, which corresponds to term-wise coefficient multiplication of corresponding polynomials in $z$-domain. For this reason, the location of roots can be derived analytically only for some elementary signals ($i.e.$ power series, damped sinusoidal, impulse train, $etc$). For more complex signals such

---

[1] The formulation in Equation (3) is referred to as the ZZT (zeros of the $z$-transform) representation [8]. It is a direct factorisation of the polynomial ($i.e.$ root finding), not a low degree moving average (MA) modelling for the signal.

as speech, the analytical solution becomes intractable and the roots should be estimated numerically. It allows then to observe their location in the $z$-plane. At first sight, it was almost impossible to get an intuition about where the zeros/roots could be located on the $z$-plane for a given speech signal. However, some patterns can be inferred for speech signals and have been presented in detail in [8]. Here we provide a short review due to space limitations.

## 2.2  ZZT and the Source-Filter Model of Speech

In Fig. 2, we present the source-filter model of voiced speech in various domains: the first row is in the time domain, the second row is in the ZZT domain and the third row is in the log-magnitude spectrum domain. In each domain, the different contributions of the source-filter model of speech interact with each other through some operator: convolution (*), union (U) and addition (+), respectively.

Consider the second row of Fig. 2. The ZZT pattern for the impulse train is such that zeros are equally spaced on the unit circle with the exception that there exist gaps at all harmonics of the fundamental frequency, which create the harmonic peaks on the magnitude spectrum (third row of Fig. 2).

The ZZT representation of the differential glottal flow signal (LF model [9]), which is shown in second column of Fig. 2, contains two groups of zeros: a group of zeros below R=1 (inside the unit circle) and a group of zeros above R=1 (outside the unit circle) in polar coordinates. The group of zeros inside the unit circle is due to the return phase of the glottal flow excitation waveform and the group outside the unit circle is due to the first phase of the LF signal.

The zeros of the vocal tract filter response are mainly located inside the unit circle due to the decreasing exponential shape of this signal and there are gaps for the formant locations, which create formant spectral peaks. We observe a wing-like shape for the ZZT pattern of the vocal tract response depending on the location of the truncation point for the time-domain response (demonstrated in movie 2 on our demo website [10]).

It is interesting to note here that the ZZT set of speech is just the union of ZZT sets of its three components. This is due to the fact that the convolution operation in time-domain corresponds to multiplication of the z-transform polynomials in z-domain. What is interesting is that the ZZT of each component appear at a different area on the z-plane and have effect on the magnitude spectrum relative to their distance to the unit circle. The closest zeros to the unit circle are the impulse train zeros and they cause the spectral dips on the magnitude spectrum, which give rise to harmonic peaks. Vocal tract zeros are the second closest set and the zero-gaps due to formants contribute to the magnitude spectrum with formant peaks on the spectral envelope. Differential glottal flow ZZT are further away from the unit circle and their contribution to the magnitude spectrum is rather vague and distributed along the frequency axis.

We have shown that most of the roots are located close to the unit circle (as if there was a 'zero-cloud' around the unit circle) and that they can be further decomposed into contributions of impulse train, glottal flow and vocal tract filter components in the

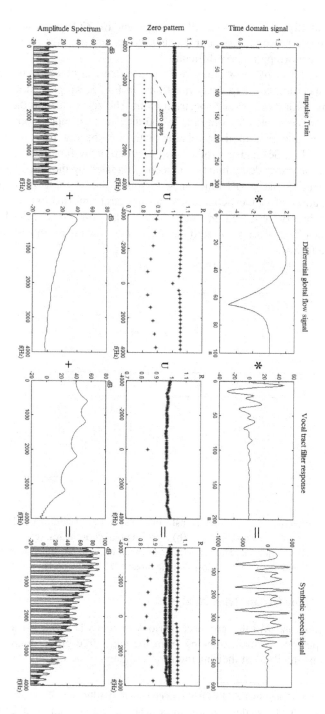

**Fig. 2.** ZZT and source-filter model of speech. Note that magnitude spectra added are in dB.

speech signal [8][2]. The 'zero-cloud' arrangement of ZZT patterns is an important obstacle in phase processing since it results in many spikes in the group delay function (making phase unwrapping very difficult).

In fact, the effect of zeros close to the unit circle can be easily observed both on magnitude spectra and group delay functions. In Fig. 3, we present a windowed real speech frame with its zeros and spectrum plots. The zeros close to the unit circle are shown in between dashed lines in Fig. 3b and they are also superimposed on spectrum plots to draw attention to their relation with the spectral dips in the magnitude spectrum (see Fig. 3c) and the spikes on the group delay function (see Fig. 3d). We observe that the group delay function is merely dictated by the zeros close to the unit circle and appears like a DC function with spikes due to these zeros (see Fig. 3d). This domination of spikes conceals other spectral information and the formant structure is hardly observed in such group delay functions. For the magnitude spectrum, the effect of zeros close to the unit circle (dips) is much smaller and we can still observe formants.

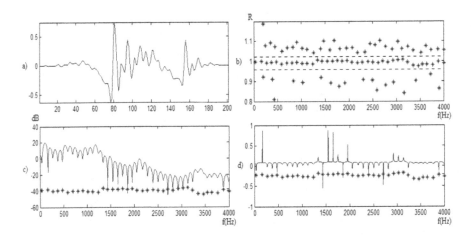

**Fig. 3.** Effects of zeros on the Fourier Transform of a signal: (a) Hanning windowed real speech frame (phoneme /a/ in the word "party"), (b) zeros in polar coordinates, (c) magnitude spectrum and (d) group delay function. The zeros close to the unit circle are superimposed on spectrum plots to show the link between the zeros and the dips/spikes on the plots.

### 2.3 Methods for Group Delay Analysis

Yegnanarayana and Murthy proposed various methods [1], [2], [3] to remove these spikes and perform formant tracking from the spike-free group delay function. The common steps involved in their methods are: obtaining the magnitude spectrum for a

---

[2] It should be noted here that ZZT of real speech signals hardly look like the ZZT plot in Fig. 2. This is mainly due to windowing, window synchronization problems and the mismatches of the source-filter model with the actual speech signal. However, with appropriate windowing, similar patterns are obtained for speech signals [8].

short-time windowed speech frame, smoothing the magnitude spectrum via cepstral lifting and computing smooth minimum-phase group delay from this representation through cepstrum. Note that the resulting group delay function is a kind of smoothed magnitude spectrum but the advantage of this representation compared to the magnitude spectrum is that the formant peaks appear with better resolution [2]. The authors propose formant tracking algorithms by picking peaks on this representation.

Other recent studies address the spike problem and propose group delay based features: the modified group delay function (MODGDF) [7] and the product spectrum (PS) [11]. These representations are obtained by modifying one term in the group delay computation, which is supposed to be the main source of spikes in the group delay function. These rather recent representations are further discussed in the following sections.

### 2.3.1  Modified Group Delay Function (MODGDF)

As exposed previously, spikes in group delay can be explained by the very low values of the $|X(\omega)|^2$ term as defined in Equation (2). The basic idea behind the modified group delay function (MODGDF) [7] consists in smoothing the magnitude spectrum $|X(\omega)|$ in order to avoid extremely low values. Such smoothing can be easily performed through cepstral processing. However, this modification alone cannot remove all spikes but some formant peaks can be enhanced. To further reduce spikes, two other parameters have been introduced: $\alpha$ and $\gamma$ which need to be fine-tuned according to the nature of the signals[3]. The modified group delay function is eventually defined as:

$$MODGDF(\omega) = \left(\frac{\tau_p(\omega)}{|\tau_p(\omega)|}\right)\left(|\tau_p(\omega)|\right)^{\alpha} \tag{5}$$

with

$$\tau_p(\omega) = \left(\frac{X_R(\omega)Y_R(\omega) + X_I(\omega)Y_I(\omega)}{S(\omega)^{2\gamma}}\right) \tag{6}$$

where $S(\omega)$ is the cepstrally smoothed version of $|X(\omega)|$.

### 2.3.2  Product Spectrum (PS)

In [11], another group delay function is proposed, the so-called product spectrum (PS). It is a version of Equation (2) where the denominator $|X(\omega)|^2$, which is considered to be a source of spikes, is simply removed. The product spectrum $PS(\omega)$ is simply defined as the product of the power spectrum and the group delay function:

$$PS(\omega) = |X(\omega)|^2 GDF(\omega) = X_R(\omega)Y_R(\omega) + X_I(\omega)Y_I(\omega) \tag{7}$$

---

[3] In all tests/plots of this study, we have set the parameters as in [17], namely $\alpha=0.4$ and $\gamma=0.9$.

## 3   Chirp Group Delay Processing

In [8], we have presented various ways of avoiding spikes on the group delay spectrum mainly by: modifying the zero/root locations (or suppressing some of the zeros) and changing the analysis circle to guarantee certain distance to the closest zero/root, namely using Chirp Group Delay (CGD) representations[4].

We define the chirp group delay (CGD) as the negative derivative of the phase spectrum (the group delay function) computed from chirp z-transform [12], that is, from z-transform computed on a circle/spiral other than the unit circle. Given a short-term discrete-time signal $\{x(n)\}$, $n=0,1,...,N-1$, the chirp Fourier transform $\tilde{X}(\omega)$ is defined as:

$$\tilde{X}(\omega) = X(z)\big|_{z=\rho e^{j\omega}} = \sum_{n=0}^{N-1} x(n)\left(\rho e^{j\omega}\right)^{-n} = \left|\tilde{X}(\omega)\right| e^{j\tilde{\theta}(\omega)} \tag{8}$$

where $\rho$ is the radius of the analysis circle. Similarly to Equation (1), the chirp group delay function $CGD(\omega)$ is defined as:

$$CGD(\omega) = -\frac{d(\tilde{\theta}(\omega))}{d\omega} \tag{9}$$

Interestingly enough, a fast Fourier transform (FFT) can be used to compute $\tilde{X}(\omega)$ by re-writing Equation (8) as:

$$\tilde{X}(\omega) = \sum_{n=0}^{N-1} \left(x(n)\rho^{-n}\right)\left(e^{j\omega}\right)^{-n} = \sum_{n=0}^{N-1} \tilde{x}(n)\left(e^{j\omega}\right)^{-n} \tag{10}$$

Therefore, for the computation of the $CGD(\omega)$ of a given short-term signal, it is sufficient to term-wise multiply the signal samples with an exponential time-series and compute the group delay with direct formula in Equation (2).

For applications like formant tracking and feature estimation for speech recognition, we propose to use CGD with some rough control on the zero/root locations so that group delay is computed on a zero-free region. Three CGD representations were proposed in [8] which apply various ways of controlling zero/root locations. Here we will only discuss *Chirp Group Delay of the Zero-Phase version of a signal (CGDZP)*, which is more suited to practical applications than the other CGD two representations, due to computational and robustness issues.

The procedure consists of two steps for the computation of CGDZP[5]: computation of the zero-phase version of the signal by taking the inverse Fourier transform of its magnitude spectrum $|X(\omega)|$ and computation of the CGD on a circle outside the unit circle. The conversion to zero-phase guarantees that all of the zeros occur very close to the unit circle [8] therefore the resulting chirp group delay representation is very

---

[4] The first presentation of Chirp Group Delay can be found in [22]. Initially the term "differential phase spectrum" has been used, then we switched to "chirp group delay", which is more accurate.

[5] Our Matlab code for CGDZP computation is shared on [23].

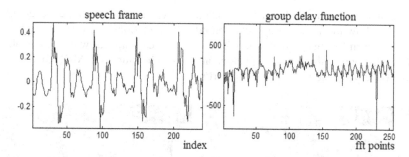

**Fig. 4.** A 30 ms speech frame and its group delay function. The frame example is extracted from the noise-free utterance "mah_4625" of the test set A of the AURORA-2 speech database [13] and corresponds to vowel /i/ in word "six".

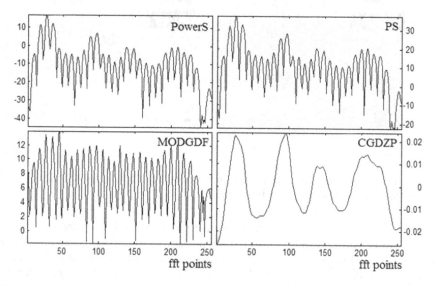

**Fig. 5.** Power spectrum (PowerS) and group delay representations (Product Spectrum, Modified Group Delay Function and Chirp Groupd Delay of Zero-Phased signal) for the speech signal frame in Fig. 3

smooth with well-resolved formant peaks. However, the phase information is destroyed and the representation contains only the information available in the magnitude spectrum as for the group delay representations proposed by Yegnanarayana and Murthy [1], [2], [3]. They also have the same property that formant peak resolutions appear with higher resolution than in the magnitude spectrum. However it should be noted that there is important difference in the final representations obtained (as it clearly appears when the methods to compute them are compared). For comparing CGDZP with rather recent group delay based representations as explained in Section 2, we present example plots hereafter.

Fig. 4 presents a typical time-domain speech signal and its classical group delay function. As expected, the group delay function computed directly on the speech frame contains mainly spikes and resonance information cannot be observed. In Fig. 5, we show the three group delay based representations together, as well as the power spectrum for this speech frame. The formant peaks appear with high resolution in CGDZP, whereas the spectral envelope appears to be blurred in MODGDF, and PS is actually very similar to the power spectrum (as in [11]).

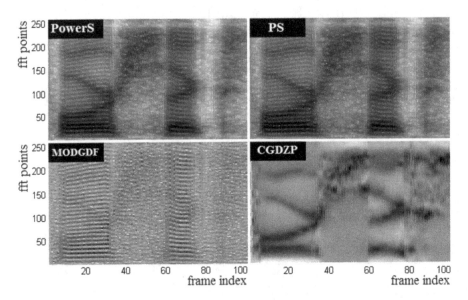

**Fig. 6.** Spectrogram plots of a noise-free utterance. Only the first half of the file, "mah_4625a", that contains the digit utterance "4 6" is presented.

In Fig. 6, we also present spectrogram-like plots obtained using the same group delay representations as well as the classical power spectrum. The formant tracks can be well observed on all of the spectrograms except for MODGDF, and PS is again very close to PowerS (as in Fig. 1 of [11]). These observations suggest that the CGDZP has some potential for formant tracking and ASR feature extraction. In the following sections we present our tests in these two applications.

## 4 Application in Formant Tracking

Automatic tracking of acoustic resonance frequencies of the vocal tract filter, the formant frequencies, has been an important speech analysis problem for a long time. Many proposed algorithms exist and they show large variety. The reader is referred to [8] for a list of some of the approaches. Moderate-good quality formant tracking has been achieved with most of the recently proposed technologies and further improvement is necessary for increasing robustness of applications based on formant tracking.

SPEECH DATA

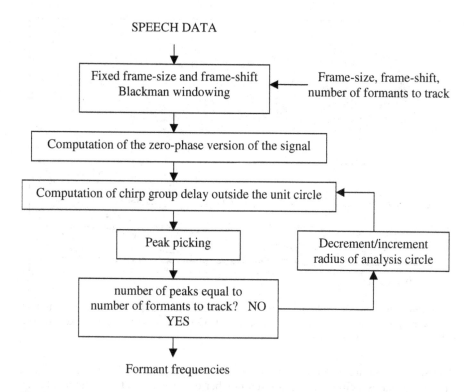

Fig. 7. Formant tracking algorithm using peak picking on chirp group delay computed outside the unit circle

## 4.1 The Formant Tracking Algorithm

Formant tracking can simply be achieved by tracking the peaks of the CGDZP of constant frame size/shift windowed speech frames. The flow chart of the proposed method is presented in Fig. 7. Note that the radius $\rho$ of the analysis circle is continuously adapted to properly track all formants.

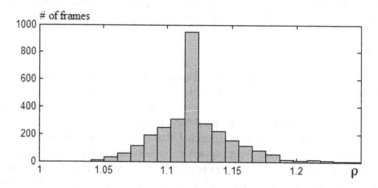

Fig. 8. Histogram of $\rho$ values obtained by the iterative procedure

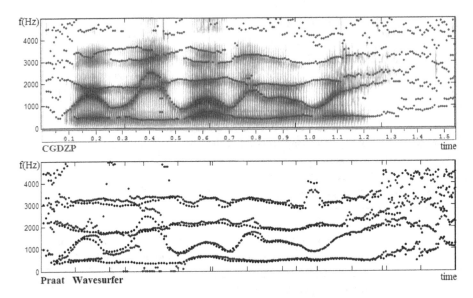

CGDZP

Praat  Wavesurfer

**Fig. 9.** Formant tracking example: male speech, 1SX9.wav file from [14] corresponding to text "where were you while we were away". Upper plot: CGDZP-based formant tracker. Lower plot: Praat and WaveSurfer formant trackers.

The smoothness and resolution of peaks of the chirp group delay varies with the radius of the analysis circle. Given a fixed number of formants to track, the $\rho$ value is iteratively optimized by decrementing/incrementing it with steps of 0.01: if the number of peaks picked is higher than the number of formants to be tracked, $\rho$ is incremented and vice versa. For tracking of five formants on a 30 ms frame-size analysis (at 16000Hz sampling frequency), the optimum value found for most of the examples is $\rho=1.12$, so this value is taken as the optimum initial value for the iterative procedure. In Fig. 8, we present the histogram of results for iteration of $\rho$ on 2865 speech frames (1453 male, 1412 female). The initial value is set to $\rho=1.12$ and the limits of the iteration are [1.05 1.25] where the number of formants is fixed to five. This figure shows that $\rho=1.12$ is an appropriate value for tracking five formant peaks. To reduce computational time of the algorithm one can remove the iteration block and set $\rho=1.12$ for frame size of 30 ms. with 16000Hz sampling frequency.

## 4.2  Tests

As commonly done, we compare our formant tracker with well-known, publicly available techniques on a few examples, namely the formant tracker of Praat [15] and the formant tracker of Wavesurfer [16]. Five female and five male (real speech) examples with large formant movements were used for comparing the trackers. In Fig. 9, we present one example plot for one male speech. Other plots are available in [8].

The overall results for the three systems are comparable; they all provide high quality formant tracks. For some examples, the formant trackers of Praat and WaveSurfer provide more continuous plots since a smoothest path finding algorithm is included in their procedures, which is not the case for the CGDZP based formant tracker. The fact that high quality formant tracking can be performed on CGDZP with a simple algorithm, as presented here, shows that CGDZP reveals clearly formant peaks and can potentially be used in various other applications.

# 5 Application to Speech Recognition

## 5.1 ASR Feature Extraction

In this section, we investigate the possibilities of using group delay representation for ASR feature extraction. The idea that comes naturally to mind is to replace the power spectrum by any group delay function in an MFCC-like feature extraction algorithm. Two recent studies have already considered this approach using the modified group delay function [17] or the product spectrum [11], which are reviewed in Section 2. Here, we compare these two representations as well as the standard power-based MFCC with our proposed CGDZP. In Table 1, we list all the feature extractions that are considered in the ASR experiments in next section.

## 5.2 ASR Experiments

The ASR system that is considered in this work is based on the STRUT toolkit [18]. It relies on the hybrid Multi Layer Perceptron / Hidden Markov Model (MLP/HMM) technology [19] where the phonemes of the language under consideration are modeled by HMM's whose observation state probabilities are estimated as the outputs of a MLP. Such an acoustic model is trained beforehand in a supervised fashion on a large database of phonetically segmented speech material and is naturally dependent on the nature of the extracted acoustic features. Therefore, an acoustic model was built for every feature extraction of Table 1.

The AURORA-2 database [13] was used in this work. It consists of connected English digit utterances sampled at 8kHz. More exactly, we used the clean training set, which contains 8440 noise-free utterances spoken by 110 male and female speakers, for building our acoustic models. These models were evaluated on the test set A. It has 4004 different noise-free utterances spoken by 104 other speakers. It also contains the same utterances corrupted by four types of real-world noises (subway, babble, car, exhibition hall) at various signal-to-noise ratios (SNR) ranging from 20dB to -5dB. During the recognition experiments, the decoder was constrained by a lexicon reduced to the English digits and no grammar was applied.

Table 2 gives the word error rates (WER) for the ASR system tested with the feature extractions described in Table 1. Errors are counted in terms of word substitutions, deletions and insertions, and error rates are averaged over all noise types. In Table 3, the results are also provided when combining MFCC feature extraction with the features used in Table 2. The combination is simply performed by taking a weighted geometric average of the outputs probabilities of the combined acoustic models:

$$p_{12} = p_1^{\lambda} \cdot p_2^{1-\lambda} \tag{11}$$

where $p_{12}$, $p_1$ and $p_2$ denote the combined probability and the probability provided by the two combined acoustic models, respectively. The combination parameter λ takes its value in the range (0,1) and is optimized for every combination.

The results show that CGDZP-CC outperforms the other representations. It should be noted however that for computation of MODGDF-CC we used the same parameter values as in [17], while the authors mention that the parameters need to be tuned for the specific system and data. For this reason our comparison is limited in the sense that only one set of parameters is used for comparison with MODGDF-CC.

One of our main targets in these experiments was to test whether a phase/group delay representation carries complementary information to that of the power spectrum in the framework of feature extraction for ASR systems. The values corresponding to CGDZP-CC combined with MFCC, compared to the MFCC-only results on the first row in Table 2 are in all cases lower except for the extreme noise setting SNR=-5dB. This demonstrates that CGDZP-CC features extraction does indeed provide complementary information to MFCC and is potentially useful for improving ASR performance.

Noise robustness is definitively a sensitive issue and neither MFCC nor the group delay representations are effectively robust to additive noise. The degradation of the recognition performances in the presence of noise is primarily due to the mismatch

**Table 1.** Methods for ASR feature extraction based on power spectrum or group delay function. All methods are applied on 30ms-long frames, shifted every 10 ms.

| Feature extraction | Description |
| --- | --- |
| MFCC | Mel-warped Frequency Cepstral Coefficients: 1st-13th order cepstral coefficients obtained by inverse discrete cosine transform of the log-compressed outputs of a Mel-spaced 24-band filterbank applied to the power spectrum. The feature vector is augmented by delta coefficients and the delta(-delta) log-compressed frame energy. |
| MODGDF-CC | Modified Group Delay Function - Cepstral Coefficients: 1st-13th order cepstral coefficients obtained by inverse discrete cosine transform of the outputs of a Mel-spaced 24-band filterbank applied to the modified group delay function. The feature vector is augmented by delta coefficients and the delta(-delta) log-compressed frame energy. |
| PS-CC | Product Spectrum - Cepstral Coefficients: 1st-13th order cepstral coefficients obtained by inverse discrete cosine transform of the outputs of a Mel-spaced 24-band filterbank applied to the product spectrum. The feature vector is augmented by delta coefficients and the delta(-delta) log-compressed frame energy. |
| CGDZP-CC | Chirp Group Delay of Zero-Phased Signal - Cepstral Coefficients: 1st-13th order cepstral coefficients obtained by inverse discrete cosine transform of the outputs of a Mel-spaced 24-band filterbank applied to the chirp group delay ($\rho=1.12$) of a zero-phase version of frame signal. The feature vector is augmented by delta coefficients and the delta(-delta) log-compressed frame energy. |

**Table 2.** ASR performances for various feature extractions on the AURORA-2 task. Results are given in terms of word error rate (WER) in percent.

| Feature extraction | SNR(dB) | | | | | | | |
|---|---|---|---|---|---|---|---|---|
| | ∞ | 20 | 15 | 10 | 5 | 0 | -5 | ∞ |
| MFCC | 1.9 | 6.7 | 18.6 | 45.2 | 75.1 | 88.8 | 91.5 | 1.9 |
| MODGDF-CC | 3.2 | 19.0 | 41.7 | 68.7 | 86.1 | 91.0 | 92.3 | 3.2 |
| PS-CC | 2.0 | 6.7 | 19.4 | 45.3 | 75.5 | 89.0 | 92.2 | 2.0 |
| CGDZP-CC | 1.8 | 5.8 | 12.2 | 29.4 | 62.6 | 88.7 | 97.6 | 1.8 |

**Table 3.** ASR performances for features combined with MFCC on the AURORA-2 task. Results are given in terms of word error rate (WER) in percent.

| Feature extraction | SNR(dB) | | | | | | | |
|---|---|---|---|---|---|---|---|---|
| | ∞ | 20 | 15 | 10 | 5 | 0 | -5 | ∞ |
| MODGDF-CC | 2.1 | 8.5 | 23.9 | 52.7 | 79.5 | 89.5 | 91.5 | 2.1 |
| PS-CC | 1.9 | 6.7 | 18.6 | 44.4 | 74.6 | 88.5 | 91.6 | 1.9 |
| CGDZP-CC | 1.7 | 5.0 | 10.4 | 24.8 | 52.7 | 82.3 | 91.1 | 1.7 |

between the training conditions (clean speech) and the test conditions (noisy speech). Several approaches can be adopted to reduce these acoustics discrepancies [20], [21]. First, the speech signal can be captured with as less noise as possible by using spatially selective microphone or arrays of microphones. Further techniques can be applied to enhance speech signals. These techniques concentrate on enhancing the amplitude spectrum and can be hardly generalized to the phase spectrum. Other techniques aim at adapting the acoustic models to noisy conditions and could clearly be used for group delay representations.

## 6 Conclusion

In this chapter, we have presented the CGDZP representation and demonstrated its successful utilization in two speech processing problems: formant tracking and feature extraction for speech recognition.

The main motivation for processing chirp group delay (CGD) of speech frames computed on circles other than the unit circle is to get rid of spikes created by zeros of their z-transform (ZZT) close to the unit circle, which actually mask formant peaks on classical group delay functions. By both manipulating the zeros/roots (ZZT) by zero-phasing and adjusting the analysis circle radius for CGD computation, we can guarantee a certain distance between zeros and the analysis circle. The choice of the circle radius is definitively a sensitive issue and its value should be tuned for every application. When the analysis circle is set too far away from the areas on z-plane where zeros are located, the resolution of formant peaks become poorer (*i.e.* CGD gets too smooth). As the analysis circle gets closer to those areas, the resolution of formant peaks gets higher but also the risk of having spurious spikes. For this reason, in our experiments with formant tracking and ASR feature estimation, we first searched for some optimum value for the radius (by incrementing the radius by 0.1 in the range [0.9,2] and checking the system performance) and found that $\rho=1.12$ appears to be a good choice.

We have shown that formant tracking can be performed succesfully by just picking peaks in the CGDZP representation. In addition the speech recognition test results are very promising and should be confirmed on more challenging speech recognition tasks. Although the tests applied were limited, they are sufficient to demonstrate that CGDZP is potentially a very useful function for spectral processing of speech signals.

**Acknowledgments.** Baris Bozkurt was funded by Region Wallonne/Belgium, grant FIRST EUROPE #215095. Laurent Couvreur was funded by Region Wallonne/Belgium in the project WIST IC&C.

# References

1. Yegnanarayana, B., Duncan, G., Murthy, H. A.: Improving formant extraction from speech using minimum-phase group delay spectra. Proc. of European Signal Processing Conference (EUSIPCO). vol. 1, Sep. 5–8, Grenoble, France, (1988) 447–450
2. Murthy, H. A., Murthy, K. V., Yegnanarayana, B.: Formant extraction from phase using weighted group delay function. Electronics Letters. vol. 25, no. 23, (1989) 1609–1611.
3. Murthy, H. A., Yegnanarayana, B.: Formant extraction from group delay function. Speech Communication. vol. 10, no. 3, (1991) 209–221.
4. Bozkurt, B., Doval, B., D'Alessandro, C., Dutoit, T.: Appropriate windowing for group delay analysis and roots of z-transform of speech signals. Proc. of European Signal Processing Conference (EUSIPCO), Sep. 6–10, Vienna, Austria, (2004).
5. Oppenheim, A. V., Schafer, R. W., Buck, J. R.: Discrete-Time Signal Processing. Second edition, Prentice-Hall, (1999).
6. Yegnanarayana, B., Saikia, D. K., Krishnan, T. R.: Significance of group delay functions in signal reconstruction from spectral magnitude or phase. IEEE Trans. on Acoustics, Speech and Signal Processing. vol. 32, no. 3, (1984) 610–623.
7. Hegde, R. M., Murthy H. A., Gadde, V. R.: The modified group delay feature: A new spectral representation of speech. Proc. of International Conference on Spoken Language Processing (ICSLP), Oct. 4–8, Jeju Island, Korea, (2004)
8. Bozkurt, B.: New spectral methods for analysis of source/filter characteristics of speech signals. PhD Thesis, Faculté Polytechnique De Mons, Presses universitaires de Louvain, ISBN: 2-87463-013-6, (2006).
9. Fant, G.: The LF-model revisited. Transformation and frequency domain analysis. Speech Trans. Lab.Q.Rep., Royal Inst. of Tech. Stockholm, vol. 2-3, (1995) 121-156
10. Demo Page for Zeros of the Z-Transform (ZZT) Representation: http://tcts.fpms.ac.be/demos/zzt.
11. Zhu, D. Paliwal, K. K.: Product of power spectrum and group delay function for speech recognition. Proc. of International Conference on Acoustics, Speech and Signal Processing (ICASSP), May 17–21, Montreal, Canada, (2004) 125–128
12. Rabiner, L. R., Schafer R. W., Rader, C. M.: The chirp z-transform algorithm and its application. Bell System Tech. J. vol. 48, no. 5, (1969) 1249–1292

13. Hirsch, H. G., Pearce, D.: The AURORA experimental framework for the performance evaluation of speech recognition Systems under noisy conditions. Proc. of ASR 2000, Sep. 18–20, Paris, France, (2000)
14. http://www.ldc.upenn.edu/readme_files/timit.readme.html
15. http://www.praat.org
16. http://www.speech.kth.se/wavesurfer/
17. Hegde, R. M., Murthy H. A., Gadde, V. R.: Continuous speech recognition using joint features derived from the modified group delay function and MFCC. Proc. of International Conference on Spoken Language Processing (ICSLP), Oct. 4–8, Jeju Island, Korea, (2004)
18. J.-M. Boite, L. Couvreur, S. Dupont and C. Ris, Speech Training and Recognition Unified Tool (STRUT), http://tcts.fpms.ac.be/asr/project/strut.
19. Bourlard, H., Morgan, N.: Connectionist Speech Recognition: A Hybrid Approach, Kluwer Academic Publisher, (1994)
20. Gong, Y.: Speech recognition in noisy environments: a survey. Speech Communication. vol. 16, no. 3, (1995) 261–291
21. Junqua, J. C.: Robust Speech Processing in Embedded Systems and PC Applications, Kluwer Academic Publishers,( 2000)
22. Bozkurt, B., Dutoit, T.: Mixed-phase speech modeling and formant estimation, using differential phase spectrums. Proc. of ISCA ITRW VOQUAL. Aug, 21–24, (2003)
23. Introduction page for Chirp Group Delay processing: http://tcts.fpms.ac.be/demos/zzt/cgd.html
24. Bozkurt, B., Doval, B., d'Alessandro, C., Dutoit, T.: Zeros of z-transform representation with application to source-filter separation in speech. IEEE Signal Processing Letters. vol. 12, no. 4, (2005) 344–347
25. Fant, G.: Acoustic Theory of Speech Production, Mouton and Co. Netherlands, (1960)

# Towards Neurocomputational Speech and Sound Processing[*]

Jean Rouat[1], Stéphane Loiselle[1], and Ramin Pichevar[1,2]

[1] Université de Sherbrooke
http://www.gel.usherbrooke.ca/necotis
[2] Communications Research Centre, Ottawa

**Abstract.** From physiology we learn that the auditory system extracts simultaneous features from the underlying signal, giving birth to simultaneous representations of audible signals. We also learn that pattern analysis and recognition are not separated processes (in opposition to the engineering approach of pattern recognition where analysis and recognition are usually separated processes). Furthermore, in the visual system, it has been observed that the sequence order of firing is crucial to perform fast visual recognition tasks (Rank Order Coding). The use of the Rank Order Coding has also been recently hypothesized in the mammalian auditory system. In a first application we compare a very simplistic speech recognition prototype that uses the Rank Order Coding with a conventional Hidden Markov Model speech recognizer. It is also shown that the type of neurons being used should be adapted to the type of phonemes (consonants/transients or vowels/stable) to be recognized.

In a second application, we combine a simultaneous auditory images representation with a network of oscillatory spiking neurons to segregate and bind auditory objects for acoustical source separation. It is shown that the spiking neural network performs unsupervised auditory images segmentation (to find 'auditory' objects) and binding of the objects belonging to the same auditory source (yielding automatic sound source separation).

**Keywords:** Auditory modelling, Source separation, Amplitude Modulation, Auditory Scene Analysis, Spiking Neurons, Temporal Correlation, Cochlear Nucleus, Corrupted Speech Processing, Rank Order Coding, Speech recognition.

## 1 Introduction

Speech recognition and separation of mixed signals is an important problem with many applications in the context of audio processing. It can be used to assist a robot in segregating multiple speakers, to ease the automatic transcription of video via the audio tracks, to separate musical instruments before automatic

---

[*] This work has been funded by NSERC and Université de Sherbrooke. S. Loiselle has been funded by FQRNT of Québec for the year 2006.

Y. Stylianou, M. Faundez-Zanuy, A. Esposito (Eds.): WNSP 2005, LNCS 4391, pp. 58–77, 2007.

transcription, to clean the signal and performs speech recognition, etc. The ideal instrumental set–up is based on the use of an array of microphones during recording in order to obtain many audio channels. In fact, in the latter-mentioned situation, very good separation can be obtained.

In many situations, only one channel is available to the audio engineer and no training data are easily available. The automatic separation, segregation of the sources and speech recognition are, then, much more difficult.

From the scientific literature, most of the proposed monophonic systems perform reasonably well on specific signals (generally voiced speech), but fail to efficiently segregate and recognize a broad range of signals if there is no sufficient training data to estimate the feature distributions.

In the present paper we present two speech processing systems based on an auditory motivated approach. One system is a prototype speech recognizer that uses the sequence of spikes, as a recognition feature, in a network of spiking neurons. When compared with a Hidden Markov Models recognizer, preliminary results show that the approach as a great potential for transients recognition and situations where no sufficient data are available to train the speech recognizer. The second system shows that separation and segregation of simultaneous audio sources can be performed by using the temporal correlation paradigm to group auditory objects coming from the same source.

## 1.1   Suitable Representations

We know that, for source separation and speech recognition, an efficient and suitable signal representation has first to be found. Ideally the representation should be adapted to the problem in hand and has not to be the same for both systems (as the separation and recognition cues are different). We briefly review some of the most important common features that should be preserved and enhanced when analysing the speech signals.

**Voiced Speech.** With at least two interfering speakers and voiced speech, it is observed that the separation is relatively easy – speakers with different fundamental frequencies – since spectral representations or auditory images exhibit different regions with structures dominated by different pitch trajectories. Hence, amplitude modulation of cochlear filter outputs (or modulation spectrograms) are discriminative. In situations where speakers have similar pitches, the separation is difficult and features, like the phase, should be preserved by the analysis to increase the discrimination. Most conventional source segregation or recognition systems use an analysis that is effective, as long as speech segments under the analysis window are relatively stationary and stable. Furthermore, these systems need a sufficient amount of data to be trained.

**Unvoiced Speech.** For segregation with at least 2 simultaneous speakers and overlapping unvoiced speech segments, a signal-dependent and fine analysis is required. In this situation, separation and recognition cannot be performed with conventional speech analysis that are usually based on spectral and time-averaged features. It is very likely that this kind of system would fail. Hence, adaptive (or at least multi-features) and dynamic signal analysis is required.

**So, Which Signal Representation?** The question is still open, but the signal representation should enhance speech structured features that ease discrimination and differentiation.

Based on the literature on auditory perception, it is possible to argue that the auditory system generates a multi–dimensional spatio-temporal representation of the one dimensional acoustic signal. One view of this can be found in the remarkable work by Shamma and his team [1,2] with a recent work in source separation [3].

In the first half of the paper (speech recognition application) we propose a simple time sequence of 2D auditory images (cochlear channels – neuron thresholds) or we use the time sequence of 3D Shamma's multiscale analysis (tonotopic frequency – temporal rate – modulation of the auditory spectrum). In the second half of the paper we use 2D auditory image (AM modulation and spectrum of cochlear envelops) sequences and we treat them as videos.

## 1.2   Adaptative and Unsupervised Recognition

Most conventional source separation approaches require segregation and/or fusion (integration) usually based on correlation, statistical estimation or binding of features while recognition systems require the use of reference templates with training or explicit estimation with supervision and huge signal databases such as documented in [4], [5] (AURORA database), and [6]. Therefore, the design and training of such systems is heavy and very costly. There is obviously a need for fast and easy training with autonomy.

In the present work, we integrate auditory-based features with unconventional pattern recognizers or segregation and fusion systems based on spiking neurons.

## 2   Perceptive Approach

From physiology we know that the auditory system extracts simultaneous features from the underlying signal, giving birth to simultaneous multi-representation of speech. We also learn that fast and slow efferences can selectively enhance speech representations in relation to the auditory environment. This is in opposition with most conventional speech processing systems that use a systematic analysis [1] that is effective only when speech segments under the analysis window are relatively stationary and stable.

Psychology observes and attempts to explain the auditory sensations by proposing models of hearing. The interaction between sounds and their perception

---

[1] A systematic analysis extracts the same features independently of the signal context. Frame by frame extraction of Mel Frequency Cepstrum Coefficients (MFCC) is an example of a systematic analysis.

can be interpreted in terms of auditory environment or auditory scene analysis. We also learn from psycho-acoustics that the time structure organisation of speech and sounds is crucial to perception. In combination with physiology, suitable hearing models can also be derived from psycho-acoustic research.

## 2.1   Physiology: Multiple Features

In the cochlea inner and outer hair cells establish synapses with efferent and afferent fibres. The efferent projections to the inner hair cells synapse on the afferent connection, suggesting a modulation of the afferent information by the efferent system. On the contrary, other efferent fibres project directly to the outer hair cells, suggesting a direct control of the outer hair cells by the efferences. It has also been observed that all afferent fibres (inner and outer hair cells) project directly into the cochlear nucleus. It has a layered structure that preserves frequency tonotopic organisation where one finds very different neurons that response to various features [2].

It is clear from physiology that multiple and simultaneous representations of the same input signal are observed in the cochlear nucleus [7] [8]. In the remaining parts of the paper, we call these representations, *auditory images*.

## 2.2   Rank Order Coding, Temporal Correlation

VanRullen et *al.* [9] discuss the importance of the relative timing in neuronal responses and have shown that the coding of the Rank Order of spikes can explain the fast responses that are observed in the human somatosensory system. Along the same line, Nätschlager and Maass [10] have technically shown that information about the result of the computation is already present in the current neural network state long before the complete spatio-temporal input patterns have been received by the neural network. This suggests that neural networks use the temporal order of the first spikes yielding ultra-rapid computation in accordance with the physiology [11,9]. As an example, we can cite the work by DeWeese et *al.* [12], where the authors observe in the auditory cortex of the rat that transient responses in auditory cortex can be described as a binary process, rather than as a highly variable Poisson process. Once again, these results suggest that the spike timing is crucial. As the Rank Order Coding is one of the potential neural codes that respects these spike timing constraints, we explore here a possible way of integration in the context of speech recognition.

On the other hand, we explore, in the context of source separation, the use of the *Temporal Correlation* to compute dynamical spatio–temporal correlation between features obtained with a bank of cochlear filters. This time the coding is made through the synchronization of neurons. Neurons that fire simultaneously will characterize the same sound source. The implementation we made is based on the Computational Auditory Scene Analysis that derives from the work of Al. Bregman [13]. In our work we were interested in pushing ahead the study of

---

[2] Onset, chopper, primary–like, etc.

the source separation problem by relying on similarities between features coming from the same sound source. We also constrained the system to be fully adaptive and unsupervised.

## 3   Exploration in Speech Recognition

### 3.1   Rank Order Coding

Rank Order Coding has been proposed by Simon Thorpe and his team from CERCO, Toulouse to explain the impressive performance of our visual system [14,15]. The information is distributed through a large population of neurons and is represented by spikes relative timing in a single wave of action potentials. The quantity of information that can be transmitted by this type of code increases with the number of neurons in the population. For a relatively large number of neurons, the code transmission power can satisfy the needs of any visual task [14]. There are advantages in using the relative order and not the exact spike latency: the strategy is easier to implement, the system is less subject to changes in intensity of the stimulus and the information is available as soon as the first spike is generated.

### 3.2   System Overview

We now explore the feasibility of a speech recognizer based on spiking neurons and Rank-Order Coding (ROC). In this work, we use the temporal order of spikes at the output of two auditory models. One is a very simple peripheral auditory channels representation (which we call *cochlear channels* model) while the second is a far more complete model that includes mid–brain and cortical representations of sounds (which we call *complete* model).

We also use two models of neurons. In the first model, spikes are obtained with simple fixed thresholds (which we call *threshold* model), without integration. Different neurons can have a different internal threshold value. The second model is the conventional leaky integrate and fire representation of neurons (LIAF) with an adaptive internal threshold.

### 3.3   Speech Analysis Modules

**Simple Cochlear Peripheral Model.** The peripheral auditory system is crudely modelled by a gammatone filter-bank [16] followed by rectification and compression with a square-root law. It is intended to represent the average firing probability in primary auditory nerve fibres, without taking into account adaptation and loss of phase-locking.

**A More Complete Auditory Model.** We use here the model proposed by Shamma and his team [1]. The signal remains analyzed by a model of the cochlea where each cochlear filter output is rectified. However, the compression has been replaced by a pre-accentuation and a spatial first difference operation to imitate the function of a lateral inhibitory network (LIN) where higher frequency channels inhibit low frequency channels to enhance the frequency selectivity of the cochlear filters [17]. Then, an integration over a short window is used to model the slow adaptation of the central auditory neurons [2] and we use Shamma's cortical multiscale analysis with various spectro-temporal response fields (SRTF).

Spike trains are generated by feeding the neuronal models (described in next subsections) with one of the two analysis modules described here.

## 3.4   Neuronal Models

**Simple Threshold Neuronal Model.** For each envelop signal from each cochlear channel, we use three neurons with different thresholds (denoted 1, 2 and 3). A spike is generated when the envelop signal exceeds one of the internal neuron's threshold. After producing a spike, a neuron becomes inactive for the remaining time of the stimulus. With such model we only capture the first instant for which the envelop signal is sufficiently high and we ignore the other spikes.

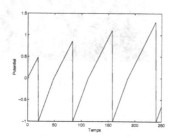

**Fig. 1.** Example of time evolution of the potential from the leaky IF neuron model with a constant input

**The Leaky Integrate and Fire Neuronal Model.** Our simple Integrate-and-Fire neuron model has four parameters: adaptive threshold, leaky current, resting potential and reset potential. At the beginning of the simulation, the internal potential is at the resting potential. Throughout the simulation, the neuron integrates the input to determine the neuron's internal potential evolution. Once the internal potential is sufficient (it reaches the threshold), a spike is generated. The internal potential is then set at the reset potential (which is below the resting potential) and the threshold is increased. The threshold adaptation and the reset potential are used to avoid generating multiple spikes in a short time window. However, with time the threshold will slowly decrease to its original value as long as the internal potential is smaller. Furthermore, without excitation the internal potential also slowly decreases to its resting value. A similar evolution applies when the internal potential is below the resting value where it will slowly increase with time to reach the resting potential. Thus, a neuron which is continuously excited will have difficulty in generating new spikes. On the other hand, a neuron that is not excited or that has a low excitation level will be more sensitive to an increase in its excitation.

### 3.5   Illustration with the Simple Analysis and Thresholding

We illustrate the sequence generation and processing with the cochlear channels analysis used in conjunction with the threshold neuronal models. Figure 2, page 64, sumarizes the preprocessing and the generation of spikes with the threshold neuronal model. Left columns of table 1 gives the list of spikes for the situation illustrated in figure 2.

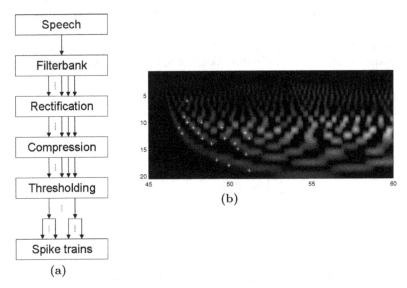

**(a)**

**(b)**

**Fig. 2.** Illustration of spike sequence generation on a French digit 'un' [ɛ̃] with the cochlear channel analysis and threshold neurons. **(a)** The signal is first filtered through a cochlear gammatone filter-bank. It is then rectified and compressed with a square-root law. For each channel, three threshold neurons are used with different threshold values. If the amplitude in the channel reaches one of the neuron's threshold, a spike is generated. After firing, a neuron becomes inactive for the remaining time of the stimulus. **(b)** White stars represent spikes. The x-axis is the time samples (sampling frequency of 16 kHz) and the y-axis shows the filter-bank channels. Center frequencies of channels 1 and 20 are respectively equal to 8000 and 100 Hz.

### 3.6   Learning and Recognition Modules

The same training and recognition procedure has been used with the simple thresholding and leaky integrate and fire neuronal models. During training a template is generated for each reference word. It is a sequence of the first most likely N cochlear "channel/threshold" numbers. For the French digit "UN" ([ɛ̃]),

**Table 1.** First four columns: Sequence with the spike order of the first 20 cochlear channels/threshold numbers to produce a spike; Last columns: Generated weights $k_i$ – illustration for the *cochlear channels* analysis module with *threshold* neurons. Channels 1 to 5 and channels greater than 19 are not taken into account (threshold neurons firing too lately).

| Channel | Sequence order Threshold index 1 | 2 | 3 | Weight $(k_{(i)})$ Threshold index 1 | 2 | 3 |
|---|---|---|---|---|---|---|
| 5 | | | | | | |
| 6 | 5 | | | 16 | | |
| 7 | | | | | | |
| 8 | | | | | | |
| 9 | 3 | | | 18 | | |
| 10 | 4 | 8 | | 17 | 13 | |
| 11 | 1 | 6 | 12 | 20 | 15 | 9 |
| 12 | 2 | 7 | 17 | 19 | 14 | 4 |
| 13 | 9 | 13 | 19 | 12 | 8 | 2 |
| 14 | 10 | 15 | | 11 | 6 | |
| 15 | 16 | | | 5 | | |
| 16 | 18 | | | 3 | | |
| 17 | 11 | | | 10 | | |
| 18 | 14 | | | 7 | | |
| 19 | 20 | | | 1 | | |
| 20 | | | | | | |

the pronunciation sequence (figure 2 and table 1, columns **Sequence order**) obtained by using the cochlear channels analysis and the threshold models, is :
11, 12, 9, 10, 6, $11_{(2)}$, $12_{(2)}$, $10_{(2)}$, 13, 14, 17, $11_{(3)}$, $13_{(2)}$, 18, $14_{(2)}$, 15, $12_{(3)}$, 16, $13_{(3)}$ and 19, where the $(l)$ indices stands for threshold levels (i.e. threshold index) 2 or 3 in the corresponding channel.

Afterwards, a weight vector $K$

$$K = \begin{vmatrix} k_1 \\ k_2 \\ \vdots \\ k_N \end{vmatrix}$$

(column **Weight**, table 1) is evaluated by computing the $k_i$ associated to each of these channels/thresholds according to Equ. 1.

$$k_i = (N - i) + 1, \tag{1}$$

with $i = 1, \ldots, N$ beeing the rank in the sequence of the considered "channel/threshold". Therefore, the weight $k_i$ depends on the "channel/threshold" position in the sequence. The first "channel/threshold" that gives a spike has the highest weight. We keep going downwards until we reach the $N$th. "channel/threshold". Since there are more than one neuron per channel, more than one weight can be given to a single channel (see table 1). The procedure is independent of the neuronal model.

During recognition, for each isolated word test $T_j$, a sequence of "channel/thresholds" $S_j(n)$ (which contains the "channel/thresholds" numbers that generated each corresponding spike) is generated. From this sequence, we keep the first $N$ "channel/thresholds" to be compared with each existing templates. During comparison with a given template, a scalar product is computed between the weight vector $K$ of that template and the weighted rank order vector of the test $T_j$. That weighted rank order vector $RO_j$ is obtained from the sequence $S_j(n)$ :

$$
RO_j = \left|
\begin{array}{c}
I^{[\text{rank of the "channel/threshold" number 1 from } S_j(n)]-1} \\
\vdots \\
I^{[\text{rank of the "channel/threshold" number i from } S_j(n)]-1} \\
\vdots \\
I^{[\text{rank of the "channel/threshold" number N from } S_j(n)]-1}
\end{array}
\right|
$$

where $I$ stands for a constant inhibition factor (lower than or equal to one).

This gives a similarity measure between the test and the reference template that depends on the "channel/threshold" rank in the sequence (Equ. 2) [18].

$$
\text{Similarity} = \sum_{i=1}^{N} k_i I^{(\text{rank\_of\_spike\_i}-1)} \tag{2}
$$

Finally, the template with the highest similarity with the test $T_j$ is selected from the dictionary. The maximum similarity, with an inhibition factor of 0.9, would be computed as follows : $20 \times 0.9^0 + 19 \times 0.9^1 + 18 \times 0.9^2 + ... + 2 \times 0.9^{18} + 1 \times 0.9^{19}$. It corresponds to the situation where the test is equal to the reference.

### 3.7   Experiments

**Speech Database.** We performed a proof-of-concept test of speech recognition using in house speech databases made of 10 French digits spoken by 5 men and 4 women and of the French vowels spoken by the same 5 men and 5 women (including the 4 women from the digits database). Each speaker pronounced ten times the same digits (from 0 to 9) and vowels. The speakers were presented with random sequences of digits and vowels to be read. The speech was recorded at 16 kHz using a microphone headset.

**Training and Recognition.** For each digit (or vowel), two reference models are used for the recognizer (one pronunciation for each sex). For each digit (or vowel), for each sex and for each pronunciation inside the same sex group, a preliminary comparison between the same digits (or vowels) is performed using the very simple peripheral auditory channels representation and thresholds neurons. The comparison is made by computing the similarity measure (Equ. 2) between all pronunciations of the same digit (or vowel) inside the same sex group. The pronunciation with the highest similarity will be used as a reference model for all simulations [3]. These reference models possess the highest similarity with the pronunciations in their respective group (digit, male or female). It should be noted that the impact of a digit model on the pronunciations of the other digits (e.g., false recognition of other digit) is not taken into account.

Recognition has been performed on all pronunciations of each speaker. During recognition and for a given digit (or vowel), only two speakers were represented in the reference models.

Experiments have been conducted with two combinations: cochlear filter–bank analysis with simple threshold neurons (noted as Cochlear–Threshold) and the complete auditory model with LIAF neurons (noted as Complete–LIAF).

**Reference System.** A conventional MFCC and Hidden Markov Model speech recognizer has been trained with the same training set than with the ROC prototype [4]. The system uses hidden Markov models with 5 states and twelve Mel Frequency Cepstral Coefficients (MFCC) for each time frame. The sliding window length is 32 ms with an overlap of 16 ms. For each state of the HMM, a mean and a variance are estimated during training. We use one Gaussian distribution of the observations (instead of the conventional mixture of Gaussians) to reduce the number of parameters [5] to be estimated during training).

## 3.8   Recognition Scores with Limited Training Data

*Recognition of vowels.* The 5 French vowels [aəioy] recognition has been made with three recognizers. The conventional reference HMM, one ROC prototype with the cochlear analysis and the threshold neuron model and another ROC prototype with the complete auditory model with LIAF neurons. The average recognition rates are reported on table 2. The HMM and the Cochlear–Threshold recognizers have comparable performance while the complete model (Complete-LIAF) is better. The Cochlear–Treshold recognizer does relatively well (recall that it uses only one spike per channel/threshold neuron) even if it uses only the first signal frames. On the opposite, the HMM and the Complete-LIAF systems

---

[3] For example, the model of digit 1 for the male speakers is obtained as:
For $j = 1$ to 50 do (each digit 1 pronounced by a male – 50 pronunciations):

1. Compute the similarity with the other digits (49 similarities)
2. Compute the average

The pronunciation with the highest average similarity will be the model for digit "un" [ɛ̃] pronounced by the male speakers.

[4] The same reference pronunciation has been used for each digit (or vowel).

[5] Approximately 130 parameters for each Markovian Model: Mean and Variance of a twelve dimensional vector for each state, 5 states and transitions between states.

**Table 2.** Averaged recognition rates on the five French vowels [aəioy] for the HMM speech recognizer, the Cochlear–Treshold and Complete-LIAF speech recognizers

| HMM | Cochlear–Treshold | Complete-LIAF |
|-----|-------------------|---------------|
| 90% | 89% | 94% |

use the full vowel signal. However, since the ROC is used with the Complete-LIAF systems, the first part of the vowel remains the most important for this prototype.

*French digit recognition.* In this paragraph we further push the evaluation of the simple Cochlear–Treshold model on the 10 French digits. We respectively report in tables 3 and 4 the results for the very simple system (Cochlear–Treshold) and those from the HMM recognizer. Each row model gives the number of recognized pronunciations; each line is the pronounced digit to be recognized.

With the Cochlear–Threshold system, the best score is obtained for digit "un" [ɛ̃] (usually short and difficult to be recognized with conventional speech recognizers). On the other hand, digits beginning with similar fricatives (like "cinq" [sɛ̃k], "six" [sis] and "sept" [sɛt]) or plosives ("trois" [tRwa ] and "quatre" [katR]) are often confused. Since the neurons in this prototype fire only once, the emphasis is made on the first frames of the signal. Therefore, it is coherent that the Cochlear–Threshold system bases the recognition on the consonants of the digits (except digit 1 that begins with the vowel).

The best score for the MFCC-HMM (table 4) is obtained with digit 5 (relatively long digit) and the worst with 1 (the best with our prototype) and 8 [ɥit].

**Table 3.** Confusion table and recognition for each pronunciation of the ten French digits – Cochlear filter analysis combined with the one time threshold neuron (Cochlear–Threshold system)

| Digits | Models | | | | | | | | | | % |
|--------|---|---|---|---|---|---|---|---|---|---|---|
| | 1 | 2 | 3 | 4 | 5 | 6 | 7 | 8 | 9 | 0 | 65 |
| 1 ("un") | 84 | 1 | 4 | | | | | | | 1 | 93 |
| 2 ("deux") | | 69 | 2 | 1 | | | | 3 | 13 | 2 | 76 |
| 3 ("trois") | 10 | | 58 | 18 | | | | 1 | 1 | 2 | 64 |
| 4 ("quatre") | | | 22 | 68 | | | | | | | 75 |
| 5 ("cinq") | 11 | | 1 | 2 | 42 | 21 | 6 | | | 7 | 46 |
| 6 ("six") | | | | 1 | 68 | 13 | 2 | 1 | 5 | | 75 |
| 7 ("sept") | | 1 | 1 | 2 | 11 | 49 | 12 | 1 | 1 | 12 | 13 |
| 8 ("huit") | | 1 | | | | | | 68 | 16 | 5 | 75 |
| 9 ("neuf") | | | 4 | | | | | 9 | 54 | 23 | 60 |
| 0 ("zéro") | | | | | 15 | 2 | 3 | 3 | 9 | 61 | 67 |

**Table 4.** Confusion table and recognition for each pronunciation of the ten French digits. MFCC analysis with *HMM*s.

| Digits | Models | | | | | | | | | | % |
|---|---|---|---|---|---|---|---|---|---|---|---|
|  | 1 | 2 | 3 | 4 | 5 | 6 | 7 | 8 | 9 | 0 | 52 |
| 1 ("un") | 15 |  |  | 1 | 20 |  |  |  | 28 | 16 | 16 |
| 2 ("deux") |  | 55 |  |  | 11 |  |  | 1 | 9 | 14 | 61 |
| 3 ("trois") |  |  | 42 |  |  |  |  |  |  | 48 | 46 |
| 4 ("quatre") |  |  |  | 33 | 32 |  |  |  | 10 | 15 | 36 |
| 5 ("cinq") |  | 2 |  |  | 81 | 1 |  |  | 1 | 5 | 90 |
| 6 ("six") |  |  |  |  | 13 | 72 |  | 1 |  | 4 | 80 |
| 7 ("sept") |  |  |  |  | 40 | 8 | 30 |  |  | 12 | 33 |
| 8 ("huit") |  | 31 |  |  | 5 | 8 |  | 5 | 38 | 3 | 5 |
| 9 ("neuf") |  | 4 |  | 10 | 19 | 3 |  |  | 44 | 10 | 49 |
| 0 ("zéro") |  |  |  |  |  |  |  |  |  | 90 | 100 |

It is clear that digit model 8 is not correctly trained and that the HMM speech recognizer did not have enough data to correctly estimate the HMM parameters (approximately 130 parameters for each Markovian reference model).

**Recognition with Larger Training Sets.** Of course, when using a longer training set (with all 9 speakers in the training set), the HMM recognizer outperforms our Rank Order Coding prototype yielding an overall recognition rate close to 100%. For now, the automatic creation of template models for the ROC is not trivial as it requires a new training rule to be created.

### 3.9   Discussion

Both ROC based speech recognizer prototypes do surprisingly well when compared with a state of the art HMM recognizer.

The Complete–LIAF system uses a shorter test signal (the spike sequence length being limited to N spikes) than the HMM system but without the stationary assumption of the MFCC analysis and yields better results on the vowels when the training set is limited (only 1 reference speaker for each sex). The simple Cochlear–Threshold system has comparable results than the HMM on stationary signals (vowels) and much better results on the consonants of the digits. Clearly, one reference speaker per sex with only one occurrence is not sufficient to train the HMM. Furthermore, the transient cues from the consonants are spread out with the stationary MFCC analysis.

Apart from the fact that the Rank Order Coding scheme could be a viable approach to the recognition it is important to notice that with only one spike per neuronal model (reported results with the Cochlear–Threshold system) the recognition is still promising. It is interesting to link our preliminary results with the arguments of Thorpe and colleagues [11] [18]. They argue that first spike relative latencies provide a fast and efficient code of sensory stimuli and that natural vision scene reconstructions can be obtained with very short durations.

If such a coding is occuring in the auditory system, the study conducted here could be a good start point in the design of a speech recognizer.

The statistical HMM speech recognizer and our ROC prototypes are complementary. The ROC prototypes seem to be robust to transient and unvoiced consonants recognition (which is known to be difficult for statistical based speech recognizers) while the HMM based systems are know to be very robust for stationary voiced speech segments. Also, an important aspect to consider is that the HMM technology dates from the middle of the seventies and plenty of good training algorithms are available which is not yet the case for the ROC. For now, a mixed speech recognizer, that relies *i)* on a Perceptive & ROC approach for the transients and *ii)* on the MFCC & HMM approach for the voiced segments could be viable.

While the HMM recognizer performance can be improved by increasing the training set, the performance of our prototypes could benefit from various pre- or post-processing schemes that are currently under investigation.

## 4   A Sound Source Separation System Based on Synchronisation of Neurons

In this second half of the paper we present a work that explores the feasibility of sound source separation without any priori knowledge on the interfering sources. In other words we begin to pave the road to answer to the question: "How far can we go in the separation of sound sources without integrating any prior knowledge on the sources?".

### 4.1   Binding of Features

We assume here that sound segregation is a generalised classification problem, in which we want to bind features – extracted from the auditory image representations – in different regions of a neural network map. This generalized classification problem was first addressed by Rosenblatt [19]. Suppose that we have two sources S1 and S2 and two features to classify. In the case of static conventional neuronal models (i.e., perceptrons) we can implement a network in which one neuron is triggered by the existence of S1 (Source 1), another one by S2 (Source 2), a third one with F1 (a specific speech feature like a modulation frequency, an onset/offset time, a modulation phase, etc.) and the final one with F2 (another feature). Suppose that we apply the preprocessed signal from S1 (that contains the F1 feature) to the network. neurons "S1" and "F1" should be activated. Now suppose that a mixture of S1 and S2 (that comprises both F2 and F1 features) are applied to the inputs of the network. In this case, all four neurons will be turned on. The network is now confused: It doesn't know whether S1 is associated to F1 or to F2. In other words, what is the correct binding

[(S1, F1), (S2, F2)] or [(S1, F2), (S2, F1)]? Three solutions to this problem are proposed in the literature:

- The most straightforward solution is the hierarchical coding of the information. One neuron is triggered when the stimulus (S1, F1) is present and another one turned on when the input (S1, F2) is applied and so on, for all possible combinations [20]. The problem with this approach is an exponential increase in the number of neurons with an increase in the number of classes and a lack of autonomy for new (not previously seen) classes.
- Another solution is the use of attentional models [21]. In this method, attention is focused on one of the elements in the stimulus, ignoring the others. When the classification of this element is completed, it is dismissed and other elements in the input are analyzed.
- The third solution is the *temporal correlation*. We use that approach as suggested by Milner [22] and Malsburg [23,19] who observed that synchrony is a crucial feature to bind neurons associated to similar characteristics. Objects belonging to the same entity are bound together in time. In this framework, synchronization between different impulse (or spiking) neurons and desynchronization among different regions perform the binding.

## 4.2   System Overview

In this work physiology, psychoacoustic and signal processing are integrated into a same framework to design a multiple sources sound separation when only one recorded channel is available (Fig. 3, page 72). The system combines a spiking neural network with a reconstruction analysis/synthesis cochlear filterbank along with auditory image representations of audible signals. The segregation and binding of the auditory objects (coming from different sound sources) is performed by the spiking neural network (implementing the *temporal correlation* [22,24]) that also generates the mask [6] to be used in conjunction with the synthesis filterbank to generate the separated sound sources.

The neural network uses third generation neural networks, where neurons are usually called *spiking* neurons [25]. In our implementation, neurons firing at the same instants (same firing phase) are characteristic of similar stimuli or comparable input signals [7]. *Spiking* neurons, in opposition to *formal* neurons, have usually a constant firing amplitude. This coding yields noise and interference robustness while facilitating adaptive and dynamic synapses (link between neurons) for unsupervised and autonomous system design. Numerous spike timing coding scheme are possible (and observable in physiology) [26]. Among them, we decided to use here synchronisation and oscillatory coding schemes in combination with competitive unsupervised framework (obtained with input dependent synapses), where group of synchronous neurons are observed. This decision has the advantage of allowing design of unsupervised systems with no training (or

---

[6] Mask and masking refer here to a binary gain and should not be confused with the conventional definition of masking in psychoacoustics.

[7] The information is coded in the firing instants.

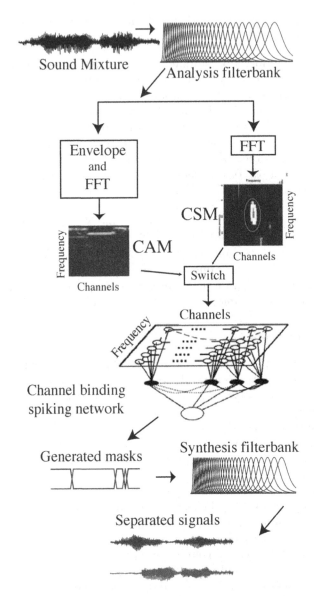

**Fig. 3.** Source Separation System. Two auditory images are simultaneously generated – a Cochleotopic/AMtopic map (CAM) and a Cochleotopic/Spectrotopic map (CSM) – in two different paths. Based on the neural synchrony of the lower layer neurons, a binary mask is generated to mute – in time and across channels – the synthesis filterbank's channels that do not belong to the desired source. The first layer of the neural layer segregates the auditory objects on the CAM/CSM maps and the second layer binds the channels that are dominated by the same stream. For now, the user decides which representation (CAM or CSM) is being presented to the neural network.

learning) phase. To a certain extend, the neural network can be viewed as a map where links between neurons are dependent on the input signals. In our implementation of the *temporal correlation*, two neurons with similar inputs on their dendrites will have increased soma to soma synaptic weights, forcing synchronous response. On the opposite, neurons with dissimilar dendritic inputs will have reduced soma to soma synaptic weights yielding reduced coupling and asynchronous neural responses.

While conventional signal processing computation of correlation have difficulties in taking simultaneously into account the spatial aspect (multi-step correlation have to be evaluated), the spiking neural network is able to compute a **spatio**-temporal correlation of the input signals in one step. With an adequate implementation of the neural network (event driven architecture) the temporal correlation computation can be faster than the conventional one.

## 4.3   Proposed System Strategy

In our life we are confronted to situations in which a mixture of sound sources is present in the environment and our goal is to extract one of the sources among others. While the auditory system may not always succeed in this goal, the range of situations in which recognition is possible in the presence of competing sources highlights the flexibility and robustness of human in speech perception. Here we propose a technique that roughly simulates the behavior of the auditory pathway.

The sound mixture is processed by an enhanced FIR Gammatone filterbank that mimics the behavior of the cochlea [27]. From the output of the cochlear channels two different anthropomorphic maps are generated (figure 3). The amplitude modulation map, that we call Cochleotopic/AMtopic (CAM) Map and the Cochleotopic/Spectrotopic Map (CSM) that encodes the averaged spectral energies of the cochlear filterbank output. These maps partially and very crudely mimic the behavior of the peripheral auditory pathway. These maps are based on the computation of the FFT (Fast Fourier Transform) and envelope detection [28] (figure 3).

The first representation somehow reproduces the AM processing performed by multipolar cells (Chopper-S) from the anteroventral cochlear nucleus [8], while the second representation is closer to the spherical bushy cell processing from the ventral cochlear nucleus [7].

For now, we assume that different sources are disjoint in the auditory image representation space and that masking (binary gain) of the undesired sources is feasible. Speech has a specific structure that is different from that of most noises and perturbations. Also, when dealing with simultaneous speakers, separation is possible when preserving the time structure (the probability at a given instant $t$ to observe overlap in pitch and timbre is relatively low). Therefore, a binary gain could be used to suppress the interference (or separate all sources with adaptive masks).

Our separation technique uses the Computational Auditory Scene Analysis [29] that is based on the computational implementation of ideas exposed by Bregman [13]. A two-layered network of spiking neurons is used to perform cochlear channel selection (figure 3) based on temporal correlation: neurons associated to those channels belonging to the same sound source synchronize. A more detailed description of the system is given in [30,27]. It has been tested on two-sources and three-sources sound source separation situations. Results can be found in [30,27,31]. Different criteria such as PEL (Percentage of Energy Loss), PNR (Percentage of Noise Reduction), LSD (Log Spectral Distortion), and PESQ (Perceptual Evaluation of Speech Quality) have been used for the evaluation of the quality of separation. According to these criteria, it has been shown [30,27,31] that the proposed system outperforms other state of the art systems that do need to be trained to know the source characteristics.

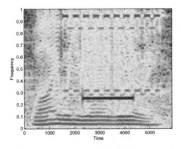

**Fig. 4.** The spectrogram of the mixture of an utterance, a tone, and a telephone ring

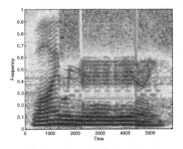

**Fig. 5.** The spectrogram of the extracted utterance. The telephone and the tone have been suppressed, while the voice has been preserved.

**Illustration of the Separation on Three Simultaneous Sources.** Figure 4 is the spectrogram of the mixture of three sources: an utterance, a tone, and a telephone ring. Figure 5 is the spectrogram of the utterance extracted by our method. One can see that the tone and the telephone ring have been extracted successfully. Results can be heard and evaluated on one of the authors' web page: [32] [33].

## 4.4 Discussion

We have presented a system that comprises a perceptive analysis to extract multiple and simultaneous features to be processed by an unsupervised neural network. There is no need to tune-up the neural network when changing the nature of the signal. Furthermore, there is no training or recognition phase.

Even with a crude approximation such as binary masking, non overlapping and independent time window [8], we obtain relatively good synthesis intelligibility.

## 5 Conclusion

Starting in the mid '80s, auditory models were already proposed and tested on corrupted speech but with limited success because of pattern recognizers' inabilities to exploit the rich time-structured information generated by these models. Spiking neural networks open doors to new systems with a stronger integration between analysis and recognition.

For now, the presented systems are relatively limited and have been tested on limited corpus. Many improvements should be made before considering an extensive use of these approaches in real situations.

Still, the experimental results led us to the conclusion that computational neuroscience in combination with speech processing offers a strong potential for unsupervised and dynamic speech processing systems.

## Aknowledgments

Many thanks to Simon Thorpe and Daniel Pressnitzer for receiving S. Loiselle during his 2003 summer session in CERCO, Toulouse. The authors would also like to thank DeLiang Wang and Guoning Hu for fruitful discussions on oscillatory neurons, Christian Feldbauer, Gernot Kubin for discussions on filterbanks and software exchanges.

## References

1. Shibab Shamma. Physiological foundations of temporal integration in the perception of speech. *Journal of Phonetics*, 31:495–501, 2003.
2. Dmitry N. Zotkin, Taishih Chi, Shihab A. Shamma, and Ramani Duraiswami. Neuromimetic sound representation for percept detection and manipulation. *EURASIP Journal on Applied Signal Processing*, Special Issue on Anthropomorphic Processing of Audio and Speech:1350–1364, June 2005.
3. Mounya Elhilali and Shihab Shamma. A biologically-inspired approach to the cocktail party problem. In *ICASSP*, volume V, pages 637–640, 2006.
4. Special Issue. Speech annotation and corpus tools. *Speech Communication Journal*, 33(1–2), Jan 2001.
5. http://www.elda.fr, 2004.
6. B. L. Karlsen, G. J. Brown, M. Cooke, M. Crawford, P. Green, and S. Renals. *Analysis of a Multi-Simultaneous-Speaker Corpus*. L. Erlbaum, 1998.

---

[8] Binary masks create artifacts by placing zeros in the spectrum where the interfering source was. The absence of energy at these locations could be heard (hearing of absent signal or musical noise).

7. C. K. Henkel. The Auditory System. In Duane E. Haines, editor, *Fondamental Neuroscience*. Churchill Livingstone, 1997.
8. Ping Tang and Jean Rouat. Modeling neurons in the anteroventral cochlear nucleus for amplitude modulation (AM) processing: Application to speech sound. In *Proc. Int. Conf. on Spok. Lang. Proc.*, page Th.P.2S2.2, Oct 1996.
9. Rufin VanRullen, Rudy Guyonneau, and Simon J. Thorpe. Spike times make sense. *Trends in Neurosciences*, 28(1):4, January 2005.
10. Thomas Natschläger and Wolfgang Maass. Information dynamics and emergent computation in recurrent circuits of spiking. In *NIPS*, December 2003.
11. S. Thorpe, D. Fize, and C. Marlot. Speed of processing in the human visual system. *Nature*, 381(6582):520–522, 1996.
12. Michael DeWeese, Michael Wehr, and Anthony Zador. Binary spiking in auditory cortex. *The Journal of Neuroscience*, 23(21):7940–7949, 2003.
13. Al Bregman. *Auditory Scene Analysis*. MIT Press, 1994.
14. Rufin VanRullen and Simon J. Thorpe. Surfing a spike wave down the ventral stream. *Vision Research*, 42(23):2593–2615, August 2002.
15. Laurent Perrinet. *Comment déchiffrer le code impulsionnel de la Vision ? Étude du flux parallèle, asynchrone et épars dans le traitement visuel ultra-rapide.* PhD thesis, Université Paul Sabatier, 2003.
16. R.D. Patterson. Auditory filter shapes derived with noise stimuli. *JASA*, 59(3):640–654, 1976.
17. Xiaowei YANG, Kuansan WANG, and Shihab SHAMMA. Auditory representations of acoustic signals. *IEEE Tr. on information theory*, 38(2):824–839, 1992.
18. S. Thorpe, A. Delorme, and R. Van Rullen. Spike-based strategies for rapid processing. *Neural Networks*, 14(6-7):715–725, 2001.
19. Ch. v. d. Malsburg. The what and why of binding: The modeler's perspective. *Neuron*, pages 95–104, 1999.
20. M. Riesenhuber and T. Poggio. Are cortical models really bound by the binding problem? *Neuron*, 24:87–93, 1999.
21. J. Reynolds and R. Desimone. The role of neural mechanisms of attention in solving the binding problem. *Neuron*, 24:19–29, 99.
22. P.M. Milner. A model for visual shape recognition. *Psychological Review*, 81:521–535, 1974.
23. Ch. v. d. Malsburg and W. Schneider. A neural cocktail-party processor. *Biol. Cybern.*, pages 29–40, 1986.
24. Ch. v. d. Malsburg. The correlation theory of brain function. Technical Report Internal Report 81-2, Max-Planck Institute for Biophysical Chemistry, 1981.
25. W. Maass. Networks of spiking neurons: The third generation of neural network models. *Neural Networks*, 10(9):1659–1671, 1997.
26. Duane E. Haines, editor. *Fondamental Neuroscience*. Churchill Livingstone, 1997.
27. R. Pichevar, J. Rouat, C. Feldbauer, and G. Kubin. A bio-inspired sound source separation technique in combination with an enhanced FIR gammatone Analysis/Synthesis filterbank. In *EUSIPCO Vienna*, 2004.
28. R. Pichevar and Jean Rouat. Cochleotopic/AMtopic (CAM) and Cochleotopic/Spectrotopic (CSM) map based sound source separation using relaxation oscillatory neurons. In *IEEE Neural Networks for Signal Processing Workshop, Toulouse, France*, 2003.
29. Computational Auditory Scene Analysis: Principles, Algorithms, and Applications. DeLiang Wang (Editor) and Guy J. Brown (Editor) Wiley-IEEE Press, 2006.

30. Jean Rouat and Ramin Pichevar. Source separation with one ear: Proposition for an anthropomorphic approach. *EURASIP Journal on Applied Signal Processing*, Special Issue on Anthropomorphic Processing of Audio and Speech:1365–1373, June 2005.

31. Ramin Pichevar and Jean Rouat. A Quantitative Evaluation of a Bio-Inspired Sound Source Segregation Technique Based for two and three Source Mixtures. In G. Chollet, A. Esposito, M. Faundez-Zanuy, and M. Marinaro, editors, *Advances in Nonlinear Speech Modeling and Applications*, volume 3445 of *Lectures Notes in Computer Science*, pages 430–434. Springer Verlag, 2005.

32. Ramin Pichevar. http://www-edu.gel.usherbrooke.ca/pichevar/Demos.htm

33. J. Rouat. http://www.gel.usherb.ca/rouat

# Extraction of Speech-Relevant Information from Modulation Spectrograms

Maria Markaki, Michael Wohlmayer, and Yannis Stylianou

University of Crete, Computer Science Department, Heraklion Crete, Greece, 71409
{mmarkaki, micki_w, yannis}@csd.uoc.gr

**Abstract.** In this work, we adopt an information theoretic approach - the Information Bottleneck method - to extract the relevant modulation frequencies across both dimensions of a spectrogram, for speech / non-speech discrimination (music, animal vocalizations, environmental noises). A compact representation is built for each sound ensemble, consisting of the maximally informative features. We demonstrate the effectiveness of a simple thresholding classifier which is based on the similarity of a sound to each characteristic modulation spectrum.

## 1   Introduction

One of the most technically challenging issues in speech recognition is to handle additive (background) noises and convolutive (e.g. due to microphone and data acquisition line) noises, in a changing acoustic environment. The performance of most speech recognition systems, degrades when these two types of noises corrupt speech signal simultaneously. General methods for signal separation or enhancement, require multiple sensors. For a monaural (one microphone) signal, intrinsic properties of speech or interference must be considered [1].

The auditory system of humans and animals, can efficiently extract the behaviorally relevant information embedded in natural acoustic environments. Evolutionary adaptation of the neural computations and representations, has probably facilitated the detection of such signals with low SNR over natural, coherently fluctuating background noises [2,3].

The neural representation of sound undergoes a sequence of substantial transformations going up to the primary auditory cortex (A1) via the midbrain and thalamus. The representation of the physical structure of simple sounds seems to be "degraded" [4,5]. However, certain features, such as spectral shape information, are greatly enhanced [6]. Auditory cortex maintains a complex representation of the sounds, which is sensitive to temporal [5,7] and spectral [8,9] context over timescales of seconds and minutes [10]. Auditory neuroethologists have discovered pulse-echo tuned neurons in the bat [11], song selective neurons in songbirds [12], call selective neurons in primates [13]. It has been argued [14] that the statistical analysis of natural sounds - vocalizations, in particular - could reveal the neural basis of acoustical perception. Insights in the auditory processing then, could be exploited in engineering applications for efficient sound

Y. Stylianou, M. Faundez-Zanuy, A. Esposito (Eds.): WNSP 2005, LNCS 4391, pp. 78–88, 2007.

identification, e.g. speech discrimination. Robust automatic audio classification and segmentation in real world conditions, is a research area of great interest as the available audio data increases.

Speech is characterized by the joint spectro-temporal energy modulations in its spectrogram; these oscillations in power across spectral and temporal axes, reflect the formant peaks, their transitions, spectral edges, and fast amplitude modulations at onsets-offsets. Of particular relevance to speech intelligibility, are the slowly varying amplitude and frequency modulations of sound [15]. Slow temporal modulations (few Hz) correspond to the phonetic and syllabic rates of speech [16]. Measurement of detection thresholds for these spectro-temporal modulations have revealed the lowpass character - in both dimensions - of the modulation transfer functions (MTF) of our auditory system [17]: 50% bandwidths of 2 cycles/octave and 16 Hz over the perceptually important range of $0.25 - 8$ cycles/octave and $1 - 128$ Hz, respectively.

Shamma et al [18,19] have proposed a computational auditory model based on wavelet decomposition, which reproduces the main trends in the experimentally determined spectro-temporal MTFs [17]. The model has been successfully applied in the assessment of speech intelligibility [20], the discrimination of speech from non-speech [21], and in simulations of various psychoacoustical phenomena [22]. During early stage of the model, spectrum estimation is performed, while at later stages spectrum analysis occurs: fast and slow modulation patterns are detected by arrays of filters with spectrotemporal response functions resembling the receptive fields (STRFs) of auditory midbrain neurons [23]. These STRFs are complicated enough, selective for specific frequency sweeps, bandwidth, etc., in order to provide a suitable basis set for speech stimuli.

However, all natural sounds are characterized by slow spectral and temporal modulations [14]. The neural mechanism then, for discriminating the behaviorally relevant sound ensembles, is the tuning to the auditory features that differ most across them [24]. In order to adopt the same approach in a principled framework, we should estimate the power distribution in the spectrogram modulations of speech signals, and contrast them to other sounds' modulation statistics, if we are interested for speech-nonspeech discrimination. Or, identify those features of the modulation spectrum which distinguish some attributes of speech signals (phonemes, speaker's identity, prosody, accent, etc.) from all the others. The information bottleneck method (IB) of Tishby et al (1999), enables the construction of a compact representation for each class, which maintains its most relevant features. Hecht and Tishby [25] have recently presented a speech-oriented implementation of IB, where a small subset of Mel frequency cepstral coefficients is selected according to the recognition task - speech or speaker recognition. The efficiency of the recognition system that follows is greatly improved, since the reduced feature set contains all the relevant-to-the-target information.

In this work, we estimate the power distribution in the modulation spectrum of speech signals, and compare it to the modulation statistics of other sounds. The auditory model of Shamma et al [19] is the basis for these estimations. Using IB method, we show that an efficient dimensionality reduction is achieved while modulation frequencies which distinguish speech from other sounds are preserved (and estimated). A simple thresholding classifier, referred to as the relevant response ratio, is proposed, measuring the similarity of sounds to the compact modulation spectra.

The auditory model of Shamma et al [17] is briefly presented in the next section. In Section 3 we describe the information theoretic principle, the sequential information bottleneck procedure applied to auditory features. Finally, we present some preliminary evaluations of these ideas in section 4.

## 2   Computational Auditory Model

Early stages of the model estimate an enhanced spectrum of sounds, while at later stages spectrum analysis occurs: fast and slow modulation patterns are detected by arrays of filters centered at different frequencies, with Spectro-Temporal Response Functions (STRFs) resembling the receptive fields of auditory midbrain neurons [20]. These have the form of a spectro-temporal Gabor function, selective for specific frequency sweeps, bandwidth, etc., performing actually a multi-resolution wavelet analysis of the spectrogram [19]. The auditory based features are collected from an audio signal in a frame-per-frame scheme. For each time frame, the auditory representation is calculated on a range of frequencies, scales (of spectral resolution) and rates (temporal resolution). In this study, the scales are set to $s = [0.5, 1, 2, 4, 8]$ cyc/oct, the rates to $r = [1, 2, 4, 8, 16, 32]$ Hz. The extracted information is averaged over time, therefore resulting in a 3-dimensional array, or third-order tensor. The dimensionality of this set covers 128 logarithmic frequency bands $\times$ 5 scales $\times$ 6 rates.

## 3   Information Bottleneck Method

In Rate Distortion theory a quantitative measure for the quality of a compact representation is provided by a *distortion function*. In general, definition of this function depends on the application: in speech processing, the relevant acoustic distortion measure is rather unknown, since it is a complex function of perceptual and linguistic variables [25]. IB method provides an information theoretic formulation and solution to the tradeoff between compactness and quality of a signal's representation [26,27,25]. In the supervised learning framework, features are regarded as relevant if they provide information about a target. IB method assumes that this additional variable $y$ (the target) is available. In the case of speech processing systems, the available tagging $y$ of the audio signal (as speech / non speech class, speakers or phonemes) guides the selection of features during training. The relevance of information in the representation of an audio signal, denoted by $x$, is defined as the amount of information it holds about the other variable $y$. If we have an estimate of their joint distribution $p(x, y)$, a natural measure for the amount of relevant information in $x$ about $y$ is given by Shannon's mutual information between these two variables:

$$I(x; y) = \sum_{x,y} p(x, y) \log \frac{p(x, y)}{p(x)p(y)} \tag{1}$$

where the discrete random variables $x \in X$ and $y \in Y$ are distributed according to $p(x)$, and $p(y)$, respectively. Further, let $\tilde{x} \in \tilde{X}$ be another random variable which denotes the compressed representation of $x$; $x$ is transformed to $\tilde{x}$ by a (stochastic) mapping $p(\tilde{x}|x)$. Our aim is to find an $\tilde{x}$ that compresses $x$ through minimization of $I(\tilde{x}; x)$, i.e. the mutual information between the compressed and the original variable. At the same time, the compression of the resulting representation $\tilde{x}$ should be minimal *under the constraint* that the relevant information in $\tilde{x}$ about $y$, $I(\tilde{x}; y)$ stays above a certain level. This constrained optimization problem can be expressed via Lagrange multipliers, with the minimization of the *IB variational functional*:

$$\mathscr{L}\{p(\tilde{x}|x)\} = I(\tilde{x}; x) - \beta I(\tilde{x}; y) \tag{2}$$

where $\beta$, the positive Lagrange multiplier, controls the tradeoff between compression and relevance. The solution to this constrained optimization problem has yielded various iterative algorithms that converge to a reduced representation $\tilde{x}$, given $p(x, y)$ and $\beta$ [27]. We choose the *sequential optimization algorithm* (sIB), as we want a fixed number of hard clusters as output. The input consists of the joint distribution $p(x, y)$, the tradeoff parameter $\beta$ and the number of clusters $M = |\tilde{X}|$. During initialization, the algorithm creates a random partition $\tilde{X}$, i.e. each element $x \in X$ is randomly assigned to one of the $M$ clusters $\tilde{x}$. Afterwards, the algorithm enters an iteration loop. At each iteration step, it cycles through all $x \in X$ and tries to assign them to a different cluster $\tilde{x}$ in order to *increase* the IB functional:

$$\mathscr{L}_{max} = I(\tilde{x}; y) - \beta^{-1} I(\tilde{x}; x) \tag{3}$$

This is equivalent to minimization of the functional defined in 2, and it is used for consistency with [27]. The algorithm terminates when the partition does not change during one iteration. This is guaranteed because $\mathscr{L}_{max}$ is always upper bounded by some finite value. To prevent the convergence of the algorithm to a local maximum (i.e., a suboptimal solution), we perform several runs with different initial random partitions [27].

## 3.1   Application to Cortical Features

The feature tensor $\mathcal{Z}$ represents a discrete set of *continuous* features $z_{i_1,i_2,i_3} = \mathcal{Z}_{i_1,i_2,i_3} \in \mathbb{R}^{+F \times R \times S}$. Since each response $z_{i_1,i_2,i_3}$ is collected over a time frame, it can be interpreted as the average count of an inherent binary event (in the case of a neural classifier, this would be a spike). We therefore consider each response at *location* indexed by $i_1, i_2$, and $i_3$, as a binary feature whose number of occurences in a time interval is represented by $z_{i_1,i_2,i_3}$.

Let the location of a response be denoted by $c_i$, $i = 1, \ldots, F \times R \times S$, such that $z_{i_1,i_2,i_3} = z_{c_i}$. The 3 - dimensional modulation spectrum (frequency - rate - scale) is divided then into $F \times R \times S$ bins centered at $(f_{i_1}, r_{i_2}, s_{i_3})$. Given a training list of $M$ feature tensors $Z^{(k)}$, $k = 1, \ldots, M$ and its corresponding targets $y^{(j)}$, $j = 1, 2$ (speech - nonspeech tags), we can now build a count matrix $K(c, y)$ which indicates the frequency of occupancy of the $i^{th}$ discrete subdivision of the modulation spectrum in the presence of a certain target value $y$. Normalizing this count matrix such that its elements sum to 1, provides an estimate of the joint distribution $p(c, y)$, which is all the IB framework requires. We assume that $M$ is large enough such that the estimate of $p(c, y)$ is reliable, although it has been reported that satisfactory results were achieved even in cases of extreme undersampling [27].

For the purpose of discrimination, the target variable $y$ has only two possible values, $y_1$ and $y_2$. We choose to cluster the features $c$ into 3 groups, one composed of features relevant to $y_1$, the second of features relevant to $y_2$, whereas the third cluster includes features that are not relevant for a specific $y$. Let us denote a compressed representation (a reduced feature set) by $t$ and the deterministic mapping obtained by sIB algorithm as $p(t|c)$. We discard the cluster $t_j$ whose contribution :

$$C_{I(t;y)}(t_j) = \sum_y p(t_j, y) \log \frac{p(t_j, y)}{p(t_j)p(y)} \tag{4}$$

to $I(t, y)$ is minimal, because its features are mostly irrelevant in this case. Therefore, we don't even have to estimate the responses at these locations of the modulation spectrum. This implies an important reduction in computational load, still keeping the maximally informative features with respect to the task of speech-nonspeech discrimination. To find out the identity of the remaining two clusters, we compute:

$$p(t, y) = \sum_c p(c, y)p(t|c) \tag{5}$$

$$p(t) = \sum_y p(t, y) \tag{6}$$

$$p(y|t) = \frac{p(t, y)}{p(t)} \tag{7}$$

The cluster that maximizes the likelihood $p(y_1|t)$ contains all relevant features for $y_1$; the other for $y_2$. We denote, hence, the first cluster as $t_1$ and the latter as $t_2$. The typical pattern (3-dimensional distribution) of features relevant for $y_1$ is given by $p(c|t = t_1)$, while for $y_2$ is given by $p(c|t = t_2)$. According to Bayes rule, these are defined as:

$$p(c|t = t_j) = \frac{p(t = t_j|c)p(c)}{p(t = t_j)}, \quad j = 1, 2 \tag{8}$$

Figure 1 presents an example of the relevant modulation spectrum of each sound ensemble, speech and non-speech (music, animal sounds and various noises).

Speech examples were taken from the TIMIT Acoustic-Phonetic Continuous Speech Corpus. Music examples were selected from the authors' music collection. Animal vocalizations consist of bird sounds and were taken from [28]. The noise examples (taken from Noisex) consist of background speech babble in locations such as restaurants and railway stations, machinery noise and noisy recordings inside cars and planes. Training set consists of 500 speech and 560 non-speech samples. One single frame of 500ms is extracted from each example, starting at a certain sample offset in order to skip initial periods of silence.

In some sense, figure 1 presents the statistical structure of the modulation spectrum of each sound ensemble. Speech class is more homogeneous since it consists exclusively of TIMIT samples. It is characterized by a triangular-like structure corresponding to the pitch of the voices and their harmonics; due to the logarithmic frequency axis (in octaves), an upward change in scale is matched

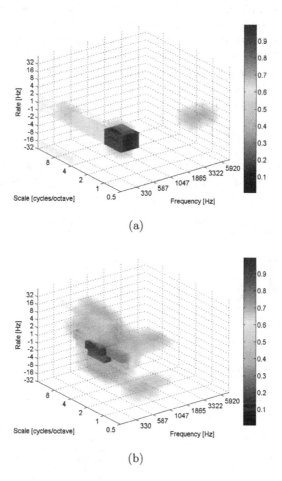

**Fig. 1.** $p(c|t = t_1)$ for non-speech (a) and $p(c|t = t_2)$ for speech class (b). Cluster $t_1$ holds 37.5% and $t_2$ holds 24.7% of all responses. The remaining 37.8% are irrelevant.

to the same increase in frequency band. The harmonic structure due to voiced speech segments is mainly depicted at the higher spectral modulations (2-6 cycles/octave). Scales lower than 2 cycles/octave represent the spectral envelope or formants [29]. Temporal modulations in speech spectrograms are the spectral components of the time trajectory of spectral envelope of speech. They are dominated by the syllabic rate of speech, typically close to 4 Hz, whereas most relevant temporal modulations are below 8 Hz in the figure. It can also be noticed that the lower frequencies - between 330 and 1047 Hz - are more prominent than higher ones, in accordance to the analysis in [30], due to the dominance of voice pitch over these lower frequency bands [29].

Non-speech class consists of quite dissimilar sounds - natural and artificial ones. Therefore, its modulation spectrum has quite "flat" structure, rather reflecting points in the modulation spectrum not occupied by speech: rates lower than 2 Hz in combination with frequencies lower than 330 Hz and scales less than 1 cycle/octave; frequency-scale distribution hasn't any structure as in the case of speech.

Knowledge of such compact modulation patterns allows us to classify new incoming sounds based on the similarity of their cortical-like representation (the feature tensor $\mathcal{Z}$) to the typical pattern $p(c|t = t_1)$ or $p(c|t = t_2)$. We assess the similarity (or correlation) of $\mathcal{Z}$ to $p(c|t = t_1)$ or $p(c|t = t_2)$, by their inner (tensor) product (a compact one dimensional feature). We propose the ratio of both similarity measures, denoted as *relevant response ratio*:

$$R(\hat{Z}) = \frac{< \hat{Z}, p(c|t = t_2) >}{< \hat{Z}, p(c|t = t_1) >} \gtrless \lambda \tag{9}$$

together with a predefined threshold, $\lambda$, for an effective classification of sounds. Large values of $R$ give strong indications towards target $y_2$, small values toward $y_1$.

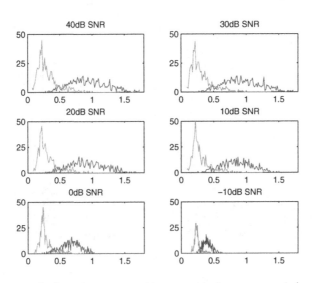

**Fig. 2.** Histogram of relevant response ratios computed on nonspeech (gray/green) and speech examples (black/red)

We calculate the relevant response ratio $R$ for all training examples and noise conditions. Figure 2 shows the histograms of $R$ computed on speech and non-speech examples. It is important to note that the histograms form two distinct clusters, with a small degree of overlap. For the purpose of classification, a threshold has to be defined such that any sound whose corresponding relevant response ratio $R$ is above this treshold is classified as speech, otherwise as non-speech. Obviously, this treshold is highly dependent on the SNR condition under which the features are extracted. This is especially true for low SNR conditions (0dB, -10dB).

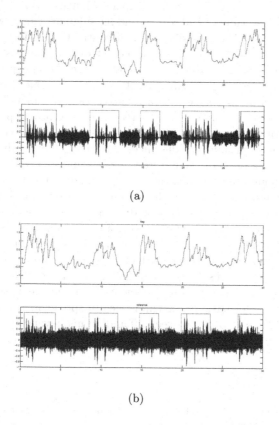

(a)

(b)

**Fig. 3.** Indexing of concatenated speech/nonspeech segments using relevant response ratio with a threshold: (a) additive white noise at SNR = 40dB and (b) SNR = 0dB

We give an example of a signal consisting of concatenations of test sounds with random length between 2 and 8 seconds, variance one, and alternating class membership, speech and nonspeech (music, various noise sources and animal vocalizations). Sentences and speakers in test examples are different from the training examples. The signal is corrupted by additive white noise at 40 dB and 0 dB SNR. The length of frames from which features are extracted is quite long

(500ms), such that within one such frame speech and nonspeech events might be concatenated. From each of these frames, a feature tensor $\mathcal{Z}$ holding the cortical responses is extracted. Figure 3 shows the indexing of the concatenated speech/nonspeech segments using relevant response ratio with a threshold for these two different SNR conditions.

## 4   Conclusions

Classical methods of dimensionality reduction seek the optimal projections to represent the data in a low - dimensional space. Dimensions are discarded based on the relative magnitude of the corresponding singular values, without testing if these could be useful for classification. In contrast, an information theoretic approach enables the selection of a reduced set of auditory features which are maximally informative in respect to the target - speech or non-speech class in this case. A simple thresholding classifier, built upon these reduced representations, could exhibit good performance with a reduced computational load.

The method could be tailored to the recognition of other speech attributes, such as speech or speaker recognition. We propose to use perceptual grouping cues, i.e., sufficiently prominent differences along any auditory dimension, which eventually segregate an audio signal from other sounds - even in cocktail party settings [31]. A sound source - a speaker, e.g. - could be identified within a time frame of some hundreds of ms, by the characteristic statistical structure of his voice (estimated using IB method). The dynamic segregation of the same signal could proceed using unsupervised clustering and Kalman prediction as in [32].

Hermansky has argued in [30] that Automatic Speech Recognition (ASR) systems should take into account the fact that our auditory system processes syllable-length segments of sounds (about 200 ms). Analogously, ASR recognizers shouldn't rely on short (tens of ms) segments for phoneme classification, since phoneme-relevant information is asymmetrically spread in time, with most of supporting information found between 20 and 80 ms beyond the current frame. This is also reflected in the prominent rates in speech modulation spectrum [30].

## References

1. BA Pearlmutter, H Asari, and AM Zador. Sparse representations for the cocktail-party problem. *unpublished*, 2004.
2. H Barlow. *Possible principles underlying the transformation of sensory messages*, pages 217–234. MIT, Cambridge, MA, 1961.
3. I Nelken, Y Rotman, and O Bar Yosef. Responses of auditory-cortex neurons to structural features of natural sounds. *Nature*, 397:154–7, 1999.
4. PX Joris, CE Schreiner, and A Rees. Neural processing of amplitude-modulated sounds. *J Physiol*, 5:257–273, 2004.
5. N Ulanovsky, L Las, and I Nelken. Processing of low-probability sounds by cortical neurons. *Nature Neurosci.*, 6:391–8, 2003.
6. L Las, E Stern, and I Nelken. Representation of tone in fluctuating maskers in the ascending auditory system. *J Neurosci*, 25(6):1503–1513, 2005.

7.  J Fritz and SA Shamma. Rapid task-related plasticity of spectrotemporal receptive fields in primary auditory cortex. *Nature Neuroscience*, 6:1216–23, 2003.

8.  DL Barbour and X Wang. Contrast tuning in auditory cortex. *Science*, 299:1073–1075, 2003.

9.  O Bar-Yosef et al. Responses of neurons in cat primary auditory cortex to bird chirps: effects of temporal and spectral context. *J. Neurosci*, 22:8619–32, 2002.

10. TD Griffiths, JD Warren, S K Scott, I Nelken, and AJ King. Cortical processing of complex sound: a way forward? *TRENDS in Neurosciences*, 27(4):181–5, 2004.

11. N. Suga, W.E. O'Neill, and T. Manabe. Cortical neurons sensitive to combinations of information-bearing elements of biosonar signals in the moustache bat. *Science*, 200:778–781, 1978.

12. D. Margoliash. Acoustic parameters underlying the responses of song-specific neurons in the white-crowned sparrow. *J. Neurosci.*, 3:1039–1057, 1983.

13. J. Newman and Z. Wollberg. Multiple coding of species-specific vocalizations in the auditory cortex of squirrel monkeys. *Brain Res.*, 54:287–304, 1978.

14. NC Singh and FE Theunissen. Modulation spectra of natural sounds and ethological theories of auditory processing. *J. Acoust. Soc. Amer.*, 114(6):3394–3411, 2003.

15. F-G Zeng, K Nie, G. S. Stickney, Y-Y Kong, M Vongphoe, A Bhargave, C Wei, and K Cao. Speech recognition with amplitude and frequency modulations. *Proc Natl Acad Sci USA*, 102(7):2293–2298, 2005.

16. TF Quatieri. *Discrete-Time Speech Signal Processing*. Prentice-Hall Signal Processing series, 2002.

17. T Chi, Y Gao, MC Guyton, P Ru, and S.A. Shamma. Spectro-temporal modulation transfer functions and speech intelligibility. *J. Acoust. Soc. Am.*, 106:2719–2732, 1999.

18. X. Yang, K. Wang, and S. A. Shamma. Auditory representations of acoustic signals. *IEEE Transactions on Information Theory*, 38(2):824–839, 1992.

19. K Wang and SA Shamma. Spectral shape analysis in the central auditory system. *IEEE Transactions on Speech and Audio Processing*, 3(5):382–396, 1995.

20. M Elhilali, T. Chi, and SA Shamma. A spectro-temporal modulation index (stmi) for assessment of speech intelligibility. *Speech communication*, 41:331–348, 2003.

21. N Mesgarani, M Slaney, and SA Shamma. Discrimination of speech from nonspeech based on multiscale spectro-temporal modulations. *IEEE Transactions on Speech and Audio Processing*, PP(99):1–11, 2006.

22. RP Carlyon and SA Shamma. An account of monaural phase sensitivity. *J Acoust Soc Am*, 114(1):333–346, 2003.

23. A Qiu, C E Schreiner, and M A Escab. Gabor analysis of auditory midbrain receptive fields: Spectro-temporal and binaural composition. *J Neurophysiol*, 90:456–476, 2003.

24. SMN Woolley, TE Fremouw, A Hsu, and FE Theunissen. Tuning for spectro-temporal modulations as a mechanism for auditory discrimination of natural sounds. *Nature Neuroscience*, 8(10):1371–1379, 2005.

25. R.M. Hecht and N Tishby. Extraction of relevant speech features using the information bottleneck method. In *Proceedings of Interspeech, Lisbon*, 2005.

26. N. Tishby, F. Pereira, and W. Bialek. The information bottleneck method. In *Proceedings of the 37-th Annual Allerton Conference on Communication, Control and Computing*, pages 368–377, 1999.

27. N. Slonim. The information bottleneck: Theory and applications. *School of Engineering and Computer Science*, 2002.

28. Raimund Specht.  Animal sound recordings, Avisoft Bioacoustics, 2006. www.avisoft.com.
29. T Chi and SA Shamma. Spectrum restoration from multiscale auditory phase singularities by generalized projections. *IEEE Transactions on Speech and Audio Processing*, pages 1–14, 2006.
30. H. Yang, S. van Vuuren, and H. Hermansky. Relevancy of time-frequency features for phonetic classification measured by mutual information. In *ICASSP Proceedings*, pages 3–27, 1999.
31. BCJ Bregman. *Auditory scene analysis*. San Diego, CA:Academic Press, 1990.
32. M Elhilali and SA Shamma. A biologically inspired approach to the cocktail party problem. *ICASSP 2006*, pages 637–640, 2006.

# On the Detection of Discontinuities in Concatenative Speech Synthesis

Yannis Pantazis and Yannis Stylianou

University of Crete, Computer Science Department, Heraklion Crete, Greece, 71409
{pantazis, yannis}@csd.uoc.gr

**Abstract.** Last decade considerable work has been done in finding an objective distance measure which is able to predict audible discontinuities in concatenative speech synthesis. Speech segments in concatenative synthesis are extracted from disjoint phonetic contexts and discontinuities in spectral shape and phase mismatches tend to occur at unit boundaries. Many feature sets—most of them of spectral nature—and distances were tested. However there were significant discrepancies among the results. In this paper, we tested most of the distances that were proposed using the same listening experiment. Best score were given by AM&FM decomposition of the speech signal using Fisher's linear discriminant.

## 1 Introduction

Modern Text-to-Speech(TTS) systems are based on concatenated segments of speech units selected from a large inventory [1] [2] [3] [4]. Different instances of each speech segment (or unit) are occurred in the inventory with various prosodic and spectral characteristics. Selection of the appropriate speech units results in high-quality and natural-sounding synthesized speech. In order to select the best units, a combination of two costs is attributed to each candidate unit. The first cost, called target cost, expresses the closeness between the context of the target and the candidate unit [3]. The other cost, called join or concatenation cost, describes how well speech units are concatenated.

Segment mismatches may be caused by various sources such as discrepancies in fundamental frequencies, different levels of loudness (energy of the segments), or variability in spectral contents. The two first, which are of prosodic nature, can be easily adjusted with little degradation in naturalness [5] while spectral mismatches, which are caused by coarticulation phenomena, cannot be changed. Unit selection tries to avoid spectral mismatches by selecting appropriate segments which minimize the concatenation cost. On the other hand, the solution of smoothing usually results in deterioration of the naturalness of the final synthetic speech. Therefore, it is necessary to find an objective spectral distance measure that is able to predict these spectral mismatches. Then, such an objective measure should be the major part of the concatenation cost.

Y. Stylianou, M. Faundez-Zanuy, A. Esposito (Eds.): WNSP 2005, LNCS 4391, pp. 89–100, 2007.

Concatenation cost is usually computed as a distance on a feature vector which is extracted from speech segments [6] (Fig. 1). Recently, a lot of research work has been developed for addressing this problem. However no definite conclusion can be made from these studies since the results were reported on different databases, and conclusions varied. Moreover, each study has conducted each own listening test (i.e. phoneme dependent/independent analysis, with or without signal processing modifications) and, with different setups (i.e. diphone/unit selection synthesizers). This, dramatically influences the quality of the opinions of the perceptual tests. Also, because of the limited duration of the acoustic stimuli (i.e. 100ms) presented to listeners, they usually argued that the assessment of a synthetic segment was difficult. Furthermore, the number of listeners participating in each test is rather limited and thus safe conclusions from only one listening test can not be extracted.

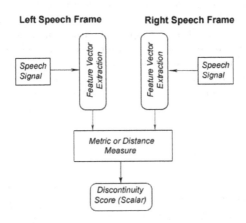

**Fig. 1.** Flow diagram for measuring the discontinuity of two successive speech units

In this paper we attempted to make a comparison of all these results under a common "space", i.e. compare the methods proposed in a database previously used for the same research purpose. Various spectral features coming from speech coding, speech recognition, speech analysis and synthesis were tested. Distances such as absolute difference metric, Euclidean distance, Kullback-Leibler divergence as well as statistical methods were used for the evaluation of perceived discontinuity.

The paper is organized as follows. In Section 2, the different methods of psychoacoustic experiments are presented while Section 3 presents the various speech features that were used in the current study. Section 4 describes the different distance measures used in the evaluation of discontinuities. Section 5 describes how speech naturalness is improved using these discontinuity measures, while in Section 6 the database where the evaluation has been performed is briefly presented. Finally, in Section 7 results and major conclusions are presented.

## 2  Review of Perceptual Listening Experiments

Since the purpose of unit selection is to locate segments (units) that will make the synthetic speech to sound natural, much effort has been devoted to finding the relation between objective distance measures and perceptual impressions. Searching for an objective distance measure that is able to predict perceptual discontinuities or is able to measure the variations of allophones, a subjective measure need to be obtained. For this purpose listeners are asked to decide for the existence of discontinuity or to judge speech quality, which may be evaluated for intelligibility, naturalness, voice pleasantness, liveness, friendliness, etc. Because of the expected variability in the human responses Mean Opinion Score (MOS) is usually used to determine the quality of the synthetic speech.

### 2.1  Perceptual Evaluation of Discontinuity

One approach for the evaluation of perceptual tests is to generate monosyllabic words with a change point at the middle of the vowel [7]. Every word pair in the perceptual test consists of a reference word and a modified version of this word. Instead of monosyllabic words sentences can be also used as in [8]. Listeners have to assess how close these pairs are in a five-point scale. Then correlations are computed between perceptual test and objective distance measures. A variant of this method is to synthesize sentences (or words) with different objective distance measures and ask listeners which sentence is more sonorant [9].

Another approach for the evaluation of objective distance is to construct a concatenation and ask the listeners whether or not a discontinuity is perceived [10], [11]. A less rigid task for the listener was to rate the discontinuity at the concatenation in a five-point scale [12], [13].

### 2.2  Test Stimuli

An issue which also determines the quality of the perceptual experiment is the contents and the duration of the stimuli. The contents of the stimuli varies from few vowels [7], [10] and diphthongs [13] to the 336 monosyllabic test words that constitute the Modified Rhyme Test [11]. The vowels used in these experiments, were selected in such a way that they corresponded to distinct tongue positions. Few studies have used consonants in their stimuli [9]. Duration also varies from few milliseconds [10], [12] to monosyllabic words [7], [11] and even entire sentences [13], [9].

## 3  Spectral Feature Representations

Due to the spectral nature of the problem, many spectral feature representations were tested.

## 3.1   Well Known Feature Sets

FFT-based spectrum (D1) as well as LPC-based spectrum (D2) were tested by many researchers. Another common feature representation of a speech magnitude spectrum is that of Line Spectral Frequencies (LSF) [14] (D3). Depending on the sampling frequency of the speech signal, a few number (i.e. 18–20) of LSFs are usually extracted from the signals. LSFs encode speech spectral information efficiently and provide good performance both in speech coding and speech recognition.

Borrowed from speech recognition systems [15], Mel-scaled Frequency Cepstral Coefficients (MFCCs) is a feature representation that has been extensively used for the detection of audible discontinuities [10] [11] [13]. Like LSFs, the number of MFCCs extracted from the speech signals, depends on the sampling frequency. The dominance of MFCCs in speech recognition as well as in speaker identification/verification systems stems from their ability to represent the amplitude spectrum in a compact form. They may be computed using two different methods; FFT spectrum (D4) and LPC spectrum (D5).

## 3.2   Less Common Features

### 3.2.1   Multiple Centroid Analysis

A spectral feature set referred as Multiple Centroid Analysis (MCA) (D6) was introduced in [13] for the prediction of discontinuities. MCA is an alternative to formant estimation techniques. If the spectral distribution within a partition of the spectrum contains a single formant then the centroid and associated variance, represent the formant frequency and bandwidth (Fig. 2). In [13] four centroid and the corresponding bandwidths were extracted from the speech signals.

The evaluation of the centroid was done by minimizing the "error" quantity

$$e(c_i, d_i) = \sum_{i=1}^{N} \sum_{k=c_{i-1}}^{c_i} P[k](k - d_i)^2$$

where $P[k]$ is the power spectrum, $c_i$ represents the bounds (bandwidth) and $d_i$ denotes the centers of the formants. $N$ determines the number of centroid, which also depends on the sampling frequency. For example, if the sampling frequency is equal to $16kHz$, four centroid are evaluated [13].

### 3.2.2   Bispectrum

Speech features obtained by linear prediction analysis as well as by Fourier analysis are determined from the amplitude or power spectrum. Thus, the phase information of the speech signal is neglected. However, phase information has been proven to play an important role in speech naturalness and signal quality in general. Furthermore, the higher order information is ignored since the power spectrum is only determined by second order statistics. If speech were a Gaussian

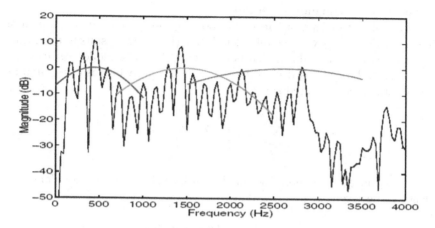

**Fig. 2.** Centers of gravity (after Vepa and King)

process, then the second order statistics would suffice for a complete description. However, evidence appears to indicate that in general, speech is non-Gaussian. To take into account phase information as well as higher order statistics bispectrum as well as Wigner-Ville transform and modified Mellin transform were tested by Chen et al. [8]. In this paper bispectrum (D7) was also tested, since it has been shown [8] that it provides high correlation scores.

Bispectrum is defined as a 2-D Fourier transform of 2-lag autocorrelation function.

$$S_{3x}(f_1, f_2) = \sum_{k=-\infty}^{\infty} \sum_{l=-\infty}^{\infty} C_{3x}(k, l) e^{-j2\pi f_1 k} e^{-j2\pi f_1 l} \tag{1}$$

where

$$C_{3x}(k, l) = \sum_{n=-\infty}^{\infty} x^*[n]x[n+k]x[n+l] \tag{2}$$

is the 2-lag autocorrelation function

### 3.2.3 Nonlinear Approaches

Another drawback of linear prediction analysis and Fourier analysis is that speech signals are considered stationary around the concatenation point. Hence, the techniques used for the extraction of the feature set do not take into account any dynamic information of the speech signal. But experimental work provided evidence that speech resonances can change rapidly within a few—even a single—speech periods [16], [17]. Therefore, in an attempt to incorporate dynamic information in the decision whether or not there is an audible discontinuity, two techniques have been introduced for the extraction of nonlinear features [18].

## a. Time-Varying Harmonic Model

The first set of features are obtained by modeling the speech signal as a sum of harmonics with time varying complex amplitude (D8). This results in representing speech signal by a nonlinear harmonic model [19]. The model assumes the speech signal to be composed by a periodic signal, h[n], which is designated as a sum of harmonically related sinusoids

$$h[n] = \sum_{k=-L(n_i)}^{L(n_i)} A_k[n]e^{j2\pi k f_0(n_i)(n-n_i)} \tag{3}$$

where $L(n_i)$ and $f_0(n_i)$ denote the number of harmonics and the fundamental frequency respectively, at n $= n_i$, while

$$A_k[n] = a_k(n_i) + (n - n_i)b_k(n_i) \tag{4}$$

where $a_k(n_i)$ and $b_k(n_i)$ are assumed to be *complex* numbers which denote the amplitude of the $k^{th}$ harmonic and the first derivative (slope) respectively.

## b. AM&FM Decomposition

The second set of features is based on a technique which tries to decompose speech signals into Amplitude Modulated (AM) and Frequency Modulated (FM) components (D9). Teager [16], [17], in his work on nonlinear modeling of speech production, has used the nonlinear operator known as Teager-Kaiser energy operator:

$$\Psi\{x[n]\} = x^2[n] - x[n-1]x[n+1] \tag{5}$$

on speech signal, $x[n]$. Based on this operator, Maragos et al. [20] have developed the Discrete Energy Separation Algorithm(DESA) for separating an AM-FM modulated signal into its components. An AM-FM modulated signal has the form

$$x[n] = a[n]cos(\Omega[n])$$

where $\Omega[n]$ is the instantaneous frequency and $a[n]$ is the instantaneous amplitude.

### 3.2.4    Phonetic Features

Prosodic and phonetic features can be used for the evaluation of concatenation cost. This is admissible since different phonetic and/or prosodic contents affect the realization of neighbouring phones —coarticulation phenomena. Phonetic features found to be more efficient than acoustic measures in predicting audible discontinuities [21] [22]. For this reason target cost may be more important since target cost is computed as a weighted sum of subcosts of prosodic and phonetic nature. However, using only the target cost, someone cannot eliminate concatenation discontinuities nor can measure the closeness of two successive speech segments.

## 4    Distance Measures

After the computation of features at the concatenated segments, the closeness of them should be somehow determined. As measures someone can use metrics, similarity measures and discriminant functions. Here, the following distance measures were tested.

(a) $l_1$ or absolute difference
(b) $l_2$ or Euclidean distance
(c) Kullback-Leibler divergence
(d) Mahalanobis Distance
(e) Fisher's linear discriminant
(f) Linear regression

Absolute and Euclidean distance are metrics that belong to the same family. Their difference rely on the fact that Euclidean distance amplifies more the difference of specific parameters of the feature vector than absolute distance.

Kullback-Leibler (KL) divergence as well as Mahalanobis distance come from statistics. Mahalanobis distance is similar to Euclidean with each parameter of the feature vector being divided by its variance. KL divergence is used to measure the distance between two probability distributions.

A symmetric version of KL divergence was used to measure the distance between two spectral envelopes and is given by,

$$D_{KL}(P,Q) = \int (P(\omega) - Q(\omega)) \, log \left( \frac{P(\omega)}{Q(\omega)} \right) d\omega \qquad (6)$$

### 4.1    Fisher's Linear Discriminant

Suppose that we have a set of N d-dimensional samples $\mathbf{x_1},...,\mathbf{x_N}$, $N_0$ samples be in the subset $D_0$ and $N_1$ samples be in the subset $D_1$. If we form a linear combination of the elements of $\mathbf{x}$, we obtain the scalar dot product

$$y = \mathbf{w}^T \mathbf{x} \qquad (7)$$

and a corresponding set of N samples $y_1,...,y_N$ that is divided into the subsets $Y_0$ and $Y_1$. This is equivalent to form a hyperplane in d-space which is orthogonal to $\mathbf{w}$ (Fig. 3).

Since Fisher's linear discriminant projects feature vectors to a line, it can also be viewed as an operator (FLD) which is defined by

$$FLD\{\mathbf{x}\} = \sum_{i=1}^{d} w_i x_i \qquad (8)$$

where $w_i$ are the elements of $\mathbf{w}$. If $x_i$ are real positive numbers, this is a kind of weighted version of $l_1$ norm (weights can be negative numbers). According to this method, features which are in different scale can now be combined or compared.

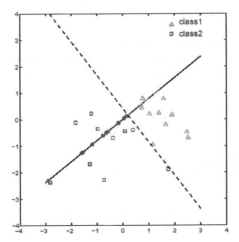

**Fig. 3.** Example of Fisher's Linear Discriminant between two classes

## 4.2  Linear Regression

Linear regression fits an input feature set to the observations (or output) using a least-squares criterion. In our case input vectors are the various feature representations and output is the Mean Opinion Score of listeners. Linear regression is similar to Fisher linear discriminant since both methods are linear and optimal for normal distributions. However, their parameters are estimated by different ways.

## 5  Improve Speech Naturalness

When the inventory is small there will be cases where the selected units are not matching very well. Moreover, the objective distance measures used in modern synthesis systems do not correlate very well with human perception, thus spectral mismatches may occur. Therefore, smoothing at the concatenation points is necessary to lower the mismatch effect.

Wouters and Macon [23] reduced concatenation mismatches by combining spectral information represented by LSFs from two sequences of speech units selected in parallel. The first sequence defined the initial spectral trajectories for a target utterance. Then, this sequence was modified by the second sequence which defined the desired transitions between concatenation units. Perceptual experiments showed that considerable amount of concatenation artifacts were removed.

Klabbers and Veldhuis [24] extended the diphone inventory with context-sensitive diphones. Using their best predictor which was based on spectral features (MFCC), they have clustered the contexts obtaining new recordings. To evaluate the improvements they have conducted further experiments and they have found that the added diphones significantly reduce the amount of audible discontinuities.

In an other study of Vepa and King [25], linear dynamical model (Kalman filter) on LSF trajectories has been used for the computation of join cost in unit selection speech synthesis. The model, after training, could be used to measure how well concatenated speech segments join together. The objective join cost is based on the error between model prediction and actual observations. Linear dynamical model was used also for smoothing the LSF coefficients reducing the audible discontinuities. An advantage of this method is that the degree and extent of the smoothing is controlled by the model parameters which are learned from natural speech.

## 6   Database and Listening Experiment

In this section we briefly present the database used for comparing all the previously reported methods and features as well as the listening experiment that was conducted. A more detailed description can be found in Klabbers et al. [24]. It is worth to note that since the same database has already been used on the same task, useful conclusions may be reached.

Five subjects with backgrounds in psycho-acoustics or phonetics participated in the listening experiment. The material was composed of 1449 $C_iVC_j$ stimuli, which were constructed by concatenating diphones $C_iV$ and $VC_j$ excised from nonsense words of the form $C@CVC@$ (where $C$ =consonant, $V$ =vowel$\in$ /a/, /i/ and /u/ and @ = schwa). The recordings were made of a semiprofessional female speaker. Speech signals have been sampled at $16kHz$.

Preliminary tests showed that discontinuities and other effects in the surrounding consonants would overshadow the effects in the vowel. Hence the surrounding consonants were removed. In addition, the duration of the vowels was normalized to 200 ms and the signal power of the second diphone was scaled to equalize the level of both diphones in the boundary. The stimuli were randomized and the subjects were instructed to ignore the vowel quality and focus on the diphone transition. Listeners' task was to make a binary decision about whether the transition was smooth (0) or discontinuous (1). The experiment was divided into six blocks, presented in three hourly sessions with a short break between two blocks. A transition was marked as discontinuous when the majority of the subjects (3 or more out of 5) perceived it as such.

## 7   Results

### 7.1   Detection Scenario

In distance measures as well as in vector projection we deal with scalars. The evaluation of the distance measures was based on the detection rate, $P_D$, given a false alarm rate, $P_{FA}$. For each measure, $y$, two probability density functions, $p(y|0)$ and $p(y|1)$ were computed depending on the results from the perceptual test: (0) if the synthetic sentence was perceived as continuous and (1) if it was perceived as discontinuous by the listeners. Then the detection rate for that measure, $y$, is computed as:

$$P_D(\gamma) = \int_\gamma^\infty p(y|1)\, dy \tag{9}$$

where $\gamma$ is defined by:

$$P_{FA}(\gamma) = \int_\gamma^\infty p(y|0)\, dy = 0.05 \tag{10}$$

which means that the false alarm rate was set to 5%.

## 7.2    Results and Discussion

In Table 1, detection rate of various measure distances are presented. For the statistical methods such as Fisher linear discriminant and linear regression, the training was done on the 80% of the database, while the testing was done on the remaining 20% of the database. Note also that the evaluation is independent of the phonemes of the database while most of previous studies were phoneme specific. Phoneme specific approaches [7] [24] [8] provide better results compared to phoneme independent approaches [11]. This is expected since in the former case the search space is smaller compared to the space generated in the phoneme independent analysis case. However, even for these phoneme specific approaches the prediction score cannot be considered to be sufficiently high.

**Table 1.** Detection Rates. False Alarm was set at 5%.

| Distance | Detection Rate (%) | Distance | Detection Rate (%) |
|----------|--------------------|----------|--------------------|
| D1a | 10.31 | D1b | 19.66 |
| D1c | 17.27 | D2a | 15.35 |
| D2b | 20.14 | D2c | 23.50 |
| D3a | 17.75 | D3b | 17.27 |
| D3d | 6.24 | D3e | 38.13 |
| D3f | 37.26 | D4a | 33.33 |
| D4b | 36.93 | D4d | 28.54 |
| D4e | 40.53 | D4f | 39.61 |
| D5a | 39.33 | D5b | 37.65 |
| D5d | 27.58 | D5e | 41.01 |
| D5f | 40.78 | D6a | 10.55 |
| D6b | 9.83 | D6d | 10.07 |
| D6e | 25.42 | D6f | 24.90 |
| D7a | 12.04 | D7b | 19.24 |
| D8e | 46.52 | D8f | 45.50 |
| D9e | 49.40 | D9f | 47.83 |

In the table, the feature sets are represented with numbers (D1, D2, ...), while the letters (a, b, ...) following the feature set correspond to the distance. For example, D3d means that LSF coefficients have been used along with the Mahalanobis distance. It is obvious from the table that none speech representation passed 50% of detection rate. Spectrum evaluated from FFT (D1), from LPC coefficients (D2) and Bispectrum (D7) gave small detection rate. LSFs and MFCCs combined with Fisher's linear discriminant performed well. Same conclusion can be made for the nonlinear harmonic model and AM&FM decomposition The latter gave the best detection rate 49.40%. Linear regression gave detection rates close to Fisher's linear discriminant as it was expected. These results show clearly that a lot of works remains to be done despite the considerable effort of many researchers on searching an optimal distance and feature representation.

From the above it is obvious that using a weighted distance the detection rates are improved independently of the features. This is explained by the fact that weights are trained from the same database. Moreover these data-driven weights can boost some particulate parameters of the feature vector and eliminate some others.

# References

1. Robert E. Donovan. *Trainable Speech Synthesis*. PhD thesis, Cambridge University, Engineering Department, 1996.
2. A. Hunt and A. Black. Unit selection in a concatenative speech synthesis system using large speech database. *Proc. IEEE Int. Conf. Acoust., Speech, Signal Processing*, pages 373–376, 1996.
3. W. N. Campbell and A. Black. Prosody and the selection of source units for concatenative synthesis. In R. Van Santen, R.Sproat, J.Hirschberg, and J.Olive, editors, *Progress in Speech Synthesis*, pages 279–292. Springer Verlag, 1996.
4. M. Beutnagel, A. Conkie, J. Schroeter, Y. Stylianou, and A. Syrdal. The AT&T Next-Gen TTS System. *137th meeting of the Acoustical Society of America*, 1999. http://www.research.att.com/projects/tts.
5. Thierry Dutoit. *An Introduction to Text-to-Speech Synthesis*. Kluwer Academic Publishers, 1997.
6. T. R. Barnwell S. R. Quackenbush and M. A. Clements. *Objective Measures of Speech Quality*. Prentice Hall, 1988.
7. J. Wouters and M. Macon. Perceptual evaluation of distance measures for concatenative speech synthesis. *International Conference on Spoken Language Processing ICSLP 98*, pages 2747–2750, 1998.
8. J.-D. Chen and N. Campbell. Objective distance measures for assessing concatenative speech synthesis. *EuroSpeech99*, pages 611–614, 1999.
9. Jerome R. Bellegarda. A novel discontinuity metric for unit selection text-to-speech synthesis. *5th ISCA Speech Synthesis Worksop*, pages 133–138, 2004.
10. E. Klabbers and R. Veldhuis. On the reduction of concatenation artefacts in diphone synthesis. *International Conference on Spoken Language Processing ICSLP 98*, pages 1983–1986, 1998.
11. Y. Stylianou and A. Syrdal. Perceptual and objective detection of discontinuities in concatenative speech synthesis. *Proc. IEEE Int. Conf. Acoust., Speech, Signal Processing*, 2001.

12. Robert E. Donovan. A new distance measure for costing spectral discontinuities in concatenative speech synthesis. *The 4th ISCA Tutorial and Research Workshop on Speech Synthesis*, 2001.

13. J. Vepa S. King and P. Taylor. Objective distance measures for spectal disconti-nuities in concatenative speech synthesis. *ICSLP 2002*, pages 2605–2608, 2002.

14. F. K. Soong and B. H. Juang. Line spectrum pairs and speech data compression. *ICCASP*, pages 1.10.1–1.10.4, 1984.

15. L. Rabiner and B. H. Juang. *Fundamentals of Speech Recognition.* Prentice Hall, 1993.

16. H. M. Teager. Some observations on oral air flow during phonation. *IEEE Trans. Acoust., Speech, Signal Processing*, Oct 1980.

17. H. M. Teager and S. M. Teager. Evidence for nonlinear sound production mecha-nism in the vocal tract. *Speech Production and Speech Modelling*, 55, Jul 1990.

18. Y. Pantazis Y. Stylainou and E. Klabbers. Discontinuity detection in concatenated speech synthesis based on nonlinear analysis. *InterSpeech2005*, pages 2817–2820, 2005.

19. Yannis Stylianou. *Harmonic plus Noise Models for Speech, combined with Statis-tical Methods, for Speech and Speaker Modification.* PhD thesis, Ecole Nationale Supérieure des Télécommunications, 1996.

20. P. Maragos J. Kaiser and T. Quatieri. On separating amplitude from frequency modulations using energy operators. *Proc. IEEE Int. Conf. Acoust., Speech, Signal Processing*, Mar 1992.

21. H. Kawai and M. Tsuzaki. Acoustic measures vs. phonetic measures as predictors of audible discontinuity in concatenative synthesis. *ICSLP*, 2002.

22. A. K. Syrdal and A. D. Conkie. Data-driven perceptually based join cost. *5th ISCA Speech Synthesis Workshop*, pages 49–54, 2004.

23. J. Wouters and M. W. Macon. Unit fusion for concatenative speech synthesis. *ICSLP*, Oct 2000.

24. E. Klabbers and R. Veldhuis. Reducing audible spectral discontinuities. *IEEE Transactions on Speech and Audio Processing*, 9:39–51, Jan 2001.

25. J. Vepa and S. Taylor. Kalman-filter based join cost for unit selection speech synthesis. *Eurospeech*, Sep 2003.

# Voice Disguise and Automatic Detection: Review and Perspectives

Patrick Perrot[1,2], Guido Aversano[1], and Gérard Chollet[1]

[1] CNRS-LTCI-Ecole Nationale Supérieure des Télécommunications (ENST)
75013 Paris, France
[2] Institut de Recherche Criminelle de la Gendarmerie Nationale (IRCGN)
93110, Rosny sous Bois, France
{perrot, aversano, chollet @tsi.enst.fr}

**Abstract.** This study focuses on the question of voice disguise and its detection. Voice disguise is considered as a deliberate action of the speaker who wants to falsify or to conceal his identity; the problem of voice alteration caused by channel distortion is not presented in this work. A large range of options are open to a speaker to change his voice and to trick a human ear or an automatic system. A voice can be transformed by electronic scrambling or more simply by exploiting intra-speaker variability: modification of pitch, modification of the position of the articulators as lips or tongue which affect the formant frequencies. The proposed work is divided in three parts: the first one is a classification of the different options available for changing one's voice, the second one presents a review of the different techniques in the literature and the third one describes the main indicators proposed in the literature to distinguish a disguised voice from the original voice, and proposes some perspectives based on disordered and emotional speech.

**Keywords:** classification disguise automatic detection.

## 1 Introduction

In the field of disguised voices, different studies have been carried out on some specific features and some specific kinds of disguise. Voice disguise is the purposeful change of perceived age, gender, identity, personality of a person. It can be realized mechanically by using some particular means to disturb the speech production system, or electronically by changing the sound before it gets to the listener. Several applications are concerned by voice disguise: forensic science, entertainment, speech synthesis, speech coding. In the case of forensic science a study [26] reveals that a voice disguise is used at a level of 52% in the case where the offender uses his voice and supposes that he is recorded. The challenge is to find indicators to detect the type of disguise and if possible the original voice. Research into voice disguise could also provide some possibilities to personalize a voice in the development of modern synthesisers. The question of voice disguise includes the voice transformation, the voice conversion and the alteration of the voice by mechanic means. The principle of

Y. Stylianou, M. Faundez-Zanuy, A. Esposito (Eds.): WNSP 2005, LNCS 4391, pp. 101–117, 2007.
© Springer-Verlag Berlin Heidelberg 2007

disguise consists in modifying the voice of one person to sound differently (mechanic alteration or transformation), or sound like another person (conversion). There are a number of different features to be mapped like voice quality, timing characteristics and pitch register. Voice modality can not be compared to digital fingerprints or DNA in terms of robustness. This is the reason why it is interesting to study this modality in order to understand invariable and variable features of the voice. So, the aim of this paper is, after a classification of voice disguise, to present the different approaches in the literature and last to indicate some directions of research to establish an automatic detection.

## 2  Classification of Voice Disguise

The difficulty in classifying the voice disguise is to determine what a normal voice is. Some people speak naturally with a creaky voice, while some others with a hoarse voice. A disguise is applied when there is a deliberate will to transform one's voice to imitate someone or just to change the sound.  Distinguish electronic and non electronic alteration appears as a good method of classification.

**Table 1.** Classification of voice disguise

|  | Electronic | Non-electronic |
|---|---|---|
| **Voice conversion** | Vector quantization<br>LMR     (Linear     Multivariate Regression)<br>GMM (Gaussian Mixture Model)<br>Indexation in a client memory<br>… | Imitation |
| **Voice transformation** | Electronic device<br>Voice changer software | Mechanic alteration<br>prosody alteration |

In the first category (electronic), there are two kinds of disguise: conversion and transformation. The first one consists in transforming a source speaker voice to sound like a target speaker voice, and the second one in modifying electronically some specific parameters like the frequency, the speaking rate and so on, in order to change the sound of the voice. There are many free software which offer to modify the register of his own voice [45].

In the second category (non-electronic), we consider as voice conversion the imitation by a professional impersonator and as voice transformation the different possibilities to change one or more parameters of the voice as described below. The impostor can use a mechanic system like a pen in the mouth for instance, or simply use a natural modification of his voice by adopting a foreign accent for example. Some features that could change are presented in table 2 as proposed in [33].

The techniques used for the both categories are detailed with references in 3.

Table 2. Non-electronic voice disguise

| Prosody | Deformation | Phonemic |
|---|---|---|
| Intonation | Pinched nostrils | Use of dialect |
| Stress placement | Clenched Jaw | Foreign accent |
| Segment lengthening or shortening | Use of bite blocks (pipe smoker speech) | Speech defect |
| Speech tempo | Pulled cheeks | Hyper-nasal (velum lowered throughout |
| | Object over mouth | |
| | Objects in mouth | |
| | Tongue holding | |

The different terms used in this table are:
Prosody: indicators of many channels of linguistic and para-linguistic information
Deformation: forced physical changes in the vocal tract
Phonemic: use of unusual allophones

# 3   State of the Art

The question of voice disguise has been studied since the 1970's [16] [18] [25]. The main field of application at the beginning of those studies was intelligence and forensic science. The first works determined some means to change the voice quality and to evaluate the ability to identify the disguise. The aim of this section is to describe these different approaches adapting them to the classification presented above. As stated previously, a deliberated intention is considered as part of the definition of the voice disguise.

## 3.1   Electronic: Voice Transformation

Voice transformation is defined as the technique of changing the voice sounds by different means but without intention of imitating another voice. In this section, our purpose focuses on a presentation of change voice techniques based on electronic devices. The interest of those changes is to conceal the identity of the speaker. This could be used by radio or television to mask the identity of a person being interviewed but also in the case of anonymous or miscellaneous calls. However these means are relatively uncommon, representing one to ten percent of voice disguise situations [26]. Today with the development of internet, more and more software is available to change the voice [45]. The main technique, proposed by these software, consists in modifying the pitch register by a simple move of the mean or the pitch contour. It is also possible to add some specific effects to your original voice. These software proposes a modification of your voice pitch or your voice timbre in real time and an unlimited number of new voices. This offers an easy way to disguise your voice in voice chat, PC Phone, online gambling, voice mail, voice message and so on.

The best way to change the voice consists in modifying the prosody by using a modification of the pitch or of the duration of the segments. There are some methods able to modify the time scale or the frequency range independently. The change of the time scale offers the possibility to alter the duration of the signal without changing the frequency properties. The change of the frequency range is the contrary, that is to say modifying the pitch of a sound without changing the duration, and keeping the position of formants.

A technique which gives some interesting results is the TD PSOLA (Time Domain Pitch Synchronous Overlapp and Add) [30] [12]. This method proposes a flexible creation and modification of high quality speech. Using PSOLA, prosodic changes are easily performed. The following figure describes this technique:

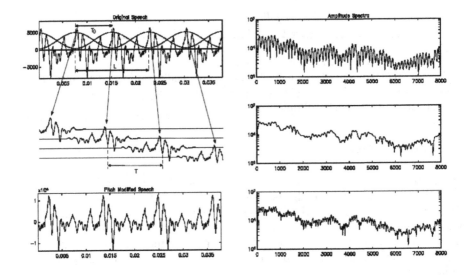

**Fig. 1.** TD PSOLA technique

## 3.2  Electronic: Voice Conversion

There are many techniques which have been developed in voice conversion because of the extended field of applications: speech synthesis, interpreted telephony or very low rate bit speech coding. Voice conversion is the process of transforming the characteristics of speech uttered by a source speaker, such that a listener would believe the speech was pronounced by a target speaker. Different techniques are possible for a voice conversion:

- spectral conversion [1][9][23][24][34][36][37][42]
- indexation in a client memory [32]

Generally the automatic method applied to convert a voice is based on a spectral conversion. From a set of features x = [x1, x2, .....xn] characterising a succession of source speaker speech sounds, and a set of features describing these same sounds but produced by a target speaker, the aim of the conversion is to find a transformation function between both sets and to apply it to a new sentence uttered by the source speaker. A spectral transformation can be performed by finding the conversion function F that minimizes the mean square error: $\varepsilon_{mse} = E[\|y - F(x)\|^2]$ , where E is the expectation. The main approach begins by the construction of a training phase (fig.2) in which the sets from source and target voice are first aligned and then used to define the function to map the acoustic space of the source to that of the target (Fig.3). So, a voice conversion system is composed of three steps:

- modelling step: this step is constituted by the parameterisation step which consists in extracting the acoustic features (MFCC: Mel frequency cepstral coefficients) and by the modelling of these features
- transformation step: this step consists in elaborating the mapping between the source and the target voice by minimizing the distance
- Synthesis step: from the transformation function, the acoustic features of source speech are mapped and the perceptual qualities of the synthesised speech are maintained.

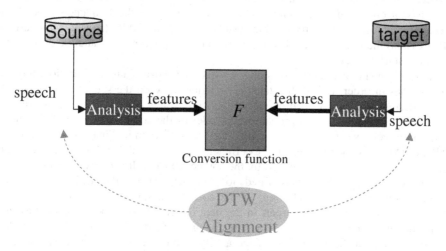

**Fig. 2.** Training step

The historical technique has been proposed by [1] who described the means to elaborate a mapping codebook between a source and a target voice. The determination of the codebook is based on vector quantization. The main problem of this method is the question of discontinuities when moving from one codebook to another over time.

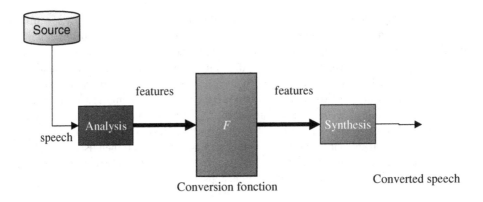

**Fig. 3.** Conversion step

Another original technique is presented in [34]. It differs from the previous by proposing a much more natural output by using the PSOLA (Pitch Synchronous Overlap and Add) synthesis and by proposing two methods to learn the spectral mapping: LMR (Linear Multivariate Regression) and DFW (Dynamic Frequency Warping). The principle of the first one is a projection of the acoustic space of the source speaker into the acoustic space of the target speaker and the second one consists in elaborating an optimal non-linear warping of the frequency axis. Both techniques provide some reasonable results even if the LMR (Linear Multivariate Regression) method is better. The main problem is the presence of audible distortions which disturb the result.

Lots of papers on voice conversion are based on GMM (Gaussian Mixture Models) approaches in order to find the statistical relation between the spectral envelopes of two different speakers who pronounced the same sentence. The works proposed in [36] [37] uses a continuous probabilistic model of the source envelope. The source and the target speech were first aligned by DTW (Dynamic Time Warping). Then MFCC (Mel Frequency Cepstral Coefficient) were calculated for each frame of speech, and a vector was produced by the source MFCC followed by the same frame target MFCC. A GMM was fitted to this data, using the EM (Expectation Maximization) algorithm. The aim of the conversion function is to transform the source data set into its counterpart in the data target set. This method increases the voice quality of the conversion by an attenuation of the discontinuities. Based on the same mapping of the spectral envelope as Stylianou and al., Kain proposes in [23] [24] another technique where he predicts the residual from the predicted spectral envelope. This technique provides a higher quality transformation.

Another work different from the previous has been proposed in [32]. The principle of this system is to encode speech by recognition and synthesis in terms of basic acoustic units that can be derived by an automatic analysis of the signal. Such analysis is not based on a priori linguistic knowledge [10]. Firstly, a collection of speech segments is constituted by segmenting a set of training sentences, all pronounced by the target voice. This step is performed using the temporal decomposition algorithm [5] on MFCC speech features. Segments resulting from temporal decomposition are then organized by vector quantization into 64 different classes. The training data is thus automatically labelled; using symbols that correspond to the above classes. A set of HMMs (Hidden Markov Models) is then trained on this data, providing a stochastic model for each class. The result of the ALISP (Automatic Language Independent Speech Processing) training is an inventory of client speech segments, divided into 64 classes according to a codebook of 64 symbols. The encode phase consists in replacing the segment of the source voice, recognized by HMM, by their equivalent of the target voice. The results (Fig.4) on an automatic speaker recognition system are proposed below where we notice a significant degradation of the recognition performance.

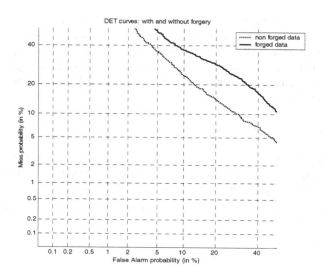

**Fig. 4.** DET curve: voice forgery

### 3.3 Non Electronic: Voice Conversion

Imitation is a well-known case of voice conversion more often used in the field of advertising. Zetterholm [38] and Mejvaldova [28] studied the different techniques used by a professional imitator to impersonate some voices. The principle is based on the impersonation of some specific characteristics of a target voice linked to prosody, pitch register, voice quality, dialect or the speech style. It is impossible for an impersonator to imitate all the voice register of the target speaker, but some specific parameters are enough to disturb the recognition. E. Zetterholm has demonstrated that the impersonator adapted his fundamental frequency and the position of his formants to the target voice. In [6] a study presents the difficulties of an automatic recognition system compared to a case of impersonation. A professional impersonator has imitated two target speakers: Blomberg and al. show the impersonator's adjustments, of the formant positions.

## 3.4  Non Electronic: Voice Transformation

This category of voice disguise includes the alteration of voice by using a mechanic system like a pen in the mouth and an handkerchief over the mouth, or by changing the prosody like dialect, accent or pitch register to get a low or high frequency voice modification, in order to trick the identity perception. Modifications in the rate of speech, the use of deliberate pause, the removal of extraneous syllables between words, the removal of frequency vocal fry and the heightening of prosodic variation (intonation and stress) are basically the more common voice transformation.

- Mechanic alteration [13] [43][44]

What we mean by mechanic alteration is the use of ways to disturb an original voice. Those are some ways like a pen in the mouth, parallel to the lips, a handkerchief or a hand over the mouth, or the action of pinching the nose. These types of disguise influence the quality of the voice by reducing or modifying for instance the zero of the transfer function of the vocal tract and actually the speech production system.

- Prosody alteration [19][29][31]

In this section we are interested in the deliberated changes of the voice prosody that is to say the supra segmental characteristics of the signal. Several parameters are able to influence the prosody of an individual such as:

- the physiological characteristics of the vocal tract (linked to the age and the gender)
- the emotion
- the social origin (accent)
- region origin (dialect)
- etc …

In theory a subject could modify all of those parameters to disguise his voice by changing the prosody. A classification of prosody is provided in [4], where three components could be proposed:

**Table 3.**

| Production | Acoustic | Perception |
|---|---|---|
| Vocal folds tension | Fundamental Frequency (F0) | Pitch - melody |
| Subglottic pressure | Intensity | Sone |
| Air flow | Interval | Rythm – duration |

Actually, the easiest prosody features to change a voice are the acoustic parameters and the perception parameters. Some of them can be easily measured.

- Fundamental frequency: estimation of the larynx frequency from a speech signal
- Duration: including speech rate, duration and distribution of the pause, syllable duration
- Intensity: the signal energy during a time interval

## 4  Research Program to Detect Voice Disguise

The question of characterizing different kinds of voice disguise and recognizing the original voice by automatic means has not been a subject of much study.

The main reason of this lack of study could be that the alteration caused by disguise has some important consequences on the voice quality and on the different features that provide a capacity for recognition. Nevertheless some studies have been published in this field, and in this section we are going to examine the different works before presenting some directions of research.

A rare work has been carried out in the field of mechanic disguise [13] by holding a pencil between the teeth, parallel to the lips. They analysed the effect of this disguise on the first three formants of seven oral vowels and detailed the proportional alteration of those formants. They noticed that perceptually the most evident effect was the lowering of the high vowels. The superimposition of settings of lips, jaw, and tongue affected speech segments to differing degrees, depending on the phoneme's susceptibility. In [26], Masthoff deals also with the problem of using a means to block some parameters of the vocal track and he notices that when more than one speech characteristic are simultaneously changed, the identification task is significantly more difficult for listeners. So we can reasonably conclude that this is the same for automatic detection.

In [20] the author proposes a study on three kinds of disguise on reading sentences: raising fundamental frequency, lowering fundamental frequency, denasalization by firmly pinching their nose. By focusing his work on F0, Künzel has showed that there is a direct and constant link between the F0 of a speaker's natural speech behaviour and the kind of disguise he will use. Speakers with higher-than-average F0 tend to increase their F0 levels. This process may involve register changes from modal voice to falsetto. Speakers with lower-than-average F0 prefer to disguise their voices by lowering F0 even more and often end up with permanently creaky voice.

A particular disguise, the whispered voice, has been studied in [31]. In this kind of disguise we can easily understand that the F0 and the pitch will be disturbed and even eliminated. There are also some influences on the available information about vocal intensity and voice quality.

The phenomenon of "creaky voice" that is to say the action of lowering the fundamental frequency has been examined in [21] [29]. S. Moosmüller studied the modifications of the vocal tract in this kind of disguise and the effect on formant frequencies. She noticed a sex difference in the analysis of the second and the third formant. Her work is based on 750 creaky and modal vowels pronounced by 5 female and four male speakers. It appears that creaky vowels uttered by women show a lower second formant as compared to the same vowels produced by the same speaker using modal phonation.

In an interesting work in [20], the authors analyse the effect of three kinds of disguise (falsetto speech, lowered voice pitch and pinched nose) on the performance of an automatic speaker recognition system. The experiment is limited to the estimation of the performance degradation when the suspect is known as being the speaker of the disguised speech. The results are depending on the reference population. If it contains speech data which exhibits the same type of disguise the influence is marginal on the performance. On the contrary, if the reference population is assembled with normal speech only, the effects have important consequences on the performance of the system for the three cases of disguise. Those different works reveal the lack of a global study on voice disguise; global in the sense of the number of disguises, the number of features studied, but also in the sense of technical approaches used.

In order to complete those different works on voice disguise, we have decided to examine the different parameters studied in the case of the pathological voice [17] and the analysis of emotion [2] [15] [35] and to determine if we could apply these works on our study. In addition, we propose to compare the classification of these features to the classification of features used in automatic speaker or speech recognition, the MFCC (Mel Frequency Ceptstral Coefficient) applied on voice disguise.

### 4.1 Principles of the Study

Our work focuses on the following disguises:

- pinched nostril voice
- high pitched voice
- low pitched voice
- a hand over the mouth
- electronic voice transformation
- electronic voice conversion

The first work consists in building a voice disguise database. According to our work we impose ourselves two major constraints. The first one is that the speech must be intelligible, and the second one is that the chosen disguise is commonly used. These conditions are necessary for work oriented towards forensic sciences. The training session and the tests will be carried out using a database developed in our lab. The speech samples will be collected in a controlled environment sampled at a 16 bit resolution. 50 French people will be recorded according to a specific protocol. Each of them will pronounce 10 phonetically balanced sentences, the different vowels of the vocalic triangle, an article from a common newspaper and a phonetically balanced text. There will be five sessions of recording: normal voice, high pitched voice, low pitched voice, hand over mouth voice, pinched nostril voice. Electronic transformation and conversion will be based on their normal voices. The database is divided in two sets: one for training (35 people) one for testing (15 people).

The following figure shows a block diagram describing the process of the automatic disguise detection system.

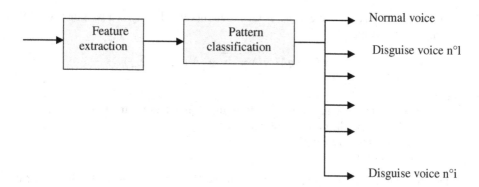

**Fig. 5.** Process of Detection system

Our aim is to compare two kinds of approaches: the first one is based on the principle of an automatic speaker recognition system by classification of cepstral coefficients: MFCC (Mel frequency Cepstral Coefficient); the second one regards the classification of each kind of disguise based on the prosodic parameters. In this second approach we plan to estimate some boundaries between the disguise (inter disguise) but also to analyse the main components for each kind of disguise (intra disguise).

### 4.2 Approach Based on Automatic Speaker Recognition System by Classification of Spectral Coefficient

The principle of this method is to build a Universal Background Model on the one hand for all disguises in order to detect if a voice is disguised or not and on the other hand for each kind of disguise in order to classify a speech sample in one of the disguises studied. The first work consists in extracting the features. We choose in this phase to use the MFCC. The mel frequency cepstral coefficient (MFCC) is one of the most important features required among various kinds of speech applications. These features represent the spectral contour of the signal and are captured from short time frame of the speech signal. Then a Fourier transform is applied to calculate the magnitude spectrum before quantifying it using a mel spaced filterbank. This last operation transforms the spectrum of each frame in a succession of coefficients which characterize the energy in each frequency bandpass of the mel range. A DCT is applied on the logarithm of those coefficients.

In addition to the MFCC, we calculate the first and the second derivatives of the MFCC in order to take into account dynamic information which introduces the temporal structure of the speech signal like for instance the phenomenon of co-articulation.

The second main step of this approach is the creation of a universal background model by training for all disguise and for each kind of disguise. The using of the first UBM (all disguise) is to discriminate a disguised voice from a normal voice. This UBM will be built on a statistic modelling based on GMM (Gaussian mixture models) on the entire disguised voice corpus. A Gaussian mixture density is a weigthed sum of M component densities:

$$f(x/disgMod) = \sum_{j=1}^{M} g_j N(x, \mu_j, \Sigma_j)$$

where

      x is a D dimensional vector resulting from the feature extraction
      j = 1 to M are the component densities
      $g_j$ are the mixture weigths
      disgMod is the disguise model

The different parameters ($g_j$, $\mu_j$, $\Sigma_j$) of the UBM will be estimated by the EM (Expectation – Maximisation) algorithm. This algorithm is a general technique for maximum likelihood estimation (MLE). The first step of the algorithm (E: estimation) consist in estimating the likelihood on all the data from the last iteration and the second step (M: maximisation) consists in maximizing the density function of the first step.

The same principle is used to estimate the specific UBM of each kind of disguise.

The last step of this approach is the verification phase which consists in knowing if an unknown recording comes from a normal voice of from a disguised voice and what kind of disguise by calculation of a likelihood ratio as follows.

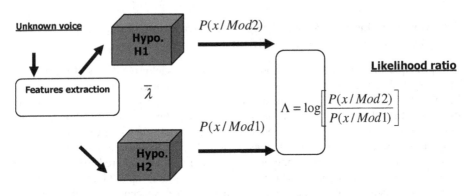

**Fig. 6.** Verification task: test phase

H1 : the unknown voice is a normal voice
H2 : the unknown voice is a disguised voice
Mod1: normal voice UBM
Mod2: disguised voice UBM

## 4.3  Approach Based on Analysis and Classification of Prosodic Features

The second objective consists in detecting the disguise by studying some specific prosody parameters. Perceptually, it is easy to notice a difference between an original voice and a voice transformed by such a technique, but the question is what the main parameters that have been changed are. We can expect that each kind of disguise will have some specific parameters that will change.

We are using PRAAT [8] for a statistical study on

F0 features:
- min, max, mean, std,
- Jitter: this parameter measures the instability of frequency in each cycle:

$$\frac{\frac{1}{n-1}\sum_{i=n-1}^{1}|F0_{i+1}-F0_i|}{F0_{mean}}$$

Energy features:

$$E(x) = \int |x(t)|^2 dt \rightarrow i\mathrm{dB} = 20\log 10(E(x))$$
$$i\mathrm{dB} = 20\log 10(E(x)/Eo).$$

- mean: Eo
- energy proportion in 5 Frequency bandwidths (0 - 1kHz - 2kHz – 3kHz – 4kHz - 5KHz).
- The shimmer: this parameter measures the instability of amplitude in each cycle.

$$\frac{\frac{1}{n-1}\sum_{i=n-1}^{1}|E_{i+1}-E_i|}{E_{\grave{a}}}$$

Rhythm features:
- Speaking rate based on the calculation of number of phoneme per second
- Voiced/unvoiced region
- Ration of speech to pause time

Formant features for each vowels of the vocalic triangle:
- F1: characteristic from the mouth opening
- F2: characteristic from the tongue position
- F3: characteristic from the lips contour

After this extraction phase, the aim is to organize and classify the different features in order to find boundaries inter disguise.

*Inter disguise*

Contrary to the first approach, where we used the MFCC which have the property of being uncorrelated, a first work in this approach consists in extracting the main information in the global distribution of the coefficient before classification. Different methods of data analysis and classification will be used in order to select the main features which influence a disguise and reduce the dimension via a PCA (Principal Component Analysis) for instance. The use of PCA allows the number of variables in a multivariate data set to be reduced, whilst retaining as much as possible of the variation present in the data set. This reduction is achieved by taking p variables $X_1$, $X_2$,..., $X_p$ and finding the combinations of these to produce principal components (PCs) $PC_1$, $PC_2$,..., $PC_p$, which are uncorrelated. These PCs are also termed eigenvectors. PCs are ordered so that $PC_1$ exhibits the greatest amount of the variation, $PC_2$ exhibits the second greatest amount of the variation, $PC_3$ exhibits the third greatest amount of the variation, and so on. The aim is to be able to describe the original number of variables (X variables) as a smaller number of new variables (PCs).

We will also apply a LDA (Linear Discriminant Analysis) in order to increase the class distribution by optimization of the ratio between the intra class the inter class. After this step of data description and organization, we will structure our database by applying supervised classification methods based on training.

The classification step planned is based on GMM clustering as previously explained. The principle is to build a GMM model for each kind of model based on a training phase and to calculate a distance which will be the likelihood function between a test vector and the model.

*Intra disguise*

From the same set of prosodic features, a study in order to evaluate the main characteristics of each of disguise has been planned. The idea is to extract the more significant components for each disguise and the influence of some specific features. The algorithm used is a PCA.

And last, we investigated a measurement of the vocalic triangle [39][40][41] moving between a normal voice and a disguise n°k voice. The study based on a limited corpus of voice disguised provides interesting results as shown by the following figure.

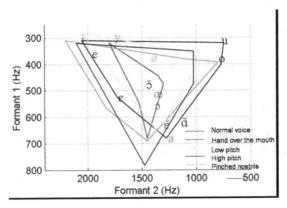

**Fig. 7.** Vocalic triangle

This vocalic triangle is based on a corpus of twenty people who pronouced the different french vowels in five disguise voice (included normal voice) .

The aim of the PCA and the comparison of vocalic triangle analysis are to find some specific clues in each kind of disguise.

Our last objective will consist in:

- Fusing both approaches in order to increase voice disguise recognition
- Synthesising a disguised voice from the original voice of the suspect and to evaluate the distance between this voice and the unknown voice.
- Or applying a transformation adapted to the type of disguise determined previously, to the disguised voice and comparing it to an undisguised voice of the suspect.

Such a goal will be certainly possible in the case of simple disguise, like a lower pitch for instance, but if the impostor uses different kinds of disguise, the task will be more complicated.

To conclude, this paper presents the problem of voice disguise under different aspects. In the first part, we propose a classification where we distinguish different possibilities of disguise depending on the means employed. The question of disguise is considered under the aspect of a deliberate action in order to falsify identity. All the problems of voice transformation caused by channel distortion are not studied. A review of different works on some particular disguises is detailed in the second part in order to understand the difficulties encountered in characterizing disguises. An important problem could be the using of different disguises in the same time. But the main studies in the forensic field reveal that in the most case the impostor has just used a specific disguise. Lastly in a third section, we first present the relative importance of specific features in different kinds of disguises and, secondly we propose some directions of research to evaluate the impact of disguise on an automatic speaker recognition system and to determine the disguise by finding out some indicators linked to study of emotional or pathological voice.

# References

1. M. Abe, S. Nakamura, K. Shikano, H. Kuwabara, "Voice conversion through vector quantization," *Proc. ICASSP 88,* New-York, 1988
2. N. Amir, "Classifying emotions in speech: a comparison of methods" in Proceedings EUROSPEECH 2001, Scandinavia
3. G. Baudoin, J. Cernocky, F. El Chami, M. Charbit, G. Chollet, D. Petrovska-Delacretaz. "Advances in Very Low Bit Rate Speech Coding using Recognition and Synthesis Techniques," *Proc. Of the 5th Text, Speech and Dialog workshop, TSD 2002*, Brno, Czech Republic, pp. 269-276, 2002
4. F. Beaugendre, "Modèle de l'intonation pour la synthèse".1995 de la parole", in "Fondements et perspectives en traitement automatique de la parole", Aupelf-Uref (ed.).
5. F. Bimbot, G. Chollet, P. Deleglise, C. Montacié, "Temporal Decomposition and Acoustic-phonetic Decoding of Speech," *Proc. ICASSP 88*, New-York, pp. 445-448, 1988
6. M. Blomberg, Daniel Elenius, E. Zetterholm, "Speaker verification scores and acoustics analysis of a professional impersonator," *Proc. FONETIK 2004*
7. R. Blouet, C. Mokbel, G. Chollet, "BECARS: a free software for speaker recognition," *ODYSSEY 2004*, Toledo, 2004
8. P. Boersma, D. Weenink, "PRAAT: doing phonetics by computer. http://www.praat.org"
9. O. Cappe, Y. Stylianou, E Moulines, "Statistical methods for voice quality transformation," *Proc. of EUROSPEECH 95*, Madrid, 1995

10. G. Chollet, J. Cernocky, A. Constantinescu, S. Deligne, F. Bimbot, "Toward ALISP: a proposal for Automatic Language Independent Speech Processing," *Computational Models of Speech Processing*, NATO ASI Series, 1997

11. V. Delvaux, T. Metens, A. Soquet. "French nasal vowels: articulary and acoustic properties", Proc. Of the 7th ICSLP, Denver, 1,53-56,2002

12. T. Dutoit, "High quality text to speech synthesis: a comparison of four candidates algorithms", Proc. ICASSP 1994 vol.1 pp 565-568, Adelaïde, Australie.

13. Figueiredo Ricardo Molina de, Britto, Helena de Souza "A report on the acoustic effects of one type of disguise", Forensic Linguistics, 1996, 3, 1, 168-175

14. D. Genoud, G. Chollet, "Voice transformations: some tools for the imposture of speaker verification systems," *Advances in Phonetics*, A. Braun (ed.), Franz Steiner Verlag, Stuttgart, 1999

15. D. Gibbon, U. Gut, "Measuring speech rhythm", Proc. Eurospeech 2001, Scandinavia

16. W. Endres, W. Balbach, G. Flösser, "Voice spectrograms as a function of age, voice disguise and voice imitation", Journal of the Acosutical Society of America, 49:1842-8, 1971

17. L. Gu, J.G. Harris, R. Shrivastav, C. Sapienza, "Disordered speech evaluation using objective quality measures", Proc. ICASSP 2005, Philadelphie

18. M. Hall, "Spectrographic analysis of interspeaker and intraspeaker variability of professional mimicry", MA dissertation, Michigan State University. 1975

19. Hermann J. Künzel "Effects of voice disguise on fundamental frequency", Forensic linguistics 7:149-179, 2000

20. H. Künzel, J.Gonzalez-Rodriguez, J. Ortega-Garcia, "Effect of voice disguise on the performance of a forensic automatic speaker recognition system", Proc. Odyssey 2004

21. A. Hirson, Duckworth M, "Glottal fry and voice disguise: a case study in forensic phonetics", Journal of Biomedical Enginering vol 15:193-200, 1993

22. D.Jiang, W. Zhang, L. Shen, L. Cai, "Prosody analysis and modelling for emotional speech synthesis", Proc. ICASSP 2005, Philadelphie

23. A. Kain, M. W. Macon, "Spectral voice conversion for text to speech synthesis," *Proc. ICASSP 98,* New-York, 1998

24. A. Kain, M. W. Macon, "Design and evaluation of a voice conversion algorithm based on spectral envelope mapping and residual prediction," *Proc. ICASSP 01,* Salt Lake City, 2001

25. R.C. Lummis, A.E Rosenberg, "Test of an automatic speaker verification method with intensively trained professional mimics", Journal of Acoustical Society of America, vol 9, number 1, 1972

26. H. Masthoff. « A report on voice disguise experiment, Forensic Linguistics", 3(1) :160-167. 1996

27. A. Martin, G. Doddington, T. Kamm, M. Ordowski, M. Przybocki, "The DET curve in assessment of detection task performance," *Proc. EUROSPEECH 97*, Rhodes, Greece, pp. 1895-1898, 1997.

28. J. Melvaldova, "Caractéristiques temporelle de la parole imitée", Proceedings JEP (Journées d'Etudes sur la Parole) 2004

29. S. Moosmüller, "The influence of creaky voice on formant frequency changes", The International Journal of Speech, Language and the Law, vol8, n°1, 2001

30. E. Moulines, F. Charpentier, "Pitch synchronous waveform processing techniques for text to speech synthesis using diphone". Speech comm. vol.9 p 453-497

31. T. Ochard, A. Yarmey, "The effects of whispers, voice sample duration and voice distinctiveness on criminal Speaker Identification", Appl. Cogn. Psychol., 31:249-260

32. P. Perrot, G. Aversano, R. Blouet, M. Charbit, G. Chollet, « voice forgery using ALISP » Proc. ICASSP 2005, Philadelphie

33. R. Rodman, Speaker Recognition of disguised voices: a program for research, consortium on Speech Technology Conference on Speaker by man and machine: direction for forensic applications, Ankara, Turkey, COST 250, 1998

34. H. Valbret, E. Moulines, J.P. Tubach, "Voice trans-formation using PSOLA technique" *Proc. ICASSP 92*, San Francisco, 1992

35. I. Shafran, M. Mohri, "A comparison of classifiers for detecting emotion from speech", Proc. ICASSP 2005, Philadelphie

36. Y. Stylianou, O. Cappe, "A system for voice conversion based on probabilistic classification and a harmonic plus noise model," *Proc ICASSP 98*, Seattle, WA, pp. 281-284, 1998

37. Y. Stylianou, O. Cappe, E. Moulines "Continuous probalistic transform for voice conversion," IEEE Trans. Speech and Audio Processing, 6(2):131-142, March 1998.

38. Zetterholm, E. Voice Imitation. A phonetic study of perceptual illusions and acoustic success. Dissertation. Department of Linguistics and Phonetics, Lund University. 2003

39. Rostolland D., 1982a, "Acoustic features of shouted voice", Acustica 50, pp. 118-125.

40. Rostolland D., 1982b, "Phonetic structure of shouted voice", Acustica 51, pp. 80-89.

41. Rostolland D., 1985, "Intelligibility of shouted voice", Acoustica 57, pp. 103-121

42. Abboud B. Bredin H, Aversano G., Chollet G. "Audio visual forgery in identity verification" Workshop on Nonlinear Speech Processing, Heraklion, Crete, 20-23 Sept. 2005

43. B.S. Atal, "Automatic speaker recognition based on pitch contours", Journal of Acoustical Society of America, 52:1687-1697, 1972.

44. J. Zalewski, W. Maljewski, H. Hollien, "Cross correlation between Long-term speech Spectra as a criterion for speaker identification, Acoustica 34:20-24, 1975

45. http://www.zdnet.fr/telecharger/windows/fiche/0,39021313,11009007s,00.htm

# Audio-visual Identity Verification: An Introductory Overview

Bouchra Abboud, Hervé Bredin, Guido Aversano, and Gérard Chollet

CNRS-LTCI, GET-ENST, 46 rue Barrault, 75013 Paris, France
bouchra.abboud@facing-it.net - {bredin, aversano, chollet}@tsi.enst.fr

**Abstract.** Verification of identity is commonly achieved by looking at the face of a person and listening to his (her) speech. Automatic means of achieving this verification has been studied for several decades. Indeed, a talking face offers many features to achieve a robust verification of identity. The current deployment of videophones drives new opportunities for a secured access to remote servers (banking, certification, call centers, etc.). The synchrony of the speech signal and lip movements is a necessary condition to check that the observed talking face has not been manipulated and/or synthesized. This overview addresses face, speaker and talking face verification, as well as face and voice transformation techniques. It is demonstrated that a dedicated impostor needs limited information from a client to fool state of the art audio-visual identity verification systems.

## 1 Introduction

Identity verification based on talking face biometrics is getting more and more attention. As a matter of fact, a talking face offers many features to achieve a robust identity verification: it includes speaker verification, face recognition and their multimodal combination. Moreover, whereas iris or fingerprint biometrics might appear intrusive and need user collaboration, a talking face identity verification system is not intrusive and can even be achieved without the user noticing it.

Though it can be very robust thanks to the complementarity of speaker and face recognition, these two modalities also share a common weakness: an impostor can easily record the voice or photograph the face or his/her target without him/her noticing it ; and thus fool a talking face system with very little effort. Moreover, higher effort impostors might perform both voice conversion and face animation in order to perform impersonation that is even more difficult to detect or to mask his/her identity (see *Voice Disguise and Automatic Detection: Review and Perspectives* by Perrot et al. in this volume). We will show that explicit talking face modeling (i.e. the coupled modeling of acoustic and visual synchronous features) is an effective way to overcome these weaknesses.

The remaining of this chapter is organized as follows. After a short review of the most prominent methods used for speaker verification and face recognition, low and high forgery scenarios are described, including simple replay attacks,

Y. Stylianou, M. Faundez-Zanuy, A. Esposito (Eds.): WNSP 2005, LNCS 4391, pp. 118–134, 2007.

voice conversion and face animation. Finally, the particular task of replay attacks detection is addressed, based on the detection of a lack of synchrony between voice and lip motion.

## 2    Audio-Visual Identity Verification

### 2.1    Speaker Verification

Speech is a biometric modality that may be used to verify the identity of a speaker. The speech signal represents the amplitude of an audio waveform as captured by a microphone. To process this signal a feature extraction module calculates relevant feature vectors on a signal window that is shifted at a regular rate. In order to verify the identity of the claimed speaker a stochastic model for the speech generated by the speaker is generally constructed. New utterance feature vectors are generally matched against the claimed speaker model and against a general model of speech that may be uttered by any speaker called the world model. The most likely model identifies if the claimed speaker has uttered the signal or not. In text independent speaker recognition, the model should not reflect a specific speech structure, i.e. a specific sequence of words. Therefore in state-of-the-art systems, Gaussian Mixture Models (GMM) are used as stochastic models [1].

Given a feature vector $\mathbf{x}$, the GMM defines its probability distribution function as in (1).

$$\sum_{i=1}^{N} w_i \frac{1}{\sqrt{(2\pi)^d \|\Gamma_i\|}} \exp\left(-\frac{1}{2}(\mathbf{x} - \mu_i)^T \Gamma_i^{-1} (\mathbf{x} - \mu_i)\right) \qquad (1)$$

This distribution can be seen as the realizations of two successive processes. In the first process, the mixture component is selected and based on the selected component the corresponding Gaussian distribution defines the realization of the feature vector. The GMM model is defined by the set of parameters $\lambda = (\{w_i\}, \{\mu_i\}, \{\Gamma_i\})$. To estimate the GMM parameters, speech signals are generally collected. The unique observation of the feature vectors provides incomplete data insufficient to allow analytic estimation, following the maximum likelihood criterion, of the model parameters, i.e. the Gaussian distributions weights, mean vectors and covariance matrices. The Estimation Maximization (EM) algorithm offers a solution to the problem of incomplete data [2]. The EM algorithm is an iterative algorithm, an iteration being formed of two phases: the Estimation (E) phase and the Maximization (M) phase. In the E phase the likelihood function of the complete data given the previous iteration model parameters is estimated. In the M phase new values of the model parameters are determined by maximizing the estimated likelihood. The EM algorithm ensures that the likelihood on the training data does not decrease with the iterations and therefore converges towards a local optimum. This local optimum depends on the initial values given to the model parameters before training. Thus, the initialization of the model parameters is a crucial step. The LBG algorithm is used to initialize the model parameters.

The direct estimation of the GMM parameters using the EM algorithm requires a large amount of speech feature vectors. This causes no problem for the world model where several minutes from several speakers may be collected for this purpose. For the speaker model, this would constrain the speaker to talk for a long duration and may not be acceptable. To overcome this, speaker adaptation techniques may be used [3], such as Bayesian adaptation, maximum likelihood linear regression (MLLR), and the unified adaptation technique defined in [4]. Using the adaptation techniques few minutes of speech become sufficient to determine the speaker model parameters.

During recognition, feature vectors are extracted from a speech utterance. The log likelihood ratio between the speaker and world models is computed and compared to a threshold. This allows to verify the identity of the claimed speaker.

### 2.2    Face Verification

Face recognition is divided into two major areas: face identification and face verification. On the one hand, face verification is concerned with validating a claimed identity based on a frontal and/or profile image or a video sequence of the claimant's face, and either accepting or rejecting the identity claim. On the other hand, the goal of face identification is to identify a person based on the image or video of his/her face. This face has to be compared with all registered persons and hence it is desirable to represent faces in a compact yet precise manner. Many techniques exist to perform this task, some of which are reviewed below.

**Face Representation.** Traditionally two major classes of techniques exist for face representation. On the one hand, geometrical feature extraction relies on parameters of distinctive features such as eyes, mouth and nose. On the other hand, in appearance-based approaches, a face is represented as an array of intensity values suitably preprocessed; the array is then compared with a face template using an appropriate metric. The performances of both representation techniques in face recognition are compared in [5]. Our work on faces belongs to appearance-based approaches.

**Face Recognition.** Once proper face representation is accomplished, the next step consists in determining which class the represented face belongs to. In this context several approaches have been proposed.

In template matching, the extracted face information is compared with the pre-computed templates of each class [6]. The degree of similarity is measured either with the Euclidian distance or with the Mahalanobis distance in eigenspace and fisherspace [7,8]. A probabilistic similarity measure is also used in [9].

However, in distance-based classification, it is assumed that the prototypes are representative of query images under various conditions and the recognition performance depends largely on the representational capacity of the training set. Therefore, location and scale of query images are usually normalized before they are compared to the templates. Nevertheless, changes in illumination and rotation are difficult to compensate by normalization. In this context, the nearest feature line method proposed in [10] aims at expanding the representational capacity of available feature points in order to account for new conditions not represented in the training set. The method interpolates the available prototype images to build appropriate linear combinations that represent the variations in illumination and viewing angle. The decision is made based on the minimum distance between the query and each interpolated line.

Support Vector Machine (SVM) is an effective method for pattern recognition that finds the hyperplane separating the largest possible fraction of points of the same class on the same side while maximizing the distance from either classes to the hyperplane [11]. SVM is a binary classifier, and two strategies exist for solving $q$-class problems. The one-versus-all strategy involves the training of $q$ SVMs, each separating a given class from the rest of the training set, whereas pairwise classifiers involve the training of a different SVM for separating each pair of classes. The one-versus-all strategy was successfully used for facial expression recognition [12] as well as face recognition [13].

Multilayer Perceptron (MLP) neural network (NN) is a good classification tool. It searches for an acceptable local minimum in the NN weight space in order to achieve minimal error. Weights are adjusted using back-propagation which is a gradient descent supervised training procedure. During the training procedure MLP builds separating hypersurfaces in the input space. After training MLP can successfully apply acquired skills to previously unseen samples. Backpropagation trained Neural Networks were used for facial expression recognition in [14].

Hidden Markov Model (HMM) is an extension of the theory of Markov chains where the observation of a certain output is a probabilistic function of the state. Identification is achieved by selecting the HMM which obtains the highest likelihood [15]. HMM computations converge quickly making them practical for real time processing.

Finally, recent papers investigate the use of video sequences in order to perform face recognition. For instance, in [16], face features are extracted from every frame of the video, and gaussian mixture modeling is used (as in the speaker verification task). In the GMM space, an additional step is performed: one SVM is trained per client to achieve better discrimination between clients.

## 3   The Forgery Issue in Biometrics

Many databases are available to the research community to help evaluate multi-modal biometric verification algorithms, such as BANCA [17], BT-DAVID [18], XM2VTS [19] and BIOMET [20]. Different protocols have been defined for evaluating biometric systems on each of these databases, but they share the assumption that impostor attacks are zero-effort attacks. For example, in the particular framework of the BANCA database, each subject records one client access and one impostor access per session. However, the only difference between the two is the particular message that the client utters—their name and address in the first case; the target's name and address in the second. Thus the impersonation takes place without any knowledge of the target's face, age, and voice. These zero-effort impostor attacks are unrealistic—only a fool would attempt to imitate a person without knowing anything about them. In this work we adopt more realistic scenarios in which the impostor has more information about the target.

### 3.1   Replay Attacks

A major drawback of using the talking-face modality for identity verification is that an impostor can easily obtain a sample of any client's audiovisual identity. Contrast this with iris recognition: it is quite difficult to acquire a sample of another person's iris. But numerous small devices allow an impostor to take a picture of the target's face without being noticed, and some mobile phones are even able to record movies. Of course, it is even easier to acquire a recording of the target's voice. Therefore, protocols to evaluate audiovisual identity verification systems should recognize this fact, for example by adding replay attacks to their repertoire of envisaged impostor accesses [21].

### 3.2   Voice Conversion

Forgery attacks against a speaker verification system, where the voice characteristics of the impostor is modified in such a way that it resembles the voice of the client, are investigated in this section. The choice of the transformation technique is made according to the available quantity of client voice data.

If only a limited amount of client data is available for training (as in the case of BANCA protocol [17]), a spectral conversion technique should be adopted, which give some interesting results according to previous studies [22]. Consider a sequence of spectral vectors pronounced by the impostor, $X = [x_1, x_2, \ldots, x_n]$, and a sequence composed by the same words, pronounced by the client, $Y = [y_1, y_2, \ldots, y_n]$. A spectral transformation can be performed by finding the conversion function $F$ that minimizes the mean square error: $\epsilon_{mse} = \mathbb{E}[||y - F(x)||^2]$, where $\mathbb{E}$ is the expectation. This conversion method requires preliminary word-level segmentation of the training sentences.

If more client data are available (e.g. approximately 1 hour of client's speech), we can use a voice encoder based on the Automatic Language Independent Speech Processing approach (ALISP) [23]. This method is described in Sec.2.2 of the chapter untitled *Voice Disguise and Automatic Detection: Review and Program* by Perrot et al.

## 3.3    Face Transformation

Natural talking faces synthesis is a very challenging task, since a synthetic face has to be photo-realistic and represent subtle texture and shape variations that are vital to talking faces representation and recognition, in order to be considered natural.

Many modeling techniques exist which achieve various degrees of realism and flexibility. The first class of techniques uses 3D meshes to model the face shape [24,25]. To obtain natural appearance a 3D scan image of the subject face is texture-mapped on the 3D parameterized deformable model.

An alternative approach is based on morphing between 2D images. This technique produces photo-realistic images of new shapes by performing interpolation between previously seen shapes and is successfully combined with geometric 3D transformations to create realistic facial models from photos and construct smooth transitions between different facial expressions [26]. Using the same technique, multi-dimensional deformable models [27] can generate intermediate video-realistic mouth movements of a talking face from a small set of manually selected mouth samples. Morphing is also used in the context of the *video-rewrite* to change the identity of a talking face [28].

## 3.4    Talking-Face Animation

In this work we propose to use an appearance-based face tracker allowing to extract from each frame of a video sequence a set of feature points describing the face shape. These feature points are tracked from frame to frame throughout the entire sequence [29] and their motion is injected into any target image allowing to simulate a lip movement similar to the tracked sequence.

**Face Tracking.** It has already been shown that the active appearance model [30] is a powerful tool for object synthesis and tracking. It uses Principal Component Analysis (PCA) to model both shape and texture variations seen in a training set of visual objects. After computing the mean shape $\bar{\mathbf{s}}$ and aligning all shapes from the training set by means of a Procrustes analysis, the statistical shape model is given by (2)

$$\mathbf{s}_i = \bar{\mathbf{s}} + \Phi_s \mathbf{b}_{si} \tag{2}$$

where $\mathbf{s}_i$ is the synthesized shape, $\Phi_s$ is a truncated matrix describing the principal modes of shape variations in the training set and $\mathbf{b}_{si}$ is a vector that controls the synthesized shape.

It is then possible to warp textures from the training set of faces onto the mean shape $\bar{\mathbf{s}}$ in order to obtain shape-free textures. Similarly, after computing the mean shape-free texture $\bar{\mathbf{t}}$ and normalizing all textures from the training set relatively to $\bar{\mathbf{t}}$ by scaling and offset of the luminance values, the statistical texture model is given by (3)

$$\mathbf{t}_i = \bar{\mathbf{t}} + \Phi_t \mathbf{b}_{ti} \tag{3}$$

where $t_i$ is the synthesized shape-free texture, $\Phi_t$ is a truncated matrix describing the principal modes of texture variations in the training set and $\mathbf{b}_{ti}$ is a vector that controls the synthesized shape-free texture.

By combining the training shape and texture vectors $\mathbf{b}_{si}$ and $\mathbf{b}_{ti}$ and applying further PCA the statistical appearance model is given by (4) and (5)

$$\mathbf{s}_i = \bar{\mathbf{s}} + Q_s \mathbf{c}_i \tag{4}$$

$$\mathbf{t}_i = \bar{\mathbf{t}} + Q_t \mathbf{c}_i \tag{5}$$

where $Q_s$ and $Q_t$ are truncated matrices describing the principal modes of combined appearance variations in the training set, and $\mathbf{c}_i$ is a vector of appearance parameters simultaneously controlling both shape and texture.

Given the parameter vector $\mathbf{c}_i$, the corresponding shape $\mathbf{s}_i$ and shape-free texture $\mathbf{t}_i$ can be computed respectively using (4) and (5). The reconstructed shape-free texture is then warped onto the reconstructed shape in order to obtain the full appearance. Displacing each modes of the mean appearance vector $\bar{\mathbf{c}}$ changes both the texture and shape of the coded synthetic faces.

Furthermore, in order to allow pose displacement of the model, it is necessary to add to the appearance parameter vector $\mathbf{c}_i$ a pose parameter vector $\mathbf{p}_i$ allowing control of scale, orientation and position of the synthesized faces.

While a couple of appearance parameter vector $\mathbf{c}$ and pose parameter vector $\mathbf{p}$ represents a face, the active appearance model can automatically adjust those parameters to a target face by minimizing a residual image $\mathbf{r}(\mathbf{c}, \mathbf{p})$ which is the texture difference between the synthesized faces and the corresponding mask of the image it covers as shown in (6) and (7).

In the following, the appearance and pose parameters obtained by this optimization procedure will be denoted respectively as $\mathbf{c}_{op}$ and $\mathbf{p}_{op}$.

$$\mathbf{c}_{op} = \arg_{min} |r[(\mathbf{c} + \delta \mathbf{c}), \mathbf{p}]|^2 \tag{6}$$

$$\mathbf{p}_{op} = \arg_{min} |r[\mathbf{c}, (\mathbf{p} + \delta \mathbf{p})]|^2 \tag{7}$$

For this purpose, a set of training residual images are computed by displacing the appearance and pose parameters within allowable limits. These residuals are then used to compute matrices $\mathbf{R}_a$ and $\mathbf{R}_t$ establishing the linear relationships (8) and (9)

$$\delta(\mathbf{c}) = -\mathbf{R}_a\, \mathbf{r}(\mathbf{c}, \mathbf{p}) \tag{8}$$

$$\delta(\mathbf{p}) = -\mathbf{R}_t\, \mathbf{r}(\mathbf{c}, \mathbf{p}) \tag{9}$$

between the parameter displacements and the corresponding residuals, so as to minimize $|r((\mathbf{c}, \mathbf{p}) + \delta(\mathbf{c}, \mathbf{p}))|^2$.

A first order Taylor development gives the following solution (10) and (11)

$$\mathbf{R}_a = \left( \frac{\partial \mathbf{r}}{\partial \mathbf{c}}^T \frac{\partial \mathbf{r}}{\partial \mathbf{c}} \right)^{-1} \frac{\partial \mathbf{r}}{\partial \mathbf{c}}^T \tag{10}$$

$$\mathbf{R}_t = \left(\frac{\partial \mathbf{r}}{\partial \mathbf{p}}^T \frac{\partial \mathbf{r}}{\partial \mathbf{p}}\right)^{-1} \frac{\partial \mathbf{r}}{\partial \mathbf{p}}^T \tag{11}$$

These linear relationships are then used to determine the optimal appearance and pose vectors $\mathbf{c}_{op}$ and $\mathbf{p}_{op}$ using a gradient descent algorithm [31].

Hence adapting the active appearance model to each frame of a video sequence showing a speaking face allows to track the facial movements of the face as shown on Fig. 1. The experiments are conducted on the BANCA database which

**Fig. 1.** Face tracking through consecutive adaptation of AAM to each frame

contains video recordings of different speaking faces. Evaluation is conducted according to the MC evaluation protocol [32]. This database was designed in order to test multi-modal (face and voice) identity verification with various acquisition devices. For 4 different languages (English, French, Italian and Spanish), video and speech data were collected for 52 subjects on 12 different occasions. During each recording, the subject was prompted to say a random 12 digits number, their name, address and date of birth.

The consecutive frames were extracted from each video sequence of the BANCA database. An appearance model is first trained using the first 5 images of the training set, which corresponds to the world model according to the protocol, and then used to automatically detect feature points on the next 5 images. The model is subsequently rebuilt using the whole 10 annotated images and so on to annotate the whole training set in a bootstrapping mode. The obtained model is then used to automatically annotate the client verification data. This procedure allows hence to perform automatic face tracking on the client verification sequences.

**Face Animation.** Lip motion is defined by the position of the MPEG-4 compatible feature points on each frame of the tested sequence. A set of 18 features

**Fig. 2.** MPEG-4 compatible feature points located at the inner and outer contours of the training lips

**Fig. 3.** Appearance model adaptation and automatic feature point placement on the target face

Driving sequence                                    Target image

Driving sequence                                    Lip motion cloning

Driving sequence                                    Lip motion cloning

**Fig. 4.** Lip motion cloning from the driving sequence (left) to animate the static target image (right)

points were selected at key positions on the outer and inner lip contours as shown on Fig. 2. This motion can be injected to any target image showing an unknown face using the following procedure.

First the lip pixels on the target image are detected using the lip localization method described in Sec. 3.4, as shown on Fig. 1. Then, starting from this rough position, an appearance model is initialized and adapted to the target lip using the gradient descent algorithm. This procedure allows to automatically place the feature points at the correct positions of the target lips as shown on Fig. 3. An artificial motion is then obtained by displacing these feature points to match each frame of the driving sequence. A Delaunay triangulation coupled with a piecewise affine transform is used to interpolate pixels color values. An example of lip motion cloning of a driving sequence on an unknown target face is shown on Fig. 4.

## 4    Replay Attacks Detection

The main weakness of a biometric system based on the fusion of speaker verification and face recognition stays in the fact that it is easily fooled by replay attacks (as described in Sec. 3). The solution that we propose is to detect a lack of synchrony between voice and lip motion that could result from this kind of replay attacks.

In this section, we overview the most promising methods of the literature allowing to measure the degree of synchrony between audio and visual speech [33].

### 4.1    Audio-Visual Features

Most of the audio-visual features used in the relatively new field dealing with audio-visual speech synchrony are shared with the audio-visual speech recognition domain [34].

**Audio Speech.** Acoustic speech parameterization is classically performed on overlapping sliding window of the original audio signal.

In [35], the authors extract the average acoustic energy on the current window as their one-dimensional audio feature, whereas [36] uses the periodogram. The use of classical Mel-Frequency Cepstral Coefficients (MFCC) is very frequent [37,38,39,40,41]. Linear-Predictive Coding (LPC), and its derivation Line Spectral Frequencies (LSF) [42] have also been widely investigated. The latter are often preferred because shown to be strongly related to the vocal tract geometry [43].

A comparison of these different acoustic speech features is performed in [37] in the framework of the *FaceSync* linear operator. To summarize, in their specific framework, the authors conclude that MFCC, LSF and LPC parameterizations lead to a stronger correlation with the visual speech than spectrogram and raw energy features.

**Visual Speech.** Raw pixels are the visual equivalent of the audio raw energy. In [35] and [40], the intensity of gray-level pixels is used as is. In [21], their sum over the whole region of interest is computed, leading to a one-dimensional feature. Holistic methods consider and process the region of interest as a whole source of information. In [39], a two-dimensional discrete cosine transform (DCT) is applied on the region of interest. In [44], the authors perform a projection of the region of interest on vectors resulting from a principal component analysis (PCA): they call the principal components eigenlips. Lip-shape methods consider and process lips as a deformable object from which geometrical features can be derived, such as height, width openness of the mouth, position of lip corners, etc. Mouth width, mouth height and lip protrusion are computed in [45]. In [46,47], a deformable template composed of several polynomial curves follows the lip contours: it allows the computation of the mouth width, height and area. In [41], the lip shape is summarized with a one-dimensional feature: the ratio of lip height and lip width.

**Audio-Visual Subspaces.** Once these features are computed, transformation are performed in order to reduce dimensionality and keep only the dimensions that are meaningful for the specific task of measuring the degree of synchrony in audio-visual speech. Thus, in [48], Principal Component Analysis (PCA) is used in order to reduce the dimensionality of a joint audiovisual space (in which audio speech features and visual speech features are concatenated), while keeping the characteristics that contribute most to its variance. In [49], Independent Component Analysis (ICA) is applied on an audiovisual recording of a piano session: the camera frames a close-up on the keyboard when the microphone is recording the music. ICA allows to clearly find a correspondence between the audio and visual note. However, to our knowledge, ICA has never been used as a transformation of the audiovisual speech feature space. Canonical Correlation Analysis (CANCOR) is a statistical analysis allowing to jointly transform the audio and visual feature spaces while maximizing the audiovisual cross-correlation. Given two synchronized random variables, the *FaceSync* algorithm presented in [37] uses CANCOR to find canonic correlation matrices that whiten them under the constraint of making their cross-correlation diagonal and maximally compact. Co-Inertia Analysis (CoIA) is quite similar to CANCOR. However, while CAN-COR is based on the maximization of the correlation between audio and visual features, CoIA relies on the maximization of their covariance [50,46].

## 4.2   Measures

Once audio-visual speech features are extracted, the next step is to measure their degree of correspondence. The following paragraphs overview what is proposed in the literature.

**Correlation.** Let $X$ and $Y$ be two independent random variables which are normally distributed.

Assuming a linear relationship between $X$ and $Y$, the square of their Pearsons product-moment coefficient $R(X, Y)$ (defined in equation 12) denotes the portion of total variance of $X$ that can be explained by a linear transformation of $Y$ (and reciprocally, since it is a symmetrical measure).

$$R(X, Y) = \frac{\text{cov}(X, Y)}{\sigma_X \sigma_Y} \tag{12}$$

In [35], the authors compute the Pearsons product-moment coefficient between the average acoustic energy $X$ and the value $Y$ of the pixels of the video to determine which area of the video is more correlated with the audio. This allows to decide which of two people appearing in a video is talking.

In information theory, the mutual information $MI(X, Y)$ of two random variables $X$ and $Y$ is a quantity that measures the mutual dependence of the two variables. In the case of $X$ and $Y$ are discrete random variables, it is defined as in equation (13).

$$MI(X, Y) = \sum_{x \in X} \sum_{y \in Y} p(x, y) \log \frac{p(x, y)}{p(x)p(y)} \tag{13}$$

It is non-negative $(MI(X, Y) \geq 0)$ and symmetrical $(MI(X, Y) = MI(Y, X))$. One can demonstrate that $X$ and $Y$ are independent if and only if $MI(X, Y) = 0$. The mutual information can also be linked to the concept of entropy $H$ in information theory as shown in equation 15:

$$MI(X, Y) = H(X) - H(X|Y) \tag{14}$$
$$MI(X, Y) = H(X) + H(Y) - H(X, Y) \tag{15}$$

In [35,51,39,40], the mutual information is used to locate the pixels in the video which are most likely to correspond to the audio signal: the face of the person who is speaking clearly corresponds to these pixels.

**Joint Audio-Visual Models.** Let consider two discrete random variables $X = \{x_t, t \in \mathbb{N}\}$ and $Y = \{y_t, t \in \mathbb{N}\}$ of dimension $d_X$ and $d_Y$ respectively. One can define the discrete random variable $Z = \{z_t, t \in \mathbb{N}\}$ of dimension $d_Z$ where $z_t$ is the concatenation of the two samples $x_t$ and $y_t$, such as $z_t = [x_t, y_t]$ and $d_Z = d_X + d_Y$.

Given a sample $z$, the Gaussian Mixture Model (GMM) $\lambda$ defines its probability distribution function as in 16.

$$p(z|\lambda) = \sum_{i=1}^{N} w_i \mathcal{N}(z; \mu_i, \Gamma_i) \tag{16}$$

where $\mathcal{N}(\bullet; \mu, \Gamma)$ is the normal distribution of mean $\mu$ and covariance matrix $\Gamma$. $\lambda = \{w_i, \mu_i, \Gamma_i\}_{i \in [1, N]}$ are parameters describing the joint distribution of $X$ and $Y$. Using a training set of synchronized samples $x_t$ and $y_t$ concatenated into joint samples $z_t$, the Expectation-Maximization algorithm (EM) allows the estimation of $\lambda$. Given two sequences of test $X = \{x_t, t \in [1, T]\}$ and $Y = \{y_t, t \in [1, T]\}$, a measure of their correspondence $C_\lambda(X, Y)$ can be computed as in (17).

$$C_\lambda(X, Y) = \frac{1}{T} \sum_{t=1}^{T} p([x_t, y_t]|\lambda) \tag{17}$$

The authors of [39] propose to model audio-visual speech with Hidden Markov Models (HMMs). Two speech recognizers are trained: one classical audio only recognizer [52], and an audiovisual speech recognizer as described in [34]. Given a sequence of audiovisual samples ($[x_t, y_t], t \in [1, T]$), the audio only system gives a word hypothesis $W$. Then, using the HMM of the audiovisual system, what the authors call a measure of plausibility $P(X, Y)$ is computed as follows:

$$P(X, Y) = p([x_1, y_1]...[x_T, y_T]|W) \tag{18}$$

An asynchronous hidden Markov model (AHMM) for audio-visual speech recognition is proposed in [53]. It assumes that there is always an audio observation $x_t$ and sometimes a visual observation $y_s$ at time $t$. It intrinsically models the difference of sample rates between audio and visual speech, by introducing the probability that the system emits the next visual observation $y_s$ at time $t$. AHMM appears to outperform HMM in the task of audio-visual speech recognition [53] while naturally resolving the problem of different audio and visual sample rates.

The use of neural networks (NN) is investigated in [38]. Given a training set of both synchronized and not synchronized audio and visual speech features, a neural network with one hidden layer is trained to output 1 when the audiovisual input features are synchronized and 0 when they are not. Moreover, the authors propose to use an input layer at time $t$ consisting of $[X_{t-N_X}, \ldots, X_t, \ldots, X_{t+N_X}]$ and $[Y_{t-N_Y}, \ldots, Y_t, \ldots, Y_{t+N_Y}]$ (instead of $X_t$ and $Y_t$), choosing $N_X$ and $N_Y$ such as about 200 ms of temporal context is given as an input.

## 5   Conclusion

Biometric identity verification is usually used to protect the access to sensitive information or locations, which are –by definition– prone to be attacked by malevolent people. Therefore, it is very important to investigate the possible attacks that could threaten such a system. In the case of audio-visual identity verification based on talking faces, we have shown that it is possible to increase error rates by transforming the voice of the impostor so that it resembles the voice of his/her target. Moreover, an algorithm allowing to automatically animate the face of a person in order to reproduce the lip motion of an impostor was described. These high-effort forgeries are a great threat for talking face-based identity verification algorithms. However, much simpler attacks (yet very efficient if the algorithm was not originally designed to take them into account) can also be used by impostors. This is the case of replay attacks, which can be detected by measuring a possible lack of synchrony between voice and lip motion.

## Acknowledgments

This work was partially supported by the European Commission through our participation to the SecurePhone project (`http://www.secure-phone.info/`) and the BioSecure Network of Excellence (`http://www.biosecure.info/`)

## References

1. Reynolds, D.A., Quatieri, T.F., Dunn, R.B.: Speaker Verification using Adapted Gaussian Mixture Models. Digital Signal Processing **10** (2000) 19 – 41
2. Dempster, A., Laird, N., Rubin, D.: Maximum Likelihood from Incomplete Data via the EM Algorithm. J. of Royal Statistical Society **39**(1) (1977) 1 – 22
3. Blouet, R., Mokbel, C., Mokbel, H., Sanchez, E., Chollet, G.: BECARS: a Free Software for Speaker Verification. In: ODYSSEY 2004. (2004) 145 – 148
4. Mokbel, C.: Online Adaptation of HMMs to Real-Life Conditions: A Unified Framework. In: IEEE Transactions on Speech and Audio Processing. Volume 9. (2001) 342 – 357
5. Brunelli, R., Poggio, T.: Face recognition: Features versus templates. IEEE Trans. on Pattern Analysis and Machine Intelligence **15**(10) (1993) 1042–1052
6. Wiskott, L., Fellous, J.M., Krüger, N., von der Malsburg, C.: Face recognition by elastic bunch graph matching. In: Intl. Conference on Computer Analysis of Images and Patterns. Number 1296, Heidelberg, Springer-Verlag (1997) 456–463
7. Abboud, B., Davoine, F., Dang, M.: Expressive face recognition and synthesis. In: IEEE CVPR workshop on Computer Vision and Pattern Recognition for Human Computer Interaction, Madison, U.S.A. (2003)
8. Turk, M., Pentland, A.: Eigenfaces for recognition. Journal of Cognitive Neuroscience **3**(1) (1991) 71–86
9. Moghaddam, B., Pentland, A.: Beyond euclidean eigenspaces: Bayesian matching for visual recognition. In: Face Recognition: From Theories to Applications, Berlin, Springer-Verlag (1998)
10. Li, S., Lu, J.: Face recognition using the nearest feature line method. IEEE Transactions on Neural Networks **10** (1999) 439–443
11. Vapnik, V. In: Statistical Learning Theory. Wiley (1998)
12. Bartlett, M.S., Littlewort, G., Fasel, I., Movellan, J.R.: Real time face detection and facial expression recognition: Development and applications to human computer interaction. In: IEEE CVPR workshop on Computer Vision and Pattern Recognition for Human Computer Interaction, Madison, U.S.A. (2003)
13. Heisele, B., Ho, P., J.Wu, Poggio, T.: Face recognition: Component-based versus global approaches. In: Computer Vision and Image Understanding. Volume 91. (2003) 6–21
14. Padgett, C., Cottrell, G., Adolphs, R.: Categorical perception in facial emotion classification. In: Proceedings of the Eighteenth Annual Cognitive Science Conference., San Diego, CA (1996) 249–253

15. Lien, J., Zlochower, A., Cohn, J., Li, C., Kanade, T.: Automatically recognizing facial expressions in the spatio temporal domain. In: Proceedings of the Workshop on Perceptual User Interfaces, Alberta, Canada (1997)
16. Bredin, H., Dehak, N., Chollet, G.: GMM-based SVM for Face Recognition. International Conference on Pattern Recognition (2006)
17. Bailly-Baillière, E., Bengio, S., Bimbot, F., Hamouz, M., Kittler, J., Mariéthoz, J., Matas, J., Messer, K., Popovici, V., Porée, F., Ruiz, B., Thiran, J.P.: The BANCA Database and Evaluation Protocol. In: Lecture Notes in Computer Science. Volume 2688. (2003) 625 – 638
18. BT-DAVID: (http://eegalilee.swan.ac.uk/)
19. Messer, K., Matas, J., Kittler, J., Luettin, J., Maitre, G.: XM2VTSDB: The Extended M2VTS Database. Audio- and Video-Based Biometric Person Authentication (1999) 72 – 77
20. Garcia-Salicetti, S., Beumier, C., Chollet, G., Dorizzi, B., Jardins, J.L., Lunter, J., Ni, Y., Petrovska-Delacretaz, D.: BIOMET: a Multimodal Person Authentication Database including Face, Voice, Fingerprint, Hand and Signature Modalities. Audio- and Video-Based Biometric Person Authentication (2003) 845 – 853
21. Bredin, H., Miguel, A., Witten, I.H., Chollet, G.: Detecting Replay Attacks in Audiovisual Identity Verification. In: IEEE International Conference on Acoustics, Speech, and Signal Processing. (2006)
22. Stylianou, Y., Cappé, O., Moulines, E.: Statistical Methods for Voice Quality Transformation. European Conference on Speech Communication and Technology (1995)
23. Perrot, P., Aversano, G., Chollet, G., Charbit, M.: Voice Forgery Using ALISP: Indexation in a Client Memory. In: ICASSP 2005. (2005)
24. Romdhani, S., Vetter, T.: Efficient, robust and accurate fitting of a 3D morphable model. In: IEEE Intl. Conference on Computer Vision, Nice, France (2003)
25. Terzopoulos, D., Waters, K.: Analysis and synthesis of facial image sequences using physical and anatomical models. IEEE Trans. on Pattern Analysis and Machine Intelligence 15(6) (1993) 569–579
26. Pighin, F., Hecker, J., Lischinski, D., Szeliski, R., Salesin, D.: Synthesizing realistic facial expressions from photographs. In: Siggraph proceedings. (1998) 75–84
27. Ezzat, T., Geiger, G., Poggio, T.: Trainable videorealistic speech animation. In: ACM Siggraph, San Antonio, Texas (2002)
28. Bregler, C., Covel, M., Slaney, M.: Video rewrite: Driving visual speech with audio. In: Siggraph proceedings. (1997) 353–360
29. Ahlberg, J.: An active model for facial feature tracking. EURASIP Journal on applied signal processing 6 (2002) 566–571
30. Abboud, B., Davoine, F., Dang, M.: Facial expression recognition and synthesis based on an appearance model. Signal Processing: Image Communication 10(8) (2004) 723–740
31. Cootes, T., Edwards, G., Taylor, C.: Active appearance models. IEEE Trans. on Pattern Analysis and Machine Intelligence 23(6) (2001) 681–685
32. Bailly-Bailliere, E., Bengio, S., Bimbot, F., Hamouz, M., Kittler, J., Mariethoz, J., Matas, J., Messer, K., Popovici, V., Pore, F., Ruiz, B., Thiran, J.P.: The BANCA database and evaluation protocol. In: 4th International Conference on Audio- and Video-Based Biometric Person Authentication, AVBPA, Springer-Verlag (2003)
33. Bredin, H., Chollet, G.: Measuring Audio and Visual Speech Synchrony: Methods and Applications. In: International Conference on Visual Information Engineering. (2006)

34. Potamianos, G., Neti, C., Luettin, J., Matthews, I.: 10. In: Audio-Visual Automatic Speech Recognition: An Overview. MIT Press (2004)
35. Hershey, J., Movellan, J.: Audio-Vision: Using Audio-Visual Synchrony to Locate Sounds. Neural Information Processing Systems (1999)
36. Fisher, J.W., Darell, T.: Speaker Association With Signal-Level Audiovisual Fusion. IEEE Transactions on Multimedia 6(3) (2004) 406–413
37. Slaney, M., Covell, M.: FaceSync: A Linear Operator for Measuring Synchronization of Video Facial Images and Audio Tracks. Neural Information Processing Society 13 (2000)
38. Cutler, R., Davis, L.: Look Who's Talking: Speaker Detection using Video and Audio Correlation. International Conference on Multimedia and Expo (2000) 1589–1592
39. Nock, H., Iyengar, G., Neti, C.: Assessing Face and Speech Consistency for Monologue Detection in Video. Multimedia'02 (2002) 303–306
40. Iyengar, G., Nock, H., Neti, C.: Audio-Visual Synchrony for Detection of Monologues in Video Archives. International Conference on Acoustics, Speech, and Signal Processing (2003) 329–332
41. Chetty, G., Wagner, M.: "Liveness" Verification in Audio-Video Authentication. Australian International Conference on Speech Science and Technology (2004) 358–363
42. Sugamura, N., Itakura, F.: Speech Analysis and Synthesis Methods developed at ECL in NTT–From LPC to LSP. Speech Communications 5(2) (1986) 199–215
43. Yehia, H., Rubin, P., Vatikiotis-Bateson, E.: Quantitative Association of Vocal-Tract and Facial Behavior. Speech Communication (28) (1998) 23–43
44. Bregler, C., Konig, Y.: "Eigenlips" for Robust Speech Recognition. International Conference on Acoustics, Speech, and Signal Processing 2 (1994) 19–22
45. Goecke, R., Millar, B.: Statistical Analysis of the Relationship between Audio and Video Speech Parameters for Australian English. International Conference on Audio-Visual Speech Processing (2003)
46. Eveno, N., Besacier, L.: Co-Inertia Analysis for "Liveness" Test in Audio-Visual Biometrics. International Symposium on Image and Signal Processing Analysis (2005) 257–261
47. Eveno, N., Besacier, L.: A Speaker Independent Liveness Test for Audio-Video Biometrics. 9th European Conference on Speech Communication and Technology (2005)
48. Chibelushi, C.C., Mason, J.S., Deravi, F.: Integrated Person Identification Using Voice and Facial Features. IEE Colloquium on Image Processing for Security Applications (4) (1997) 1–5
49. Smaragdis, P., Casey, M.: Audio/Visual Independent Components. International Symposium on Independent Component Analysis and Blind Signal Separation (2003) 709–714
50. Dolédec, S., Chessel, D.: Co-Inertia Analysis: an Alternative Method for Studying Species-Environment Relationships. Freshwater Biology 31 (1994) 277–294
51. Fisher, J.W., Darrell, T., Freeman, W.T., Viola, P.: Learning Joint Statistical Models for Audio-Visual Fusion and Segregation. Advances in Neural Information Processing Systems (2001)
52. Rabiner, L.R.: A Tutorial on Hidden Markov Models and Selected Applications in Speech Recognition. In: IEEE. Volume 77. (1989) 257–286
53. Bengio, S.: An Asynchronous Hidden Markov Model for Audio-Visual Speech Recognition. Advances in Neural Information Processing Systems (2003)

# Text-Independent Speaker Verification: State of the Art and Challenges

Dijana Petrovska-Delacrétaz[1], Asmaa El Hannani[1,2,*], and Gérard Chollet[3]

[1] Institut National des Télécommunications, 91011 Evry, France
[2] DIVA Group, Informatics Dept., University of Fribourg, Switzerland
[3] TSI Department, CNRS-LTCI ENST, Paris, France
dijana.petrovska@int-evry.fr, asmaa.elhannani@unifr.ch,
gerard.chollet@enst.fr

**Abstract.** Speech is often the only available modality to recognize the identity of a person (over the telephone, the radio, in the dark,...). Automatic speaker recognition has been studied for several decades. In this chapter the state of the current text-independant speaker verification research is reviewed. Basic principles of speaker recognition are first summarized. The choice of the speech features and speaker models are mostly related to the individual characteristics (variability) of the speakers' voices. Besides the speaker's variability, we are faced with other factors, such as microphone or transmission channel variabilities, that degrade the performances of speaker verification algorithms. Some of these issues are illustrated on recent NIST–2005 and 2006 speaker recognition evaluation campaigns.

The field of speaker verification is also reviewed in relation to speech recognition, focusing on the usage of this new source of information. This relationship has to be seen as an important issue in the development of new services based on speaker and speech recognition. An overview of recent results in this field is given. More particularly, examples of combining baseline Gaussian Mixture Models (GMM) with high-level information extracted with data-driven speech segmentation are reported.

## 1 Introduction

Speaker verification consists of verifying a person's claimed identity. It is a sub-field of the more general speaker recognition field. In this chapter an overview of recent developments in text-independent speaker verification is presented, with a special focus on emerging techniques using high-level information. High-level information could be obtained using well known speech recognition methods, or using data-driven speech segmentation techniques.

Gaussian Mixtures Models (GMM) are widely used statistical models for text-independent speaker verification experiments. They have the advantage to represent well-understood statistical models, to be computationally inexpensive, and

* Supported by the Swiss National Fund for Scientific Research, No. 200020-108024 and NoE BioSecure, IST-2002-507634.

Y. Stylianou, M. Faundez-Zanuy, A. Esposito (Eds.): WNSP 2005, LNCS 4391, pp. 135–169, 2007.
© Springer-Verlag Berlin Heidelberg 2007

to be insensitive to the temporal variability of speech. They are used in combination with well known speech parametrization techniques based on cepstral analysis. Such systems, denoted here as acoustic GMM, have excellent performances in artificially good conditions, such as quiet environments, high-quality microphones, matched enrollment and test conditions and with cooperative speakers. When applied to more challenging real world applications, including recordings with background noise, different microphones and transmission channels, the performances of GMM using spectral level feature are degraded. Normalization techniques can be used at different levels in order to cope with such more challenging situations. Recent results have shown that high level information can be successfully extracted and combined with acoustic GMM in order to improve speaker verification performances [79].

The outline of this chapter is the following. In the introductory Sect. 1, the basic terminology of speaker recognition is summarized, introducing the two main tasks: speaker verification and indentification. The dependence of the speaker recognition task related to the nature of the speech data is also introduced. At the end of this section, the basic steps needed for speaker recogniton are presented: extraction of relevant features, speaker modeling and decision making.

In Sect. 2, the widely used spectral representation for parametrization of the speech data is summarized. Problems of choosing some additional features and their combination, as well as selecting the relevant speech frames for speaker recogntion are also introduced.

In Sect. 3, the statistical modeling algorithms for speaker verification are presented, including generative models (such as GMM) and discriminative models, such as Multiple Layer Perceptrons (MLP) and Support Vector Machines (SVM).

Section 4, introduces the problems of deciding if a test utterance was produced by the claimed speaker or by an impostor.

Issues regarding factors affecting the performance evaluation and the importance of choosing relevant evaluation speech data and common evaluation protocols are presented in Sect. 5. The difficulties of real world applications are also pointed out.

In Sect. 6 two possible directions to cope with the difficulties of widely used GMM based systems are given: to use different normalization techniques at different levels or to combine current spectral-feature GMM with high-level information systems. Summary of reported recent experiments using these two directions is also given. Section 6.1, presents the current normalization techniques at different levels (feature or score level) that are used to improve baseline text-independent speaker verification results using GMM. In the second part, Sect. 6.2, recent developments and results using high-level information for text-independent speaker verification experiments and summarized.

In Sect. 7 case studies examples of factors influencing the performances of speaker verification experiments are shown. They illustrate the difficulties of text-independent speaker verification systems. The evaluation databases and reference evaluation protocols underlying these examples are presented in Sect. 7.1. A reference (benchmarking) framework using well defined development data, reference protocols and open-source state-of-the-art algorithms is introduced in this section. The case studies examples are grouped in two parts. Results presented in Sect. 7.2, illustrate the difficulties of tuning a variety of parameters in order to achieve well performing GMM based systems. Results presented in Sect. 7.3, show the improvements that could be achieved when high-level information extracted with data-driven methods are combined with baseline GMM systems.

The conclusions and perspectives are given in Sect. 8.

Other reviews on speaker verification were published in the literature. Without being exhaustive, the following reviews and tutorials could be mentionned. In [62] a tutorial on text-dependent speaker verification is given, pointing out the advantages of text-dependent systems. [10] presents a tutorial on text-independent speaker verification. An overview of the widely used Gaussian Mixture models, and normalization techniques that are needed to deal with real world data are presented. It also addresses the applications of speaker verification including forensic applications.

In this chapter an updated summary of text-independent speaker verification is presented, with a main focus on how to solve problems arising when real world data are encountered. Two directions are given: developments concerning normalization techniques and a summary of recent experiments using high-level features. The particularity of this contribution is to illustrate this updated summary with case study experiments. These case study experiments are presented using relevant (NIST–2005 and 2006) evaluation databases, and are also compared to a bechmarking (reference) framework.

## 1.1   Task Dependence

There are two main tasks of speaker recognition: speaker identification and speaker verification. The **closed set speaker identification** task consists of determining (from a sequence of speech samples), the identity of an unknown person among N recorded speakers, called reference speakers. The identification answers the question "Who am I?". This process gives place to N possible results. The **open set** version of this task is often more realistic. It also decides if the unknown person is within the closed set or not.

The **speaker verification** task consists of deciding if a person, who claims to be a target speaker [1], is or is not this speaker. The decision will be either an acceptance or a rejection. The verification answers the question, "Am I who I claim to be?". If the person is not a target speaker, he is called an impostor.

## 1.2   Text Dependence

The speaker recognition task can be classified in three major categories according to the textual contents of the speech data. A speaker recognition system could be: (a) **text-dependent**, when the speaker must reproduce, during the

---

[1] Also referred in the literature as true, reference or client speaker.

testing phase, the same words or sentences as those pronounced during train-ing, (b)**text-prompted**, when the speaker must pronounce, during the test, words and sentences imposed by the system or (c) **text-independent** when the speaker can speak freely during the training (enrollment) and testing phases.

The choice of text dependence is related to the foreseen application. There are different classes of applications. They can be classified in various families, such as on-site access control applications, remote applications, forensic appli-cations or applications where only telephone speech data of the target speaker is available. As pointed out in [62] text-dependent (also called fixed-text) sys-tems have a much higher level of performance then text-independent (also called free-text) systems. Text-independent systems are needed in forensic and surveil-lance applications where the user is not cooperative and often not aware of the task. This chapter is focused on recent developments in text-independent speaker verification experiments.

### 1.3   Speaker Verification Modules

There are three basic steps in any speaker verification system:

- speech parametrization,
- speaker modeling, and
- decision making.

The performance of the overall system is dependent on each of the steps listed above. The choice of the feature extraction method and classifier depends on the constraints of the planned application. In the following section the speech parametrization methods commonly used to extract relevant parameters from speech data are summarized.

## 2   Spectral Features for Speaker Recognition

Speaker verification/identification tasks, commonly designed as speaker recogni-tion tasks, are typical pattern recognition problems. One important step is the extraction of relevant information from the speech data that is used to character-ize the speakers. The speaker-dependent voice characteristics can be categorized in high-level and low-level attributes [77,15].

Low-level attributes, related to the physical structure of the vocal tract, are derived from spectral measurements. High-level attributes include attributes like prosody (pitch, duration and enery) or behavioral cues like dialect, word usage, conversational patterns, topics of conversations, etc. Behavioral cues are influ-enced by many factors, such as the sociolinguistic context, the education and the socio-economic environment. These attributes are more difficult to extract by automated systems but they are less sensitive to noise and channel mismatch than the low-level cues. They begin to be used in combinations with low-level spectral features, as explained in Sect. 6.2 and Sect. 7.3.

Most of the speech parametrization used for speaker recognition systems rely on a cepstral representation of speech. In the following section Linear Prediction Coding and filter-bank cepstral parameters are summarized.

## 2.1   Linear Predictive Coding (LPC) Based Cepstral Parametrization

The basic principle of the Linear Prediction Coding (LPC) [66,31,67,58,78] method is that the speech signal can be modeled by a linear process predicting the signal at each time using a certain number of preceeding samples. Spectral analysis is done on windows of speech using an all-pole modeling constraint. Within each window, the sample at time $t$, $s(t)$, is approximated with a linear combination of the past $p$ samples, plus some excitation term, $e(t)$:

$$s(t) = \sum_{i=1}^{p} a_i.s(t-i) + e(t) \tag{1}$$

The estimation of the prediction coefficients $a_i$ is done by minimizing the prediction error between the model and the signal. The prediction coefficients can be further transformed into Linear Predictive Cepstral Coefficients (LPCC) using a recursive algorithm.

Another variant of the LPC analysis is the Perceptual Linear Prediction (PLP) [43] method. The main idea of this technique is to take advantage of some characteristics derived from the psychoacoustic properties of the human ear. Transformations of the speech signal to simulate the perceptual properties of the human ear are applied.

## 2.2   Filter-Bank Cepstral Parametrization

The second approach uses a bank of filters [13,75,78,10]. The steps needed to transform the speech signal to cepstral vectors based on filterbanks are the following: preemphasis, windowing (such as Hamming or Hanning), Fast Fourier Transform (FFT), extraction of the FFT modulus, application of the filterbank in order to perform smoothing and to get the envelope of the spectrum, log transformation to obtain the spectral vectors and cepstral transformations in order to calculate the final cepstral parameters. The filterbank is defined by the shape of the filters and by their frequency localization. The filters could be spaced uniformly according to a linear scale, to calculate the Linear Frequency Cepstral Coefficients (LFCC), or according to a Mel scale to calculate the Mel Frequency Cepstral Coefficients (MFCC). The mel-cepstrum, introduced by Davis and Mermelstein [20] exploits the human auditory principles as well as the decorrelating property of the cepstrum.

As pointed out in [77] an important property of MFCC based parameters is that the discrete cosine transform that is used for their calculation has the property of decorrelating the coefficients. Using decorrelated coefficients is important for probabilistic modeling, such as the widely used Gaussian Mixture Models [80].

## 2.3   Additional Features

In most speaker verification systems, features representing the dynamics of the speech signal are used in addition to the static cepstral coefficients. The dynamic coefficients are usually estimated using first and second order derivatives, denoted as $\delta$ and $\delta\delta$ [34].

Other coefficients such as the log–energy and its first derivative ($\delta$ log–energy) could also be added to the feature vectors. In practice, the $\delta$ log–energy is used, whereas the log-energy is discarded. An example of using these features is given in case studies in Sect. 7.2.

## 2.4   Configuration of Features

Regarding spectral parameters and additional features, many possible configurations have been experimented. Until today, there is no study showing a systematic advantage of using one or another configuration. Each approach has demonstrated some advantages in some cases but could not be generalized. The multiple choices are related to the kind of features (LPCC, LFCC, MFCC, . . . ), the numbers of coefficients, the use or not of the $\delta\delta$ coefficients, of the log–energy and of $\delta$ log–energy, etc. Experimental results using different configuratons of the feature vectors could be found in [81,9].

## 2.5   Selection of Speech Frames

Another crucial step in any speaker verification system is the selection of the frames conveying speaker information. The problem is to separate the incoming signal into speech portions versus silence and background noise. One way to separate speech from non-speech or background noise is to compute a bi-Gaussian model of the log–energy coefficients (see for example [57]). Normally, the useful frames will belong to the gaussian with the highest mean. A threshold dependent on the parameters of this gaussian, could then be used for the selection of the frames.

Another possibility to select the useful frames is to use Hidden Markov Models. Such models are implemented in current speech recognizers, and can be used to separate speech from non-speech and noisy data. This method is used for the data-driven experiments described in the case study experiments in Sect. 7.3.

# 3   Statistical Modeling Algorithms for Speaker Verification

Once the feature vectors are extracted and the irrelevant frames corresponding to non-speech or noisy data are removed, the remaining data could be used for extracting speaker specific information. This step is denoted as training (or enrollment) step of the recognition system and the associated speech data used to build the speaker model are called training (or enrollment) data. During the test phase, the same feature vectors are extracted from the waveform of a test utterance and matched against the relevant model.

As the focus of this chapter is on text-independent speaker verification, techniques based on measuring distances between two patterns are only mentioned, leaving more emphasis to statistical modeling techniques. The "distance based" methods were mainly used in systems developed at the beginning of the speaker recognition history. In the beginning (1930–1980) methods like template matching and Dynamic Time Warping and Vector Quantization were used and evaluated on small size databases recorded in "clean conditions", with few speech data and few speakers. With the evolution of storage and computers' calculating capacities, methods using statistical models such as Gaussian Mixture Models, as well as Neural Networks, began to be more widely used. Such methods are needed in order to cope with more realistic and difficult conditions of the continuously changing telecommunication environments. They cover the period between 1980–2003. Last years developments combine the well developed statistical models with methods that extract high-level information for speaker characterization.

There are several ways to build speaker models using statistical methods. They can be divided into two distinct categories: generative and discriminative models. Generative models include mainly Gaussian Mixture Models (GMM) and Hidden Markov Models (HMM). These methods are probability density estimators that model the acoustic feature vectors. The discriminative models are optimized to minimize the error on a set of training samples of the target and non-target (impostors) classes. They include Multilayer Perceptrons (MLP) and Support Vector Machines (SVM).

## 3.1 Generative Models

### Gaussian Mixture Models

The use of Gaussian Mixtures Models (GMM) for speaker modeling was introduced by D. Reynolds [80,83]. This approach has become over the past years the dominant approach for text-independent speaker verification systems. Most of the actual systems are based on GMM or use them in combination with other classifiers. Several techniques were developed around the GMM in order to improve the robustness of these systems.

GMM are probability density estimators that attempt to capture the variations of the speech data. They represent a particular case of Hidden Markov Models (HMM) and can be viewed as a single-state HMM where the probability density is estimated by a mixture of gaussians.

Given a D-dimensional feature vector, $x_t$, the probability density function $p(x_t|\lambda)$ is approximated as a weighed sum of $M$ multinormal gaussian densities:

$$p(x_t|\lambda) = \sum_{i=1}^{M} w_i \mathcal{N}(x_t, \mu_i, \Sigma_i) \qquad (2)$$

where $\mathcal{N}(x_t, \mu_i, \Sigma_i)$ is a density function with a $D \times 1$ mean vector $\mu_i$, and a $D \times D$ covariance matrix[2] $\Sigma_i$. $w_i$ are the mixture weights, with the constraint $\sum_{i=1}^{M} w_i = 1$.

The GMM are defined by the set of parameters $\lambda = w_i, \mu_i, \Sigma_i$. During the training phase, these parameters are iteratively estimated using the Expectation-Maximization (EM) algorithm [22]. Usually, only limited data is available to train the speaker model. Therefore, adaptation techniques are used. First a background model is trained. The speaker model is then derived by adapting the parameters of the background model with the speaker's enrollment speech data. Different adaptation techniques are possible, such as Maximum a Posteriori (MAP) [36] or Maximum Likelihood Linear Regression (MLLR) estimations [53].

By making the assumption of independence of the features, the likelihood of a model $\lambda$ for a sequence of feature vectors $X = x_1, ...., x_T$ is computed as follows:

$$\log p(X|\lambda) = \sum_{t=1}^{T} \log p(x_t|\lambda) \tag{3}$$

where $p(x_t|\lambda)$ is computed from (2). The $\log p(x_t|\lambda)$ is used instead of $p(x_t|\lambda)$ in order to avoid computer precision problems. Note that the average log–likelihood value is used to normalize out the duration effects.

## Hidden Markov Models

Hidden Markov Models (HMM) are statistical models, where the system being modeled is assumed to be a Markov process with unknown parameters. The goal is to determine the most probable sequence of states of the test data regarding the previously trained models. As explained in [78], there are three fundamental problems for the HMM design:

- the evaluation of the probability (or likelihood) of a sequence of observations given a specific HMM,
- the determination of a best sequence of model states, and
- the adjustment of model parameters so as to best account for the observed signal.

For speaker recognition applications, each state of the HMMs may represent phones or other longer units of speech. Temporal information is encoded by moving from one state to another regarding the allowed transitions. In this case the HMM method consists in determining for each speaker the best alignment between the sequence of test speech vectors and the Hidden Markov Model associated with the pronounced word or phrase. The probabilities of the HMM process are accumulated to obtain the utterance likelihood, in similar fashion to the GMM.

---

[2] Usually, the feature vectors are assumed independent, so only diagonal covariance matrices are used.

## GMM Versus HMM

State-of-the-art text-independent speaker verification systems use GMM. Conceptually they do not account for temporal ordering of feature vectors. The linguistic and temporal structure of the speech signal is not taken into account and all sounds are represented using a unique model. The temporal and linguistic knowledge can be incorporated by using HMM. In text-dependent speaker recognition tasks, where there is a prior knowledge of the textual content, HMM [64,92] are more accurate than GMM since the former can better model temporal variations. In text-independent tasks the GMM have proven their efficiency through consecutive NIST speaker recognition evaluations. Some recent studies [91,11,5] have looked at improving performance for text-independent speaker verification by attempting to convert the task into a text-dependent one. This was achieved by constraining the verification process to a limited set of words. The results were encouraging.

Motivated by research that have shown that voiced phones and fricatives are the most effective broad speech classes for speaker discrimination [68,25,65,72], several studies examined the combination of speech and speaker recognition for text-independent speaker verification, trying to exploit the temporal information of speech data. Most of them are based on GMM, HMM or Multi Layer Perceptrons. The idea behind all these systems is the following: first a sequence of phones is found from a given utterance using speech recognition systems, based on HMM. Then speaker verification is performed separately for each phone to obtain a verification score. Finally, the global utterance score is obtained by combining the weighted results from all phones.

In order to exploit the above ideas for text-independent speaker recognition tasks, more data and the availability of speech recognizers are necessary. Such approaches necessitate the usage of large vocabulary speech recognizers, phone recognizers, or data-driven speech segmentation methods. They can be used in two manners: to compute likelihood values at a finer temporal level or to extract high-level information, as shown in Sect. 7.3.

### 3.2  Discriminative Models

#### Multilayer Perceptrons

Multilayer Perceptrons (MPL) are feed-forward neural networks trained using the back-propagation algorithm [41]. They can be used as binary classifiers for speaker verification systems to separate the speaker and the non-speaker classes. The MLP are usually composed of several layers, each one with several nodes. Each node computes a linear weighted sum over its input connections, where the weights of the summation are the adjustable parameters. A non-linear transfer function is applied to the result to compute the output of that node. The weights of the network are estimated by gradient descent based on the back-propagation algorithm. An MLP for speaker verification would classify speaker and impostors access by scoring each frame of the test utterance. The final utterance score is the mean of the MLP's output over all the frames in the utterance. Among studies that used MLP in text-independent speaker verification task, [61] and [73] could be mentioned. Despite their discriminant power, the MLP present some disadvantages. The main ones are that their optimal configuration is not easy to select and a lot of data is needed for the training and the cross-validation steps. That could explain the fact that MLP are not widely used in speaker verification task as it can be remarked in recent NIST speaker recognition evaluations.

### Support Vector Machines (SVM)

Support Vector Machines are discriminant and binary classifiers [93]. Their basic principle is to project the non-linearly separable multidimensional data in a hyperspace, where they can be linearly separated. Given a collection of feature vectors belonging to two classes that are separable by a hyperplane, the SVM will attempt to find the hyperplane with the maximal margin. In other words, the distance between the closest labeled vectors to the hyperplane is maximal. This hyperplane could be further used (during the testing phase) to determine to which class an unknown vector belongs.

In recent years, the SVM based approach has become one of the most performing discriminant methods [87]. In speaker verification, the use of SVM has taken two directions. The first approach uses SVM in the acoustic features space [86]. The decision score is calculated by averaging the SVM scores over all the frames in the test utterance. This method gave promising results for the speaker identification task, but proved to be less successful than well trained GMM for speaker verification.

The second approach consists of combining GMM and SVM. Some results are presented in [95,96,24,48,21,16]. [95,96] incorporate generative models into a discriminative framework of an SVM so that an entire utterance is classified discriminatively instead of the constituent frames. Similar approach is presented in [24], where discriminative training of GMM is performed. [48,21,16] use SVM in order to better separate the GMM scores. All these techniques, which take advantage of both generative and discriminative models, produced better accuracy than either their purely generative or purely discriminative version.

Few attempts have been made to use discriminatively trained generative models [56,76]. The difference between the generative and discriminative models is that the former treat the samples of one speaker independently from the samples of the other group whereas the latter minimize the error on training samples of data belonging to both classes (i.e. speaker and impostors).

## 4   Decision Making

The speaker verification task is taking the decision if the speech data collected during the test phase, belongs to the claimed model or not. Given a speech segment $X$ and a claimed identity $S$ the speaker verification system should choose one of the following hypothesis:

$H_S$: $X$ is pronounced by $S$
$H_{\bar{S}}$: $X$ is **not** pronounced by $S$

The decision between the two hypothesis is usually based on a likelihood ratio given by:

$$\Lambda(X) = \frac{p(X|H_S)}{p(X|H_{\bar{S}})} \begin{cases} > \Theta & accept\ H_S \\ < \Theta & accept\ H_{\bar{S}} \end{cases} \qquad (4)$$

where $p(X|H_S)$ and $p(X|H_{\bar{S}})$ are the probability density functions (called also likelihoods) associated with the speaker $S$ and non-speakers $\bar{S}$, respectively. $\Theta$ is the threshold to accept or reject $H_S$.

In practice, $H_S$ is represented by a model $\lambda_S$, estimated using the training speech from the hypothesized speaker $S$, and $H_{\bar{S}}$ is represented by a model $\lambda_{\bar{S}}$, estimated using a set of other speakers, that cover as much as possible the space of the alternative hypothesis. There are two main approaches to select this set of other speakers.

The first one consists of choosing, for each speaker $S$ a set of speakers $\bar{S}_1, ..., \bar{S}_N$, called cohort [85]. In this case each speaker will have a corresponding non-speaker model.

A more practical approach consists of having a unique or gender dependent set of speakers representing the non-speakers, where a single (or gender dependent) non-speaker model is trained for all speakers [82]. This model is usually trained using speech samples from a large number of representative speakers. This model is referred in the literature as world model or Universal Background Model(UBM) [83]. This last approach is the most commonly used in speaker verification systems. It has the advantage of using a single non-speaker model for all the hypothesized speakers, or two gender-dependent world (background) models.

The likelihood ratio in (4) is then rewritten as:

$$\Lambda(X) = \frac{p(X|\lambda_S)}{p(X|\lambda_{\bar{S}})} \qquad (5)$$

Often the logarithm of this ratio is used. The final score is then:

$$\Lambda(X) = \log p(X|\lambda_S) - \log p(X|\lambda_{\bar{S}}) \qquad (6)$$

The values of the likelihoods $p(X|\lambda_S)$ and $p(X|\lambda_{\bar{S}})$ are computed using one of the techniques described in Sect. 3.

Once the model is trained, the speaker verification system should make a decision to accept or reject the claimed identity. This last step consists of comparing the score of the test utterance with a decision threshold.

Setting the threshold appropriately for a specific speaker verification application is still a challenging task. The threshold is usually chosen during the development phase, and is speaker-independent. However these kind of thresholds do not really reflect the speaker peculiarities and the intra-speaker variability. Furthermore, if there is a mismatch between development and test data, the optimal operating point could be different from the pre-set threshold.

There are two main approaches to deal with the problem of automatic threshold estimation. The first one consists of setting a priori speaker-dependent threshold [55], in such a way the threshold is adjusted for each speaker in order to compensate the score variability effects. In the second approach, score normalization techniques (see Sect. 6.1) make the speaker-independent threshold more robust and easy to set.

The performance of any speaker recognition system is evaluated in function of the error rate. There are two types of errors that occur in the verification task: the false acceptance when the system accepts an impostor and the false rejection when the system rejects a valid speaker. Both types of error depend on the decision threshold. With a high threshold, the system will be highly secured. In other words, the system will make very few false acceptances but a lot of false rejections. If the threshold is fixed to a low value the system will be more convenient to the users. Thus, it will make few false rejections and lots of false acceptances. The rates of false acceptance, $R_{FA}$, and false rejection, $R_{FR}$, define the operating point of the system. They are calculated as follows:

$$R_{FA} = \frac{number\ of\ false\ acceptances}{number\ of\ impostors\ access} \tag{7}$$

$$R_{FR} = \frac{number\ of\ false\ rejection}{number\ of\ targets\ access} \tag{8}$$

These rates are normally estimated on the development set and are further used to compute the Detection Cost Function (DCF). This cost function is a weighted measure of both false acceptance and false rejection rates:

$$DCF = C_{FR}P_{tar}R_{FR} + C_{FA}P_{imp}R_{FA} \tag{9}$$

where $C_{FR}$ is the cost of false rejection, $C_{FA}$ is the cost of false acceptance, $P_{tar}$ and $P_{imp}$ are the a priori probabilities of targets and impostors respectively. The DCF should be normalized by the value: $C_{FR}P_{tar} + C_{FA}P_{imp}$.

The DCF is the most used measure to evaluate the performances of operational speaker verification systems. Smaller is the value of the DCF better is the system for the given application and conditions. Thus, the decision threshold should be optimized in order to minimize the DCF. This optimization is often done during the development of the system on a limited set of data.

The measures presented above, evaluate the performances of the system at a single operating point. However, representing the performance of the speaker verification system over the whole range of operating points is also useful. A way for doing this is to use a performance curve. The Detection Error Tradeoff (DET) curve [59], a variant of the Receiver Operating Characteristic (ROC) curve [26], has been widely used for this purpose. In the DET curve the $R_{FA}$ is plotted as a function of the $R_{FR}$ and the axis follow a normal deviate scale. This representation allows an easy comparison of the performances of the systems at different operating points. The Equal Error Rate (EER) appears directly on this curve as the intersection of the DET curve with the first bisectrix.

Experimental results described in Sect. 7 will be reported in terms of DET curves and Equal Error Rates.

There are different factors that affect the performance of a speaker verification system. They can be evaluated using appropriately designed corpora that reflect the reality of the speaker characteristics and the complexity of the foreseen application. Measuring real progress achieved with new research methods and pinpointing the unsolved problems is only possible when relevent publicly available evaluation databases and protocols are associated with a benchmarking framework [18]. Such benchmarking framework should be composed of open-source state-of-the-art algorithms defined on benchmarking publicly available databases and protocols.

## 5 Evaluation Paradigm

### 5.1 Performance Factors

Speaker verification performance is dependent upon many different factors, that could be grouped in the following categories:

**Intra-Speaker Variability.** Usually the speaker model is obtained using a limited speech data, that characterizes the speaker at a given time and situation. However, the voice could change in time due to aging, illness and emotions. For these reasons the speaker model may not be representative of the speaker and may not cover all these variabilities, which affect negatively the performance of the speaker verification systems. To deal with this problem, incremental enrollment techniques could be used, in order to include the short and long-term evolution of the voice [7].

**Amount of Speech Data.** The amount of training data available to built the speaker models has also a large impact on the accuracy of the systems.

**Mismatch Factors.** The mismatch in recording conditions between the training and testing is one of the major challenges for automatic speaker recognition over the telephone communication channels. Differences in the telephone handset, in the transmission channel, and in the recording devices can introduce discepancies and decrease the accuracy of the system. Beside this, most of the statistical models do not capture only the speaker characteristics but also the environmental ones. Hence, the system decision may be biased if the verification environment is different from the enrollment. The normalization techniques (of features and scores) presented in Sect. 6.1 are useful to make speaker modeling more robust to mismatched train/test conditions. The high-level features introduced in Sect. 6.2 are also important because they are supposed to be more robust to mismatched conditions.

### 5.2 Speech Corpora

Evaluating speaker recognition algorithms on relevant speech corpora is a key issue for measuring the progress and remaining difficulties of speaker verification systems. A common evaluation framework is also a key point when comparing different systems. The speech group of the National Institute of Standards and

Technology (NIST) has been organizing evaluations of text-independent speaker verification technologies since 1997, with an increasing success over the years[3].

The main task in these NIST Speaker Recognition Evaluations (NIST–SRE) is text-independent speaker verification. It can be evaluated using increasing amount of training data (from 5 min to an hour), and with mismatched train-test conditions. In these evaluations a unique data-set and evaluation protocol are provided to each participating laboratory, so that researchers can compare their submitted results and highlight problems that require further research. As pointed out in Sect. 1 it has to be noted that NIST–SRE evaluations are mostly relevant for applications when the interest is to find if speech from a target speaker is present in the test data. Such applications include governmental surveillance applications, as well as applications for speaker segmentation, clustering or database annotations. Speaker verification has a potential for commercial applications, but in order to be convenient for the users, such systems need to be functional with short training and testing data. For such applications text-dependent systems are more suited, and relevant databases are needed. A survey of standard speech corpora that are suitable for development and evaluation of speaker recognition systems can be found in [37,14].

### 5.3   Benchmarking Framework

Measuring real progress achieved with new research methods and pinpointing the unsolved problems is only possible when relevent publicly available evaluation databases and protocols are associated with a benchmarking framework. Such benchmarking framework should be composed of open-source state-of-the-art algorithms defined on benchmarking publicly available databases and protocols. In Sect. 7.1 such reference framework is defined.

The yearly NIST–SRE evaluations have shown that Gaussian Mixture Models (using spectral features) are best suited for text-independent speaker verification experiments. In the same time, they have shown their limitations that occur mainly because of the mismatched train/test conditions using different microphnones and transmission lines. These problems are outlined in the following section, and the possible solutions including normalization at different levels (feature or score level) and using high-level information are presented.

## 6   How to Solve Some of the Remaining Problems ?

### 6.1   Normalization Techniques Useful for Speaker Recognition

#### 6.1.1   Normalization at Feature Level
**Cepstral Mean Substraction (CMS)** [33] is one of the widely used normalization methods in speech and speaker recognition. Also referred as blind deconvolution, this method consists of removing the mean cepstral coefficients from each feature, over the entire speech duration. The stationary convolution

---

[3] http://www.nist.gov/speech/tests/spk/

noises due to transmission channel effects are reduced with this method. It could also be performed over a sliding window in order to take into account the linear channel variation inside the same recording. CMS could compensate linear channel variations, however, under additive noise conditions it is less effective. It is sometimes supplemented with variance normalization [94,51]. The coefficients are transformed to fit a zero mean and a unit variance distribution, over all speech frames or using a sliding window. The mean and variance values are usually estimated only on frames belonging to speech.

**RASTA (RelAtive SpecTrA)**, introduced by [44], is a generalization of CMS. It addresses the problem of a slowly time-varying linear channel in contrast to the time-invariant channel removed by CMS. Its essence is a cepstral lifter that removes low and high modulation frequencies.

**Feature Warping** was proposed by [69] in order to construct a more robust representation of each cepstral feature distribution. This is achieved by mapping the individual cepstral feature distributions such that they follow a normal distribution over a window of speech frames. In [97] a variant of the feature warping is presented, called "short-time gaussianization". It applies a linear transformation to the features before mapping them to a normal distribution. The purpose of this linear transformation is to make the resulting features independent. Results in [69,6] have shown that feature warping slightly outperforms mean and variance normalization but it is computationally more expensive.

**The Feature Mapping** approach, introduced in [79], is another normalization method, based on the idea to minimize the channel variability in the feature domain. This method focuses on mapping features from different channels into a common channel independent feature space. The feature mapping procedure is achieved through the following steps. First, a channel independent GMM is trained using a pool of data from many different channels. Then, channel dependent GMM are trained by adapting the channel-independent GMM using channel dependent data. Finally, the feature-mapping functions are learned by examining how the channel independent model parameters change after the adaptation. During the normalization step, and for each utterance, the most likely channel dependent model is first detected and then each feature vector in the utterance is mapped to the channel independent space using the corresponding feature-mapping functions. This method showed good performances in channel compensation but its disadvantage is that a lot of data is needed to train the different channel models.

**Joint Factor Analysis** is another successful approach for modeling channel variability [47,46]. This method is quite similar to the feature mapping with the exception that in joint factor analysis the channel effect is modeled by a normal distribution of the GMM supervector space whereas in the feature mapping this effect is modeled by a discrete distribution.

The basic assumption in the joint factor analysis is that a speaker and channel-dependent supervector can be decomposed into a sum of two supervectors, one of which depends on the speaker and the other on the channel, and that speaker supervectors and channel supervectors are both normally distributed.

Suppose that a speaker $S$ is modeled by GMM with $C$ mixture components in an $F$ dimensional feature space. A speaker and channel dependent supervector, denoted by a $CF$–dimensional random vector $M$, can be decomposed as:

$$M = s + c \tag{10}$$

where $s$ is the speaker dependent supervector and $c$ is the channel dependent supervector.

Thus, the factor analysis model is specified by the hyperparameters of $s$ and $c$. To estimate these hyperparameters first a speaker independent Principal Component Analysis (PCA) model is trained from a large database in which each speaker is recorded in multiple sessions. Then the resulting model is adapted to each target speaker. Once more, representative data are needed.

**The Nuisance Attribute Projection (NAP)** technique was introduced by Solomonoff et al. in [89] to handle the problem of handset and channel variability for SVM based speaker verification systems. This approach consists of modifying the kernel function in order to increase its ability to be invariant to channel effects. For this purpose the authors propose to use a modified kernel matrix which projects out the effects of channel. The criterion for constructing this matrix is to minimize the average distance between cross-channel pairs.

The normalization methods presented above are applied at the feature level. In the following subsection the most used score normalization methods will be summarized.

### 6.1.2  Normalization at Score Level

Most of the actual score normalization techniques are based on the assumption that the impostors scores follow a gaussian distribution where the mean, $\mu_S$, and the standard deviation, $\sigma_S$, depend on the considered speaker model and/or test utterance. These mean and standard deviation values are used to normalize any incoming score $\Lambda_X(\lambda)$:

$$\Lambda_X^{norm}(\lambda) = \frac{\Lambda_X(\lambda) - \mu_S}{\sigma_S} \tag{11}$$

**The Zero Normalization (Znorm)** method [54,84] normalizes the score distribution using the claimed speaker statistics. In other words, the claimed speaker model is tested against a set of impostors, resulting in an impostor similarity score distribution which is then used to estimate the normalization parameters $\mu_S$ and $\sigma_S$. The main advantage of the Znorm is that the estimation of these parameters can be performed during the training step (offline).

**The Test Normalization (Tnorm)** technique was introduced by [3]. It is another score normalization method in which the parameters $\mu_S$ and $\sigma_S$ are estimated using the test utterance. During testing, a set of impostor models is used to calculate impostor scores for a given test utterance abd $\mu_S$ and $\sigma_S$ are estimated using these scores. The Tnorm is known to improve the performances particularly in the region of low false alarms. More details about Tnorm could be found in [63]. In contrary to the Znorm, the Tnorm has to be performed online during testing.

**Dnorm**, introduced by Ben. et al. [8], deals with the problem of pseudo-impostor data availability, by generating data using the world (background) model. Target and pseudo-impostor data are generated using Monte-Carlo methods.

**Variants of Score Normalization** were introduced in order to reduce microphone and transmission channel effects. Among the variants of Znorm, is the handset normalization (Hnorm) [84] and channel normalization (Cnorm). Handset or channel dependent normalization parameters are estimated by testing each speaker model against handset or channel dependent set of impostors. During testing, the type of handset or channel related to the test utterance is first detected and then the corresponding set of parameters are used for score normalization. The HTnorm, a variant of Tnorm, uses basically the same idea as the Hnorm. The handset-dependent normalization parameters are estimated by testing each test utterance against handset-dependent impostor models. Finally, and in order to improve speaker verification performance, different normalization methods may be combined, such as ZTnorm (Znorm followed by Tnorm) or TZnorm (Tnorm followed by Znorm).

Besides the score normalization techniques described above, another way to improve text-independent speaker verification results is to use speech recognition methods in order to extract high-level information.

## 6.2   Speaker-Specific Information Sources and Their Fusion

Speech is the product of a complex behavior conveying different speaker-specific traits that are potential sources of complementary information. One set of information reflects the spectral properties of speech (low-level) which are related to the physical structure of the vocal apparatus. These parameters are used since the beginning of the speaker recognition research, as described in Sect. 2. The second set of information reflects the behavioural traits (high-level) such as prosody, phonetic information, pronunciation, emotion, stress, idiolectal word usage, conversational patterns and topics of conversations. Usually more data are needed for such kind of information. In recent years, research on text-independent speaker verification has expanded from using only the acoustic content of speech to trying to exploit high-level information. Gains in speaker recognition accuracy are possible [79] by exploiting such high level information sources.

The various information sources for speaker recognition can be categorized as follows.

**Acoustic** features reflect the spectral properties of speech and convey information about the configuration of the vocal tract. They are extracted from short time overlapping windows (typically 10-20 ms).

**Prosodic** information is derived from the acoustic characteristics of speech and includes pitch, duration and intensity.

**Segmental** features are related to phonetic and data driven speech units, denoted here as "pseudo-phonetic" units. The phoneme is the smallest speech unit that distinguishes two words. The phonetic characteristics are related to the way the speaker pronounces different phonemes.

**Idiolectal** information is unique to each speaker and characterizes her/his speaking style. It is manifested by patterns of word selection and grammar. Every individual has an idiolect, however it could depend on the context in which the speaker is talking (such as the person to whom we are talking, the subject or the emotional situation).

**Dialogic** features are based on the conversational patterns and define the manner in which the speaker communicates. Every speaker could be characterized by the frequency and the duration of his turns in a conversation. These traits are also dependent on the conversational context.

**Semantic** characteristics of the speech are related to the signification of the utterance. The kind of subject frequently discussed by the speaker could also provide information on her/his identity.

The following paragraphs present a summary of the usefulness of high-level information for spaker verification experiments.

**Prosodic Information.** Results published in [90,1] have shown that prosodic information can be used to effectively improve the performance of speaker verification systems. In [90] the authors appended the prosodic features to a standard spectral based features and used them in a traditional distribution modeling systems. The addition of these dynamic prosodic features improved the performance of the GMM system significantly. Adami et al. proposed in [1] two approaches that use the fundamental frequency and energy trajectories to capture long-term information. The first approach uses bigrams to capture the dynamics of the fundamental frequency and energy trajectories for each speaker. The second approach uses the fundamental frequency trajectories of a pre-defined set of words as the speaker templates and then, using dynamic time warping, computes the distance between the templates and the words from the test message. They also showed that the prosodic approaches improve the performance of systems that use short-term information.

**Phonetic Information.** The phonetic information is also an important aspect of the speech signal that conveys speaker information. [60] used phoneme-specific HMM for modeling the target speakers. A speaker verification system based on broad phonetic categories was proposed in [52,45] and achieved an improvement over the baseline system. In [4], GMM and HMM were compared across different phonemes, and unlike in the above cited works, phonetic information was used only during the scoring phase. Hebert et al. [42] introduced a phonetic class-based GMM system based on a tree-like structure, which outperformed a single GMM system. Closer to what is presented in this last work, are the approaches presented in [39] and [38], where phoneme-adapted GMMs were built for each speaker. The authors concluded that the phoneme-adapted GMM system outperformed the phoneme independent GMM system. [50] present a new technique to explicitly model speaker's pronunciations. It uses time-aligned streams of phones and phonemes to model speaker's specific pronunciation.

**Idiolectal Information.** The idiolectal information was explored by several authors. [23] studied the possibility of using word n-gram statistics for speaker verification. This technique exploited the idiolectal information in a straightforward way and gave encouraging results. Motivated by this work, similar techniques have been applied to phone n-gram statistics [2]. This last approach gave good results and was found to provide features complementary to short-term acoustic features. Another variant of this approach is presented by Campbell et al. in [17]. The basic idea of this approach is to use SVM to combine the phone n-gram scores instead of the log-likelihood ratio method. The SVM based method halved the error rate of the standard phone n-gram approach [2]. Further improvements were reported by using lattice phonetic decoding instead of the 1-best decoding [40].

**Data-Driven High-Level Information.** Most of the above reported promising methods are however based on phonetic transcriptions. Two of the major problems that arise when phone based systems are being developed are the possible mismatch between the development and evaluation data and the lack of transcribed databases. Data-driven segmentation techniques provide a potential solution to these problems because they do not use transcribed data and can easily be applied on development data minimizing the mismatches. Their usage for speech recognition is not straightforward, but such methods can be used to extract speaker-specific information, for language identification [70] or for call type classification [71]. In [74] a speaker verification system, based on an automatic data-driven speech segmentation was proposed. The speech data was clustered in 8 classes and a per-class MLP were used for modeling the speaker. This data-driven segmentation is based on Automatic Language Independent Speech Processing (ALISP) tools [19]. Recently the same method was used in combination with Gaussian Mixture Models (GMM). In [27] the performances of a segmental ALISP-based and a global GMM systems were compared. Even though the ALISP classes were not explicitly modeled and the segmental information was used only during the scoring phase, the segmental system provided better performance compared to the global GMM system. In [29] the data-driven ALISP units were explicitly modeled by GMM. The data-driven segmentation was also used to capture speaker specific idiolectal information [28]. In this system, speaker specific information is captured only by analyzing sequences of ALISP units like in [2]. This system was fused with an acoustic GMM system and the resulting fused system reduced the error rate of the individual systems. In [30] the authors attempted to analyze the correlation between the automatically aligned phonemes and ALISP units. They also compare the results obtained with a speaker recognition system based on data-driven acoustic units and phonetic speaker recognition systems trained on Spanish and English data. Compared to phone, data-driven units could lead to better speaker recognition results with the additional advantage of not requiring phonetically transcribed speech. On the other hand, further improvements can be achieved by combining both approaches.

The results of combining different levels of information using such data-driven methods on NIST 2005 and 2006 evaluations are shown in the case study examples in Sect. 7.3.

**Combining Speaker Verification Systems.** As pointed out in the previous section, when using multiple systems in order to improve performance a new problem that has to be solved is how to combine these systems. The ultimate goal of fusion is to map a set of scores produced by individual systems to a combined score in order to improve the system performance. Such combinations take advantage of the heterogeneity of the systems and of their different discriminant powers. In Kittler et al. [49] comparisons between alternative combination rules are reported. For speaker verification many different techniques have been used for score combination, such as linear combination, Multiple Layer Perceptrons [79,15,28], and Support Vector Machines [35]. The basic idea of all these approaches is to estimate the parameters of the combiner to detect target and impostor access given a vector of scores from the systems being combined.

Another class-dependent score combination techniques that rely on clustering of both the target models and the test utterances are presented [88,32]. The basic idea of these approaches is to distinguish classes of target and test speakers or acoustical conditions and then use separate classifiers for each class. The class-dependent classifier scores are subsequently combined and/or selected to generate the final score.

# 7   Case Studies

In this section, some examples of factors influencing the results and presenting the difficulties of text-independent speaker verification systems are given. The evaluation databases and reference evaluation protocols underlying these examples are presented in Sect. 7.1. A reference (benchmarking) system using well defined development data is also presented. Such reference system is useful to point out the importance of different parameters. Two tasks are used in our case studies. The first task is denoted as 1conv4w-1conv4w, and uses one conversation of approximately five minutes total duration to build the speaker model and another conversation for testing. For the second task, denoted here as long training/short test conditions, or 8conv4w-1conv4w task, approximately 40 minutes total duration are used to build the speaker model and another conversation for testing.

The experimental results presented in this section are grouped in two parts. The first part, presented in Sect. 7.2, illustrates the difficulties of tuning a variety of parameters in order to achieve well performing GMM based systems. The short train/test task of the NIST–2005–SRE evaluation data is used in this part. The second part, presented in Sect. 7.3 shows the improvements that could be achieved when high level information extracted with data-driven methods are combined with well known baseline GMM systems. For these experiments, the best performing GMM from the first part are combined with data-driven high-level information systems. The results are shown on NIST–2005 and 2006 evaluation data, but using the long training/short test task, which is more suited for extracting high-level speaker-specific information.

## 7.1 Experimental Set Up

In order to evaluate text-independent speaker verification algorithms two distinct data sets are needed. They are separated into development and evaluation data. For the development part different data sets have to be defined, according to the nature of the experiments. Usually at least a world set is needed, for typical impostors/targets log-likelihood systems. If we are interested in a specific operational point, additional tuning data are necessary in order to fix the threshold between targets and impostors likelihoods or to determine the fusion parameters if multiple systems are combined. In the case of mismatched train/test conditions more data are needed in order to cope with this problem, as explained in Sect. 6.1.

### 7.1.1 Development Data

The following items describe the data that we have used as development data for the case study experiments.

**World set:** subsets from NIST–2003 and 2004 are used to define the reference (bechmarking) GMM System. Additional Fisher data (available from [4]) are used to show the influence of adding more relevant data to the reference world (background) data. They are used to train the gender dependent background models.

**Tuning set:** subsets from NIST–2004 are used to train the fusion parameters and the thresholds.

**Normalization set:** subsets from Fisher data are used for score normalization.

### 7.1.2 Evaluation Data

As already mentioned in Sect. 5 evaluating speaker recognition algorithms on relevant speech corpora is a key issue for measuring the progress and remaining difficulties of speaker verification systems. The yearly NIST–SRE evaluations have shown that Gaussian Mixture Models (using spectral features) are well suited for text-independent speaker verification experiments. In the same time, they have shown their limitations that occur mainly because of the mismatched train/test conditions of modern communication modes using different microphones and transmission lines. These problems are illustrated in the following sections, using NIST–2005 and 2006 evaluation data.

NIST–2005 and 2006 data are multilingual data. In order to eliminate the influence of this parameter, we have reported our experimental results using

---

[4] http://www.ldc.upenn.edu

English trials only. The degradation of the results when multilingual data are used is shown in Fig. 7.

The first series of experiments, reported in Sect. 7.2, are carried out on the core task of the NIST–2005 speaker recognition evaluation with a total of 646 speaker models (372 females and 274 males). In this task denoted as 1conv4w-1conv4w, one two-channel (4-wire) conversation, of approximately five minutes total duration is used to build the speaker model and another conversation for testing. There are 31′243 (2771 targets' access + 28′472 impostors' access) trials in this task, including 20′907 (2148 targets' access + 18′759 impostors' access) English trials.

For the second set of experiments, related to using data-driven speech segmentation to extract high-level speaker information, NIST–2005 and NIST–2006 evaluation data are used. These experiments are illustrated on the 8conv4w-1conv4w task, where eight two-channel (4-wire) conversations, of approximately 40 min. total duration are used to build the speaker model and another conversation for testing. In this task, 700 (402 females and 298 males) speaker models for the NIST–2006 and 497 (295 females and 202 males) for NIST–2005 are present. The systems are evaluated on 16′053 traials (1′671 targets' access + 14′382 impostors' access) for NIST–2005 and on 17′387 trials (2′139 targets' access and15′248 impostors' access) for NIST–2006.

### 7.1.3   Reference(Benchmarking) Framework

Another key issue when comparing performances of different systems is the usage of a reference framework [18] using well defined development data as a benchmarking set. Such reference system is presented here. It is composed of state-of-the-art open-source GMM based system [12], and precisely defined development data. Such benchmarking framework is useful to point out the importance of different parameters, and to measure the progress achieved with newly introduced systems, such as the data-driven high-level information systems.

### 7.2   Tuning the GMM Based Spectral Feature Systems

In this part more details and illustrative experimental results with the reference benchmarking system are given. For the evaluation data, the short train/testing task of NIST–2005–SRE is used. The proposed reference system is composed of state-of-the-art open-source ALIZE GMM based system, the LIA–SpkDet tools [12], and well defined development and evaluation data (see Sect. 7.1).

In this section we will first summarize the reported figures and their main characteristics, giving more details about each experimental configuration later.

In Fig. 1 the performance of the baseline reference system, using the LFCC+$\delta$ features, the reference world model, and a GMM with 512 gaussian mixtures is reported, with an Equal Error Rate (EER) of 10.3%.

The influence of different feature configurations is shown in Fig. 2, where better results than the reference system are obtained using also the $\delta$–energy coefficients in addition to the LLFCC+$\delta$, improving the results from 10.3% to 9.9%.

The influence of using relevant speech data for building the world(background) models is illustrated in Fig. 3, leading to improved EER of 9%, when additional Fisher data are added for building the background (world) models, over the reported 9.9% of the reference system.

The influence of different score normalization methods is illustrated in Fig. 5, leading to improved EER of 8.6% (compared with the improved world model using Fisher data). As these normalization techniques are computationally expensive, we will not use them for the remaining comparisons.

The influence of the number of gaussians in the mixture is shown in Fig. 4. Using 2048 "mixtures" leads to improved EER of 8.5%, to be compared with the 9% of the reference system described in Fig. 3.

Using all the trials (and not only the pooled English trials) degrades the performance, as shown in Fig. 7.

The influence of the duration of training data is shown in Fig. 6, where the results using NIST–2005 evaluation tasks with short and long training data are reported.

Figure 8 illustrates the influence of mismatched train/test conditions. NIST–2006 evaluation data were used for these experiments, because the relevant labels were available only for this data set.

More details about the above cited experiments that influence the performance of baseline GMM reference system are given below.

### 7.2.1   Frame Removal and Speech Parametrization

The speech parameterizations for the reference GMM system is done with Linear Frequency Cepstral Coefficients (LFCC), calculated on $20\,ms$ windows, with a $10\,ms$ shift. For each frame a 16-element cepstral vector is computed and appended with first order deltas and the delta-energy. Bandwidth is limited to the $300 - 3400Hz$ range. The parameter vectors are normalized to fit a zero mean and a unit variance distribution. The mean and variance used for the normalization are computed file by file on all the frames kept after applying the frame removal processing. The parameterizations is carried out using SPRO tools[5].

For the frame removal, the energy coefficients are first normalized using zero mean and unit variance normalization. Then the normalized energies are used to train a three component GMM. Finally, $N$% of the most energized frames are selected through the GMM, with:

$$N = w_1 + (g * \alpha * w_2) \tag{12}$$

where $w_1$ is the weight of the highest Gaussian component, $w_2$ is the weight of the middle component, $g$ is an integer ranging from 0 to 1, and $\alpha$ is a weighting parameter.

The feature vectors are modeled with gender-dependent GMM. The background GMMs are created using data from the reference world set. For each

---

[5] http://www.irisa.fr/metiss/guig/spro/spro-4.0.1/spro.html

target speaker, a Gaussian Mixture Model with diagonal covariance matrices is trained via maximum a posteriori adaptation. The verification is performed using the 10-best scoring mixture components. This system is based on the ALIZE-LIA-SpkDet tools [12].

In order to study the influence of frame removal, different configurations are evaluated. Figure 1 shows the results using the frame removal procedure explained above (by varying the $\alpha$ parameter) and using also the NIST transcripts which are produced using an automatic speech recognition (ASR) system[6]. These transcripts are errorful, with word error rates typically in the range of $15-30\%$. Table 1 gives the statistics on speech data kept in each case. These statistics are computed on English trials on NIST–2005 SRE data of each system from Fig. 1.

**Table 1.** Percentage of frames belonging to speech after applying the frame removal procedure. The corresponding speaker verification systems performances are plotted in Fig. 1.

| Frames removal | % of speech data |
|---|---|
| $\alpha = 0.9$ | 53% |
| $\alpha = 0.25$ | 36% |
| $\alpha = 0.05$ | 30% |
| $\alpha = 0$ | 28% |
| Nist transcription | 43% |

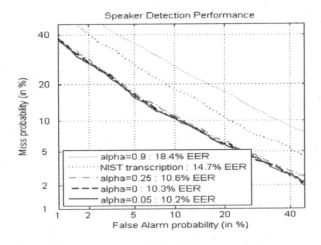

**Fig. 1.** DET plot showing the effect of frames selection. The reference GMM system is defined as LFCC+$\delta$ features, a frame removal parameter with $\alpha = 0$, a reference world model, and a GMM with 512 gaussians. The results are reported on NIST–2005 using only the English trials (20907 trails: 2148 targets access and 18759 impostors access).

---

[6] http://www.nist.gov/speech/tests/spk/2005/sre-05_evalplan-v6.pdf

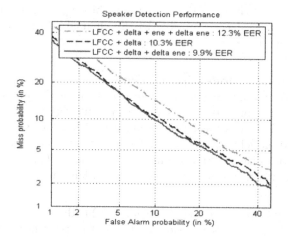

**Fig. 2.** DET plot showing the effect of the feature selection. The GMM system (512 gaussians) is evaluated on NIST–2005 using only the English trials.

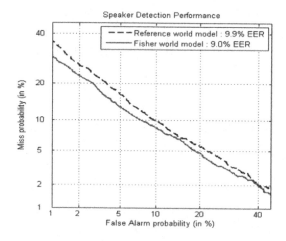

**Fig. 3.** DET plot showing the effect of background model speech data. The baseline reference system is defined with LFCC+$\delta$ features, a frame removal parameter with $\alpha = 0$, a reference world model, and a GMM with 512 gaussians. Results are reported on NIST–2005 using only the English trials.

### 7.2.2  Feature Selection

The second set of experiments is related to the feature selection. In Fig. 2 the inclusion of the $\delta$ log–energy and/or of the *log*–energy in the feature vectors is illustrated. Results show that the addition of the $\delta$ log–energy to the parameter vectors improves slightly the results in comparison to the use of the cepstral and $\delta$–cepstral coefficients only. Whereas adding the log–energy to the feature vectors degrades clearly the results. One possible explanation of this result is that the log–energy is more sensible to the channel effect and some kind of normalization should be used to eliminate this effect.

### 7.2.3   Background Model Speech Data

The third set of experiments concerns speaker modeling. Figure 3 illustrates the influence of using appropriate speech data for building the background (world model). The DET curve of using only data from NIST–2003 and 2004 to build the world GMM model is labeled as "Reference world model". Adding 600 more speakers form the Fisher data set improves the results. The speech data is balanced by the handset type (cordless, cellular and landline).

### 7.2.4   Complexity of the World/Speaker Model

The use of 2048 gaussians instead of 512 for the reference system ( Fig. 4) improves slightly the performances. Regarding the fact that GMM with 2048 gaussians need more computation, a model with 512 gaussians could be a good compromise.

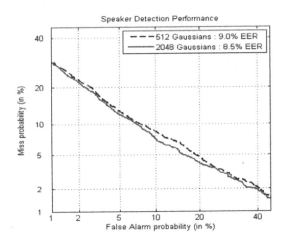

**Fig. 4.** DET plot showing the comparison of performances using 512 and 2048 gaussians in the GMM, on NIST–2005 evaluation data using only the English trials

### 7.2.5   Score Normalization

For the score normalization, the DET curves shown in Fig. 5 reveal that both ZTnorm and Tnorm are better than the baseline reference system in the area of low false acceptances and that the Znorm is better in the area of low false rejections. It shows also that ZTnorm performs better than Tnorm or Znorm alone. Taking into account that such normalizations are computationally expensive, they are not going to be used for the reference system.

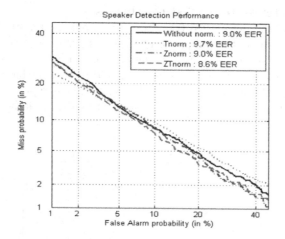

**Fig. 5.** DET plot showing the effect of the different score normalization techniques. The GMM system with 512 gaussians are evaluated on NIST–2005 using only the English trials.

### 7.2.6 Duration of Enrollment Training Data

For the following experiments, the GMM system with 2048 gaussians is used as it outperforms the one with 512 gaussians. The amount of training data available to built the speakers model has also a large impact on the accuracy of the system. Figure 6 illustrates this fact and shows that using more data (8 conversations instead of 1 conversation) to build the speaker model improves the results.

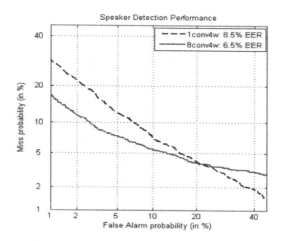

**Fig. 6.** DET plot showing the comparison of performances using one and eight conversations to build the speaker model. The GMM system (2048 gaussians) is evaluated on NIST–2005 using only the English trials.

### 7.2.7   Mismatched Train/Test Conditions

The influence of the mismathed train/test conditions are reported in this paragraph. Figure 7 shows the comparison between the performances of the system when all data (test segments and model training) are limited to English and when multilingual data are used for training and testing (including the English trials). In Fig. 8 the data were pooled by transmission type. They show that using different handset type for training and testing degrades the performances.

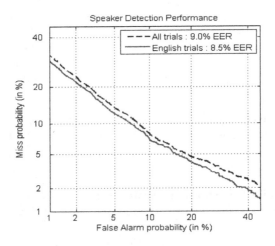

**Fig. 7.** DET plot showing language effects. The GMM systems (2048 gaussians) are evaluated on NIST–2005.

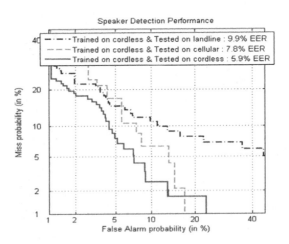

**Fig. 8.** DET plot showing the comparison of performances by transmission type. The GMM systems (2048 gaussians) are evaluated on NIST–2006 using only English trials.

### 7.3 Examples of Using Data-Driven High-Level Features as Complementary Sources of Information

The experiments presented in the previous section illustrate the difficulties of tuning a variety of parameters in order to achieve well performing GMM based systems. The best performin GMM system described in the previous experiments are used as the baseline classifier for the acoustic level features.

In this paragraph, the usefulness of high-level features described in Sect. 6.2 are shown. The particularity of our approach is that the data segmentation requires no annotated data. The speech parametrization for the data-driven AL-ISP recognizer is done with Mel Frequency Cepstral Coefficients (MFCC), using HTK[7]. Mel frequency bands are computed in the $300 - 3400\,Hz$ range. Cepstral mean substraction is applied to the 15 static coefficients, estimating the mean on the speech-detected parts of the signal. The energy and $\delta$ components are appended, leading to 32 coefficients in each feature vector. The MFCC are chosen for the parametrization of the speech data for practical reasons [8].

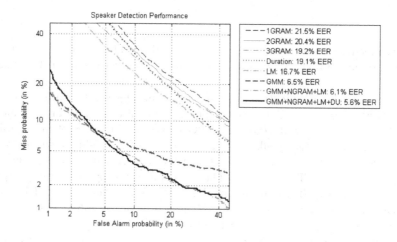

**Fig. 9.** DET plot showing the fusion results of low-level acoutic GMM with high-level systems based on ALISP speech segmentation. The fusion results are shown on the 8conv4w-1conv4w task of NIST–2005 using English trials.

The systems described here use in the first stage a data-driven Automatic Language Independent Speech Processing (ALISP) tools [19] for the segmentation step. This technique is based on units acquired during a data-driven segmentation, where no phonetic transcription of the corpus is needed. In this work we use 65 ALISP classes. Each class is modeled by a left-to-right HMM having three emitting states and containing up to 8 gaussians each. The number of gaussians

---

[7] http://htk.eng.cam.ac.uk/

[8] they can asily be used with the HTK toolkit

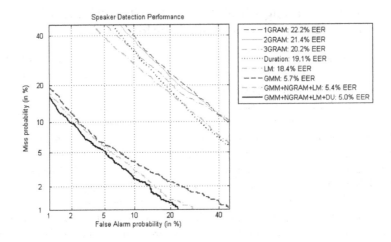

**Fig. 10.** DET plot showing the fusion results of the same systems as in Fig. 9 with the same development data, but on the 8conv4w-1conv4w task of NIST–2006 using English trials

is determined through a dynamic splitting procedure. The gender dependent AL-ISP HMMs are trained on sub-sets from NIST–1999, 2001 and 2003 evaluation data.

Various speaker verification systems using high-level information could be build starting from this data-driven speech segmentation, and are revealed in Figs. 9 and 10. Systems denoted by "NGRAM" an "LM" capture high-level information about the speaking style of each speaker. This speaker specific information is captured by analyzing sequences of ALISP units produced by the data-driven ALISP recognizer. The system denoted by "Duration" exploits speaker-specific ALISP-durations. In this case the speakers are modeled using only the duration of the ALISP units. The scores of the different systems are fused with an SVM trained on NIST-2004 data.

The fusion of these high-level systems with the reference GMM system are shown in Figs. 9 and 10. Improvements of the fused systems on NIST–2005 and 2006 evaluation data are observed. Nevertheless, the fusion is more effective on 2006 data, illustrating the sensitivity of the fusion using different evaluation data sets.

## 8    Conclusions and Perspectives

In this chapter we have summarized the recent developments of text-independent speaker verification research. As pointed out in [10] the widely used Gaussian Mixture Models need a lot of tuning and normalization in order to be efficient in mismatched train/test conditions. We have illustrated some of the parameters that influence the results of GMM systems, on NIST–2005 and 2006 evaluation data.

Recent developments try to improve the performances of the GMM based systems by incorporating high-level features. A summary of this newly developed techniques is given. In order to show an example of combining low and high-level features, we have chosen to use our data-driven approach illustrating the improvements that can be achieved on NIST–2005 and 2006 evaluation data.

This indicates that further improvements of text-independent speaker verification systems will necessitate a combined useage of low ans high-level speaker information, including compensation techiques for channel mismatch, noise, phonetic, prosodic, emotional and lexical content.

# References

1. A. Adami, R. Mihaescu, D. A. Reynolds, and J. J. Godfrey. Modeling prosodic dynamics for speaker recognition. *In Proc. ICASSP*, April 2003.
2. W. Andrews, M. Kohler, J. Campbell, and J. Godfrey. Phonetic, idiolectal, and acoustic speaker recognition. *Speaker Odyssey Workshop*, 2001.
3. R. Auckenthaler, M. J. Carey, and H. Llyod-Thomas. Score normalization for text-independent speaker verification systems. *Digital Signal Processing*, 10, 2000.
4. R. Auckenthaler, E. S. Parris, and M. J. Carey. Improving a GMM speaker verification system by phonetic weighting. *Proc. ICASSP*, 1999.
5. B. Baker, R. Vogt, and S. Sridharan. Gaussian mixture modelling of broad phonetic and syllabic events for text-independent speaker verification. *Proc. Eurospeech*, september 2005.
6. C. Barras and J. L. Gauvain. Feature and score normalization for speaker verification of cellular data. *In Proc. ICASSP*, April 2003.
7. C. Barras, S. Meignier, and J. L. Gauvain. Unsupervised online adaptation for speaker verification over the telephone. *Proc. Odyssey*, 2004.
8. M. Ben, R. Blouet, and F. Bimbot. A monte-carlo method for score normalization in automatic speaker verification using kullback-leibler distances. *2002 IEEE International Conference on Acoustics, Speech, and Signal Processing (ICASSP)*, 2002.
9. F. Bimbot, M. Blomberg, L. Boves, D. Genoud, H.-P. Hutter, C. Jaboulet, J.W. Koolwaaij, J. Lindberg, and J.-B. Pierrot. An overview of the cave project research activities in speaker verification. *Speech Communication*, 31:158–180, 2000.
10. F. Bimbot, J.F. Bonastre, C.Fredouille, G. Gravier, I. Magrin-Chagnolleau, S. Meignier, T. Merlin, J. Ortega-Garcia, D. Petrovska-Delacretaz, and D. A. Reynolds. A tutorial on text-independent speaker verification. *Eurasip Journal On Applied Signal Processing*, 4:430–451, 2004.
11. K. Boakye and B. Peskin. Text-constrained speaker recognition on a text-independent task. *Proc. Odyssey*, page 129134, June 2004.
12. J.-F. Bonastre, F. Wilsand, and S. Meignier. Alize, a free toolkit for speaker recognition. *In Proceedings of the 2005 IEEE International Conference on Acoustics, Speech and Signal Processing (ICASSP2005)*, 1, March 2005.
13. R.N. Bracewell. *The Fourier Transform and Its Applications*. McGraw-Hill, New York, NY USA, 1965.
14. J. Campbell and D. Reynolds. Corpora for the evaluation of speaker recognition systems. *Proc. ICASSP*, 1999.
15. J. Campbell, D. Reynolds, and R. Dunn. Fusing high- and low level features for speaker recognition. *In Proc. Eurospeech*, 2003.

16. W. Campbell, D. Sturim, and D. Reynolds. Support vector machines using gmm supervectors for speaker verification. *IEEE Signal Processing Letters*, 13:5, 2006.

17. W. M. Campbell, J. P Campbell, D. Reynolds, D. A. Jones, and T. R. Leek. Phonetic speaker recognition with support vector machines. *In Proc. Neural Information Processing Systems Conference in Vancouver*, pages 361–388, 2003.

18. G. Chollet, G. Aversano, B. Dorizzi, and D. Petrovska-Delacrétaz. The first biosecure residential workshop. *4th International Symposium on Image and Signal Processing and Analysis-ISPA2005*, pages 198–212, September 2005.

19. G. Chollet, J. Černocký, A. Constantinescu, S. Deligne, and F. Bimbot. Towards ALISP: a proposal for Automatic Language Independent Speech Processing. *In Keith Ponting, editor, NATO ASI: Computational models of speech pattern processing Springer Verlag*, 1999.

20. S.B. Davis and P. Mermelstein. Comparison of parametric representations for monosyllabic word recognition in continuously spoken sentences. *In Proc. ICASSP*, ASSP-28, no.4:357–366, August 1980.

21. N. Dehak and G. Chollet. Support vector gmms for speaker verification. *Proc. Odyssey*, June 2006.

22. A. Dempster, N. Laird, and D. Rubin. Maximum likelihood from incomplete data via the em algorithm. *J. Roy. Stat. Soc.*, page 138, 1977.

23. G. Doddington. Speaker recognition based on idiolectal differences between speakers. *Eurospeech*, 4:2517–2520, 2001.

24. X. Dong and W. Zhaohui. Speaker recognition using continuous density support vector machines. *ELECTRONICS LETTERS*, 37(17), 2001.

25. J.P. Eatock and J.S. Mason. A quantitative assessment of the relative speaker discriminant properties of phonemes. *Proc. ICASSP*, 1:133–136, 1994.

26. J. Egan. *Signal detection theory and ROC analysis*. Academic Press, 1975.

27. A. El Hannani and D. Petrovska-Delacrétaz. Segmental score fusion for alisp-based gmm text-independent speaker verification. *In the book, Advances in Nonlinear Speech Processing and Applications, Edited by G. Chollet, A. Esposito, M. Faundez-Zanuy, M. Marinaro*, pages 385–394, 2004.

28. A. El Hannani and D. Petrovska-Delacrétaz. Exploiting high-level information provided by alisp in speaker recognition. *Non Linear Speech Processing Workshop (NOLISP 05)*, 19-22 April 2005.

29. A. El Hannani and D. Petrovska-Delacrétaz. Improving speaker verification system using alisp-based specific GMMs. *In proc. of Conference on Audio- and Video-Based Biometric Person Authentication (AVBPA)*, July 20 - 22 2005.

30. A. El Hannani, D. T. Toledano, D. Petrovska-Delacrétaz, A. Montero-Asenjo, and Jean Hennebert. Using data-driven and phonetic units for speaker verification. *In proc. of ODYSSEY06, The Speaker and Language Recognition Workshop*, 28-30 June 2006.

31. Gunar Fant. *Acoustic Theory of Speech Production*. Mouton , The Hague, The Netherlands, 1970.

32. L. Ferrer, K. Sönmez, and S. Kajarekar. Class-dependent score combination for speaker recognition. *Proc. Interspeech*, September 2005.

33. S. Furui. Cepstral analysis technique for automatic speaker verification. *IEEE Transactions on Acoustics, Speech and Signal Processing*, 29(2):254–272, 1981.

34. S. Furui. Comparison of speaker recognition methods using static features and dynamic features. *IEEE Transactions on Acoustics, Speech and Signal Processing*, vol. 29(3):342–350, 1981.

35. D. Garcia-Romero, J. Fierrez-Aguilar, J. Ortega-Garcia, and J. Gonzalez-Rodriguez. Support vector machine fusion of idiolectal and acoustic speaker information in spanish conversational speech. *In Proc. ICASSP*, April 2003.

36. J. L. Gauvain and C.-H. Lee. Maximum a posteriori estimation for multivariate gaussian mixture observations of markov chains. *IEEE Trans. Speech Audio Process*, vol. 29:291298, 1994.

37. J. Godfrey, D. Graff, and A. Martin. Public databases for speaker recognition and verification. *ESCA Workshop on Automatic Speaker Recognition Identification and Verification*, pages 39–42, April 1994.

38. D. Gutman and Y. Bistritz. Speaker verification using phoneme-adapted gaussian mixture models. *Proc. EUSIPCO*, 2002.

39. E. G. Hansen, R. E. Slyh, and T. R. Anderson. Speaker recognition using phoneme-specific GMMs. *Proc. Odyssey*, 2004.

40. A. O. Hatch, B. Peskin, and A. Stolcke. Improved phonetic speaker recognition using lattice decoding. *In Proc. ICASSP*, March 2005.

41. S. Haykin. *Neural Networks: A Comprehensive Foundation*. IEEE Computer society Press, Macmillan, New York, NY, USA, 1994.

42. M. Hébert and L. P. Heck. Phonetic class-based speaker verification. *Proc. Eurospeech*, 2003.

43. H. Hermansky. Perceptual linear prediction (plp) analysis of speech. *Journal of the Acoustical Society of America*, vol. 87(4), 1990.

44. H. Hermansky. Rasta processing of speech. *IEEE Trans. on Speech and Audio Processing*, vol. 2(4), 1994.

45. S. S. Kajarekar and H. Hermansky. Speaker verification based on broad phonetic categories. *2001: A Speaker Odyssey - The Speaker Recognition Workshop*, June 2001.

46. P. Kenny and P. Dumouchel. Experiments in speaker verification using factor analysis likelihood ratios. *In Proceedings of Odyssey04 - Speaker and Language Recognition Workshop*, May 31 - June 3 2004.

47. P. Kenny and P. Dumouchel. Disentangling speaker and channel effects in speaker verification. *In Proceedings of the 2005 IEEE International Conference on Acoustics, Speech and Signal Processing (ICASSP2004)*, vol. 1, May 2005.

48. J. Kharroubi, D. Petrovska-Delacréraz, and G. Chollet. Combining GMM's with support vector machines for text-independent speaker verification. *Proc. Eurospeech*, pages 1761–1764, 2001.

49. J. Kittler, M. Hatef, R.P.W. Duin, and J. Matas. On combining classifiers. *IEEE Transactions on Pattern Analysis and Machine Intelligence*, vol. 20(3):226–239, 1998.

50. D. Klusacek, J. Navratil, D. A. Reynolds, and J. Campbell. Conditional pronunciation modeling in speaker detection. *In Proc. ICASSP*, April 2003.

51. J. Koolwaaij and L. Boves. Local normalization and delayed decision making in speaker detection and tracking. *Digital Signal Processing*, vol. 10, 2000.

52. J. Koolwaaij and J. de Veth. The use of broad phonetic class models in speaker recognition. *Proc. ICSLP*, 1998.

53. C.J. Leggetter and P.C. Woodland. Maximum likelihood linear regression for speaker adaptation of continuous density hidden markov models. *Comput. Speech Language*, 9:171–185, 1995.

54. K.-P. Li and J.E. Porter. Normalizations and selection of speech segments for speaker recognition scoring. *Proc. ICASSP*, 1:595598, 1988.

55. J. Lindberg, J. Koolwaaij, H. Hutter, D. Genoud, M. Blomberg, F. Bimbot, and J. Pierrot. Techniques for a priori decision threshold estimation in speaker verification. *In Speaker Verification Proceedings RLA2C, Avignon, 1998.*, 1998.

56. C. Ma and E. Chang. Comparaison of discriminative training methods for speaker verification. *In Proc. ICASSP*, April 2003.

57. I. Magrin-Chagnolleau, G. Gravier, and R. Blouet. Overview of the 2000-2001 elisa consortium research activities. *Speaker Odyssey Workshop*, June 2001.

58. J. Makhoul. Linear prediction: A tutorial review. *Proceedings of the IEEE*, 63(4):561–580, 1975.

59. A. Martin, G. Doddington, T. Kamm, M. Ordowski, and M. Przybocki. The det curve in assessment of detection task performance. *Proc. Eurospeech'97*, vol. 4:1895–1898, 1997.

60. T. Matsui and S. Furui. Concatenated phoneme models for text-variable speaker recognition. *Proc. ICASSP*, pages 133–136, 1993.

61. J. M. Naik and D. Lubensky. A hybrid hmm-mlp speaker verification algorithm for telephone speech. *Proc. ICASSP*, 1994.

62. J.M. Naik. Speaker verification: A tutorial. *IEEE Commun. Magazine*, pages 42–48, Jan. 1990.

63. J. Navratil and G. N. Ramaswamy. The awe and mystery of t-norm. *Proc. Eurospeech'03*, 2003.

64. T. Nordström, H. Melin, and J. Lindberg. A comparative study of speaker verification systems using the polycost database. *Proc. ICSLP*, December 1998.

65. J. Olsen. A two-stage procedure for phone based speaker verification. *In G. Borgefors J. Bigün, G. Chollet, editor, First International Conference on Audio and Video Based Biometric Person Authentication*, pages 199–226, 1997.

66. A.V. Oppenheim and R.W. Schafer. Homomorphic analysis of speech. *IEEE Transactions on Audio and Electroacoustics*, 16, no.2:221–226, 1968.

67. A.V. Oppenheim and R.W. Schafer. *Discrete-Time Signal Processing*. Prentice-Hall, Englewood Cliffs, NJ, USA, 1989.

68. E. S. Parris and M. J. Carey. Discriminative phonemes for speaker identification. *In ICLSP*, pages 1843–1846, 1994.

69. J. Pelecanos and S. Sridharan. Feature warping for robust speaker verification. *2001: A Speaker Odyssey - The Speaker Recognition Workshop*, June 2001.

70. D. Petrovska-Delacrétaz, M. Abalo, A. El-Hannani, and G. Chollet. Data-driven speech segmentation for speaker verification and language identification. *ITRW Non Linear Speech Processing (NOLISP 03)*, May 20-23 2003.

71. D. Petrovska-Delacrétaz, A.L. Gorin, J.H. Wright, and G. Riccardi. Detecting acoustic morphemes in lattices for speken landuage understanding. *ICSLP*, October 2000.

72. D. Petrovska-Delacretaz and J. Hennebert. Text-prompted speaker verification experiments with phoneme specific MLP's. *In Proc. ICASSP*, pages 777–780, 1998.

73. D. Petrovska-Delacrétaz, J. Černocký, and G. Chollet. Segmental approaches for automatic speaker verification. *DSP, Special Issue on the NIST'99 evaluations*, vol. 10(1-3):198–212, January/April/July 2000.

74. D. Petrovska-Delacrétaz, J. Černocký, J. Hennebert, and G. Chollet. Text-independent speaker verification using automatically labeled acoustic segments. *In ICLSP*, 1998.

75. J. Picone. Signal modeling techniques in speech recognition. *Proceedings of the IEEE*, 81(9):1214–1247, September 1993.

76. A. Preti, N. Scheffer, and J.-F. Bonastre. Discriminant approches for gmm based speaker detection systems. *In the workshop on Multimodal User Authentication,* 2006.
77. Thomas F. Quatieri. *Speech Signal Processing.* Prentice Hall Signal Processing Series, 2002.
78. L. Rabiner and B.H. Juang. *Fundamentals of Speech Recognition.* Prentice Hall, 1993.
79. D. Reynolds, W. Andrews, J. Campbell, J. Navratil, B. Peskin, A. Adami, Q. Jin, D. Klusacek, J. Abramson, R. Mihaescu, J. Godfrey, J. Jones, and B. Xiang. The supersid project: Exploiting high-level information for high-accuracy speaker recognition. *In Proc. ICASSP,* April 2003.
80. D. A. Reynolds. A gaussian mixture modeling approach to text-independent speaker identification. *Ph.D. Thesis, Georgia Institute of Technology,* 1992.
81. D.A. Reynolds. Experimental evaluation of features for robust speaker identification. *IEEE Transactions on Speech and Audio Processing,* 2(3):639–643, 1994.
82. D.A. Reynolds. Automatic speaker recognition using gaussian mixture speaker models. *Lincoln Lab. Journal 8,* (2):173–191, 1995.
83. D.A. Reynolds. Comparison of background normalization methods for text-independent speaker verification. *Proc. Eurospeech,* pages 963–966, 1997.
84. D.A Reynolds, T.F. Quatieri, and R.B. Dunn. Speaker verification using adapted gaussian mixture models. *DSP, Special Issue on the NIST'99 evaluations,* vol. 10(1-3):19–41, January/April/July 2000.
85. A. E. Rosenberg, J. DeLong, C. H. Lee, B. H. Juang, and F. K. Soong. The use of cohort normalized scores for speaker verification. *In International Conference on Speech and Language Processing,* page 599602, November 1992.
86. M. Schmidt and H. Gish. Speaker identification via support vector machines. *In Proc. ICASSP,* 1996.
87. B. Schölkopf and A.J. Smola. Learning with kernels: Support vector machines, regularization, optimization and beyond. *MIT pres,* 2001.
88. Y. A. Solewicz and M. Koppel. Enhanced fusion methods for speaker verification. *Proc. SPECOM'2004: 9th Conference Speech and Computer,* pages 388–392, 2004.
89. A. Solomonoff, C. Quillen, and W. Campbell. Channel compensation for svm speaker recognition. *Proc. Odyssey,* 2004.
90. K. Sönmez, E. Shriberg, L. Heck, and M. Weintraub. Modeling dynamic prosodic variation for speaker verification. *Proc. ICSLP98,* 1998.
91. D. Sturim, D. Reynolds, R. Dunn, and T. Quatieri. Speaker verification using text-constrained gaussian mixture models. *Proc. ICASSP,* vol. 1:677680, 2002.
92. N. Tishby. On the application of mixture ar hidden markov models to text independent speaker recognition. *IEEE Transactions on Signial Processing,* vol. 39(3):563–570, March 1991.
93. V. Vapnik. *The Nature of Statistical Learning Theory.* Springer-Verlag, New York, 1995.
94. O. Viikki and K. Laurila. Cepstral domain segmental feature vector normalization for noise robust speech recognition. *Speech Communication,* vol. 25:133–147, 1998.
95. V. Wan and S. Renals. SVMSVM: Support vector machine speaker verification methodology. *Proc. IEEE ICASSP,* 2:221–224, 2003.
96. V. Wan and S. Renals. Speaker verification using sequence discriminant support vector machines. *IEEE Trans. on Speech and Audio Processing,* 13:203–210, 2005.
97. B. Xiang, U. Chaudhari, J. Navratil, G. Ramaswamy, and R. Gopinath. Short-time gaussianization for robust speaker verification. *Proc. ICASSP,* vol. 1:681684, 2002.

# Nonlinear Predictive Models: Overview and Possibilities in Speaker Recognition

Marcos Faundez-Zanuy and Mohamed Chetouani

Escola Universitària Politècnica de Mataró (BARCELONA), Spain
Université Pierre and Marie Curie, Paris VI, France
faundez@eupmt.es, mohamed.chetouani@upmc.fr
http://www.eupmt.es/veu

**Abstract.** In this paper we give a brief overview of speaker recognition with special emphasis on nonlinear predictive models, based on neural nets. Main challenges and possibilities for nonlinear feature extraction are described, and experimental results of several strategies are provided. This paper is presented as a starting point for the non-linear model for speaker recognition.

## 1 Introduction

Recent advances in speech technologies have produced new tools that can be used to improve the performance and flexibility of speaker recognition While there are few degrees of freedom or alternative methods when using fingerprint or iris identification techniques, speech offers much more flexibility and different levels to perform recognition: the system can force the user to speak in a particular manner, different for each attempt to enter. Also, with voice input, the system has other degrees of freedom, such as the use of knowledge/codes that only the user knows, or dialectical/semantical traits that are difficult to forge.

This paper offers an overview of the state of the art in speaker recognition, with special emphasis on the pros and cons, and the current research lines based on nonlinear speech processing. We think that speaker recognition is far away from being a technology where all the possibilities have already been explored.

### 1.1 Biometrics

Biometric recognition offers a promising approach for security applications, with some advantages over the classical methods, which depend on something you have (key, card, etc.), or something you know (password, PIN, etc.). However, there is a main drawback, because it cannot be replaced after being compromised by a third party. Probably, these drawbacks have slowed down the spread of use of biometric recognition [1-2]. For those applications with a human supervisor (such as border entrance control), this can be a minor problem, because the operator can check if the presented biometric trait is original or fake. However, for remote applications such as internet, some kind of liveliness detection and anti-replay attack mechanisms should be provided. Fortunately, speech offers a richer and wider range of possibilities when

Y. Stylianou, M. Faundez-Zanuy, A. Esposito (Eds.): WNSP 2005, LNCS 4391, pp. 170–189, 2007.
© Springer-Verlag Berlin Heidelberg 2007

compared with other biometric traits, such as fingerprint, iris, hand geometry, face, etc. This is because it can be seen as a mixture of physical and learned traits. We can consider physical traits those which are inherent to people (iris, face, etc.), while learned traits are those related to skills acquired along life and environment (signature, gait, etc.). For instance, your signature is different if you have been born in a western or an Asian country, and your speech accent is different if you have grown up in Edinburgh or in Seattle, and although you might speak the same language, probably prosody or vocabulary might be different (i.e. the relative frequency of the use of common words might vary depending on the geographical or educational background).

### 1.2  Speech Processing Techniques

Speech processing techniques relies on speech signals usually acquired by a microphone and introduced in a computer using a digitalization procedure. It can be used to extract the following information from the speaker:

- Speech detection: is there someone speaking? (speech activity detection)
- Gender identification: which is his/her gender? (Male or female).
- Language recognition: which language is being spoken? (English, Spanish, etc.).
- Speech recognition: which words are pronounced? (speech to text transcription)
- Speaker recognition: which is the speaker's name? (John, Lisa, etc,)

Most of the efforts of the speech processing community have been devoted to the last two topics. In this paper we will focus on the latest one and the speech related aspects relevant to biometric applications.

## 2  Speaker Recognition

Speaker recognition can be performed in two different ways:

**Speaker identification:** In this approach no identity is claimed from the speaker. The automatic system must determine who is talking. If the speaker belongs to a predefined set of known speakers, it is referred to as closed-set speaker identification. However, for sure the set of speakers known (learnt) by the system is much smaller than the potential number of users than can attempt to enter. The more general situation where the system has to manage with speakers that perhaps are not modeled inside the database is referred to as open-set speaker identification. Adding a "none-of-the-above" option to closed-set identification gives open-set identification. The system performance can be evaluated using an identification rate. For open set identification, it is expected that some users do not belong to the database and an additional decision is necessary: "Not a known person". In this case, a threshold is needed in order to detect this situation. However, most of the published systems refer to the "closed set" identification (the input user is certainly in the database).

**Speaker verification:** In this approach the goal of the system is to determine whether the person is who he/she claims to be. This implies that the user must provide an identity and the system just accepts or rejects the users according to a successful or unsuccessful verification. Sometimes this operation mode is named authentication or detection. The system performance can be evaluated using the False Acceptance Rate (FAR, those situations where an impostor is accepted) and the False Rejection Rate (FRR, those situations where a speaker is incorrectly rejected), also known in detection theory as False Alarm and Miss, respectively. This framework gives us the possibility of distinguishing between the discriminability of the system and the decision bias. The discriminability is inherent to the classification system used and the discrimination bias is related to the preferences/necessities of the user in relation to the relative importance of each of the two possible mistakes (misses vs. false alarms) that can be done in speaker identification. This trade-off between both errors has to be usually established by adjusting a decision threshold. The performance can be plotted in a ROC (Receiver Operator Characteristic) or in a DET (Detection error trade-off) plot [3]. DET curve gives uniform treatment to both types of error, and uses a scale for both axes, which spreads out the plot and better distinguishes different well performing systems and usually produces plots that are close to linear. Note also that the ROC curve has symmetry with respect to the DET, i.e. plots the hit rate instead of the miss probability, and uses a logarithmic scale that expands the extreme parts of the curve, which are the parts that give the most information about the system performance. For this reason the speech community prefers DET instead of ROC plots. Figure 1 shows an example of DET of plot, and figure 2 shows a classical ROC plot.

In both cases (identification and verification), speaker recognition techniques can be split into two main modalities:

**Text independent:** This is the general case, where the system does not know the text spoken by person. This operation mode is mandatory for those applications where the user does not know that he/she is being evaluated for recognition purposes, such as in forensic applications, or to simplify the use of a service where the identity is inferred in order to improve the human/machine dialog, as is done in certain banking services. This allows more flexibility, but it also increases the difficulty of the problem. If necessary, speech recognition can provide knowledge of spoken text. In this mode one can use indirectly the typical word co-occurrence of the speaker, and therefore it also characterizes the speaker by a probabilistic grammar. This co-occurrence model is known as n-grams, and gives the probability that a given set of n words are uttered consecutively by the speaker. This can distinguish between different cultural/regional/gender backgrounds, and therefore complement the speech information, even if the speaker speaks freely. This modality is also interesting in the case of speaker segmentation, when there are several speakers present and there is an interest in segmenting the signal depending on the active speaker.

**Text dependent:** This operation mode implies that the system knows the text spoken by person. It can be a predefined text or a prompted text. In general, the knowledge of the spoken text lets to improve the system performance with respect to previous category. This mode is used for those applications with strong control over user input, or in applications where a dialog unit can guide the user.

One of the critical facts for speaker recognition is the presence of channel variability from training to testing. That is, different signal to noise ratio, kind of microphone, evolution with time, etc. For human beings this is not a serious problem, because of the use of different levels of information. However, this affects automatic systems in a

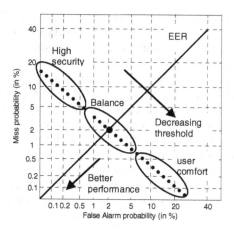

**Fig. 1.** Example of a DET plot for a speaker verification system (dotted line). The Equal Error Rate (EER) line shows the situation where False Alarm equals Miss Probability (balanced performance). Of course one of both errors rates can be more important (high security application versus those where we do not want to annoy the user with a high rejection/ miss rate). If the system curve is moved towards the origin, smaller error rates are achieved (better performance). If the decision threshold is reduced, we get higher False Acceptance/Alarm rates.

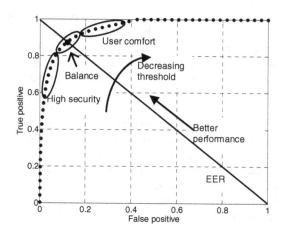

**Fig. 2.** Example of a ROC plot for a speaker verification system (dotted line). The Equal Error Rate (EER) line shows the situation where False Alarm equals Miss Probability (balanced performance). Of course one of both errors rates can be more important (high security application versus those where we do not want to annoy the user with a high rejection/ miss rate). If the system curve is moved towards the upper left zone, smaller error rates are achieved (better performance). If the decision threshold is reduced, higher False Acceptance/Alarm rates are achieved. It is interesting to observe that comparing figures 1 and 2 we get True positive = (1 – Miss probability) and False positive = False Alarm.

significant manner. Fortunately higher-level cues are not as affected by noise or channel mismatch. Some examples of high-level information in speech signals are speaking and pause rate, pitch and timing patterns, idiosyncratic word/phrase usage, idiosyncratic pronunciations, etc.

Considering the first historical speaker recognition systems, we realize that they have been mainly based on physical traits extracted from spectral characteristics of speech signals. So far, features derived from speech spectrum have proven to be the most effective in automatic systems, because the spectrum reflects the geometry of the system that generates the signal. Therefore the variability in the dimensions of the vocal tract is reflected in the variability of spectra between speakers [4]. However, there is a large amount of possibilities [5]. Figure 3 summarizes different levels of information suitable for speaker recognition, being the top part related to learned traits and the bottom one to physical traits. Obviously, we are not bound to use only one of these levels, and we can use some kind of data fusion [6] in order to obtain a more reliable recognizer [7].

Learned traits, such as semantics, diction, pronunciation, idiosyncrasy, etc. (related to socio-economic status, education, place of birth, etc.) is more difficult to automatically extract. However, they offer a great potential. Surely, sometimes when we try to imitate the voice of another person, we use this kind of information. Thus, it is really characteristic of each person. Nevertheless, the applicability of these high-level recognition systems is limited by the large training data requirements needed to build robust and stable speaker models. However, a simple statistical tool, such as the n-gram, can capture easily some of these high level features. For instance, in the case of the prosody, one could classify a certain number of recurrent pitch patterns, and compute the co-occurrence probability of these patterns for each speaker. This might reflect dialectical and cultural backgrounds of the speaker. From a syntactical point of view, this same tool could be used for modeling the different co-occurrence of words for a given speaker.

The interest of making a fusion [6] of both learned and physical traits is that the system is more robust (i.e, increases the separability between speakers), and at the same time it is more flexible, because it does not force an artificial situation on the speaker. On the other hand, the use of learned traits such as semantics, or prosody introduces a delay on the decision because of the necessity of obtaining enough speech signal for computing the statistics associated to the histograms.

Different levels of extracted information from the speech signal can be used for speaker recognition. Mainly they are:

**Spectral:** The anatomical structure of the vocal apparatus is easy-to-extract in an automatic fashion. In fact, different speakers will have different spectra (location and magnitude of peaks) for similar sounds. The state-of-the-art speaker recognition algorithms are based on statistical models of short-term acoustic measurements provided by a feature extractor. The most popular model is the Gaussian Mixture Model (GMM) [8], and the use of Support Vector Machines [9]. Feature extraction is usually computed by temporal methods like the Linear Predictive Coding (LPC) or frequencial methods like the Mel Frequency Cepstral Coding (MFCC) or both methods like Perceptual Linear Coding (PLP). A nice property of spectral methods is that logarithmic scales (either amplitude or frequency), which mimic the functional properties of

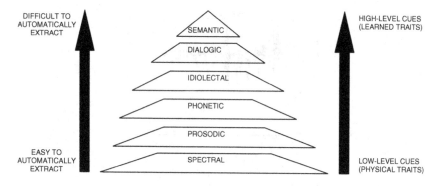

**Fig. 3.** Levels of information for speaker recognition

human ear, improve recognition rates. This is due to the fact that the speaker generates signals in order to be understood/recognized, therefore, an analysis tailored to the way that the human ear works yields better performance.

**Prosodic:** Prosodic features are stress, accent and intonation measures. The easiest way to estimate them is by means of pitch, energy, and duration information. Energy and pitch can be used in a similar way than the short-term characteristics of the previous level with a GMM model. Although these features by its own do not provide as good results as spectral features, some improvement can be achieved combining both kinds of features. Obviously, different data-fusion levels can be used [6]. On the other hand, there is more potential using long-term characteristics. For instance, human beings trying to imitate the voice of another person usually try to replicate energy and pitch dynamics, rather than instantaneous values. Thus, it is clear that this approach has potential. Figure 4 shows an example of speech sentence and its intensity and pitch contours. This information has been extracted using the Praat software, which can be downloaded from [10]. The use of prosodic information can improve the robustness of the system, in the sense that it is less affected by the transmission channel than the spectral characteristics, and therefore it is a potential candidate feature to be used as a complement of the spectral information in applications where the microphone can change or the transmission channel is different from the one used in the training phase. The prosodic features can be used at two levels, in the lower one, one can use the direct values of the pitch, energy or duration, at a higher level, the system might compute co-occurrence probabilities of certain recurrent patterns and check them at the recognition phase.

**Phonetic:** It is possible to characterize speaker-specific pronunciations and speaking patterns using phone sequences. It is known that same phonemes can be pronounced in different ways without changing the semantics of an utterance. This variability in the pronunciation of a given phoneme can be used by recognizing each variant of each phoneme and afterwards comparing the frequency of co-occurrence of the phonemes of an utterance (N-grams of phone sequences), with the N-grams of each speaker. This might capture the dialectal characteristics of the speaker, which might include geographical and cultural traits. The models can consist of N-grams of

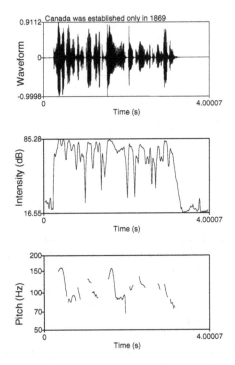

**Fig. 4.** Speech sentence "Canada was established only in 1869" and its intensity and pitch contour. While uttering the same sentence, different speakers would produce different patterns, i.e. syllable duration, profile of the pitch curve.

phone sequences. A disadvantage of this method is the need for an automatic speech recognition system, and the need for modelling the confusion matrix (i.e. the probability that a given phoneme is confused by another one). In any case, as there are available dialectical databases [11] for the main languages, the use of this kind of information is nowadays feasible.

**Idiolectal (synthactical):** Recent work by G. Doddington [12] has found useful speaker information using sequences of recognized words. These sequences are called n-grams, and as explained above, they consist of the statistics of co-occurrence of n consecutive words. They reflect the way of using the language by a given speaker. The idea is to recognize speakers by their word usage. It is well known that some persons use and abuse of several words. Sometimes when we try to imitate them we do not need to emulate their sound neither their intonation. Just repeating their "favorite" words is enough. The algorithm consists of working out n-grams from speaker training and testing data. For recognition, a score is derived from both n-grams (using for instance the Viterbi algorithm). This kind of information is a step further than classical systems, because we add a new element to the classical security systems (something we have, we know or we are): something we do. A strong point of this method is that it does not only take into account the use of vocabulary specific to the user, but also the context, and short time dependence between words, which is more difficult to imitate.

**Dialogic:** When we have a dialog with two or more speakers, we would like to segmentate the parts that correspond to each speaker. Conversational patterns are useful for determining when speaker change has occurred in a speech signal (segmentation) and for grouping together speech segments from the same speaker (clustering).

The integration of different levels of information, such as spectral, phonological, prosodic or syntactical is difficult due to the heterogeneity of the features. Different techniques are available for combining different information with the adequate weighting of evidences and if possible the integration has to be robust with respect to the failure of one of the features. A common framework can be a bayesian modeling [13], but there are also other techniques such as data fusion, neural nets, etc.

In the last years, improvements in technology related to automatic speech recognition and the availability of a wide range of databases have given the possibility of introducing high level features into speaker recognition systems. Thus, it is possible to use phonological aspects specific to the speaker or dialectical aspects which might model the region/background of the speaker as well as his/her educational background. Also the use of statistical grammar modelling can take into account the different word co-occurrence of each speaker. An important aspect is the fact that these new possibilities for improving speaker recognition systems have to be integrated in order to take advantage of the higher levels of information that are available nowadays.

Next sections of this paper will be devoted to feature extraction using non-linear features. For this goal, we will start with a short overview of nonlinear speech processing from a general point of view.

## 3  Non-linear Speech Processing

In the last years there has been a growing interest for nonlinear models applied to speech. This interest is based on the evidence of nonlinearities in the speech production mechanism. Several arguments justify this fact:

a)  Residual signal of predictive analysis [14].
b)  Correlation dimension of speech signal [15].
c)  Physiology of the speech production mechanism [16].
d)  Probability density functions [17].
e)  High order statistics [18].

Although these evidences, few applications have been developed so far, mainly due to the high computational complexity and difficulty of analyzing the nonlinear systems. These applications have been mainly applied on speech coding. [19] presents a recent review.

However, non-linear predictive models can also been applied to speaker recognition in a quite straight way, replacing linear predictive models by non-linear ones.

## 3.1 Non-linear Predictive Models

The applications of the nonlinear predictive analysis have been mainly focussed on speech coding, because it achieves greater prediction gains than LPC. The first proposed systems were [20] and [21], which proposed a CELP with different nonlinear predictors that improve the SEGSNR of the decoded signal.

Three main approaches have been proposed for the nonlinear predictive analysis of speech. They are:

a) Nonparametric prediction: it does not assume any model for the nonlinearity. It is a quite simple method, but the improvement over linear predictive methods is lower than with nonlinear parametric models. An example of a nonparametric prediction is a codebook that tabulates several (input, output) pairs (eq. 1), and the predicted value can be computed using the nearest neighbour inside the codebook. Although this method is simple, low prediction orders must be used. Some examples of this system can be found in [20], [22-24].

$$\left( \underline{x}[n-1], \hat{x}[n] \right) \tag{1}$$

b) Parametric prediction: it assumes a model of prediction. The main approaches are Volterra series [25] and neural nets [2], [26-27].

The use of a nonlinear predictor based on neural networks can take advantage of some kind of combination between different nonlinear predictors (different neural networks, the same neural net architecture trained with different algorithms, or even the same architecture and training algorithm just using a different bias and weight random initialization). The possibilities are more limited using linear prediction techniques.

On the other hand, there is an additional advantage. When dealing with linear models, the unique way to extend the number of training/ testing vectors is to overlap consecutive frames. Using nonlinear models we can also overlap consecutive frames, but we can also take advantage of different set of coefficients when using different random weights initialization. For instance, figure 5 shows the prediction gain (which is an important property for speech coding) obtained with different random initializations computed with the same speech frame. This plot represents linear case (LPC-10 and LPC-25) and two different Multi-Layer Perceptron architectures (MLP 10×2×1 and MLP 10×4×1). Figure 6 shows the histogram of the different prediction gains (extracted from [19]). It is true that there is some chance to get worse results than LPC-25 in some cases, but we can take advantage of the combination of several random initializations. This is in agreement with the philosophy explained in [41]. Instead of looking for the best set of features and the best classifier, we look for the best set of classifiers/features and then the best combination method. "It is time to stop arguing over which type of pattern classification/ parameterization is best. Instead we should look at a higher level and discover how to build managerial systems to exploit the different virtues and evade the different limitations of each of these ways of comparing things".

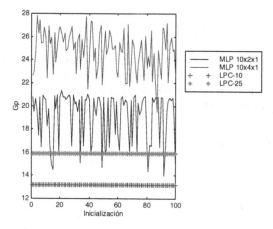

**Fig. 5.** Prediction gain for a given frame using 100 different random initializations for Multi-Layer Perceptrons and linear analysis

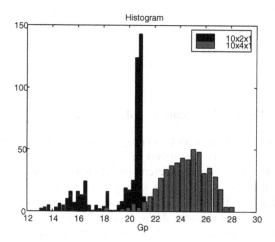

**Fig. 6.** Prediction gain (*Gp*) histograms for 500 random initializations for the MLP 20x2x1 and MLP 10x4x1 architectures

However, there is a strong limitation when trying to compare two different set of features. While the comparison of two linear sets such as (2) and (3) is straightforward (4), this is not the case with nonlinear sets.

$$x[n] \cong \hat{x}[n] = \sum_{k=1}^{P} a_k x[n-k] = a_1 x[n-1] + a_2 x[n-2] \tag{2}$$

$$x[n] \cong \hat{x}'[n] = \sum_{k=1}^{P} a_k' x[n-k] = a_1' x[n-1] + a_2' x[n-2] \tag{3}$$

$$d\left[\{a_1,a_2\},\{a_1',a_2'\}\right] \tag{4}$$

For instance, figure 7 represents two MLP, which have been trained using the same speech frame. It is clear that both networks perform exactly the same transfer function. However, a direct comparison will reveal that they differ. Obviously, much more analogous examples can be stated.

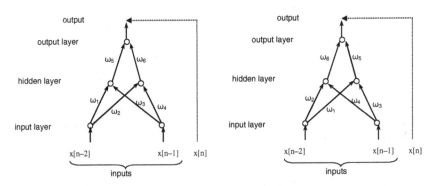

**Fig. 7.** Example of two different MLP, which perform the same transfer function. It is interesting to observe that the hidden layer neurons order has been interchanged. Thus a direct weight comparison would reveal that they are different.

### 3.2 Non-linear Feature Extraction: Method 1

With a nonlinear prediction model based on neural nets it is not possible to compare the weights of two different neural nets in the same way that we compare two different LPC vectors obtained from different speech frames. This is due to the fact that infinite sets of different weights representing the same model exist, and direct comparison is not feasible. For this reason one way to compare two different neural networks is by means of a measure defined over the residual signal of the nonlinear predictive model. For improving performance upon classical methods a combination with linear parameterization must be used.

The main reason of the difficulty for applying the nonlinear predictive models based on nets in recognition applications is that it is not possible to compare the nonlinear predictive models directly. The comparison between two predictive models can be done alternatively in the following way: the same input is presented to several models, and the decision is made based on the output of each system, instead of the structural parameters of each system.

For speaker recognition purposes we propose to model each speaker with a codebook of nonlinear predictors based on MLP. This is done in the same way as the classical speaker recognition based on vector quantization [30]. Figure 8 summarizes the proposed scheme, where each person is modeled by a codebook. This VQ system has been recently applied to online signature recognition, and is specially suitable for situations with a small amount of training vectors [42].

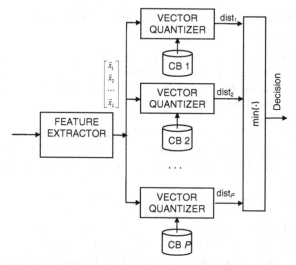

**Fig. 8.** Proposed scheme for identification based on VQ. There is one codebook per person.

We obtained [28-29] that the residual signal is less efficient than the LPCC coefficients. Both in linear and nonlinear predictive analysis the recognition errors are around 20%, while the results obtained with LPCC are around 6%. On the other hand we have obtained that the residual signal is uncorrelated with the vocal tract information (LPCC coefficients) [28]. For this reason both measures can be combined in order to improve the recognition rates.

We proposed:

a) The use of an error measure defined over the LPC residual signal, (instead of a parameterization over this signal) combined with a classical measure defined over LPCC coefficients. The following measures were studied:

- measure 1 (1): Mean Square Error (MSE) of the LPCC.
- measure 2 (2): Mean Absolute difference (MAD) of the LPCC.

b) The use of a nonlinear prediction model based on neural nets, which has been successfully applied to a waveform speech coder [19]. It is well known that the LPC model is unable to describe the nonlinearities present in the speech, so useful information is lost with the LPC model alone. The following measures were studied, defined over the residual signal:

- measure 3 (3): MSE of the residue.
- measure 4 (4): MAD of the residue.
- measure 5 (5): Maximum absolute value (MAV) of the residue.
- measure 6 (6): Variance ($\sigma$) of the residue.

Our recognition algorithm is a Vector Quantization approach. That is, each speaker is modeled with a codebook in the training process. During the test, the input sentence is quantized with all the codebooks, and the codebook which yields the minimal accumulated error indicates the recognized speaker.

The codebooks are generated with the splitting algorithm. Two methods have been tested for splitting the centroids:

a) The standard deviation of the vectors assigned to each cluster.

b) A hyperplane computed with the covariance matrix.

The recognition algorithm in the MLP's codebook is the following:

1. The test sentence is partitioned into frames.

For each speaker:

2. Each frame is filtered with all the MLP of the codebook (centroids) and it is stored the lowest Mean Absolute Error (MAE) of the residual signal. This process is repeated for all the frames, and the MAE of each frame is accumulated for obtaining the MAE of the whole sentence.

3. The step 2 is repeated for all the speakers, and the speaker that gives the lowest accumulated MAE is selected as the recognized speaker.

This procedure is based on the assumption that if the model has been derived from the same speaker of the test sentence then the residual signal of the predictive analysis will be lower than for a different speaker not modeled during the training process.

Unfortunately the results obtained with this system were not good enough. Even with a computation of a generalization of the Lloyd iteration for improving the codebook of MLP.

### Nonlinear codebook generation

In order to generate the codebook a good initialization must be achieved. Thus, it is important to achieve a good clustering of the train vectors. We have evaluated several possibilities, and the best one is to implement first a linear LPCC codebook of the same size. This codebook is used for clustering the input frames, and then each cluster is the training set for a multilayer perceptron with 10 input neurons, 4 neurons in the first hidden layer, 2 neurons in the second hidden layer, and one output neuron with a linear transfer function. Thus, the MLP is trained in the same way as in our speech coding applications [19], but the frames have been clustered previously with a linear LPCC codebook. After this process, the codebook can be improved with a generalization of the Lloyd iteration.

### Efficient algorithm

In order to reduce the computational complexity and to improve the recognition rates a novel scheme that consists of the pre-selection of the $K$ speakers nearest to the test sentence was proposed in [28-29]. Then, the error measure based on the nonlinear predictive model was computed only with these speakers. (In this case a reduction of 3.68% in error rate upon classical LPC cepstrum parameterization was achieved).

The LPCC used for clustering the frames is used as a pre-selector of the recognized speaker. That is, the input sentence is quantized with the LPCC codebooks and the K codebooks that produce the lowest accumulated error are selected. Then, the input sentence is quantized with the K nonlinear codebooks, and the accumulated distance of the nonlinear codebook is combined with the LPCC distance.

### 3.3  Non-linear Feature Extraction: Method 2

As mentioned previously, neural predictive models are not easily comparable in terms of parameters (i.e. the weights). However, it is well-known that the neural weights can be considered as a representation of the input vector even if it is not a singular one. To overcome this limitation, we propose a model optimized by original constraints: The Neural Predictive Coding (NPC) model [31, 32].

The Neural Predictive Coding (NPC) model is basically a non-linear extension of the well-known LPC encoder. As in the LPC framework with the Auto-Regressive (AR) model, the vector code is estimated by prediction error minimization. The main difference relies in the fact that the model is non-linear (connectionist based):

$$\hat{y}_k = F(\mathbf{y}_k) = \sum_j a_j \sigma(\mathbf{w}^T \mathbf{y}_k) \tag{5}$$

Where $F$ is the prediction function realized by the neural model. $\hat{y}_k$ is the predicted sample. $\mathbf{y}_k$ the prediction context: $\mathbf{y}_k = [y_{k-1}, y_{k-2}, \cdots, y_{k-\lambda}]^T$ and $\lambda$ the length of the prediction window. $\mathbf{w}$ and $\mathbf{a}$ represent the first and the last (output) layer weights. $\sigma$ is a non-linear activation function (the sigmoid function in our case).

The key idea of the NPC model is to use it as a nonlinear autoregressive model. As in the LPC framework, the NPC weights (predictor coefficients) represent the vector code. It is well-known that neural weights can be considered as a representation of the input vector. A drawback of this method is that nonlinear models have no clear physical meanings [33]. The solution weights can be very different for a same minimum of the prediction error. To overcome this limitation, we exploit the neural feedforward interpretation of the Kolmogorov superposition algorithm [34, 35, 36, 37]. This interpretation states that any continuous function:

$$f(x_1, x_2, \cdots, x_n) = \sum_{j=1}^{2n+1} g_f \left( \sum_{i=1}^{n} \lambda_i Q_j(x_i) \right) \tag{6}$$

Where $\{\lambda_i\}_1^n$ are universal constants that no depend on $f$. $\{Q_j\}_1^{2n+1}$ are universal transformations which also do not depend on $f$. And $g_f$ is a continuous function which totally characterizes $f(x_1, x_2, \cdots, x_n)$. Following this interpretation, and under convergence and structure (i.e. the number $n$ of hidden cells [34,36], the output layer weights $\mathbf{a}$ completely describe the signal $\hat{y}_k$. The NPC model is based on this assumption [38] and consequently these only output layer weights can be used as features from the speech signal.

*Description*
The NPC model is a Multi-Layer Perceptron (MLP) with one hidden layer. Only the output layer weights are used as the coding vector instead of all the neural weights. For that, we assume that the function $F$ realized by the model, under convergence

assumptions, can be decomposed into two functions:    $G_{\mathbf{w}}$ (**w** being the first weights) and $H_{\mathbf{a}}$ (**a** output layer weights):

$$F_{\mathbf{w,a}}(\mathbf{y}_k) = H_{\mathbf{a}} \circ G_{\mathbf{w}}(\mathbf{y}_k) \tag{7}$$

With $\hat{\mathbf{y}}_k = H_{\mathbf{a}}(\mathbf{z}_k)$ and $\mathbf{z}_k = G_{\mathbf{w}}(\mathbf{y}_k)$.

The learning phase is realized in two stages (cf. figure 9). First, the *parameterization phase* involves the learning of all the weights by the prediction error minimization criterion:

$$Q = \sum_{k=1}^{K} \left( y_k - \hat{y}_k \right)^2 = \sum_{k=1}^{K} \left( y_k - F(\mathbf{y}_k) \right)^2 \tag{8}$$

With $y_k$ the speech signal, $\hat{y}_k$ the predicted speech signal, $k$ the samples index and $K$ the total number of samples.

In this phase, only the first layer weights **w** (which are the NPC encoder parameters) are kept. Since the NPC encoder is set up by the parameters defined in the previous phase, the second phase, called the *coding phase*, involves computation of the output layer weights **a** : representing the phoneme coding vector. This is done also by prediction error minimization but only the output layer weights are updated. One can notice that the output function is linear (cf. equation 5), so it can use simple LMS-like algorithms. Here, for consistency with the *parameterization phase*, it is done by the backpropagation algorithm.

*Linear initialization of non-linear model*
The proposed feature extraction, i.e. the NPC model, can be viewed as the optimization of the prediction error with the respect of the weights (features). The quality of such methods, which can be evaluated in terms of prediction gain, largely depends on the local minimum. In recognition tasks, the purpose is different. Indeed, those systems are based on the comparison of features usually by machine learning approaches (GMM, neural networks ...). The performances are directly related to the stability of the features. For instance the features produced by the MFCC process for one frame is always the same. To avoid the stability which results from the NPC *coding phase,* we propose an original *initialization phase* exploiting speech knowledge.

We used the LPC coding method for the initialization of the non-linear coding model (cf. figure 10). By this way, one can see the NPC as a non-linear feature extractor initialized by a linear model. By neglecting biaises and removing the non-linear activation functions (for linear approximation), one obtains the following equivalence:

$$\Theta = \mathbf{w} \bullet \mathbf{a} \tag{9}$$

Where $\Theta$ are the LPC parameters of the speech signal, **w** first layer weights (determined in the previous phase: the *parameterization phase*) and **a** second layer weights.

If the NPC vector code dimension is $\rho$ and the prediction window is $\lambda$ then the LPC vector code dimension has to be set to $\lambda$. The second layer weights **a** are given by:

$$\mathbf{a} = \mathbf{w}^+ \bullet \Theta \tag{10}$$

Where $\mathbf{w}^+$ is the pseudo-inverse of **w** .

**Parameterization phase**
= Computation of the first
layer weights

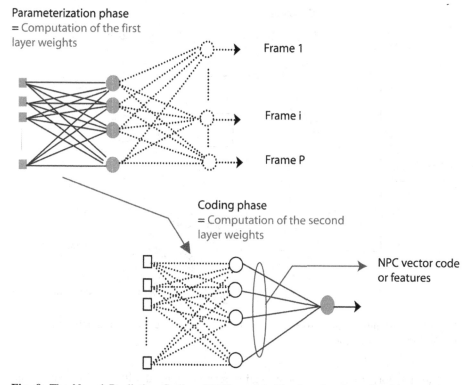

Frame 1

Frame i

Frame P

**Coding phase**
= Computation of the second
layer weights

NPC vector code
or features

**Fig. 9.** The Neural Predictive Coding (NPC) model. The learning is realized in two times namely the *parameterization* and the *coding* phases.

The initialized weights are determined by a simple LPC analysis with an $\lambda$ order. Once the initialization is accomplished, the coding process (prediction error minimization) proceeds as well as the original NPC *coding phase* by the backpropagation algorithm.

Initialization of non-linear models by linear ones has been already investigated [39] but with matrices decomposition methods (SVD, QR,...). The main limitation relies in the multiplicity of the solution. Ref. [40] proposes a new method which guarantees a single solution.

*Application to speaker identification*

The new initialization method has been successfully applied to speaker identification. In [32, 39], random initialization gives the worst results in comparison to standard methods such as MFCC or LPCC. However, the use of linear initialization clearly improves the results since they are better than MFCC and LPCC ones.

We also investigated the importance of non-linear modeling by the comparison of identification rates obtained by linear (LPC) and non-linear feature extraction (NPC) methods. Within the proposed method, the initial features are the LPC ones which give better results than the random initialization. Indeed, as it has been previously pointed out, a direct comparison of the weights even if they perform the same function.

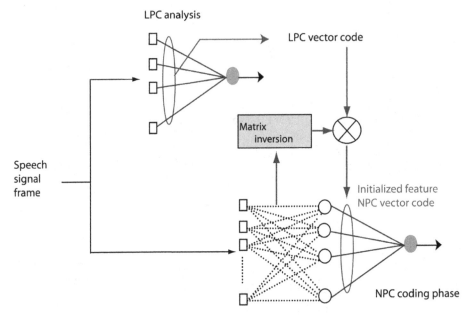

**Fig. 10.** Linear initialization process. The LPC vector code is used as an initial feature vector for the NPC *coding phase*.

Tab. 1 reports the speaker identification results obtained with the Covariance Matrix method for different parameterization methods [32]. The results highlight of both non-linear modeling (LPC vs NPC) and the improvement of data-driven initialization of non-linear models such as the NPC (random vs linear).

**Table 1.** Experimental results for different parameterizations

| PARAMETERIZATION | IDENTIFICATION RATE (%) |
|---|---|
| LPC | 90.61 |
| LPCC | 96.73 |
| MFCC | 97.55 |
| PLP | 86.12 |
| NPC (random initialization) | 61.63 |
| NPC (linear initialization | 100 |

## 4   Conclusions

In this paper we have presented an overview of speaker recognition application with special emphasis on nonlinear speaker models. We feel that the scientific community of speaker recognition has reached a saturation point about feature extraction, and nonlinear techniques offer a wide range of possibilities to be explored. This paper should serve as a starting point for discovering this topic.

## Acknowledgement

This work has been supported by FEDER and the Spanish grant MCYT TIC2003-08382-C05-02. I want to acknowledge the European project COST-277 "nonlinear speech processing", that has been acting as a catalyzer for the development of nonlinear speech processing since middle 2001. I also want to acknowledge Prof. Enric Monte-Moreno for the support and useful discussions of these years.

## References

1. Faundez-Zanuy M. "On the vulnerability of biometric security systems" IEEE Aerospace and Electronic Systems Magazine Vol.19 n° 6, pp.3-8, June 2004
2. Faundez-Zanuy M. "Biometric recognition: why not massively adopted yet?". IEEE Aerospace and Electronic Systems Magazine. Vol.20 n° 8, pp.25-28, August 2005
3. Martin A., Doddington G., Kamm T., Ordowski M., and Przybocki M., "The DET curve in assessment of detection performance", V. 4, pp.1895-1898, European speech Processing Conference Eurospeech 1997
4. Furui S., Digital Speech Processing, synthesis, and recognition. Marcel Dekker, 1989.
5. Campbell J. P., Reynolds D. A. and Dunn R. B. "Fusing high- and low-level features for speaker recognition". Eurospeech 2003 Geneva.
6. Faundez-Zanuy M. "Data fusion in biometrics". IEEE Aerospace and Electronic Systems Magazine Vol. 20 n° 1, pp.34-38. January 2005.
7. Faundez-Zanuy M., Monte-Moreno E., IEEE Aerospace and Electronic Systems Magazine. Vol. 20 n° 5, pp 7-12, May 2005.
8. Reynolds D. A., Rose R. C. "Robust text-independent speaker identification using Gaussian mixture speaker models". IEEE Trans. On Speech and Audio Processing, Vol. 3 No 1, pp. 72-83 January 1995
9. Cristianini, N., Shawe-Taylor, J., An Introduction to Support Vector Machines, Cambridge University Press, (2000).
10. http://www.praat.org
11. Ortega-García J., González-Rodríguez J. and Marrero-Aguiar V. "AHUMADA: A Large Speech Corpus in Spanish for Speaker Characterization and Identification". Speech communication Vol. 31 (2000), pp. 255-264, June 2000
12. Doddington G., "Speaker Recognition based on Idiolectal Differences between Speakers," Eurospeech, vol. 4, p. 2521-2524, Aalborg 2001
13. Manning C. D., Schtze H. Foundations of Statistical Natural Language Processing, MIT Press; 1st edition (June 18, 1999).
14. Thyssen, J., Nielsen, H., Hansen S.D.: Non-linear short-term prediction in speech coding. IEEE ICASSP 1994, pp.I-185 , I-188.
15. Townshend, B.: Nonlinear prediction of speech. IEEE ICASSP-1991, Vol. 1, pp.425-428.
16. Teager, H.M.: Some observations on oral air flow vocalization. IEEE trans. ASSP, vol.82 pp.559-601, October 1980

17. Kubin, G.: Nonlinear processing of speech. Chapter 16 on Speech coding and synthesis, editors W.B. Kleijn & K.K. Paliwal, Ed. Elsevier 1995.

18. Thyssen, J., Nielsen, H., Hansen, S.D.: Non-linearities in speech. Proceedings IEEE workshop Nonlinear Signal & Image Processing, NSIP'95, June 1995

19. Faundez-Zanuy M., "Nonlinear speech processing: Overview and possibilities in speech coding", Lecture Notes in Computer Science LNCS Vol. 3445, pp.16-45. G. Chollet et al. Ed. 2005

20. Kumar, A., Gersho, A.: LD-CELP speech coding with nonlinear prediction. IEEE Signal Processing letters Vol. 4 N°4, April 1997, pp.89-91

21. Wu, L., Niranjan, M., Fallside, F.: Fully vector quantized neural network-based code-excited nonlinear predictive speech coding. IEEE transactions on speech and audio processing, Vol.2 n° 4, October 1994.

22. Wang, S., Paksoy E., Gersho, A.: Performance of nonlinear prediction of speech. Proceedings ICSLP-1990, pp.29-32

23. Lee Y.K., Johnson, D.H.: Nonparametric prediction of non-gaussian time series. IEEE ICASSP 1993, Vol. IV, pp.480-483

24. Ma, N., Wei, G.:Speech coding with nonlinear local prediction model. IEEE ICASSP 1998 vol. II, pp.1101-1104.

25. Pitas, I., Venetsanopoulos, A. N.: Non-linear digital filters: principles and applications. Kluwer ed. 1990

26. Lippmann, R. P.,: An introduction to computing with neural nets. IEEE trans. ASSP, 1988, Vol.3 N° 4, pp.4-22

27. Jain, A.K., Mao, J.: Artificial neural networks: a tutorial. IEEE Computer, March 1996, pp. 31-44.

28. Faundez-Zanuy M., Rodriguez D., "Speaker recognition using residual signal of linear and nonlinear prediction models". 5th International Conference on spoken language processing. Vol.2 pp.121-124. ICSLP'98, Sydney 1998

29. Faundez-Zanuy M., "Speaker recognition by means of a combination of linear and nonlinear predictive models ". Vol. 2 pp. 763-766. EUROSPEECH'99, Budapest 1999

30. Soong F. K., Rosenberg A. E., Rabiner L. R. and Juang B. H. " A vector quantization approach to speaker recognition". pp. 387-390. ICASSP 1985

31. B. Gas, J.L. Zarader, C. Chavy, M. Chetouani, "Discriminant neural predictive coding applied to phoneme recognition", Neurocomputing, Vol. 56, pp. 141-166, 2004.

32. M. Chetouani, M. Faundez-Zanuy, B. Gas, J.L. Zarader, "Non-linear speech feature extraction for phoneme classification and speaker recognition", Lecture Notes in Computer Science LNCS Vol. 3445, pp.340-350. G. Chollet et al. Ed. 2005.

33. W.B. Kleijn, "Signal processing representations of speech", IEICE Trans. Inf. And Syst., E86-D, 3, 359-376, March (2003).

34. A.N. Kolmogorov, "On the representation of continuous functions of several variables by superposition of continuous functions of one variable and addition," Dokl, 679-681 (1957).

35. V. Kurkova,"Kolmogorov's theorem is relevant," Neural Computation, 3(4), pp. 617-622.

36. R. Hecht-Nielsen, "Kolmogorov's mapping neural network existence theorem", Proc. of International Conference on Neural Networks, pp. 11-13 (1987).

37. C. Bishop, "Neural Networks for Pattern Recognition", Oxford University Press (1995).

38. B. Gas, M. Chetouani, J.L. Zarader and F. Feiz, "The Predictive Self_Organizing Map: application to speech features extraction," WSOM'05 (2005).

39. T.L. Burrows, "Speech processing with linear and neural networks models", PhD Cambridge, 1996.
40. M. Chetouani, M. Faundez-Zanuy, B. Gas, J.L. Zarader, "A new nonlinear speaker parameterization algorithm for speaker identification", Speaker Odyssey'04: Speaker Recognition Workshop, May 2004, Toledo, Spain.
41. Arun A. Ross, Karthik Nandakumar, and Anil K. Jain *Handbook of multibiometrics*. Springer Verlag 2006
42. M. Faundez-Zanuy "On-line signature recognition based on VQ-DTW". Pattern Recognition 40 (2007) pp.981-992. Elsevier. March 2007.

# SVMs for Automatic Speech Recognition: A Survey

R. Solera-Ureña, J. Padrell-Sendra, D. Martín-Iglesias, A. Gallardo-Antolín,
C. Peláez-Moreno, and F. Díaz-de-María

Signal Theory and Communications Department
EPS-Universidad Carlos III de Madrid
Avda. de la Universidad, 30, 28911-Leganés (Madrid), Spain

**Abstract.** Hidden Markov Models (HMMs) are, undoubtedly, the most
employed core technique for Automatic Speech Recognition (ASR). Nevertheless, we are still far from achieving high-performance ASR systems. Some alternative approaches, most of them based on Artificial
Neural Networks (ANNs), were proposed during the late eighties and
early nineties. Some of them tackled the ASR problem using predictive
ANNs, while others proposed hybrid HMM/ANN systems. However, despite some achievements, nowadays, the preponderance of Markov Models is a fact.

During the last decade, however, a new tool appeared in the field of
machine learning that has proved to be able to cope with hard classification problems in several fields of application: the Support Vector
Machines (SVMs). The SVMs are effective discriminative classifiers with
several outstanding characteristics, namely: their solution is that with
maximum margin; they are capable to deal with samples of a very higher
dimensionality; and their convergence to the minimum of the associated
cost function is guaranteed.

These characteristics have made SVMs very popular and successful.
In this chapter we discuss their strengths and weakness in the ASR context and make a review of the current state-of-the-art techniques. We
organize the contributions in two parts: isolated-word recognition and
continuous speech recognition. Within the first part we review several
techniques to produce the fixed-dimension vectors needed for original
SVMs. Afterwards we explore more sophisticated techniques based on
the use of kernels capable to deal with sequences of different length.
Among them is the DTAK kernel, simple and effective, which rescues
an old technique of speech recognition: Dynamic Time Warping (DTW).
Within the second part, we describe some recent approaches to tackle
more complex tasks like connected digit recognition or continuous speech
recognition using SVMs. Finally we draw some conclusions and outline
several ongoing lines of research.

## 1   Introduction

Hidden Markov Models (HMMs) are, undoubtedly, the most employed core
technique for Automatic Speech Recognition (ASR). During the last decades,

Y. Stylianou, M. Faundez-Zanuy, A. Esposito (Eds.): WNSP 2005, LNCS 4391, pp. 190–216, 2007.

research in HMMs for ASR has brought about significant advances and, consequently, the HMMs are currently very accurately tuned for this application. Nevertheless, we are still far from achieving high-performance ASR systems. One of the most relevant problems of the HMM-based ASR technology is the loss of performance due to the mismatch between training and testing conditions, or, in other words, the design of robust ASR systems.

A lot of research efforts have been dedicated to tackle the mismatch problem; however, the most successful solution seems to be using larger databases, trying to embed in the training set all the variability of speech and speakers. At the same time, speech recognition community is aware of the HMM limitations, but the few attempts to move toward other paradigms did not work out. In particular, some alternative approaches, most of them based on Artificial Neural Networks (ANNs), were proposed during the late eighties and early nineties ([1, 2, 3, 4] are some examples). Some of them dealt with the ASR problem using predictive ANNs, while others proposed hybrid ANN/HMM approaches. Nowadays, however, the preponderance of HMMs in practical ASR systems is a fact.

In this chapter we review some of the new alternative approaches to the ASR problem; specifically, those based on Support Vector Machines (SVMs) [5, 6]. One of the fundamentals reasons to use SVMs was already highlighted by the ANN-based proposals: it is well known that HMM are generative models, i.e., the acoustic-level decisions are taken based on the likelihood that the currently evaluated pattern had been generated by each of the models that comprise the ASR system. Nevertheless, conceptually, these decisions are essentially classification problems that could be approached, perhaps more successfully, by means of discriminative models. Certainly, algorithms for enhancing the discrimination abilities of HMMs have also been devised. However, the underlying model keeps being generative.

There are other reasons to propose the use of SVMs for ASR. Some of them will be discussed later; now, we focus on their excellent capacity of generalization, since it might improve the robustness of ASR systems. SVMs rely on maximizing the distance between the samples and the classification boundary. Unlike others, such as neural networks or some modifications of the HMMs that minimize the empirical risk on the training set, SVMs minimize also the structural risk [7], which results in a better generalization ability. In other words, given a learning problem and a finite training database, SVMs properly weight the learning potential of the database and the capacity of the machine.

The maximized distance, known as the margin, is the responsible of the outstanding generalization properties of the SVMs: the maximum margin solution allows the SVMs to outperform most nonlinear classifiers in the presence of noise, which is one of the longstanding problems in ASR. In a noise-free system, this margin is related to the maximum distance a correctly classified sample should travel to be considered as belonging to the wrong class. In other words, it indicates the noise that added to the clean samples is allowed into the system.

Nevertheless, the use of SVMs for ASR is not straightforward. In our opinion, three are the main difficulties to overcome, namely: 1) SVMs are originally static classifiers and have to be adapted to deal with the variability of duration of speech utterances; 2) the SVMs were originally formulated as a binary classifier while the ASR problem is multiclass; and 3) current SVM training algorithms are not able to manage the huge databases typically used in ASR; in spite of the appearance of techniques as Sparse SVM, the number of training samples is still limited to a few thousands.

In this Chapter we will review the solutions that during the last years have been proposed to solve the mentioned problems. Nowadays, it can be said that SVMs have been successfully used in simple ASR tasks, especially in presence of noise. On the other hand, the research work focused on more complex task is still incipient, though the results are encouraging.

This Chapter is organized as follows. Section 2 briefly reviews the ANN- and hybrid ANN/HMM-based approaches proposed during the late eighties and early nineties. First, some of the difficulties of using ANNs for ASR (that SVMs share) are revealed. Later, as a consequence of the study of the hybrid systems, some of HMM limitations are illustrated and how ANNs can be used to complement HMMs is discussed (again the lessons apply to SVMs). Section 3 summarizes the SVM fundamentals, emphasizing those aspects relevant from the ASR perspective. Section 4 is the core of the Chapter. The expected advantages of SVMs in ASR are reviewed. The limitations to be overcome are discussed. The most relevant research works dealing with SVMs for ASR are briefly described. For that purpose, the different contributions are organized in two subsections depending on the ASR task complexity: first, isolated-phone, -letter or -word recognition and after connected-words or continuous speech recognition. Finally, some conclusions are drawn and future lines of research are outlined in Section 5.

## 2   ANNs for ASR

In next paragraphs, we briefly introduce the application of Artificial Neural Networks (ANNs) to the speech recognition problem. This section does not try to be an exhaustive review of this matter. On the contrary, its aim is to outline the main alternatives proposed for the integration of ANNs into ASR systems in order to illustrate their similarities with the use of SVMs for the same purpose, especially in the context of hybrid HMM-based ASR systems.

During the last two decades some alternative approaches to HMMs, most of them based on ANNs, have been proposed for ASR as an attempt to overcome the limitations of the HMMs. ANNs represent an important class of discriminative techniques, very well suited for classification problems. In particular, ANNs exhibit several properties that have motivated their application to the implicit pattern classification problem in ASR, namely [4]:

- They learn according to discriminative criteria. Although other classifiers like HMMs can be trained in a discriminative framework, ANN training is inherently discriminative.
- ANNs are the universal approximators, i.e., they can approximate any continuous function with a simple structure.

- ANNs do not require strong assumptions about the underlying statistical properties of the input data and the functional form of the output density. On the contrary, HMMs usually assume that successive acoustic vectors are uncorrelated and follow a Gaussian (or mixture of Gaussians) distribution.

Despite of the good performance of ANNs on static classification problems, they present notable limitations to deal with the classification of time sequences as is the case of speech signals. In fact, this has been one of the fundamental problems to solve in the application of ANNs to speech recognition tasks.

## 2.1  ANN-Based ASR Systems

In order to deal with the time sequence classification problem, the first ANN-based ASR systems pursued the adaptation of the neural network architecture to the temporal structure of speech. In this context, two different classes of neural networks which consider the correlation between the temporal structures in the speech patterns were proposed: Time-Delay Neural Networks (TDNNs) [8] and Recurrent Neural Networks (RNNs) [9].

TDNNs can be considered as a special type of the well-known Multilayer Perceptron (MLP) in which input nodes integrate shift registers (or time delays). This way, the TDNN training is performed over a time sequence of acoustic vectors and the network is capable of incorporating a local acoustic context into the whole process. RNNs are a generalization of the MLP network in which feedback connections are allowed. As a consequence, the network behavior is based on its history providing a mechanism to model time sequence patterns.

Although these systems have shown to achieve good results on phoneme or isolated word recognition tasks, ANNs have not been successful on more complex tasks as continuous speech recognition. The main reason for this lack of success has been their inability to model the time variability of the speech signal even when recurrent structures are used.

## 2.2  Hybrid ANN/HMM-Based ASR Systems

To overcome these difficulties, several researchers have proposed the so-called Hybrid ANN/HMM-based ASR systems. The basic idea underlying these schemes is to combine HMMs and ANNs into a single system to get profit from the best properties of both approaches: the ability of HMMs to model the time variability of the speech signal and the discrimination ability provided by ANNs. Following this principle, different classes of hybrid ANN/HMM systems have been developed. In next paragraphs, we briefly describe some of the most relevant ones. A complete survey about this subject can be found in [10].

The most common approach to hybrid systems is the initially proposed in [11, 4] in which an ANN is used to estimate jointly all the HMM state emission probabilities. Several types of neural networks have been used for this purpose: MLPs [4], RNNs [12] and even Radial Basis Function (RBF) networks [13].

Other approaches for speech recognition use Predictive Neural Networks, one per class, to predict a certain acoustic vector given a time window of observations centered in the current one [2], [3]. This way Predictive Neural Networks capture the temporal correlations between acoustic vectors.

Finally, in the hybrid ANN/HMM system proposed in [14], ANNs are trained to estimate phone posterior probabilities and these probabilities are used as feature vectors for a conventional GMM-HMM recognizer. This approach is called Tandem Acoustic Modeling and it achieves good results in context-independent systems.

Numerous studies show that hybrid systems achieve comparable recognition results than equivalent (with a similar number of parameters) HMM-based systems or even better in some tasks and conditions. Also, they present a better behavior when a little amount of training data is available. However, hybrid ANN/HMM have not been yet widely applied to speech recognition, very likely because some problems still remain open, for example: the design of optimal network architectures or the difficulty of designing a joint training scheme for both, ANNs and HMMs.

## 3   SVM Fundamentals

### 3.1   SVM Formulation

A SVM is essentially a binary nonlinear classifier capable of guessing whether an input vector $\mathbf{x}$ belongs to a class 1 (the desired output would be then $y = +1$) or to a class 2 ($y = -1$). This algorithm was first proposed in [15] in 1992, and it is a nonlinear version of a much older linear algorithm, the optimal hyperplane decision rule (also known as the generalized portrait algorithm), which was introduced in the sixties.

Given a set of separable data, the goal is to find the optimal decision function. It can be easily seen that there is an infinite number of optimal solutions for this problem, in the sense that they can separate the training samples with zero errors. However, since we look for a decision function able to generalize for unseen samples, we can think on an additional criterion to find the best solution among those with zero errors. If we knew the probability densities of the classes, we could apply the maximum a posteriori (MAP) criterion to find the optimal solution. Unfortunately, in most practical cases this information is not available, so we can adopt another simpler criteria: among those functions without training errors, we will choose that with the *maximum margin*, being this margin the distance between the closest sample and the decision boundary defined by that function. Of course, optimality in the sense of maximum margin does not imply necessarily optimality in the sense of minimizing the number of errors in test, but it is a simple criterion that yields to solutions which, in practice, turn out to be the best ones for many problems [16].

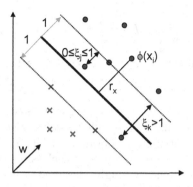

**Fig. 1.** Soft-margin decision

As can be inferred from the Figure 1, the nonlinear discriminant function $f(\mathbf{x}_i)$ can be written as:

$$f(\mathbf{x}_i) = \mathbf{w}^T \cdot \phi(\mathbf{x}_i) + b, \qquad (1)$$

where $\phi(\mathbf{x}_i) : \Re^n \mapsto \Re^{n'}$, $(n << n')$, is a nonlinear function which maps the vector $\mathbf{x}_i$ into what is called a *feature space* of higher dimensionality (possibly infinite) where classes are assumed to be linearly separable. The vector $\mathbf{w}$ represents the separating hyperplane in such a space. It is worth noting that the meaning of *feature space* here has nothing to do with the space of the speech features that within the kernel methods nomenclature belong to the *input space*.

On the other hand, $r_x$ is the distance between the transformed sample $\phi(\mathbf{x}_i)$ and the separating hyperplane, and $\| \mathbf{w} \|$ the Euclidean norm of $\mathbf{w}$. We call *support vectors* those closest to the decision boundary. These vectors define the margin and are the only samples that are needed to find the solution. Thus, we have that for every sample $\mathbf{x}_i$, $r_x = f(\mathbf{x}_i)/ \| \mathbf{w} \|$. Hence, the goal to find the optimum classifier is achieved by minimizing $\| \mathbf{w} \|$ with the restriction of all samples being correctly classified, i.e.:

$$y_i \left( \mathbf{w}^T \cdot \phi(\mathbf{x}_i) + b \right) \geq 1. \qquad (2)$$

This can be formulated as a problem of quadratic optimization:

$$\min_{\mathbf{w},b} \quad \frac{1}{2} \| \mathbf{w} \|^2,$$

$$\text{subject to} \quad y_i(\mathbf{w}^T \cdot \phi(\mathbf{x}_i) + b) \geq 1$$

In order to get a classifier with a better generalization ability and capable of handling the non-separable case, we should allow a number of misclassified data. This is accomplished by introducing a penalty term in the function to be minimized:

$$\min_{\mathbf{w},b,\xi_i} \quad L_P = \frac{1}{2} \parallel \mathbf{w} \parallel^2 + C \sum_{i=1}^{N} \xi_i,$$

$$\text{subject to} \quad y_i(\mathbf{w}^T \cdot \phi(\mathbf{x}_i) + b) \geq 1 - \xi_i,$$

$$\xi_i \geq 0, \text{ for } i = 1, \cdots, N, \tag{3}$$

where $\mathbf{x}_i \in \Re^n$ $(i = 1, \dots, N)$ are the training vectors corresponding to the labels $y_i \in \{\pm 1\}$, and the variables $\xi_i$ are called *slack variables* and allow a certain amount of errors that contribute to obtain solutions in the non-separable case. $\xi_i$ verifies $0 \leq \xi_i \leq 1$ for those samples well classified but inside the margin, and $\xi_i > 1$ for those samples wrongly classified. The $C$ term, on the other hand, expresses the trade-off between the number of training errors and the generalization capability.

This problem is usually solved introducing the restrictions in the function to be optimized using Lagrange multipliers, leading to the maximization of the Wolfe dual:

$$\max_{\alpha_i} \quad L_D = \sum_{i=1}^{n} \alpha_i - \frac{1}{2} \sum_{i=1}^{n} \sum_{j=1}^{n} y_i y_j \alpha_i \alpha_j \phi^T(\mathbf{x}_i)\phi(\mathbf{x}_j),$$

$$\text{subject to} \quad \sum_{i=1}^{n} \alpha_i y_i = 0 \text{ and } 0 \leq \alpha_i \leq C. \tag{4}$$

This problem is quadratic and convex, so its convergence to a global minimum is guaranteed using quadratic programming (QP) schemes. The resulting decision boundary $\mathbf{w}$ will be given by:

$$\mathbf{w} = \sum_{i=1}^{N} \alpha_i y_i \phi(\mathbf{x}_i). \tag{5}$$

According to (5), only vectors with an associated $\alpha_i \neq 0$ will contribute to determine the weight vector $\mathbf{w}$ and, therefore, the separating boundary. These are the support vectors that, as we have mentioned before, define the separation border and the margin.

Generally, the function $\phi(\mathbf{x})$ is not explicitly known (in fact, in most of the cases its evaluation would be impossible as long as the feature space dimensionality can be infinite). However, we do not actually need to know it, since we only need to evaluate the dot products $\phi^T(\mathbf{x}_i) \cdot \phi(\mathbf{x}_j)$ which, by using what has been called the *kernel trick*, can be evaluated using a kernel function $K(\mathbf{x}_i, \mathbf{x}_j)$. Many of the SVM implementations compute this function for every pair of input samples producing a *kernel matrix* that is stored in memory.

By using this method and replacing $\mathbf{w}$ in (1) by the expression in (5), the form that a SVM finally adopts is the following:

$$f(\mathbf{x}) = \sum_{i=1}^{N} \alpha_i y_i K(\mathbf{x}_i, \mathbf{x}) + b. \tag{6}$$

The most widely used kernel functions are:

- the simple *linear* kernel

$$K_L(\mathbf{x}_i, \mathbf{x}_j) = \mathbf{x}_i^T \cdot \mathbf{x}_j; \tag{7}$$

- the *radial basis function kernel* (RBF kernel),

$$K_{RBF}(\mathbf{x}_i, \mathbf{x}_j) = \exp\left(-\gamma \|\mathbf{x}_i - \mathbf{x}_j\|^2\right), \tag{8}$$

  where $\gamma$ is proportional to the inverse of the variance of the Gaussian function and whose associated feature space is of infinite dimensionality; and

- the polynomial kernel

$$K_P(\mathbf{x}_i, \mathbf{x}_j) = \left(1 + \mathbf{x}_i^T \cdot \mathbf{x}_j\right)^p, \tag{9}$$

  whose associated feature space are polynomials up to grade $p$, and

- the sigmoid kernel

$$K_{SIG}(\mathbf{x}_i, \mathbf{x}_j) = \tanh\left(a\mathbf{x}_i^T \cdot \mathbf{x}_j + b\right), \tag{10}$$

It is worth mentioning that there are some conditions that a function should accomplish to be used as a kernel. These are often denominated KKT (Karush-Kuhn-Tucker) conditions [17] and can be reduced to check the kernel matrix is symmetrical and positive semi-definite.

## 3.2 Pros and Cons of SVMs

The reason that makes SVMs more effective in many applications than other methods based on linear discriminants is its learning criterion. The goal of any classifier must be minimizing the number of misclassifications in any possible set of samples. This is known as Risk Minimization (RM). However, in typical classification problems we only have a limited number of samples available (in some cases we can have an unlimited number of samples but, anyway, we only can deal with a subset), and so, all we can do is trying to minimize the number of misclassifications within the training set. This is known as Empirical Risk Minimization (ERM), and most classifiers base their learning process on it.

However, having the classifier with the best ERM is not enough (or even desirable). The complexity of the classifiers normally must be fixed a priori, and so, we can choose a too simple structure unable to model correctly the classification boundaries of our problem, or a too complex one, overfitted to our training set and unable to generalize to unseen samples. This is known as Structural Risk, and a good classifier must maintain a compromise between the ERM and the SRM (Structural Risk Minimization).

In SVMs, we do not need to previously fix the complexity of the resultant machine, but there is a parameter (the $C$ in equation 3) which establishes this compromise between ERM and SRM. Unfortunately, there is no method to know a priori the most adequate value for this parameter, so we must find it by means of a search process.

Other advantages of SVMs are:

- They have a unique solution and its convergence is guaranteed (the solution is found by minimizing a convex function). This is an advantage compared to other classifiers as ANNs that often fall in local minima or does not converge to a stable version.
- The solution is that with maximum margin, what makes these machines robust and, in our opinion, very well suited for applications as ASR in noisy environments.
- Since in the minimization process only the kernel matrix is involved, they can deal with input vectors of very high dimensionality, as long as we are capable of calculating their corresponding kernels. In practice, they can deal with vectors of thousands of dimensions.

Among the disadvantages, we can highlight the following:

- Most implementations of SVM algorithm require to compute and store in memory the complete kernel matrix of all the input samples. This task have a space complexity $O(n^2)$, and is one of the main problems of these algorithms that prevent their application on very large speech databases. Most implementations allow us to work with some thousands of samples. However, some modifications of the algorithm are being developed which would allow us to work with millions of samples [18].
- The optimality of the solution found can depend on the kernel we have used, and there is not a method to know a priori which will be the best kernel for a concrete task. Although kernels as RBF are considered *universal*, it is still necessary to perform a grid-based search to fix all the parameters of the SVM.
- As we have mentioned, the best value for the parameter C is also unknown a priori.
- Like ANNs, the input vectors of an SVM with the formulation we have seen, must have a fixed size. This is a problem in speech recognition where each sequence to be recognized has a different duration. There are some solutions to this problem that we will discuss later.

However, despite these troubles, SVMs are attractive enough to be used in a variety of applications and, specifically, in speech recognition.

## 4   SVMs for ASR

As already discussed in the Introduction and in the previous section, SVMs are state-of-the-art tools for solving classification problems that seems to be very promising from the speech recognition perspective. They offer a discriminative solution to the pattern classification problem involved in ASR. Furthermore, the maximum margin SVM solution exhibits an excellent generalization capability, what might notably improve the robustness of ASR systems.

In fact, the improved discrimination ability of SVMs has attracted the attention of many speech technologists. Though this paper focuses on speech recognition, it is worth noticing that SVMs have already been employed in speaker identification [19] and verification [20], or to improve confidence measurements that can help in dialogue systems [21], among other applications.

However, its application to ASR is by no means straightforward. Here follows a review of the most important problems that has motivated the structure of the present section.

- *The variable time duration of the speech utterances*: The Automatic Speech Recognition involves the solution of a pattern classification problem. However, the variable time duration of the speech signals has prevented the ASR from being approached as a simple static classification problem. In fact, this has been for many decades one of the fundamental problems faced by the speech processing community and the main responsible for the success of the HMMs. The main problem stems from the fact that conventional kernels can only deal with (sequences of) vectors of fixed length. Standard parameterization techniques, on the other hand, generate variable length sequences of feature vectors depending on the time duration of each speech utterance.

  Different approaches have been proposed to deal with the variable time duration of the acoustic speech units. Basically, solutions can be divided into three groups: 1) the ones that aim at performing a previous dimensional (time) normalization to fit the SVM input; 2) those that explore string-related or normalizing kernels [5] to adapt the SVMs to make them able to use variable dimension vectors as inputs; and 3) those that avoid this problem by working in a framewise manner. As we will see later in section 4.2, the latter is specially well suited for continuous speech recognition while the first two are more appropriate for lower complexity tasks and will be addressed in section 4.1.

- *Multiclass SVMs*: ASR is a multiclass problem, whereas in the original formulation an SVM is a binary classifier. Although some of the proposed approaches to multiclass SVMs make a reformulation of the SVM equations to consider all classes at once, this option is very computationally expensive. A more usual approach to cope with this limitation involves combining a number of binary SVMs to achieve the multiclass classifier by means of a subsequent voting scheme. Two different versions of this method are usually considered. The first consists of comparing each class against all the rest (*1-vs-all*), while in the second each class is confronted against all the other classes separately (*1-vs-1*). Although the number of SVMs is greater for the *1-vs-1* approximation (namely, $\frac{k(k-1)}{2}$ vs. $k$ SVMs, with $k$ denoting the number of classes), the size of the training set needed for each SVM in the *1-vs-1* solution leads to a smaller computational effort with comparable accuracy rates [22].

- *The size of the databases*: most SVM implementations do not allow to deal with the huge databases typically used in medium- and high-complexity ASR task.

Having reviewed the fundamental challenges we now devote the next subsections to the exposition of the main solutions described in the literature, from the most simple tasks, such as isolated phonemes, letters or words recognition (low-complexity ASR tasks) to approaches to connected digits and continuous speech recognition (medium-complexity ASR tasks).

## 4.1  Isolated-Word Recognition

In this subsection we summarize some of the most relevant approaches to isolated unit (phonemes, letters or words) recognition by means of SVMs. We will distinguish between solutions that involve a preprocessing of the speech feature sequences and SVM-specific solutions capable of working with samples of variable dimensionality. The later are most of the times based on what is called *sequence kernels* that, in our opinion, show a great potential even for the their application to more complex task. Therefore, we will provide a more detailed overview of two instances of those kernels, namely, the DTAK and Fisher kernels.

### 4.1.1  Preprocessing of the Speech Feature Sequences

When dealing with this type of ASR tasks, the main problem of SVM-based approaches is the time normalization of the different utterances of the acoustic units (to get a fixed-dimension input space). On the other hand, the complexity of the SVM implementation (training or testing) is not a problem because the lexicon is usually quite limited.

Several authors use different variations of the the so-called *triphone model approach*. This model is motivated by the three-state HMMs used in most state-of-the-art speech recognition systems that amounts to assume that the speech segments (phones or triphones in most cases) can be decomposed into a fixed number of sections. The first and third sections model the transition into and out of the segment, whereas the second section models the stable portion. The main variants of this approach are summarized below:

- In [23] they show significant improvement in performance on a static pattern classification task based on the Deterding vowel data as well as on a continuous alphadigit one (OGI Alphadigits). The vector resulting from the concatenation of the three segments corresponding to the triphone model is augmented with the logarithm of the duration of the phone instance to explicitly model the variability in duration. The composite feature vectors are based on the alignments from a baseline three-state Gaussian-mixture HMM system. SVM classifiers are trained on these composite vectors, and recognition is also performed using these segment-level composite vectors. They have also used this model in a large vocabulary conversational speech task (Switchboard) as we will review in next subsection.
- In [24] they use SVMs for two different tasks, namely: Thai tone and Thai vowel recognition, using different feature length normalization procedures for each of them. The first one is Thai tone recognition in which they try to classify the five different lexical tones in that language: mid, low, falling,

high and rising. A fixed number of measures of the pitch evolution is chosen in this case. However for the classification of Thai vowels they also divide each vowel into three regions.

- In [25], the authors evaluate the performance of SVMs showing advantages when compared with GMM (Gaussian Mixture Models) in both vowel-only and phone classification tasks. It is worth noting that a significant difference is observed in the problem of length adaptation between these two tasks. In the vowel case, it is acknowledged that regardless of the duration of each utterance, the acoustic representations are almost constant. Therefore simple features as the formant frequencies or LPC coefficients corresponding to any time window are representative of the whole sequence. However, the representation of the variations taking place in non-vowel utterances is essential for obtaining an adequate input to SVMs. Thus, again the triphone model approach has been applied in this case, segmenting the number of frames obtained for each phone into three regions in the ratio 3-4-3 and subsequently averaging the features corresponding to the resulting regions.

- Similar distinctions have been observed in [26], where a comparison between the performance of classical HMMs and SVMs as sub-word units recognition is assessed for two different languages: 41 monophone units are classified in a Japanese corpus and 86 consonant-vowel units are considered for an Indian language. In this case, two different strategies have been devised to provide the SVMs with a fixed-length input: for the Japanese monophones, a similar technique to that proposed in [25] has been used. The frames comprising each monophone have been divided into a fixed number of segments. An averaged feature vector is then obtained for each segment. Each feature vector is subsequently concatenated to those resulting from other segments to form input vector for the SVM classifier. For the Indian consonant-vowel classification, however, a different approach has been designed to account for the variations of the acoustic characteristics of the signal during the consonant-vowel transition. In this case the fixed length patterns are obtained by linearly elongating or compressing the feature sequence duration. For both Indian and the previously mentioned Japanese tasks the SVMs have shown a better performance than HMMs with the standard MFCCs (Mel-Frequency Cepstral Coefficients) [27] plus energy and delta and acceleration coefficients.

In [28] several ways of preprocessing the speech sequence to obtain a fixed dimension vector are analyzed for a noisy digit recognition task. Two methods of sequence uniform resampling are assessed performing variations on the size of the analysis window and the frame period: a variable window size method that makes it possible to include the whole digit utterance for a given number of windows per digit by adjusting the size of the window to the digit duration, and a fixed window size one, that maintains the window size around a fixed number of analysis instants regardless of the coverage of the digit it does.

In [29] their primary goal is to solve the problem of the computational complexity of the SVM classical formulation by using an alternative Lagrangian one on the TIMIT database. Their feature representation uses the previously explained variable window size method using different window lengths based on the duration of the phoneme being classified. Therefore they concatenate 5 windows of the same size chosen from the set {32, 64, 128, 256, 400} covering the whole phoneme.

Another possible solution is showed in [28, 30, 31], where the non-uniform distribution of analysis instants provided by the internal states transitions of an HMM with a fixed number of states and a Viterbi decoder is used for dimensional normalization. The rationale behind this proposal is that the uniform resampling methods are produced without any consideration about the information (or lack of information) that speech analysis segments were providing. Selecting the utterance segments in which the signal is changing, it is hoped that a bigger amount of information is preserved in the feature vector.

Related to the previous approach, in [32] they acknowledge the fact that the classification error patterns from SVM and HMM classifiers can be different and thus their combination could result in a gain in performance. They assess this statement on a classification task of consonant-vowel units of speech in several Indian languages obtaining a marginal gain by using a sum rule combination scheme of the two classifiers evidences. As for feature length normalization they select segments of fixed duration around the vowel onset point, i.e., the instant at which the consonant ends and the vowel begins.

### 4.1.2    Isolated-Digit Recognition with DTAK-SVMs

This method was introduced in [33] and [34], and belongs to the family of methods based on *sequence kernels*, which try to solve the problem of different length sequences by adapting the kernel of the SVM to one capable of working with samples of variable dimensionality. This seems to be a more natural approach than performing a previous segmentation.

Summarizing, this technique uses as a kernel the score obtained by means of a Dynamic Time Warping (DTW) algorithm. DTW algorithms were one of the first techniques used in speech recognition and they were widely used in the 70s [35].

DTW measures the distance between a target signal and a template, expanding or contracting the temporal axis of the target to find the *path* or *warping function* which maximizes the similarity between the two signals (Figure 2). The distance of the signals is computed at each instant along the warping function, and the final score given by the algorithm is the accumulated similarity. Any metric can be used to compute this distance but usually the Euclidean is employed. In the case of DTAK, the inner product is used and therefore this distance can be interpreted as a linear kernel that is employed internally for the computation of the DTAK Kernel. With such an interpretation, it is now possible to substitute this distance metrics for the one provided by non-linear kernels such as RBF as we will introduce further on.

Specifically, for the computation of the linear kernel we use the following procedure: if $X$ and $Y$ are the two sequences of feature vectors to be compared, and $\psi_I(k)$ and $\psi_J(k)$ are warping functions which normalize the temporal axis

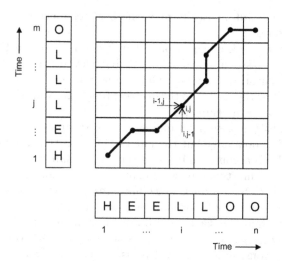

**Fig. 2.** Dynamic Time Warping

of the sequences in the instant k, we must find the solution to the new *inner product*:

$$K_{DTA}(X,Y) = X \circ Y = \max_{\psi_I,\psi_J} \frac{1}{M_\psi} \sum_{k=1}^{L} m(k) \mathbf{x}_{\psi_I(k)}^T \cdot \mathbf{y}_{\psi_J(k)},$$

$$\text{subject to } 1 \le \psi_I(k) \le \psi_I(k+1) \le |X|,$$
$$1 \le \psi_J(k) \le \psi_J(k+1) \le |Y|, \qquad (11)$$

where $|\cdot|$ denotes the length of the sequences, $M_\psi$ is a normalization factor which normally has the value $M_\psi = |X| + |Y|$, $L$ is a normalized length that can be either $|X|$, $|Y|$ or arbitrary positive integer, and $m(k)$ is a non negative scale factor which gives more importance to some particular "steps" in the "path".

This optimization problem is normally solved by means of *dynamic programming*, using the following recursive equation:

$$D(i,j) = \max \begin{cases} D(i-1,j) + \mathbf{x}_i^T \cdot \mathbf{y}_j, \\ D(i-1,j-1) + 2\mathbf{x}_i^T \cdot \mathbf{y}_j, \\ D(i,j-1) + \mathbf{x}_i^T \cdot \mathbf{y}_j. \end{cases} \qquad (12)$$

where the scale factor '2' favors translations along the diagonal, which should be the most probable ones. Therefore, the DTA Kernel gets reduced to,

$$K_{DTA}(X,Y) = X \circ Y = D(|X|,|Y|)/(|X| + |Y|) \qquad (13)$$

It is worth mentioning that in contrast with the classical template-based ASR solutions where the difficulty of finding an appropriate template was the main drawback that lead to the supremacy of the model based approaches like HMM, the DTAK solution automatically finds the best reference templates using the max-margin criterion.

Effectively, if we look at equation (5) in section 3, we see that only those templates with an associated $\alpha_i \neq 0$ will be relevant and will contribute to determine the separating boundary. Only a few templates will have a non-zero $\alpha_i$, and these will be the closest to the decision function. Now, the *support vectors* are *support sequences* or templates.

Furthermore, the algorithm not only selects those appropriate templates that define the decision boundary but the number of them that minimise the structural risk, and this is accomplish by giving an appropriate value to the parameter $C$ in equation (3). Unfortunately, we do not have a method to calculate the best value for this parameter *a priori*, so we must resort to cross-validation.

With the previous formulation it is now easy to consider the generalization that allows us to find the separating border in a higher dimension space (the feature space) by means of a non-linear kernel like an RBF. We have said that, basically, DTAK consists in using DTW as the kernel of an SVM. However, a generalization consisting in performing the time-warping in the feature space can be considered. In other words, in equation (11), we could use a kernel function (for example, an RBF) instead of a conventional dot product and the DTAK kernel would have the following form:

$$K_{sDTA}(X,Y)$$

$$= \phi(X) \circ \phi(Y) = \max_{\psi_I, \psi_J} \frac{1}{M_\psi} \sum_{k=1}^{L} m(k) K_{RBF}(\mathbf{x}_{\psi_I(k)}, \mathbf{y}_{\psi_J(k)}). \quad (14)$$

Now, we have to demonstrate that $K_{sDTA}$ fulfills the KKT conditions. As we mentioned in section 3, the only thing we have to prove is that $K_{sDTA}$ is symmetrical and positive semidefinite. The former is obvious, since the warping function is the same if we interchange the sequences $X$ and $Y$. Regarding the latter, we must demonstrate that:

$$\mathbf{u}^t \mathbf{K}_s \mathbf{u} \geq 0 \ \ \forall \mathbf{u}. \quad (15)$$

This is easily proved if we consider that DTW is the (weighted) sum of the inner products (kernels) of the vectors composing the sequences X and Y at the instants defined by the optimal warping function $\psi^*(k)$. That is (omitting the scale factors):

$$\mathbf{K}_s = \mathbf{K}_{(1)} + \cdots + \mathbf{K}_{(L)}, \quad (16)$$

where $\mathbf{K}_{(k)}$ is the kernel at the instant defined by $\psi^*(k)$. So,

$$\begin{aligned} \mathbf{u}^t \mathbf{K}_s \mathbf{u} &= \mathbf{u}^t (\mathbf{K}_{(1)} + \cdots + \mathbf{K}_{(L)}) \mathbf{u} \\ &= \mathbf{u}^t \mathbf{K}_{(1)} \mathbf{u} + \cdots + \mathbf{u}^t \mathbf{K}_{(L)} \mathbf{u} \\ &\geq 0, \end{aligned} \quad (17)$$

since $\mathbf{K}$ is a valid kernel and, therefore, positive semidefinite.

## Experimental Results

Results for the well-known SpeechDat-4000 database are presented in [31]. The whole database is not used: specifically, only the isolated-digit utterances are used for the experiments. The reported results depend on the noise level: on the one hand, the DTAK-based system achieves excellent performance, clearly superior to that achieved by the HMM-based system, for low SNRs; on the other hand, it incurs in some performance losses for high SNRs. The improvements due to DTAK (using either linear or RBF kernels) with respect to HMMs are statistically significant for white noise at 3, 6 and 9 dB and for F16-plane noise at 3 and 6 dB. On the contrary, the HMM-based system outperforms the DTAK-based one in clean conditions and several noisy cases at 12 dB. In the remaining conditions, which correspond to medium SNRs, the system performances do not exhibit statistically significant differences. Please refer to [31] for more details about the DTAK-based system and the experimental setup.

In summary, the reported results [31] show that SVMs exhibit a robust behaviour, as expected. In particular, the DTAK-based system turns out to be effective in noisy scenarios. In fact, the advantage due to the DTAK algorithm is higher as the noise conditions worsen. On the other hand, direct application of DTAK-based systems to continuous speech recognition is by no means straightforward, as the length of the sequences in eq. (13) must be known. In our opinion, some alternative segmentation techniques such as that proposed in [36], should be revisited to deal with this limitation.

### 4.1.3   Other Types of Sequence Kernels: The Fisher Kernels

DTAK is an instance of the so called *sequence kernels* that try to solve the problem of the different duration of the input sequences by looking for kernels capable of working with vectors of variable dimensionality. In this section we outline one of the most popular ones: the *Fisher kernel* and all its derivative family.

The Fisher kernel was first used in the biology field, in the context of DNA and protein sequence analysis [37], although there are also some interesting results in the field of speech recognition. Thus, in [38, 39, 40], this method is evaluated on a speaker-independent isolated letter task, outperforming the standard HMMs. Much more promising, however, are the results in speaker verification. In [41], the presented SVM system outperforms up to 34% the rates obtained with a GMM model.

The idea behind this method is to use as a kernel a score function computed by using the a posteriori probabilities of the observations obtained with a generative model (GMM, HMM...). Therefore the Fisher kernels takes advantage of the capability of the generative models to work with sequences of different lengths.

Let $P(X \mid \theta)$ be the a posteriori probability obtained with a generative model with parameters $\theta$. The set of all the $P(X \mid \theta)$ corresponding to all the different $\theta \in \Theta$ (being $\Theta$ the set of all possible parameters of the model), forms a Riemann manifold $M_\Theta$. In such a space, the inner product is given by $U_{X_i}^T F^{-1} U_{X_j}$, where $F = E_X \left[ U_X U_X^T \right]$ is the Fisher information matrix, and $U_X = \nabla_\theta \log P(X \mid \theta)$ is named the Fisher score .

Summarizing, the steps to calculate the Fisher kernel are:

- Get $P(X \mid \theta)$ from a generative model.
- Calculate $U_X = \nabla_\theta \log P(X \mid \theta)$. This can be quite complex but the steps to obtain this expression from an HMM are especified in [39].
- Calculate $F = E_X \left[ U_X U_X^T \right]$ (in some texts, this matrix is approximated by the identity, or by $\sigma^2 I$ therefore implying a conventional inner product and a Euclidean space).
- $K(X_i, X_j) = U_{X_i}^T F^{-1} U_{X_j}$.

It is easy to demonstrate that K is symmetrical and positive semi-definite and, hence, a kernel, since F fulfils those conditions.

In the same way that in the conventional kernels it is also possible to modify this kernel to obtain RBF or polynomial kernels. For example, the polynomial Fisher kernel would be:

$$\tilde{K} = (1 + K(X_i, X_j))^p \tag{18}$$

In [37] it is demonstrated that a discriminative classifier based on the Fisher kernel is at least so good as the Maximum A Posteriori (MAP) classifier of the generative model associated.

We can further generalize the Fisher kernel by substituting the logarithm and $\nabla$ operators of the score for other types of operations. For example a modification specially useful in speaker verification, employs the logarithm of the ratio between the a posteriori probabilities generated by two different models.

A final remark concerning both types of sequence kernels we have presented is that the support vectors they compute act as templates against which the incoming sequences are compared. For DTAK kernels these support vectors were particular sequences and here they are scores. This templates, however, are not the most representative instance of a class, as in the conventional template based pattern recognition but are the smaller set of vectors that we can combine to define the border between two classes.

However, the main problem that, thought they are capable of comparing different duration acoustic units, the boundaries of these units must be previously determined. This is their major drawback that prevents their application to continuous speech recognition.

## 4.2    Connected-Digit and Continuous Speech Recognition

Either connected-word recognition or continuous speech recognition are obviously more complex tasks than isolated-word recognition. In particular, the successful application of SVMs to more complex ASR tasks requires solving two additional problems. First, neither the time position of each word nor the number of words to be sought in the utterance are known. And second, the more complex it is the ASR task, the larger is the speech data base required for the design of the system; consequently, the size of the databases used in more complex tasks turns out to be huge compared to the maximum number of training samples that a SVM can deal with. Nevertheless, the very valuable characteristics of SVM classifiers have encouraged several authors to try to solve these problems.

As briefly mentioned in a previous section, some authors [42] have tried to overcome the problem of the variability of duration of speech utterances using HMMs to perform a time segmentation prior to classification. Other works cope with the variability of duration of speech utterances by embedding either an HMM [38] or a Dynamic Time Warping algorithm [33] in the kernel of the SVM. It is not easy, however, to apply these last two techniques to the problem of continuous speech because a previous word (or phoneme) segmentation of the utterance is still required. Another solution to overcome the mentioned difficulties is proposed in [43]. This method consists in classifying each frame of voice as belonging to a basic class (a phone) and using the Token Passing algorithm [44] to go from the classification of each frame to the word chain recognition. This is a similar approach to that presented in [45] by Cosi. The main difference is that Cosi uses Neural Networks (NNs) instead of SVMs.

In this section the approaches due to Ganapathiraju [42], who proposed a hybrid HMM/SVM system, and Padrell [43], who presented a pure SVM-based ASR system, are explained in detail.

Although it will not be described in this Chapter, it is worth to briefly mention a segmentation method for continuous speech presented in [46]. In particular, articulatory features are used to segment speech into broad manner classes using the probability-like outputs of SVMs to perform the classification every 5 ms over a 10 ms duration frame. They found that for this task, SVMs perform significantly better than HMM.

### 4.2.1  Hybrid HMM/SVM-Based Continuous Speech Recognition [42]

In this case the HMMs are used to generate phonetic level alignments that are treated individually by the SVM to perform phoneme identification. Since each segment will have a different duration, some method is needed to convert them to fixed length vectors. These methods were revised in 4.1. Here we illustrate with some more detail the method proposed in [42] for a continuous speech recognition task. These authors suggest dividing the segment into three regions according to a pre-established proportion; thus, the vectors of the parameterized signal can be split into three groups according to a distribution of 30%-40%-30%. Then the vectors into every region are averaged and finally concatenated as depicted in Figure 3.

### 4.2.2  SVM-Based Continuous Speech Recognition [43]

The hybrid HMM/SVM system previously described is not able to fully exploit the improved generalization capabilities of SVMs due to that SVMs are fed with a segmentation provided by the HMMs. Consequently, the the potential effectiveness of the SVMs is limited by the errors committed in the segmentation stage.

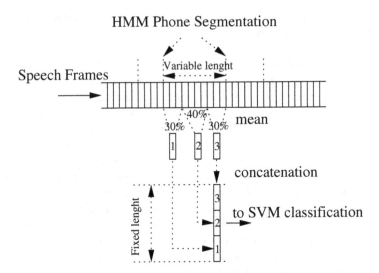

**Fig. 3.** Example of a vector construction for an HMM/SVMs hybrid system

The method suggested in [43] consists in classifying each frame of voice as belonging to a basic class (a phone). Following this approach the need to locate each word in time is avoided and its duration becomes unimportant. In order to go from the classification of each frame to the word chain recognition, The Token Passing algorithm [44] common in HMM-based speech recognition is used. LIBSVM [47] was the software chosen to train the SVMs. The reasons were the following: First, it implements the SMO algorithm [48] that allows a fast SVM training with a fairly high number of samples. And second, it provides an estimated probability value for each frame and candidate phone [49, 50], that will be described later. The main parts of this SVM-based ASR system are described in the following paragraphs.

**SVM-based frame by frame classification.** Many of the first articles dealing with speech recognition using SVMs mention the possibility of classifying the voice frames directly as a possible method to solve the problem of the variability of duration of speech utterances (different length of the input vectors in the SVM context). This approach was initially rejected because of its high computational cost. Let us make some coarse calculations to gain insight into the problem. Let us consider 31 phones to be identified (typical for Spanish), i.e., a classification problem of 32 classes (the silence is the additional one). If the considered task is a speaker-independent one, the training set should include a high number of speakers: let us consider 100 speakers, though it is a low number. In addition, in order to assure that the phones appear in several contexts and are enough to achieve statistical convergence, we should train with a few minutes of speech from each speaker, for example 10 minutes per speaker. This makes a total of 33.3 hours of voice.

If we divided them in frames (computed every 10ms), we would obtain a total of 12.000.000 frames or, in our case, training samples. If we take into account that, in a typical implementation, the entire matrix should be put in memory for training (and that a frame requires, for example, 156 bytes), we would need 1872 GBytes. Furthermore, the CPU time to solve the quadratic problem with so many points should also be considered. At first sight, it seems that this is not a feasible solution. Nevertheless, it is worthwhile to study if the solution is good and, if it was, to worry later about the memory consumption and the computational cost.

In [43] the SVMs are used on a frame by frame basis in order to determine which class (phone) every frame belongs to. They use as many classes as phones. In particular, for Spanish digits there are 17 phones plus the silence, i.e., every individual voice frame is classified as belonging to one of the 18 classes.

**Probability estimations.** The SVMs only classify, but they do not give us a reliable measure of the probability of the correctness of the classification. Several ways to estimate this probability can be found in the literature. All of them are based on some kind of mapping between the distances provided by the SVM and the sought probability. The approach followed by LIBSVM considers the actual distances as a measure of "probability". Thus, the posterior probability $S_i(x)$ that a vector $x$ belongs to class $i$ is calculated as

$$S_i(x) = \sum_{\forall j \neq i} f_{ij}(x), \tag{19}$$

where $f_{ij}(x)$ is the distance between the vector $x$ and the hyperplane used to classify between class $i$ and class $j$. This estimation can be improved using a softmax function as follows:

$$\hat{S}_i(x) = \frac{\exp(S_i(x)/k)}{\sum_j \exp(S_j(x)/k)}, \tag{20}$$

where $k$ is a constant to avoid the function saturation towards 1 or 0.

A more elaborated method makes the assumption that the probability follows a sigmoid function, whose parameters are estimated from the training samples. Thus, the probability $p_i$ that $x$ belongs to class $i$ considering classes $i$ and $j$ can be written as follows [49]:

$$p_i(x) = \frac{1}{1 + \exp(A_{ij} f_{ij}(x) + B_{ij})}, \tag{21}$$

$$p_j(x) = 1 - p_i(x), \tag{22}$$

where in order to avoid severe bias towards the training data, the free parameters, $A_{ij}$ and $B_{ij}$ are estimated on a cross-validation set.

Finally, the conversion of this two-class probability $p_{ij}$ to a multiclass probability $P_i$ is obtained by means of a variation of the Refregier and Vallet method [50].

**The Token Passing algorithm** [44] transforms a stream of acoustic classifications to a stream of recognized words. Its input is a matrix of probabilities: one row per phone (or subword unit) and one column per frame.

The Token Passing algorithm is an extension of the Viterbi algorithm typically used in continuous speech recognition devised to manage the uncertainty about the number of words in a sentence. Figure 4 illustrates the use of this algorithm for a very simple grammar which allows any concatenation of two Spanish words: "uno" and "tres". Classes are represented by circles, while word-ends are represented by squares. Two columns of circles are shown corresponding to two consecutive frames, $i$ and $j$. The possible transitions allowed by this grammar and explored by the Viterbi algorithm are represented either by solid or dashed lines (the mean of the line types is explained later). Each circle and transition could have an associate cost or probability. Every Viterbi node (circle) has an associated structure called *Token*. Each token stores the accumulated cost of reaching the corresponding node.

The *Token* not only stores the accumulated cost but also a *Link* to the last recognized word. The *Link* is only modified when the algorithm passes through word-ends (squares in Figure 4). The transitions among classes that

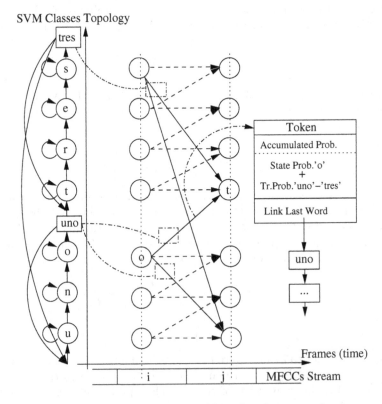

**Fig. 4.** An illustration of the Token Passing Algorithm for a very simple grammar

modify this *Link* are represented by solid-lines, while those that do not modify it are represented by dashed-lines. Proceeding as usually in the Viterbi algorithm, only the path leading to the highest probability for every node is kept.

When the Viterbi algorithm has explored all the frames, the *Token* with a higher accumulated probability is chosen and its *Link* to the (sequence of) word-ends provides us the sequence of recognized words.

**The number of training samples** that the system is able to use becomes a practical problem for the SVM system, for both training and testing. In the training process, typically, all the Kernels (or a high percentage of them) should be allocated in the computer memory. This limits the number of training samples in function of the available memory. A large training set also implies a high computational cost from the classification (test) point of view, since the number of Support Vectors (SV) increases linearly with the number of training samples.

**The Multiclass problem.** In order to solve it, the $1 - vs - 1$ approach is used. This method allows to train all the system using a maximum number of different samples for each class, and to keep limited the use of computer memory. For 18 classes, this method implies to train and use $\frac{18 \cdot (18-1)}{2} = 153$ SVMs, where each SVM classifies each frame between two of the possible phones, deciding the winning class by voting.

**The definition of classes.** When each class is a phone the time variation typically exhibited by actual phones is not taken into account. Some time variation can be embedded through the delta parameters, but better solutions should be considered; for example: either extending the time-window covered by the parameterization (for example, considering for each time instant the concatenation of two or three consecutive features vectors) or changing the definition of classes considered to deal with parts of phones.

The last alternative has been chosen because it helps to deal with another SVM-related problem: the practical limitation of the number of samples for training a single SVM. Increasing the number of classes and maintaining constant the number of samples used to train each SVM, the total number of samples used to train the whole system is effectively increased. The natural choice consists in defining a class for the beginning of the phone, a class for the center of the phone, and finally, a class for the end of the phone. This new approach transforms the 18 initial classes into $18 \cdot 3 = 54$. Therefore, the number of SVM classifiers to perform the $1 - vs - 1$ multiclass implementation moves from 153 to 1431.

To use these new classes, an allowed-transition matrix should be included to actually constrain the class transitions allowed during the Viterbi-based exploration. Furthermore a probability-transition matrix can be used instead of the previously mentioned allowed-transition matrix. The transition probabilities, $a_{ij}$, can be estimated from the number of transitions from $i$ to $j$ occurring when considering the samples in the available training set.

**The results** using this approach shows that SVMs can become a competitive alternative to HMMs in continuous speech recognition [43]. With a very small

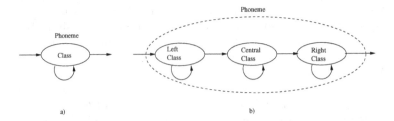

**Fig. 5.** a) Identifying an SVM class per phone; b) Identifying an SVM class as a part of a phone: three SVM classes per phone

database, 100 utterances, SVMs improve the recognition accuracy of HMMs. Furthermore, they also achieve a similar performance with a large database (100 hours), although at the expense of a huge computational effort. This last result is very encouraging since, due to current training limitations, the SVM-based system only uses the 1.5% of the training database used by HMM-based one.

## 5    Conclusions and Further Work

In this Chapter we have reviewed the research work dealing with SVMs for ASR. We have started by reviewing the reasons reported in the literature to support the use of SVMs for ASR. Thus, we have explained the characteristics of SVMs that make them valuable from the ASR point of view: first, SVMs are discriminative models, thus more appropriate for classification problems; second, as opposed to ANNs, they have the advantage of being capable to deal with samples of a very higher dimensionality; and third, they exhibit an excellent generalization ability that makes them especially suitable to deal with noisy speech.

After motivating the theme of research, we have described the problems that the attempt to use SVMs in this context has arisen: first, SVMs were originally formulated to process fixed-dimension input vectors and consequently it is not straightforward to manage the speech time variability; second, the SVMs were formerly devised as binary classifiers while the ASR problem is multiclass; and third current SVM training algorithms are not able to manage the huge databases typically used in ASR.

The larger Section of the Chapter is dedicated to present an overview of the solutions that have been proposed to the previously mentioned problems. The exposition have been organized into two subsections, depending of the complexity of the tackled ASR tasks: low- and medium-complexity ASR tasks.

Within the low-complexity tasks subsection, the most relevant alternatives to overcome the problem of speech time variability have been described, highlighting the one based on DTAK-SVMs, that is a genuine SVM-based system able to manage the variable input dimension. The experimental results reveal that the

DTAK clearly outperforms the HMM-based system in moderate to highly noisy environments. In conclusion, we believe that SVMs should be considered as a promising paradigm for the development of robust speech recognition systems. The maximum margin solution provided by SVMs, responsible for their good generalization properties, can be successfully applied to the speech recognition problem.

On the other hand, however, DTAK-SVMs incurs in some performance losses for clean speech or high SNRs. The improvement of the DTAK results for high SNRs remains an open problem for future research: some analysis should be done to gain more insight into the behavior of the DTAK algorithm.

In contrast to low-complexity tasks, the research work is still incipient in the case of medium-complexity ASR tasks. However, the results reported in [43] allow to conclude that the SVMs can be an alternative to the HMMs in continuous speech recognition. On the hand, with a very small database (100 utterances) the SVMs improve the recognition accuracy of HMMs. In addition, similar results are achieved for a large database (100 hours), although at the expense of a huge computational effort. This last result is encouraging since, due to current limitations, the SVM-based system only has used the 1.5% of the training database used by HMM-based one.

There are several proposals to overcome the current difficulties that SVM's algorithms have for handling effectively very large databases [51, 52, 18, 53]. Mega-GSVCs [53], for example, are capable of training classifiers with millions of data while keeping under control the complexity of the resulting machines.

Another way to raise the number of frames that can be used for training is to increase the number of considered classes. For example, different classes could be defined for different phonetic contexts.

Finally, in order to reduce the CPU time consumed in classification, a technique like FC-GSVC [54] or some type of Viterbi pruning could be used.

## Acknowledgement

This work has been partially supported by the regional grant (Comunidad Autónoma de Madrid-UC3M) UC3M-TEC-05-059.

## References

[1] H. Sakoe, R. Isotani, K. Yoshida, K. Iso, and T. Watanabe. Speaker-Independent Word Recognition using Dynamic Programming Neural Networks. In *Proceedings of the International Conference on Acoustics, Speech and Signal Processing (ICASSP)*, pages 439 – 442, Glasgow, Scotland, 1989.

[2] K. Iso and T. Watanabe. Speaker-Independent Word Recognition using a Neural Prediction Model. In *Proceedings of the International Conference on Acoustics, Speech and Signal Processing (ICASSP)*, pages 441–444, Alburquerque, New Mexico (USA), 1990.

[3] J. Tebelskis, A. Waibel, B. Petek, and O. Schmidbauer. Continuous Speech Recognition using Predictive Neural Networks. In *Proceedings of the International Conference on Acoustics, Speech and Signal Processing (ICASSP)*, pages 61–64, Toronto, Canada, 1991.

[4] H. Bourlard and N. Morgan. *Connectionist speech recognition: a hybrid approach.* Boston: Kluwer Academic, Norwell, MA (USA), 1994.

[5] B. Schlkopf and A. Smola. *Learning with kernels.* MIT Press, Cambridge, MA (USA), 2002.

[6] V. Vapnik. *Statistical Learning Theory.* Wiley, Chichester, GB, 1998.

[7] V. Vapnik. *The Nature of Statistical Learning Theory.* Springer Verlag, New York, 1995.

[8] A. Waibel, T. Hanazawa, G. Hinton, K. Shikano, and K. Lang. Phoneme recognition using time-delay neural networks. *IEEE Transactions on Acoustics, Speech and Signal Processing*, 37:328–339, 1989.

[9] T. Robinson and F. Fallside. A recurrent error propagation network speech recognition system. *Computer, Speech and Language*, 5:259–274, 1991.

[10] E. Trentin and M. Gori. A survey of hybrid ann/hmm models for automatic speech recognition. *Neurocomputing*, 37:91–126, 2001.

[11] H. Bourlard and N. Morgan. Continuous speech recognition by connectionist statistical methods. *IEEE Transactions on Neural Networks*, 4:893–909, 1993.

[12] T. Robinson, M. Hochberg, and S. Renals. *Automatic Speech and Speaker Recognition - Advanced Topics*, chapter The Use of Recurrent Neural Networks in Continuous Speech Recognition (Chapter 19), pages 159–184. Kluwer Academic Publishers, Norwell, MA (USA), 1995.

[13] W. Reichl and G. Ruske. A hybrid rbf-hmm system for continuous speech recognition. In *Proceedings of the International Conference on Acoustics, Speech and Signal Processing (ICASSP)*, pages 3335–3338, Detroit, MI (USA), 1995.

[14] D. Ellis, R. Singh, and S. Sivadas. Tandem-acoustic modeling in large-vocabulary recognition. In *Proceedings of the International Conference on Acoustics, Speech and Signal Processing (ICASSP)*, pages 517–520, Salt Lake City, Utah (USA), 2001.

[15] B.E. Boser, I. Guyon, and V. Vapnik. A training algorithm for optimal margin classifiers. In *Computational Learning Theory*, pages 144–152, 1992.

[16] F. Pérez-Cruz and O. Bousquet. Kernel Methods and Their Potential Use in Signal Processing. *IEEE Signal Processing Magazine*, 21(3):57–65, 2004.

[17] R. Fletcher. *Practical Methods of Optimization.* Wiley-Interscience, New York, NY (USA), 1987.

[18] A. Navia-Vázquez, F. Pérez-Cruz, A. Artés-Rodríguez, and A.R. Figueiras-Vidal. Weighted Least Squares Training of Support Vector Classifiers leading to Compact and Adaptive Schemes. *IEEE Transactions on Neural Networks*, 12(5):1047–1059, 2001.

[19] S. Fine, J. Navratil, and R.A. Gopinath. A hybrid gmm/svm approach to speaker identification. In *Proceedings of the International Conference on Acoustics, Speech and Signal Processing (ICASSP)*, volume 1, pages 417–420, Salt Lake City, Utah (USA), 2001.

[20] Q. Le and S. Bengio. Client Dependent GMM-SVM Models for Speaker Verification. In *International Conference on Artificial Neural Networks, ICANN/ICONIP,Springer-Verlag*, pages 443–451, 2003.

[21] C. Ma, M.A. Randolph, and J. Drish. A support vector machines-based rejection technique for speech recognition. In *Proceedings of the International Conference on Acoustics, Speech and Signal Processing (ICASSP)*, volume 1, pages 381–384, Salt Lake City, Utah (USA), 2001.

[22] C.W. Hsu and C.J. Lin. A Comparison of Methods for Multi-class Support Vector Machines. *IEEE Transactions on Neural Networks*, 13(2):415–425, 2002.

[23] A. Ganapathiraju, J.E. Hamaker, and J. Picone. Applications of support vector machines to speech recognition. *IEEE Transactions on Signal Processing*, 52:2348–2355, 2004.

[24] N. Thubthong and B. Kijsirikul. Support vector machines for thai phoneme recognition. *International Journal of Uncertainty, Fuzziness and Knowledge-Based Systems*, 9:803–13, 2001.

[25] P. Clarkson and P.J. Moreno. On the use of support vector machines for phonetic classification. In *IEEE International Conference on Acoustics, Speech and Signal Processing (ICASSP)*, volume 2, pages 585–588, Phoenix, Arizona (USA), 1999.

[26] C. Sekhar, W.F. Lee, K. Takeda, and F. Itakura. Acoustic modelling of subword units using support vector machines. In *Workshop on spoken language processing*, Mumbai, India, 2003.

[27] S. Young. *HTK-Hidden Markov Model Toolkit (ver 2.1)*. Cambridge University, 1995.

[28] J.M. García-Cabellos, C. Peláez-Moreno, A. Gallardo-Antolín, F. Pérez-Cruz, and F. Díaz-de-María. SVM Classifiers for ASR: A Discusion about Parameterization. In *Proceedings of EUSIPCO 2004*, pages 2067–2070, Wien, Austria, 2004.

[29] A. Ech-Cherif, M. Kohili, A. Benyettou, and M. Benyettou. Lagrangian support vector machines for phoneme classification. In *Proceedings of the 9th International Conference on Neural Information Processing (ICONIP '02)*, volume 5, pages 2507–2511, Singapore, 2002.

[30] D. Martín-Iglesias, J. Bernal-Chaves, C. Peláez-Moreno, A. Gallardo-Antolín, and F. Díaz-de-María. *Nonlinear Analyses and Algorithms for Speech Processing*, volume LNAI 3817 of *Lecture Notes in Computer Science*, chapter A Speech Recognizer based on Multiclass SVMs with HMM-Guided Segmentation, pages 256–266. Springer, 2005.

[31] R. Solera-Ureña, D. Martín-Iglesias, A. Gallardo-Antolín, C. Peláez-Moreno, and F. Díaz-de-María. Robust ASR using Support Vector Machines. *Speech Communication, Elsevier (submitted)*, 2006.

[32] S.V. Gangashetty, C. Sekhar, and B. Yegnanarayana. Combining evidence from multiple classifiers for recognition of consonant-vowel units of speech in multiple languages. In *Proceedings of the International Conference on Intelligent Sensing and Information Processing*, pages 387–391, Chennai, India, 2005.

[33] H. Shimodaira, K.I. Noma, M. Nakai, and S. Sagayama. Support vector machine with dynamic time-alignment kernel for speech recognition. In *Proceedings of Eurospeech*, pages 1841–1844, Aalborg, Denmark, 2001.

[34] H. Shimodaira, K. Noma, and M. Nakai. *Advances in Neural Information Processing Systems 14*, volume 2, chapter Dynamic Time-Alignment Kernel in Support Vector Machine, pages 921–928. MIT Press, Cambridge, MA (USA), 2002.

[35] L. R. Rabiner, A.E. Rosenberg, and S.E. Levinson. Considerations in Dynamic Time Warping Algorithms for Discrete Word Recognition. *IEEE Transactions on Acoustics, Speech and Signal Processing*, 26(6):575–582, 1978.

[36] J. R. Glass. A probabilistic framework for segment-based speech recognition. *Computer Speech and Language*, 17:137–152, 2003.

[37] T. Jaakkola and D. Haussler. Exploiting generative models in discriminative classifiers. Technical report, Dept. of Computer Science, Univ. of California, 1998.

[38] N.D. Smith and M.J.F. Gales. Using SVMs and discriminative models for speech recognition. In *IEEE International Conference on Acoustics, Speech and Signal Processing (ICASSP)*, volume 1, pages 77–80, Orlando, Florida (USA), 2002.

[39] N.D. Smith and M.J.F. Gales. *Advances in Neural Information Processing Systems 14*, volume 14, chapter Speech recognition using SVMs, pages 1197–1204. MIT Press, Cambridge, MA (USA), 2002.

[40] N.D. Smith and M. Niranjan. Data-dependent Kernels in SVM Classification of Speech Patterns. In *Proceedings of the International Conference on Spoken Language Processing (ICSLP)*, volume 1, pages 297–300, Beijing, China, 2000.

[41] V. Wan and S. Renals. Speaker verification using sequence discriminant support vector machines. *IEEE Transactions on Speech and Audio Processing*, 13:203–210, 2005.

[42] A. Ganapathiraju, J. Hamaker, and J. Picone. Hybrid SVM/HMM Architectures for Speech Recognition. In *Proceedings of the 2000 Speech Transcription Workshop*, volume 4, pages 504–507, Maryland (USA), May 2000.

[43] J. Padrell-Sendra, D. Martín-Iglesias, and F. Díaz-de-María. Support vector machines for continuous speech recognition. In *Proceedings of the 14th European Signal Processing Conference*, Florence, Italy, 2006.

[44] S. J. Young, N. H. Russell, and J. H. S. Thornton. Token Passing: a Conceptual Model for Connected Speech Recognition Systems. Technical report, CUED Cambridge University, 1989.

[45] Piero Cosi. Hybrid HMM-NN architectures for connected digit recognition. In *Proceedings of the International Joint Conference on Neural Networks*, volume 5, pages 85–90, 2000.

[46] A. Juneja and C. Espy-Wilson. Segmentation of continuous speech using acoustic-phonetic parameters and statistical learning. In *Proceedings of the 9th International Conference on Neural Information Processing, (ICONIP '02)*, volume 2, pages 726–730, 2002.

[47] Ch. Chih-Chung and L. Chih-Jen. *LIBSVM: a library for support vector machines*, 2004.

[48] J. C. Platt. *Advances in Kernel Methods: Support Vector Learning*, chapter Fast Training of Support Vector Machines Using Sequential Minimal Optimization, pages 185–208. MIT Press, Cambridge, MA (USA), 1999.

[49] J. C. Platt. *Advances in Large Margin Classifiers*, chapter Probabilities for SV Machines, pages 61–74. MIT Press, 1999.

[50] T. F. Wu, C. J. Lin, and R. C. Weng. Probability estimates for multi-class classification by pairwise coupling. *The Journal of Machine Learning Research*, 5:975–1005, 2004.

[51] C.J.C. Burges. Simplified support vector decision rules. In *Proceedings of the Thirteenth International Conference on Machine Learning*, pages 71–77, Bari, Italy, 1996.

[52] E. Osuna, R. Freund, and F. Girosi. An improved training algorithm for support vector machines. In *IEEE Workshop on Neural Networks for Signal Processing*, pages 276–285, Amelia Island, Florida (USA), 1997.

[53] D. Gutiérrez, E. Parrado, and A. Navia. Mega-GSVC: Training SVMs with Millions of Data. In *Proceedings of the Learning'04 International Conference*, 2004.

[54] E. Parrado, J. Arenas, I. Mora, A. Figueiras, and A. Navia. Growing Support Vector Classifiers with Controlled Complexity. *Pattern Recognition*, 36:1479–1488, 2003.

# Nonlinear Speech Enhancement: An Overview

A. Hussain[1], M. Chetouani[2], S. Squartini[3], A. Bastari[3], and F. Piazza[3]

[1] Department of Computing Science & Mathematics, University of Stirling, Stirling FK9 4LA,
Scotland, UK
[2] Laboratoire des Instruments et Systemes d'Ile-De-France Université Paris Pierre and Marie
Curie, 4 Place Jussieu, 75252 Paris Cedex 05, France
[3] Dipartimento di Elettronica, Intelligenza Artificiale e Telecomunicazioni Università
Politecnica delle Marche Via Brecce Bianche 12, I-60121 Ancona, Italy
`ahu@cs.stir.ac.uk`, `mohamed.chetouani@upmc.fr`,
`sts@deit.univpm.it`, `a.bastari@univpm.it`, `upf@deit.univpm.it`

**Abstract.** This paper deals with the problem of enhancing the quality of speech signals, which has received growing attention in the last few decades. Many different approaches have been proposed in the literature under various configurations and operating hypotheses. The aim of this paper is to give an overview of the main classes of noise reduction algorithms proposed to-date, focusing on the case of additive independent noise. In this context, we first distinguish between single and multi channel solutions, with the former generally shown to be based on statistical estimation of the involved signals whereas the latter usually employ adaptive procedures (as in the classical adaptive noise cancellation scheme). Within these two general classes, we distinguish between certain sub-families of algorithms. Subsequently, the impact of nonlinearity on the speech enhancement problem is highlighted: the lack of perfect linearity in related processes and the non-Gaussian nature of the involved signals are shown to have motivated several researchers to propose a range of efficient nonlinear techniques for speech enhancement. Finally, the paper summarizes (in tabular form) for comparative purposes, the general features, list of operating assumptions, the relative advantages and drawbacks, and the various types of nonlinear techniques for each class of speech enhancement strategy.

**Keywords:** Single-channel/Multi-channel Speech Enhancement, Noise Reduction, Noise Cancellation, Microphone array, Non-linear techniques.

## 1 Introduction

The goal of speech enhancement systems is either to improve the perceived quality of the speech, or to increase its intelligibility [1-3]. There is a large variety of real world applications for speech enhancement in audio signal processing – for example, we experience the presence of degraded speech both in military and commercial communications, induced by different transmission channels (telephony) or produced in various noisy environments (vehicles, home-office etc.). Due to the growing interest in this subject, numerous efforts have been made over the past 20 years or so by the scientific community in order to find an effective solution for the speech enhancement problem. The different nature of interfering sounds, the admissible assumptions on the generating process of speech degradation and on the available observables, and the

Y. Stylianou, M. Faundez-Zanuy, A. Esposito (Eds.): WNSP 2005, LNCS 4391, pp. 217–248, 2007.

various operating conditions involved require us to make a preliminary distinction between the various speech enhancement approaches proposed to-date.

The principal aim of this work is to give an overview and a preliminary comparison of the main up to date techniques found in the literature for the noise reduction problem, focusing on non-linear techniques in particular. However, wherever required, some linear techniques are also outlined in order to better introduce certain non-linear extensions of interest. Because of the huge amount and diverse range of works reported in this field, we only introduce certain families of algorithms, considering the case when the noise is additive and independent of the clean speech. Note that speech de-reverberation and separation case studies, which can also be classified as speech enhancement problems, are not addressed here. The mathematics behind the reviewed methods is also omitted for lack of space, only the main formulae being introduced. Experimental numerical results and direct comparisons of the different introduced techniques are avoided firstly, because standard benchmark data have not been proposed or used in the literature, and secondly because the various reported methods all make use of different and individually optimized operating assumptions. Instead, the main details of the important reviewed methods will be summarized and compared in tabular form at the end of this paper.

Initially, we make a rough distinction between the different techniques by considering the number of available noisy speech channels: in the next paragraphs of this Section, the single channel speech enhancement problem and the multi channel speech enhancement problem are introduced; Section II further discusses the main nonlinear approaches developed for the monaural speech enhancement problem including supervised and unsupervised neural network based techniques. Section III addresses the two-channel/binaural speech enhancement case. Section IV reviews the general multi-channel non-linear speech enhancement case and finally, Section V presents the concluding summary by highlighting the main features, list of operating assumptions, the relative advantages and drawbacks and the various types of non-linear techniques for each class of speech enhancement strategy reviewed in this paper.

## 1.1  Basic Concepts

The degradation of the speech signal can be modeled, in a quite general manner, as follows:

$$y[k] = h[k] * s[k] + n[k] = s^h[k] + n[k] \tag{1}$$

where $s^h$ is the observed degraded speech, $s$ is the original signal to be recovered, and $n$ is the additive noise, $h[k]$ is the impulse response of the room where the sensor is placed and $*$ represents the convolution operator. Obviously, one can think of other types of degradation models that require specific enhancing methods. For the most part of this work, the convolutive term is not considered ($h[k] = \delta[k]$), with only the additive term $n[k]$ considered present. In addition, we shall consider background noise as interference in our studies, and the cases of speech separation (cocktail party problem), impulse or transient noises [1] will not be dealt with here due to space restrictions.

A first rough distinction between speech enhancement techniques can be made by looking at the number and type of observables available for:

1. single channel speech enhancement: where only one degraded version of the original speech is available and modeled by (1);
2. multi-channel speech enhancement: where the noisy observations are obtained from two or more sensors.

In conventional approaches [4], speech and noise signals are considered as unknown random processes and the objective is to perform an adequate statistical estimation of one random process (the speech signal) from the sum of speech and the noise. Such a task is hard because we have neither a precise statistical model of the signals nor a reliable measure to evaluate the effectiveness of the enhancement process. Moreover the non-stationarity of speech (and possibly of noise as well) [5] requires tracking of its time-varying statistical properties by means of adaptive solutions. Next, we present an overview of single-channel and multi-channel speech enhancement problems, followed by their non-linear extensions.

## 1.2 Brief Overview of the Single-Channel Speech Enhancement Problem

Spectral Subtraction (SS) [6] is probably the earliest and most well-known technique for single channel speech enhancement: it is often still used due to its efficacy and simplicity. In its most basic form (involving subtraction/filtering of power spectral density/amplitudes), the noise power spectral density is estimated, but the method introduces musical noise and other distortions in the recovered signal [1],[3]. Some interesting solutions involving nonlinear techniques have been proposed in the literature to overcome such drawbacks [1], [7]. However, as widely agreed, the best algorithm from this perspective is the one proposed by Ephraim and Malah [8-10] that is closely related to the pioneering work of McAulay and Malpass [11]. This is based on the minimum mean square error (MMSE) estimation of the speech spectrum in the logarithmic domain; and it is a natural extension of the one in the linear domain [8]. Further improvements have been achieved through the employment of better performing MMSE estimators, as in Xie and Compernolle [12], or by making the spectral subtraction procedure dependent on the properties of the human auditory system [13].

Another interesting derivative of SS is the signal subspace approach [14], [15] based on an estimation of the clean speech, as also done in the case of the Bayesian approach for speech enhancement using Hidden Markov Models (HMM) [16], [17]. Since this approach in its basic form is essentially linear and thus out of the intent of this work, it is not described in the following. HMM have also been successfully implemented in nonlinear estimation frameworks [18], [19] where some speech data is assumed available for training. Other methods relying on the availability of a suitable training set have also been developed. Among these, we can cite the time domain and transform domain nonlinear filtering methods employing neural networks [20-26].

On the other hand, unsupervised single-channel speech enhancement techniques have received significant attention recently. Examples here include the Extended Kalman Filtering [15] [27-28] Monte-Carlo simulations [4], Particle filtering [4], [21], [30] and the Noise-Regularized Adaptive Filtering [15], [31] approaches, that can enable significant noise reduction even in difficult situations (involving noise non-gaussianity or system nonlinearity).

### 1.3  Brief Overview of the Multi-channel Speech Enhancement Problem

The multi-channel speech enhancement problem can be modelled as follows [1]:

$$y_m[k] = h_m[k] * s[k] + n_m[k] = s_m^h[k] + n_m[k] \qquad (2)$$

where $m$ is the sensor index. When $m = 2$ we refer to the so called binaural case if the spacing between the microphones is comparable to that between human's ears.

In the last years the scientific community has particularly focused its attention on multichannel techniques, as they virtually provide remarkable outcomes on the single channel ones. As highlighted in some recent works [3], using a single channel it is not possible to improve both intelligibility and quality of the recovered signal at the same time. Quality can be improved at the expense of sacrificing intelligibility. A way to overcome this limitation is to add some spatial information to the time/frequency information available in the single channel case. We can get this additional information using two or more channel of noisy speech.

Adaptive noise cancellation [32-33] can be viewed as a particular case of the multi-channel speech enhancement problem. Indeed, we have two observables, the noisy speech and the reference noise, and the goal is to get an enhanced output speech adaptively according to the scheme in Fig.1. Classical methods based on full-band multi-microphone noise cancellation implementations can produce excellent results in anechoic environments with localized sound radiators, however performance deteriorates in reverberant environments. Adaptive sub-band processing has been found to overcome these limitations [34]. The idea of involving sub-band diverse processing to take account of the coherence between noise signals from multiple sensors has been implemented as part of the so-called Multi-Microphone Sub-Band Adaptive (MMSBA) speech enhancement system [35-38].

The main limitation of these linear approaches is that they are not able to deal effectively with non-gaussianity of the involved signals or the non-linear distortions arising from the electro-acoustic transmission systems. As a result, several nonlinear approaches have been proposed to-date mainly employing Neural Networks (NN) and Volterra Filtering (VF), see for example,[39-42], [25]. Such non-linear processing approaches have also been successfully implemented within the MMSBA architecture, as will be highlighted later on.

If available, more than two microphones (resulting in a microphone array) can be used in order to achieve better performance for noise reduction. The most common approaches here are represented by the delay-and-sum array and the adaptive beamformer [43]. Among the large variety of linear approaches that have appeared in the literature so far for speech enhancement, some nonlinear microphone arrays have also been proposed [44-46], which seem to exhibit relevant performance improvements with respect to their linear counterparts. Another interesting nonlinear approach in the microphone array area is represented by the idea of estimating the log spectra of involved signals (as in the single channel case), taking advantage of the availability of more sensors [47-51].

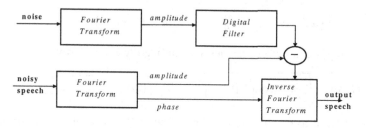

**Fig. 1.** Spectral Subtraction when two microphones are available (subtraction of amplitudes)

## 2 Nonlinear Monaural Speech Enhancement

In this section some well-known nonlinear methods for single-channel speech enhancement are outlined, without any intention of being exhaustive. Indeed, many other relevant contributions are present in the literature: our attempt here is to highlight the main approaches that have received much attention recently.

### 2.1 Spectral Subtraction (SS): Linear and Nonlinear Methods

Spectral Subtraction is a simple and effective method for reduction of stationary background noise [1-2], [6]. The processing is done on a frame-by-frame basis in the frequency domain. Speech and noise are assumed to be uncorrelated. The estimated speech short-time magnitude $|\hat{S}(\omega)|$ is obtained by subtracting from the noisy speech short-time magnitude |Y(ω)| a noise spectral magnitude estimate |Ñ(ω)| computed during speech pauses. This is what is essentially depicted in Fig.1, keeping in mind that the two-microphone SS scheme is equivalent to the monaural case with an effective Voice Activity Detector to allow the estimation of noise statistics during noise-alone periods. Taking into account the power spectral subtraction case study, we have

$$\left|\hat{S}(\omega)\right|^2 = \begin{cases} \left|Y(\omega)\right|^2 - \left|\hat{N}(\omega)\right|^2 & \text{if } \left|Y(\omega)\right|^2 > \left|\hat{N}(\omega)\right|^2 \\ 0 & \text{otherwise} \end{cases} \tag{3}$$

where $\left|\hat{N}(\omega)\right|^2$ is the noise power spectral estimate. The phase of noisy speech is left unchanged, so the enhanced signal in time domain is obtained as:

$$\hat{s}(k) = IFFT\left[\left|\hat{S}(\omega)\right| e^{j\arg(Y(\omega))}\right]. \tag{4}$$

Subtractive-type algorithms can be studied using a second approach termed *filtering of noisy speech*, involving the use of a time-varying linear filter dependent on the characteristics of the noisy signal spectrum and on the estimated noise spectrum. The noise suppression process becomes a product of the short-time spectral magnitude of the noisy speech $|Y(\omega)|$ with a gain function $G(\omega)$ as follows:

$$\left|\hat{S}(\omega)\right| = G(\omega)\left|Y(\omega)\right| \qquad with \quad 0 < G(\omega) < 1. \tag{5}$$

In terms of power spectral densities and considering (3) we have:

$$G(\omega) = \sqrt{1 - \left(\left|\hat{N}(\omega)\right|^2 / \left|Y(\omega)\right|^2\right)} = \sqrt{R_{post}(\omega)/\left(1 + R_{post}(\omega)\right)} \tag{6}$$

that is constrained to be null if the estimated noise power level is superior to that of the noisy speech. $R_{post}(\omega) = \left(\left|Y(\omega)^2\right| / \left|N(\omega)^2\right|\right) - 1$ is the a posteriori SNR. In other words, such a subtractive scheme results in emphasizing the spectral components proportionally to the amount by which they exceed noise. As can be seen in (6), $G(\omega)$ can be written as a function of the a-posteriori SNR, and many different rules, namely suppression curves, have been proposed so far. Their aim is to make the application of $G(\omega)$ more flexible in order to reduce the effect of musical noise that is characteristic of the classical SS approach [1-2], [6]. From this perspective, an interesting solution has been proposed as the so-called nonlinear SS [7], according to which a nonlinear estimation of noise power spectral density $\left|\hat{N}(\omega)\right|^2_{nl}$ is used in (3) as follows:

$$\left|\hat{N}(\omega)\right|^2_{nl} = \Phi\left(\max_{over\ M\ frames}\left(\left|\hat{N}(\omega)\right|^2\right), R_{post}(\omega), \left|\hat{N}(\omega)\right|^2\right) \tag{7}$$

where $\Phi(.)$ is the nonlinearity involved in the estimation process. A possible formulation for this is:

$$\Phi\left(\max_{over\ M\ frames}\left(\left|\hat{N}(\omega)\right|^2\right), R_{post}(\omega)\right) = \frac{\displaystyle\max_{over\ M\ frames}\left(\left|\hat{N}(\omega)\right|^2\right)}{1 + \gamma R_{post}(\omega)} \tag{8}$$

with $\gamma$ being a design parameter. Equation (8) says that as the SNR decreases the output of the nonlinear estimator approaches the maximum value of noise spectrum over $M$ frames, and as SNR increases it approaches zero. One can consider more complicated $\Phi(.)$, depending also on $\left|\hat{N}(\omega)\right|^2$, which can be useful if one is interested in over-subtraction for example.

## 2.2   The Ephraim-Malah SS Algorithm and Some of Its Variants

The Ephraim Malah algorithm [8-10] has received much attention by the scientific community. This is mainly due to its ability to achieve a highly satisfying overall quality of the enhanced speech which is appreciatively artifacts-free, and these characteristics makes it suitable for practical implementations in digital hearing aids. Such an approach has been down to outperform the conventional SS schemes as it is based on an estimation of the short-time spectral amplitude (STSA) of the speech signal. The same is also the case with the Soft-Decision Noise Suppression filter of McAulay and Malpass [11] where the STSA estimator is derived from an optimal (in the Maximum-Likelihood sense) variance estimator. In Ephraim and Malah (1985), an MMSE (minimum mean square error) STSA estimator is derived and applied in a SS scheme. The basic assumptions are the statistical independence of speech and noise, along with the spectral components of each of these two processes considered as zero mean statistically independent Gaussian random variables.

As pointed out in several papers, the main difference between the two STSA based approaches, i.e. [8] and [11], is that the former is able to yield colourless residual noise, whereas musical noise is still present after processing the observable through the latter procedure. In the following only the main formulae constituting the Ephraim-Malah noise suppressor are reported. Omitting the time and frequency indexes $(l, \omega)$ in order to shorten the notation, the suppression curve $G(l, \omega)$ to be applied to the short-time spectrum value $|Y(l, \omega)|$ can be expressed as:

$$G(l, \omega) = \frac{\sqrt{\pi}}{2} \cdot \sqrt{\left(\frac{1}{1+R_{post}}\right)\left(\frac{R_{prio}}{1+R_{prio}}\right)} \cdot M\left((1+R_{post})\left(\frac{R_{prio}}{1+R_{prio}}\right)\right) \tag{9}$$

where $M(.)$ is the nonlinearity based on $0^{th}$ and $1^{st}$ order Bessel functions:

$$M(\theta) = \exp\left(-\frac{\theta}{2}\right)\left[(1+\theta)I_0\left(\frac{\theta}{2}\right) + \theta I_1\left(\frac{\theta}{2}\right)\right]. \tag{10}$$

The formulations of the a-priori SNR and a-posteriori SNR respectively (for each value of the time and frequency indexes) are given below:

$$R_{post}(l, \omega) = \left(|Y(l-1, \omega)|^2 / |\hat{N}(\omega)|^2\right) - 1$$

$$R_{prio}(l, \omega) = (1-\alpha)P\left[R_{post}(l, \omega)\right] + \alpha \frac{|G(l-1, \omega)Y(l-1, \omega)|^2}{|\hat{N}(\omega)|^2} \tag{11}$$

with $P[x] = x$ if $x \geq 0$ and $P[x] = 0$ otherwise. $R_{prio}$ is an estimate of the SNR that takes into account the current short-term frame with weight $(1-\alpha)$ and the noise reduced previous frame with weight $\alpha$. Compared to other noise suppression rules based on averaging the short-time spectrum or on calculating the gain function over successive frames, one advantage of the Ephraim-Malah algorithm lies in the nonlinear averaging process. When the signal level is well above the noise level, the a-priori SNR becomes almost equivalent to the a-posteriori SNR with one frame delay, with the result that $R_{prio}$ is no longer a smoothed SNR estimate (which is important for preventing the deterioration of the speech signal which is rather non-stationary).

The original version of the Ephraim-Malah rule does not take the signal presence uncertainty into account, in contrast to the procedure developed in [11]. This is a relevant aspect, since the speech signal is not always present in the noisy mixture and the energy of some voiced type spectral contributions is negligible in comparison to the corresponding noise.

An interesting generalization to the rule described by (9) has also been derived to address this problem. However it is not reported here, as it has been shown to behave similarly to the log-spectral estimator developed in [9]. Such an approach comprises a nonlinear spectral estimator performing the MMSE of the log-spectra. The underlying motivation is that a distortion measure based on the MSE of the log spectra is more subjectively meaningful than the counterpart based on the MSE of the common spectra. The spectral gain $G_{\log}(l,\omega)$ of the MMSE log spectral amplitude estimator is

$$G_{\log}(l,\omega) = \frac{R_{prio}}{1+R_{prio}} \cdot \exp\left[\frac{1}{2}\int_{\kappa(\omega)}^{+\infty} \frac{e^{-t}}{t} dt\right] \tag{12}$$

where $R_{prio}$ and $R_{post}$ are defined as above and the following holds:

$$\kappa(\omega) = \frac{R_{prio}}{1+R_{prio}}\left(1+R_{post}\right). \tag{13}$$

As observed by the authors, the rule (12) allows higher noise suppression, leaving unchanged the quality of the output speech with respect to the gain function in (9).

Further improvement in the performance achievable through this approach has been demonstrated in [12], who employ an empirical approach to yield a numerical solution to the MMSE estimate in the log spectral domain. Assuming that the speech and noise log spectra have normal distributions, it can be shown that the MMSE estimate of the speech log spectrum at certain time instant and frequency bin $(l,\omega)$ is a function of noisy observations and the probabilistic model parameter (mean and variance $\{\mu_s,\sigma_s,\mu_n,\sigma_n\}$). Such a function must be approximated, and the authors in [12] propose the novel use of a multi-layer perceptron (MLP) neural network. Monte Carlo simulations are used to get an adequate input/output training set for the network under the assumed statistics; and the approximation problem then turns out to be a curve fitting one by considering the MMSE estimation as a gain function. Considering the presence of a VAD to ensure the calculation of noise statistics during silence periods (even in slowly time-varying environments), assuming fixed and known the variance of the speech log spectra, and reformulating the parameter model after proper normalization, we can formulate the scheme of approximation of MMSE estimation as shown in Fig.2.

### 2.3   Overview of Supervised Neural Network Based Approaches

Other important nonlinear methods for single channel speech enhancement are proposed and analyzed in this section. These generally provide a suitable estimation of the clean speech signal, by means of nonlinear models in order to take into account the nonlinearities within the dynamic process determining the speech signal production. We shall consider here some techniques assuming the availability of a clean speech training data for the underlying nonlinear model. The classical techniques using Neural Networks as nonlinear filters mapping the noisy speech to clean speech in the time domain or in different domains [20], allow to get good estimations only

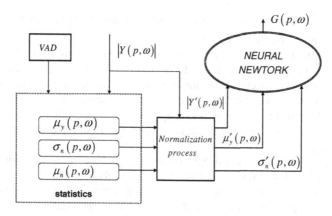

**Fig. 2.** Approximation process of the MMSE estimation in the log spectral domain

assuming speech and noise stationarity. A time variant model can be achieved by creating different fixed models for corresponding dynamical regimes of the signals and switching between these models during the speech enhancement process.

We start therefore from a straightforward neural extension of the work by Ephraim [16-17] which is represented by the principled switching method proposed by Lee [18], that incorporates the extended Kalman filtering approach (which will be discussed later). HMMs have been shown to be an effective tool in presence of signal uncertainty [16], due to their capability of dividing the received speech signal into various classes automatically. With reference to [18], each HMM state provides a maximum-likelihood estimate $\hat{s}(k)$ under the assumption that the windowed observation vector $\mathbf{y}(k)$ belongs to class $i$. The overall estimate is given by

$$\hat{s}(k) = \sum_i p\left(class_i \middle| \mathbf{y}(k)\right) \cdot \left[\hat{s}(k) \middle| \mathbf{y}(k), class_i\right] \tag{14}$$

where $p\left(class_i \middle| \mathbf{y}(k)\right)$ is the probability of being in class $i$ given the window of noisy observations $\mathbf{y}(k)$ and the second term in the sum represents the maximum-likelihood estimate of the speech given class $i$ and the data. The posterior class probability $p\left(class_i \middle| \mathbf{y}(k)\right)$ is easily calculated using standard forward-backward recursive formulas for HMMs. Alternatively, the estimate $\hat{s}(k)$ may be simply taken as the estimate for the single filter whose posterior class probability is maximum:

$$\hat{s}(k) = \left[\hat{s}(k) \middle| class_m\right] \quad with \quad p\left(class_m \middle| \mathbf{y}(k)\right) \geq p\left(class_i \middle| \mathbf{y}(k)\right) \ \forall i . \tag{15}$$

The Extendend Kalman Filter (EKF) technique, involving an autoregressive model for each class, can be used to provide the maximum-likelihood estimation for speech. On purpose, a suitable set of clean speech data has to be employed to train the autoregressive neural models, whereas the speech innovations variance $\sigma_n^2$ can be estimated from the clean speech for each class.

A recent variant has been proposed [19] to the above approach of Lee et al [18]: wherein the nonlinear prediction model is based on a Recurrent Neural Network (RNN). The enhanced speech is the output of an architecture, namely RNPHMM (Recurrent Neural Predictive Hidden Markov Model), resulting from the combination of RNN and HMM. Similar to the previous approach [18], the unknown parameters are estimated by a learning algorithm derived from the Baum-Welch and RNN backpropagation algorithms.

As previously outlined Neural Networks can also be used as non-linear time domain filters, fed with the noisy speech signal to yield the estimate of the clean speech. The training is performed by using clean speech (from a known database) artificially corrupted to create noisy input data and presented to the network sliding the observation window over the available signal. The Tamura approach [22-23] is one of the oldest and most representative of this category: a four-layered neural network is used and trained for hetero-association, employing noisy speech signal patterns at the input and the corresponding noise free signal patterns at the output. Obtained results have been compared to those obtained with spectral subtraction through subjective listening tests, concluding that most listeners preferred the neural network filtered speech.

Another classical scheme is the one used in [24] where the noise signal is filtered through a feedforward network with a $M$-unit hidden layer and a single output unit, whose notation is used on e following. For each time instant $k$, the hidden unit computes the weighted sum of its input and subsequently applies a compressor function $f : \mathbb{R} \to \mathbb{R}$ to produce its output activation. It can be shown that for every desired input-output mapping in the form of a real valued continuous function $\tilde{f}_d : \mathbf{x} \in \mathbb{R}^K \to \mathbb{R}$ and, for a non constant bounded and monotonically increasing activation function $f(\cdot)$ at all hidden elements, an integer $M$, an $M \times K$ matrix $\mathbf{U} = \left[ u_{ij} \right]$ and $M$-dimensional vectors $\mathbf{v} = \left[ v_j \right]$ and $\mathbf{b} = \left[ b_j \right]$ exist such that

$$\max_{\mathbf{x} \in \Gamma} \left| \tilde{f}_d(\mathbf{x}) - \mathbf{v}^T f(\mathbf{U}\mathbf{x} - \mathbf{b}) \right| < \varepsilon \tag{16}$$

where $\varepsilon$ is an arbitrarily small positive constant and $\Gamma$ is a bounded close subset of $\mathbb{R}^K$. Note that even if it may be theoretically possible to find the network weights that make the output error as small as desired, in real situations the parameters' optimization is very hard due to the fact that in supervised learning the adjustment of parameters is generally based on a limited number of training pairs $\left( \mathbf{x}, \tilde{f}_d(\mathbf{x}) \right)$. Moreover in noise filtering applications, the mapping of the noise signal to the corresponding clean signal is not usually a mathematical function $\tilde{f}_d(\cdot)$, and this violates one of the existence conditions of the above-stated theorem. For the filter adaptation, a backpropagation approach is usually used.

Neural network structures can also be successfully used in the transformed domain [28] to carry out the enhancement process, following a suitable training phase. The approach followed is generally based on a multistage architecture, comprising:

1. processing of the original data into a transform domain
2. nonlinear enhancement mapping performed by a neural network

The phase information is typically left unchanged through the overall process. From this perspective, if we give an estimate of noise power spectral density as input to the NN, we can see such a method as a form of nonlinear SS. This helps to address the nonlinear link between noise and speech due to the nature of transform that is not necessarily the one attainable through the Fourier transform (like log-power spectral, cepstral, LPC, and so on).

Several researchers have performed interesting studies on this subject. We can cite as examples the one employing time delay neural network for Mel-scaled spectral estimation [21] and the one with missing data technique using Reurrent Neural Networks [52]. Furthermore, the SS technique based on nonlinear spectral estimation [12] described above can also be interpreted within this framework.

## 2.4 Overview of Nonlinear Unsupervised Techniques

The problem of finding the maximum likelihood estimates of the speech and the model parameters, given the noisy data, has been successfully addressed by Wan and Nelson [16] [28] using neural autoregressive models and the Extended Kalman Filtering (EKF) method. The speech model in the time domain is the following non-linear autoregressive model:

$$s(k) = f\left(s(k-1), \cdots, s(k-K), \mathbf{w}\right) + v(k)$$
$$y(k) = s(k) + n(k) \tag{17}$$

where $v(k)$ is the process noise in state equation, usually assumed to be white, and K is the model time length. A different model is used for each frame into which the noisy signal is segmented. The EKF method is able to yield the ML optimal estimate if the model is known. However, if no suitable data set for training is provided, the model parameters have to be learnt from the available observable sequence. Kalman Filter theory can be directly applied to the autoregressive model above, if we rewrite it in the state-space form and $f(.)$ is assumed to be linear:

$$\mathbf{s}(k) = F\left[\mathbf{s}(k-1)\right] + Bv(k)$$
$$y(k) = C\mathbf{s}(k) + n(k) \tag{18}$$

where the following hold:

$$\mathbf{s}(k) = \left[s(k), \cdots, s(k-K+1)\right]^T$$
$$F\left[\mathbf{s}(k)\right] = \left[f\left(s(k), \cdots, s(k-K+1), \mathbf{w}\right), s(k), \cdots, s(k-K+2)\right]^T . \tag{19}$$
$$C = \left[1 \ 0 \ \cdots \ 0\right] \qquad B = C^T$$

The EKF algorithm is simply a generalization of the well-known KF when $f(.)$ is nonlinear, providing an approximation of $f(.)$ with a time-varying linear function. The EKF formulas are listed below, where $\sigma_v^2(k), \sigma_n^2(k)$ represent the variances of the process and observation noises respectively.

$$\hat{s}^-(k) = F\left[\hat{s}(k-1), \hat{w}(k-1)\right]$$

$$P_{\hat{s}}^-(k) = A P_{\hat{s}}(k-1) A^T + B\sigma_v^2(k) B^T \qquad A = \frac{\partial F\left[\hat{s}(k-1), \hat{w}\right]}{\partial \hat{s}(k-1)}$$

$$G(k) = P_{\hat{s}}^-(k) C^T \left(C P_{\hat{s}}^-(k) C^T + \sigma_n^2(k)\right)^{-1} \tag{20}$$

$$P_{\hat{s}}(k) = \left(I - G(k) C\right) P_{\hat{s}}^-(k)$$

$$\hat{s}(k) = \hat{s}^-(k) + G(k)\left(y(k) - C\hat{s}^-(k)\right)$$

However, note that one cannot exclusively rely on such a procedure to get what is required, i.e. a simultaneous estimation of the speech model and speech signal. As a result, a new set of state-space equations for neural networks weights **w** (used for nonlinearity parameterization) are formulated as follows:

$$\mathbf{w}(k) = \mathbf{w}(k-1) + \alpha(k)$$
$$y(k) = f\left(\mathbf{s}(k-1), \mathbf{w}(k)\right) + v(k) + n(k) \tag{21}$$

The neural system f(.) allows a nonlinear time-varying observation on **w**. An EKF algorithm can be applied to yield an ML estimate of the current state assuming the other state **s** is known. The result is that we have two EKFs running in parallel (see Fig.3), one for state and the other for weights estimation. At each time step, the

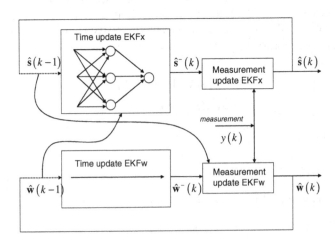

**Fig. 3.** The Dual Extended Kalman Filter method for speech enhancement

present state estimate $\hat{\mathbf{x}}(k)$ is used by the weight filter EKFw and the present weight estimate $\hat{\mathbf{w}}(k)$ feeds the state filter EKFx.

This approach, as is the case with SS, does not depend on the type of signal that we are dealing with and requires a suitable estimation of noise statistics. The main drawback is represented by the high computational cost occurring in training neural networks on-line, and some partial solutions have been proposed in order to reduce the computational complexity and obtain a faster convergence.

The Noise-Regularized Adaptive Filtering (NRAF) approach for speech enhancement [28] [31] involves a window based and iterative process that is similar to the dual EKF method, but does not use an AR model for the speech. It can be considered as a direct time-domain mapping filter (in the sense developed in [31]) avoiding the need for a clean dataset to train the network.

The objective of direct filtering approaches is to map the noisy vector y(k) to an estimate of the speech signal $\hat{s}(k) = f(\mathbf{y}(k))$. The neural network performing the mapping is trained by minimizing the mean-square error (MSE) cost function:

$$\min_f E\left\{\left[s(k) - f(\mathbf{y}(k))\right]^2\right\}. \tag{22}$$

We will now show how to minimize such a quantity without assuming that the clean signal s(k) is known. Consider the expansion:

$$E\left\{\left[s(k) - f(\mathbf{y}(k))\right]^2\right\} = E\left\{\left[y(k) - f(\mathbf{y}(k))\right]^2\right\} + 2E\left\{n(k)f(\mathbf{y}(k))\right\} +$$
$$-2E\left\{y(k)n(k)\right\} + E\left\{n^2(k)\right\} \tag{23}$$

Since the last two terms are independent of f(.), it suffices to minimize the following alternative cost function to get the optimal solution:

$$\min_f \left\{E\left\{\left[y(k) - f(\mathbf{y}(k))\right]^2\right\} + 2E\left\{\left[n(k)f(\mathbf{y}(k))\right]^2\right\}\right\}. \tag{24}$$

A relevant advantage arises: the clean speech is not needed. Indeed the first term (corresponding to the cost associated with filtering the noisy signal itself) only depends on the observables, whereas the second term (namely the regularization term) on the noise statistics. An approximate solution is typically used for the latter. It is obtained by using the Unscented Transformation (UT), a method for calculating the statistics of a random variable going through a nonlinear transformation. Then, at each time instant, the network input is a suitable set of $K$ vectors carrying the information related to the first and second order signal statistics, whereas the corresponding output is a weighted sample mean. A standard gradient based algorithm like backpropagation can be used to accomplish the minimization. The effectiveness of the method relies on the assumption that the accuracy of the second-order UT based approximation to the regularization term is good enough to achieve the network convergence to the true minimum MSE. Moreover, as in the Dual EKF approach, also in NRAF the speech non-stationarity can be dealt with by windowing the noisy data into short overlapping frames with a new filter for each frame.

In addition, Monte-Carlo simulation based approaches for audio signal enhancement have been recently proposed in some scientific works [4] [29-30]. Here their basic principles shall be discussed. Considering the clean and noisy speech as sequences of scalar random variables, we can assume they satisfy some kind of time-varying state-space equations, as previously done in (17). With a superior degree of generality, we can characterize our system by three deterministically nonlinear transition functions, here denoted as $f, g, h$. Function $f$ is also dependent on discrete time $k$ (therefore it will be represented as $f_k$), whereas the other two are in general dependent on the system parameter vector $\mathbf{w}(k)$ (and we will denote them as $g_{\mathbf{w}_k}, h_{\mathbf{w}_k}$ respectively). It follows that the state space equations are:

$$
\begin{aligned}
\mathbf{w}(k) &= f_k\left(\mathbf{w}(k-1), u(k)\right) \\
s(k) &= g_{\mathbf{w}_k}\left(s(k-1), v(k)\right) \\
y(k) &= h_{\mathbf{w}_k}\left(s(k), n(k)\right)
\end{aligned}
\tag{25}
$$

where $u(k), v(k), n(k)$ are the innovation processes of the dynamical system, usually assumed to be statistically independent and identically distributed (i.i.d). As mentioned earlier, the involved functions in (25) are not linear, the parameter vector is not known (and possibly non-stationary) and the model is non-Gaussian. This results in severe computational difficulties in estimating the system parameters and/or the state signal (speech), and favors the usage of Monte Carlo simulations according to which the probability distributions are sampled and replaced by empirical distributions. It follows that the filtering and smoothing recursions occurring in state estimation can be simulated by means of the so called particle filters and smoothers developed through the point masses (particles) obtained from distribution sampling.

In [4], [30] and [31], speech signal process is modeled as a time-varying autoregressive (TVAR) model (as for the case of the Dual EFK method discussed above). Moreover the noise is assumed to be Gaussian and the coefficients of TVAR model a Gaussian random walk process. It can be shown that the following holds:

$$
p\left(\mathbf{w}(k)\big|y^{1:k}\right) \propto \int p\left(y(k)\big|\mathbf{w}^{1:k}, y^{1:k-1}\right) p\left(\mathbf{w}(k)\big|\mathbf{w}(k-1)\right) p\left(\mathbf{w}^{1:k-1}\big|y^{1:k-1}\right) d\mathbf{w}^{1:k-1}
\tag{26}
$$

where $y^{1:k}$ stands for $\{y(1), \cdots, y(k)\}$, and accordingly for other variables occurring with same notation. The quantity $p\left(\mathbf{w}(k)\big|y^{1:k}\right)$ is the filtering distribution, namely the objective of our estimation problem. Now, let us suppose to have an estimate of $p\left(\mathbf{w}^{1:k-1}\big|y^{1:k-1}\right)$ at time instant $k-1$. This probability density function (pdf) can be sampled $N$ times producing $N$ different sample paths of $\mathbf{w}^{1:k-1}$, namely $\left\{ \mathbf{w}_i^{1:k-1}, i=1, \cdots, N \right\}$. Hence, the particle approximation to $p\left( \mathbf{w}^{1:k-1} \middle| y^{1:k-1} \right)$ is given by:

$$p\left( \mathbf{w}^{1:k-1} \middle| y^{1:k-1} \right) \approx \sum_{i=1}^{N} \delta\left( \mathbf{w}^{1:k-1} - \mathbf{w}_i^{1:k-1} \right) \tag{27}$$

where $\delta(.)$ denotes the Dirac function. For each $i$, we can get the $N$ samples $\left\{ \mathbf{w}_i(k), i=1, \cdots, N \right\}$ from a proposal distribution $\pi\left( \mathbf{w}_i(k) \middle| \mathbf{w}_i^{1:k-1}, y^{1:k} \right)$, namely the importance distribution. Then we can use the latter samples to augment the former and generate the new sample paths at time instant $k$: $\left\{ \mathbf{w}_i^{1:k}, i=1, \cdots, N \right\}$. A typical assumption is to set:

$$\pi\left( \mathbf{w}_i(k) \middle| \mathbf{w}_i^{1:k-1}, y^{1:k} \right) = p\left( \mathbf{w}(k) \middle| \mathbf{w}(k-1) \right) \tag{28}$$

It must be said that $p\left( \mathbf{w}(k) \middle| \mathbf{w}(k-1) \right)$ is fixed once we have chosen to apply a constrained Gaussian random walk in the TVAR coefficient domain.

Equation (27) can be substituted into (26), resulting in:

$$p\left( \mathbf{w}(k) \middle| y^{1:k} \right) \approx \sum_{i=1}^{N} \theta_i(k) \delta\left( \mathbf{w}^{1:k} - \mathbf{w}_i^{1:k} \right) \tag{29}$$

where $\theta_i(k)$ are the importance weights and $\theta_i(k) \propto p\left( y(k) \middle| \mathbf{w}_i^{1:k}, y^{1:k-1} \right)$ holds, as a direct consequence of (28). Under the assumption of conditionally linear Gaussian structure, the distribution $p\left( y(k) \middle| \mathbf{w}_i^{1:k}, y^{1:k-1} \right)$ can be evaluated efficiently using the Kalman filter and the prediction error decomposition. Indeed, our system model satisfies such a condition, as confirmed by (18). This ensures also $O(N)$ computational complexity and storage requirements for our algorithm. We have now an estimate of $p\left( \mathbf{w}(k) \middle| y^{1:k} \right)$ and we can iterate the procedure for all subsequent time instants. Furthermore, it follows that the MMSE estimate of the clean speech plus parameter vector of our system model ( $f_{k|k}\left( \mathbf{s}(k), \mathbf{w}^k \right) = \left( \mathbf{s}(k), \mathbf{w}^k \right)$ ) is

$$\hat{I}_N\left( f_{k|k} \right) \triangleq \sum_{i=1}^{N} \tilde{\theta}_i^{0:k} E_{p\left( \mathbf{s}(k) \middle| \mathbf{w}^{1:k}, y^{1:k} \right)} \left[ f_{k|k}\left( \mathbf{s}(k), \mathbf{w}_i^k \right) \right] \tag{30}$$

where $p\left( \mathbf{s}(k) \middle| \mathbf{w}^{1:k}, y^{1:k} \right)$ is a Gaussian distribution whose parameters may be computed using the Kalman filter and $E$ is the expectation operator. According to the principle of Sequential Importance Sampling (SIS), satisfied by our choice of the proposal distribution, a recursive evaluation of the importance weights is allowed, which implies: $\theta(\mathbf{w}_{1:k}) = \theta(\mathbf{w}_{1:k-1})\theta(k)$. Finally, the normalized importance weights appearing in (30) are given by $\tilde{\theta}_i^{0:k} \triangleq \theta(\mathbf{w}_{1:k}^i) \Big/ \sum_{j=1}^{N} \theta(\mathbf{w}_{1:k}^j)$.

## 3   Binaural Nonlinear Noise Cancellation for Speech Enhancement

### 3.1   Review of Adaptive Noise Cancellation (ANC)

The classical scheme for the Adaptive Noise Cancellation (ANC) was originally proposed by Widrow et al. [32], and has been the subject of numerous studies involving a wide range of applications. In contrast to other enhancement techniques, no a priori knowledge of signal or noise is required for the method to be applied, but this advantage is paid for by the need of a secondary or *reference* input. This reference input should contain little or no signal but it should contain a noise measurement which is correlated, in some unknown way, with the noise component of the *primary* input. An important step in ANC is obtaining a reference signal which satisfies the above mentioned requirements. Referring to Fig.4, given a noisy speech (primary) signal $y[k]$, and assuming that $s[k]$ is uncorrelated with $n_1[k]$ and $n_2[k]$, and that $n_2[k]$ is processed by a linear filter $h[k]$ (generally non-causal), it is easy to show that $E\{e^2[k]\}$ is minimized when $v[k] = n_1[k]$, so that the output speech $e[k] = s[k]$ is the desired clean signal. Hence, the adaptive filter in classical linear methods is designed to minimize $E\{n_1[k] - v[k]\}$, using standard algorithms, like the least mean squares (LMS) technique.

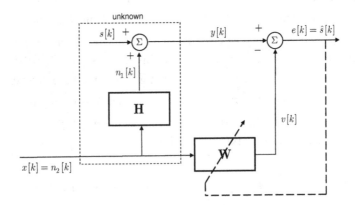

**Fig. 4.** Adaptive noise cancellation scheme for general nonlinear environments

### 3.2   Nonlinear ANC: Review of Approaches

Linear adaptive filtering, previously described, with the mean squared error (MSE) criterion is a standard signal processing method, and the reason for its success is the relative simplicity of design and ease of implementation. Nevertheless it can not often realize the Bayes conditional mean, which is the optimal filter for the MSE criterion, and generally a nonlinear function of the observed data. An important exception is if the observed data and the data to be estimated are jointly Gaussian: in this case the Bayes filter is a linear function. Since many real world signal processing applications have to deal with non-Gaussian signals, the use of a linear finite impulse response (FIR) or infinite impulse response (IIR) filter does not permit to obtain an acceptable level of noise or interference cancellation, because it can not efficiently approximate the nonlinear mapping between the known reference and the unknown interference signal. With reference to Fig.4, we say that the reference noise is related to the interference signal by an unknown nonlinear operator $\mathbf{H}$, approximated by a nonlinear feed-forward network. The objective is to determine the unknown nonlinear operator $\mathbf{H}$ by a nonlinear filter $\mathbf{W}$, so that we can optimally estimate the noise $n_1[k]$ and subtract it from the signal $y[k]$. In this way the primary source signal can be estimated. In the literature, a number of different techniques to design the filter $\mathbf{W}$ can be found which can be conveniently grouped in three principal classes: higher order-statistic filters, polynomial filters (in particular Volterra filters) and different kinds of neural networks. Higher order statistics (HOS) filters are based on ordering properties of input signals. A well-known member of this family is the Median filter, that is useful in removing impulsive noise, but poor in case of Gaussian noise. In [41] third-order statistics are used to derive novel design techniques which are more insensitive to corruption of the primary signal by additive Gaussian noise, compared to the second-order statistics ones. Referring to Fig.4, under the hypothesis that all signals are zero mean and stationary, and that $s[k]$ is independent of both $n_1[k]$ and $n_2[k]$ and that $n_1[k]$ and $n_2[k]$ are someway correlated, the optimal filter $\mathbf{W}$ can be determined using the third-order moment by solving the following

$$\sum_{i=0}^{q} w_3[i] R_{n_2}^{(3)}(m+i, l+i) = R_{yn_2}^{(3)}(m, l) \tag{31}$$

where

$$
\begin{aligned}
R_{n_2}^{(3)}(m, l) &\triangleq E\{n_2[k] n_2[k+n] n_2[k+l]\} \\
R_{yn_2}^{(3)}(m.l) &\triangleq E\{y[k] n_2[k+n] n_2[k+l]\}
\end{aligned} \tag{32}
$$

and different estimates can be obtained for different values of $(m, l)$. Furthermore, if $n_1$ is linearly related to $n_2$ (i.e. if $\mathbf{H}$ in Fig.4 can be modeled by a linear time invariant (LTI) filter) then theoretically $w_3[k]$ obtained from (31) is equivalent to those obtained by classical MSE methods, and it leads to complete cancellation of the interference, by identifying the true $\mathbf{H}$ filter. In practice, the theoretical auto- and cross-correlations are substituted by consistent sample estimator computed from the available data. The Volterra Filter (VF) has the important property to be linear in its parameters. So the identification of vector $\mathbf{H}$ in the MMSE sense can be obtained through the resolution of a linear equation. To find the optimal filters, we can operate both in the time and in the frequency domain [53]. An adaptive resolution of this equation is the RLS algorithm, which is based on the recursive calculation of the co-variance matrix of the input signal of the filter. For the application of VF to the problem of noise cancellation, we refer to Fig.4 [42]. If $n_2[k]$ and $s[k]$ are independent and zero mean, then the previously mentioned algorithms can be used, if we replace $x[k]$ with $n_2[k]$ and $y[k]$ by $s[k]+n_1[k]$.

Next, a number of selected approaches to the interference cancellation problem using neural network filters are briefly analyzed, though other techniques can of course be found in the literature too.

As previously noticed, the problem of noise filtering can be viewed as the problem of finding the mapping of noisy signal patterns $y[k]$ to the corresponding noise-free signal patterns $s[k]$. According to this perspective, different kinds and topologies of neural networks can be used relating to the different relations between $n_1[k]$ and $n_2[k]$. Since a two layer feed-forward network has been proven capable of approximating any continuous non-linear mapping, assuming there are a sufficient number of hidden units, various implementations of this structure (with different contrast functions and number of hidden units) can be found in the literature. In [42], for example, a perceptron with one hidden layer and one output unit is used for the filter $\mathbf{W}$ (referencing to Fig.4 for the notation).

Denoting $\mathbf{n}_2[k] = [n_2[k], n_2[k-1], \cdots, n_2[k-K]]$, the mapping is described by

$$v[k] = \sum_{m=1}^{M} c_m \tanh\left(\mathbf{w}_m^T \mathbf{n}_2[k] - b_m\right) \tag{33}$$

where $M$ is the number of hidden units, $c_m$ and the vectors $\mathbf{w}_m$ are the weights coefficients, and $b_m$ are the biases. The training is performed using the classical back-propagation technique. No method currently exists to precisely determine the optimal solution. Performance depends on the initial weights, the learning rate and the amount of training, but for small $K$ from (33) the perceptron seems to perform a good approximation of the optimum Bayes filter.

The last kind of neural network analyzed in this work for the problem of noise cancellation is the Hyper Radial Basis Function (HRBF) neural network, following the approach described in [40]. The main idea is to consider the mapping $\mathbf{W}$ in Fig.4 to be approximated as the sum of various radial basis functions, each one with its own prior. Defining $f_m$, $m = 1, \cdots, M$ as these functions, the function to minimize is:

$$L(n_1) = \sum_{k=1}^{K} \left( \sum_{m=1}^{M} f_m(n_2[k]) - n_1[k] \right)^2 + \sum_{m(1)}^{M} \gamma_m \|P_m f_m\|^2 \tag{34}$$

where $P_m$ are stabilizers in Tikhonov's stabilization theory and $\gamma_m$ are regularization parameters (real and positive). The approximate solution of (34) is given by:

$$\tilde{n}_1 = \sum_{m=1}^{M} \sum_{j=1}^{K} w_j^m G_j^m \left( \bar{n}_2, \mathbf{q}_j^m \right) \tag{35}$$

where $w_j^m$ are weight parameters and $G_j^m$ are Green's functions. Choosing a set of stabilizers whose Green's functions are Gaussian, the HRBS neural network becomes formally equivalent to a two layer neural network the hidden layer of which realizes an adaptive nonlinear transformation (with adjustable weight and center parameters).

### 3.3  Multi-(sub)band Processing for Binaural Speech Enhancement

Some researchers have looked to the human hearing system as a source of engineering models to approach the enhancement problem, with some modelling the cochlea and others utilizing a model of the lateral inhibition effect. Two or more relatively closely spaced microphones have been used in an adaptive noise cancellation scheme [35], to identify a differential acoustic path transfer function during a noise only period in intermittent speech. The extension of this work, termed the Multi-Microphone Sub-band Adaptive (MMSBA) speech enhancement system, applies the method within a set of sub-bands provided by a filter bank. The filter bank can be implemented using various orthogonal transforms or by a parallel filter bank approach. The idea of employing multi-band processing for speech enhancement has also been considered in other contributions focusing on the spectral subtraction technique [54-55]. In the MMSBA approach [36-38], the sub-bands are distributed non-linearly according to a cochlear distribution, as in humans, following the Greenwood model [56]. The conventional MMSBA approach considerably improves the mean squared error (MSE) convergence rate of an adaptive multi-band LMS filter compared to both the conventional wideband  time-domain and  frequency domain LMS filters, as shown in [36-38]. It is assumed that the speaker is close enough to the microphones so that environmental acoustic effects on the speech are insignificant, that the noise signal at the microphones may be modelled as a point source modified by two different acoustic path transfer functions, and that an effective voice activity detector (VAD) is available. In practice, the MMSBA based speech-enhancement systems have been shown to give the important benefit of supporting adaptive diverse parallel processing in the sub-bands, namely Sub-band Processing (SBP), allowing signal features within the sub-bands, such as the noise power, the coherence between the in-band signals from multiple sensors and the convergence behaviour of an adaptive algorithm, to influence the subsequent processing within the respective frequency band. The SBP can be accomplished with no processing, intermittent coherent noise canceller, or incoherent noise canceller. In the conventional MMSBA approach, linear FIR filtering is performed within the SBP unit and the LMS algorithm is used to perform the adaptation. In the non-linear MMSBA, Volterra Filtering based SBP has been applied (together with the RLS algorithm), leading to a significant improvement of results, especially in real noisy environments. The Magnitude Squared Coherence (MSC) has been applied by [58] to noisy speech signals for noise reduction and also successfully employed as a VAD for the case of spatially uncorrelated noises. A modified MSC has been used for selecting an appropriate SBP option within the MMSBA system [36].

   In the newly proposed modified MMSBA architecture [38], Wiener filtering (WF) operation has been applied in two different ways: at the output of each sub-band adaptive noise canceller, and at the global output of the original MMSBA scheme. The employment of such post-processing (WF) within the MMSBA allows to deal with residual incoherent noise components that may result from the application of conventional MMSBA schemes, similar to the approach adopted in [57]. In both the proposed architectures, the role of WF is to further mitigate the residual noise effects on the original signal to be recovered, following application of MMSBA noise-cancellation processing.

Finally, the MMSBA framework also allows incorporation of cross-band effects to mimic human lateral inhibition effects. One possibility seems to extend the recently reported promising work of Bahoura and Rouat [59], who have shown that non-linear masking of a time-space representation of speech can be used to achieve simulated noise suppression for the monaural case, by discarding or masking the undesired (noise) signals and retaining the desired (speech) signals. They have demonstrated that this non-linear masking can enhance single-sensor or monaurally recorded speech by performing non-linear filtering with adaptive thresholding (based on the Teager Energy operator Bahoura and Rouat [60]) on a time-frequency (multi-band) representation of the noisy signal. In [61] the MMSBA system with linear filtering and two different adaptive sub-band binaural structures have been compared in the noise reduction problem.

## 4  General Multi-channel Nonlinear Speech Enhancement

This section deals with those nonlinear techniques for enhancement of speech signals when more than one microphone is present, specifically when an $M$-element microphone array is available. Compared to the single-channel case discussed in Section 2, the multiple sensors allow suitable spatial filtering of the incoming signals thereby gaining a relatively enhanced capability of interference suppression. Two main categories of works can be identified in this area. One is based on the development of a nonlinear microphone array system, where both complementary beamforming and nonlinear SS are carried out to yield the final enhancement. The other approach deals with Log-Spectra estimation within different noise reduction frameworks.

Let us start from the former [44]. The goal here is to enhance the speech signal through a spatial spectral subtraction method by using a complementary beamformer. The presence of two complementary directivity patterns results in nonlinear SS processing that avoid use of a speech pause detector - which is normally employed in a typical SS scheme (see above). As depicted in Fig.5, the observed signals pass through two different weight vectors, then summed in order to produce primary and reference signals defined as:

$$\tilde{Y}^{(p)}(l,\omega) = 2S_0(l,\omega) + \sum_{d\in\Omega}\left(\mathbf{ga}_d(l,\omega) - \mathbf{ha}_d(l,\omega)\right)\cdot N_d(l,\omega)$$
$$\tilde{Y}^{(r)}(l,\omega) = \sum_{d\in\Omega}\left(\mathbf{ga}_d(l,\omega) - \mathbf{ha}_d(l,\omega)\right)\cdot N_d(l,\omega)$$

(36)

where $S_0$ is the speech signal coming from the look direction (so coinciding with $S$ if we consider the model (2)), $\mathbf{g},\mathbf{h}$ are the $M$-element complementary weight vectors,

$\Omega$ is the set of directions relative to the different interfering signals approaching the beamformer, $N_d$ is the noise signal corresponding to the $d$-th direction. The quantities $\mathbf{ga}_d, \mathbf{ha}_d$ describe the directivity patterns, and $\mathbf{a}_d$ is the steering vector:

$$\mathbf{a}_d(l,\omega) = \left[ a_{1,d}(l,\omega), a_{2,d}(l,\omega), \cdots, a_{M,d}(l,\omega) \right]$$
$$a_{m,d}(l,\omega) = \exp\left( j\omega x_m \sin\left(\theta_d(l)\right)/c \right) \tag{37}$$

where c is the sound velocity, $\theta_d$ the $d$-th direction of arrival, $x_m$ the coordinate of the $m$-th element of the array. The term $\sin\left(\theta_d(l)\right)$ in (37) implies that the steering vector depends on the frame number $l$ due to the non-stationary location of noise contributions (hence such a dependency can be neglected in the case of "static" noise). It can be easily proved that, under assumptions of complementary directivity patterns and uncorrelation of arriving signals, the reference signal can be subtracted from the primary to yield $S_0$ without any speech pause detector. In formulas:

$$\hat{S}(l,\omega) = \frac{1}{2}\left[ \left|\tilde{Y}^{(p)}(l,\omega)\right|^2 - E\left[\left|\tilde{Y}^{(r)}(l,\omega)\right|^2\right] \right]^{1/2} \cdot \exp\left( j\phi(\omega) \right) \tag{38}$$

where $\hat{S}(l,\omega)$ is the estimated speech signal and $\phi(\omega)$ a suitable phase function, coming from a conventional beamformer (delay-and-sum, DS) in the above approach (see Fig.5). In order to avoid occurrence of over-subtraction, a better performing frame-by-frame SS rule has been used in [44].

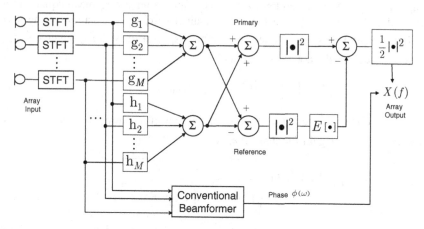

**Fig. 5.** Block diagram of the nonlinear mic array based on complementary beamforming

The directivity patterns are designed under the constraint of keeping the terms $\left|\mathbf{ga}_d(\omega) \cdot \mathbf{ha}_d(\omega)\right|$ as small as possible, for all $\omega, d$, in order to have low noise contribution to the primary signal. This results in a nonlinear constrained least squares minimization problem, tackled by a suitable iterative procedure. The approach is supervised and the common choice made for the target directivity pattern involves setting the value 1 for the look direction and 0 otherwise. In such a way, it is possible to get lower sidelobes with respect to the DS array, resulting in a significant improvement of speech enhancement capability. However, the optimization procedure employed is not specifically oriented to minimize the average gain in each direction, causing a certain difficulty to reduce directional noise. That is why another optimization scheme, within the complementary beamforming based framework described above and depicted in Fig.5, has been proposed in [45]. According to this, the power spectrum of the estimated speech $\left|\hat{S}(l,\omega)\right|^2$ is calculated through a block averaging technique, giving origin to the quantity $\left|\hat{S}_B(\omega)\right|^2$ (where $B$ is the number of blocks involved) that becomes the minimization criterion (assuming speech absence conditions). Again a relatively superior performance is obtained with respect to the conventional DS in situations where well-located noise sources (undesired speeches) are present. This occurs also when sound sources outnumber the microphones.

For the sake of completeness, we can mention the work of Dahl and Claesson [36], within the category of nonlinear microphone arrays. The approach followed in [46] is the one of nonlinear time-domain filtering, previously addressed in Section 2, and from this perspective it can be seen as a generalization of the single-channel approach described above. Hence no further details will be provided here.

Let us move now to address the Spectral Amplitude estimation based approach. The first contribution to consider here is the work of Lotter et al. [47] which provides two short-time spectral amplitude estimators generalizing the single-channel MMSE (Ephraim-Malah) and MAP [62] estimators. The method is based on the usual assumption that both speech and noise DFT coefficients have zero-mean equal-variance independent Gaussian pdfs. In the multi-channel case, the estimation of the speech spectral amplitudes is conditioned on complex spectra of M noisy channels $Y_m(\cdot)$, taking into account the notation used in (2):

$$\left|\hat{S}_m\right| = E\left\{\left|S_m\right| \mid Y_1, Y_2, \cdots, Y_M\right\} \tag{39}$$

The above is calculated at each point of the time-frequency grid $(p,\omega)$. It can be showed that the new gain for channel $m$ is:

$$G_{\bar{m}}(p,\omega) = \Gamma(1.5) \cdot \sqrt{\frac{R_{prio,\bar{m}}}{\left(1+R_{post,\bar{m}}\right)\left(1+\sum_{m=1}^{M}R_{prio,m}\right)}} \cdot$$

$$\cdot F_1\left(-0.5, 1, -\frac{\left|\sum_{m=1}^{M}\sqrt{\left(1+R_{post,m}\right)R_{prio,m}}\,e^{i\vartheta_m}\right|^2}{1+\sum_{m=1}^{M}R_{prio,m}}\right) \tag{40}$$

where $F_1$ is the confluent hypergeometric series, $\Gamma$ the Gamma function and $\vartheta_m$ the $m$-$th$ noisy channel phase. Eq. (40) turns to (9) when $M=1$, since (9) can be shown to be equal to:

$$G(p,\omega)=\Gamma(1.5)\cdot\sqrt{\frac{R_{prio}}{\left(1+R_{post}\right)\left(1+R_{prio}\right)}}\cdot F_1\left(-0.5,1,-\frac{\left(1+R_{post}\right)R_{prio}}{1+R_{prio}}\right) \tag{41}$$

It must be observed that (40) is obtained if perfect DOA (Direction of Arrival) correction is assumed within the microphone-array when the short-term spectral amplitude estimation $\left|\hat{S}(p,\omega)\right|$ is performed. As pointed out in [51], for DOA independent speech enhancement, the amplitude estimation has to be calculated by conditioning the expectation of the joint observation of noisy amplitudes, i.e. (39) turns to:

$$\left|\hat{S}_m\right| = E\left\{\left|S_m\right|\,\big|\,\left|Y_1\right|,\left|Y_2\right|,\cdots,\left|Y_M\right|\right\}. \tag{42}$$

In order to do the above in a simple and effective way, the authors in [47] suggested to employ the MAP estimator proposed originally for the single-channel case in [62]. It follows that, denoting $p(\cdot)$ as the probability density function (pdf) of a generic random variable, the following has to be maximized

$$\log(L)=\log\left(p\left(\left|Y_1\right|,\left|Y_2\right|,\cdots,\left|Y_M\right|\,\big|\,\left|S_m\right|\right)\cdot p\left(\left|S_m\right|\right)\right) \tag{43}$$

from which the following resulting gain can be derived:

$$G_{\bar{m}}(p,\omega)=\frac{\sqrt{R_{prio,\bar{m}}\big/\left(1+R_{post,\bar{m}}\right)}}{2\cdot\left(1+\sum_{m=1}^{M}R_{prio,m}\right)}\cdot\mathrm{Re}\Bigg(\sum_{m=1}^{M}\sqrt{\left(1+R_{post,m}\right)R_{prio,m}}+$$
$$+\sqrt{\left(\sum_{m=1}^{M}\sqrt{\left(1+R_{post,m}\right)R_{prio,m}}\right)^2+\left(2-M\right)\left(1+\sum_{m=1}^{M}R_{prio,m}\right)}\Bigg) \tag{44}$$

which turns to the single-channel gain as follows:

$$G(p,\omega)=\frac{R_{prio}+\sqrt{R_{prio}^{\,2}+\left(1+R_{prio}\right)R_{prio}\big/\left(1+R_{post}\right)}}{2\cdot\left(1+R_{prio}\right)} \tag{45}$$

observing that the argument of $\mathrm{Re}(\cdot)$ is always a real number when $M=1$.

Experimental results show how the new estimators allow a significant improvement of noise reduction performances (using segmental SNR as quality index) with respect to the single-channel EM rule in several operating conditions. Moreover as expected, the multi-channel MAP estimation approach turns out to be less sensitive to the phase errors (which are likely introduced by reverberation environments in rear-world applications) compared to the MMSE based method.

Along this direction we must cite the approach recently proposed by Cohen and Berdugo [49] that focused on the minimization of the Log-Spectra amplitude (LSA) distortion in environments where time-varying noise is present. The overall scheme (Fig.6) comprises an adaptive beamforming system (made of a fixed beamformer, a blocking matrix and a multi-channel adaptive noise canceller) and a suitable LSA estimation chain acting on the beamformer outputs, written as (in STFT domain):

$$V(l,\omega) = S_1(l,\omega) + \tilde{N}_{1,st}(l,\omega) + \tilde{N}_{1,ns}(l,\omega)$$
$$U_m(l,\omega) = S_m(l,\omega) + \tilde{N}_{m,st}(l,\omega) + \tilde{N}_{m,ns}(l,\omega) \qquad m = 1, \cdots, M \tag{46}$$

where $st$ and $ns$ stand for stationary and non-stationary respectively. The objective is to find a suitable estimator of $S_1(l,\omega)$ minimizing the LSA distortion.

The noise cancellation system is responsible for reducing the stationary contribution and yielding the signal $V(l,\omega)$ on which the *optimally-modified log-spectral amplitude* (OM-LSA) gain function will be applied to achieve the goal. The evaluation of the nature of transient occurrences is performed through a suitable estimation of speech presence probability, which is based on a Gaussian statistical model and in particular on the transient beam-to-reference ratio (TBRR) defined as:

$$\Omega(l,\omega) = \frac{\mathcal{S}\big[V(l,\omega)\big] - \mathcal{M}\big[V(l,\omega)\big]}{\max_{2\le m\le M}\big\{\mathcal{S}\big[U_m(l,\omega)\big] - \mathcal{M}\big[U_m(l,\omega)\big]\big\}} \tag{47}$$

where S[.], M[.] are the smoothing operator and the noise spectrum estimator arising by recursively averaging past spectral power values [48]. Assuming that the beamformer steering error is low and that the interfering noise is uncorrelated with speech, it can be said that a high TBRR means speech presence. When this is not the case, the noise estimation can be fast updated and then given to the OM-LSA [5] estimator for final speech enhancement. As confirmed by experimental results, such an approach seems to provide an adequate estimation of the time-varying noise spectral components and so a significant reduction of noise impact without degrading the speech

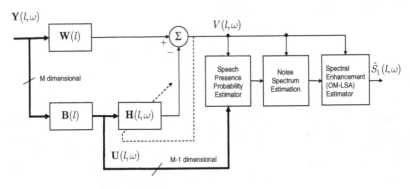

**Fig. 6.** Block diagram of the multi-microphone log-spectral amplitude estimation

information. Moreover, a significant improvement of performances is obtained through this multi-channel algorithm w.r.t. the single channel counterpart.

Another interesting approach based on Log-Spectra Amplitude estimation is the one employing a Supervised Regression technique, both in linear and nonlinear fashions. The method is termed Multiple Regression of the Log Spectrum (MRLS) [46] and has the objective of approximating the Log-Spectral Amplitude of the close-talking microphone (i.e. the original speech signal $s[k]$) by means of the Log-Spectral Amplitude of noisy signals emanating from other sensors. Mathematically, (taking (2) into account):

$$\log\left(S^{(d)}\right) \approx \sum_{m=1}^{M} \lambda_m \log\left(Y_m^{(d)}\right). \tag{48}$$

Let us first assume that the model (2) is written as:

$$y_m[k] = h_m[k] * s[k] + g_m[k] * n[k]. \tag{49}$$

Moving to the STFT domain, we can approximate the log-power spectrum of the $m$-th mic signal by a two-dimensional Taylor-series expansion around the reference $Y_m^0$ so that:

$$\log\left(Y_m\right) - \log\left(Y_m^0\right) \approx a_m\left(\log\left(S\right) - \log\left(S^0\right)\right) + b_m\left(\log\left(N\right) - \log\left(N^0\right)\right) \tag{50}$$

where it can be shown that the coefficients $a_m, b_m$ depends on the SNR at $m$-th location. Now, considering $(\bullet)^{(d)}$ the deviation from $(\bullet)^{(0)}$, (50) turns to:

$$\log\left(Y_m^{(d)}\right) \approx a_m\left(\log\left(S^{(d)}\right)\right) + b_m\left(\log\left(N^{(d)}\right)\right). \tag{51}$$

The regression error is then given by the difference between the two terms in (48). The optimal weights $\lambda_m$ can be obtained by minimizing such an error over a suitable number $T$ of training samples, i.e.:

$$\varepsilon = \frac{1}{T}\sum_{t=1}^{T}\left\{\left[\log\left(S^{(d)}\right)\right]_t - \left[\sum_{m=1}^{M}\lambda_m \log\left(Y_m^{(d)}\right)\right]_t\right\}^2. \tag{52}$$

The supervised optimization approach followed requires the employment of a close-talking microphone added to the available microphone array during the training phase the speech captured by the close talking mic is used as the speech signal $S$. The log-power spectrum is calculated though mel-filter bank (MFB) analysis and log operator. A cepstral based implementation has been also implemented, since the orthogonality of the Discrete Cosine Transform (DCT) transform ensures that minimization of (52) is equivalent to minimization in the cepstral domain. Several experimental results have shown that the MRLS approach allows a good approximation of the close-talking microphone and outperforms the adaptive beamformer from the perspective of speech recognition performance, ensuring also a low computational cost. Further improvements have been obtained when nonlinear regression (through Multi-Layer Perceptrons and Support Vector Machines) is employed [51]. A drawback is likely represented by the supervised optimization procedure that can be adopted within a speech recognition scheme, but turns out to be limiting in a more general framework for speech enhancement. An alternative approach to multi-channel non-linear speech enhancement has been described in [63], which applies neural network based sub-band processing (within the MMSBA processing framework) with promising initial results using real automobile reverberant data. This interesting approach warrants further investigation.

## 5  Concluding Summary

In this section, we summarize in tabular form for comparative purposes, the general features, list of operating assumptions, the relative advantages and drawbacks, and the various types of non-linear techniques for each class of speech enhancement strategy reviewed in this paper. Some references related to the methods not specifically described in the paper, are not included in the table.

### 5.1  Spectral Subtraction/Filtering Techniques

| BASIC (LINEAR) TECHNIQUES [1], [2], [6] | |
|---|---|
| General Features | - based on MMSE estimator<br>- optimal solution only for Gaussian statistics<br>- frame by frame processing<br>- linear subtraction/filtering in the noisy signal spectral domain |
| Assumptions | -speech and noise incorrelated<br>- stationarity of noise signal<br>- availability of a VAD system<br>- zero mean Gaussian signals (for optimal estimation) |
| Advantages | - ease of implementation<br>- computationally low demanding |
| Drawbacks | -non optimal estimate of clean speech<br>- high level musical noise |
| NON LINEAR EXTENSIONS | |
| Ephraim Malah [8],[9], [10] | - nonlinear MMSE-STSA estimator<br>- higher noise suppression compared to linear SS/SF<br>- lower musical noise on the enhanced speech |
| Xie-Compernolle [12] | - empirical approach for the MMSE-STSA estimation<br>- MLP to approximate the $Y$->$X$ mapping<br>- computationally more demanding (Monte Carlo simulations)<br>- it requires the knowledge of the log spectral variance of the clean speech (supposed fixed) |

## 5.2  Supervised NN Based Techniques

| BASIC TECHNIQUES [21], [26], [52] | |
|---|---|
| **General Features** | - NN used to get the nonlinear mapping $Y \rightarrow X$<br>- off line training stage needed<br>- standard training strategies (e.g. BP) to minimize MSE<br>- different NN topologies can be used<br>- iterative algorithms<br>- filtering can be realized both in time and in different domains<br>- speech parameters extracted form clean speech and used for enhancement |
| **Assumptions** | - additive Gaussian noise<br>- both noise and speech stationarity<br>- availability of clean speech data for off-line training<br>- Gaussian signal statistics (for optimal estimation)<br>- speech and noise stats representative of the training set<br>- SNR or measures of joint noise-signal stats available |
| **Advantages** | - better estimation of clean speech<br>- reduction of musical noise effect<br>- good for fixed noise type |
| **Drawbacks** | - higher computational complexity<br>- availability of a clean speech training set |
| **OTHER EXTENSIONS** | |
| **Kalman Filter** [3], [20] | - speech modeled as AR process<br>- noise and speech variances available<br>- no colored noise<br>- involved parameters availability (noise gain, LPC parameters) |
| **Switching Methods** [16-19] | - a posteriori probability available for each class<br>- suitable for non stationary signals<br>- HMM estimate form noisy signal using Bayesian estimator form noisy speech<br>- number of sates must be sufficient to model all ranges of signal and noise statistics |
| **Extended KF** [3], [20] | - non linear AR model for speech<br>- ML convergence to AR parameters (off line training)<br>- AR parameters available during enhancement<br>- noise and speech variances must be known |

## 5.3  Unsupervised Techniques

| BASIC METHODS | |
|---|---|
| **General Features** | - NN used to get the nonlinear mapping $Y \rightarrow x$<br>- different topologies of NN can be used<br>- iterative algorithm<br>- joint estimation of signal and noise parameters<br>- classical methods make use of EM technique |
| **Assumptions** | - noise less correlated than speech<br>- short term stationarity of involved signals |
| **Advantages** | - no need of clean speech data |
| **Drawbacks** | - computationally demanding |
| **OTHER EXTENTIONS** | |
| **Dual EKF** [20], [26] | - ML estimates for both enhanced speech and parameters<br>- can be used also with colored noise<br>- usually used in the EM algorithm<br>- high computational cost<br>- frame by frame iteration |

| | - quasi stationarity for speech signal needed |
| | - possible initialization using HOS |
| **NRAF** [20], [28], [31] | - similar to dual EKF but no AR model for speech |
| | - time domain MMSE filtering (no clean speech needed) |
| **Ephraim Cohen** [4] | - speech modeled as TVAR system |
| | - Gaussian noise |
| | - lower computational complexity ($O(N)$) |
| **Monte Carlo/Particle Filtering** [4], [29], [30] | - computationally demanding |

## 5.4  Adaptive Noise Cancellation (ANC)

| ADAPTIVE NOISE CANCELLATION [31-33] | |
|---|---|
| **General Features** | - 2 channels available |
| | - no a priori knowledge on noisy signals required |
| | - reference channel contains no speech (ideally) |
| | - $s$ and $n$ incorrelated |
| | - linear or nonlinear filter can be used |
| | - ease of implementation and low computational cost (for linear filter) |
| | - using linear filter with MMSE estimator does not allow to get the Bayes conditional mean (optimal solution) |
| | - MMSE optimal filter: usually a nonlinear function of noisy data |
| **NON-LINEAR ANC** | |
| **General Features** | - non gaussian signal allowed |
| | - can deal with more complex mappings |
| | - higher computational complexity |
| **HOS Filters** [41] | - better to remove impulse noise |
| | - stationary zero mean signals |
| | - $s$ and $n$ independent |
| **Volterra and NN** [39-40], [42] | - different topologies allowed |
| | - training using classical algorithms |
| **MMSBA** [35-38] | - sub-band processing of noisy speech |
| | - different solution for the filter bank (DFT FB or Orthogonal transform) |
| | - sub-band distribution can be non linear |
| | - MMSE convergence improved |
| | - VAD available |
| | - different processing possible for different sub-bands |
| | - non linear filters can be used in the sub-bands processing |

## 5.5  Multi-channel Speech Enhancement

| MULTI CHANNEL TECHNIQUES | |
|---|---|
| **General Features** [43] | - array of $M$ channel available |
| | - more degree of freedom |
| | - spatial filtering |
| | - enhanced capabilities of noise suppression |
| **Complementary Beamforming and SS** [44-45] | - spatial non linear SS technique |
| | - two complementary beamformers |
| | - no speech pause detector needed |
| | - incorrelation of arriving signals |
| | - nonlinear constrained least squares minimization |
| | - supervised approach |
| | - significant improvement of speech enhancement capability |
| | - optimized for directional noise in [44] |

| Dahl Cleasson [46] | - based on nonlinear time filtering<br>- employment of supervised neural networks<br>- generalization of the single channel case |
|---|---|
| Lotter [47] | - generalization of the single channel MMSE (Ephraim-Malah)<br>- speech and noise DFT coefficients zero mean independent Gaussian pdfs<br>- significant improvements of noise reduction performances<br>- less sensitive to phase errors with MAP estimators |
| Cohen Berdugo [49] | - based on log-spectra amplitude (LSA) estimation<br>- unsupervised approach<br>- adaptive beamformer plus LSA estimation chain<br>- noise cancellation system after the beamformer<br>- suitable for environments with time-varying noises |
| Multiple Regression [50-51] | - supervised technique, both in linear and nonlinear fashion<br>- based on LSA estimation of the speech signal, coming from the close-talking mic<br>- implementation in the cepstral domain<br>- suitable as front-end for speech recognition |

# References

1. Vaseghi, S.V.: Advanced Signal Processing and Digital Noise Reduction (2nd ed.). John Wiley & Sons, 2000

2. O'Shaughnessy, D.: Speech Communications – Human and Machine. IEEE Press, 2nd ed, Piscataway, NJ, 2000

3. Benesty, J, Makino, S., and Chen, J.,: Speech Enhancement. Signal and Communication Technology Series, Springer Verlag, 2005

4. Ephraim, Y., Cohen, I.: Recent Advancements in Speech Enhancement. The Electrical Engineering Handbook, CRC Press, 2005

5. Cohen, I. and Berdugo, B.H.: Speech enhancement for non-stationary noise environments. Signal Processing, vol. 81, pp. 2403-2418, 2001.

6. Boll S.: Suppression of acoustic noise in speech using spectral subtraction. IEEE Trans. Acoust. Speech, Signal Process., ASSP-27:113-120, April 1979.

7. Lockwood, P., Boudy, J.: Experiment with a Nonlinear Spectral Subtractor (NSS). Hidden Markov Models and the Projection, for Robust Speech Recognition in Cars. Speech Communications, 11, 215-228, 1992.

8. Ephraim, Y. Malah, D.:. Speech Enhancement Using a Minimum Mean Square Error Short Time Spectral Amplitude Estimator. IEEE Trans. Acoust., Speech, Signal Processing, vol. ASSP-32, pp. 1109-1121, 1984

9. Ephraim, Y. Malah, D.: Speech enhancement using a minimum mean square log spectral amplitude estimator. IEEE Trans. Acoust., Speech, Sig.Proc., vol 33, no 2, pp 443-445, 1985

10. Cappè, O.: Elimination of the musical noise phenomenon with the Ephraim and Malah noise suppressor. IEEE Trans. Speech and Audio Proc., vol. 2, pp. 345 -349, April 1994

11. McAulay, R.J. and Malpass, M.L.: Speech Enhancement Using a Soft-Decision Noise Suppression Filter. IEEE Trans.on Acoust., Speech and Sig.Proc., vol. ASSP-28, no. 2, 1980

12. Xie, F. and Compernolle, D. V.: Speech enhancement by nonlinear spectral estimation - a unifying approach. EUROSPEECH'93, 617-620, 1993

13. Virag, N.: Single channel speech enhancement based on masking properties of the human auditory system. IEEE Trans. Speech Audio Processing, vol. 7, pp. 126–137, March 1999

14. Ephraim, Y. and Van Trees, H.L.: A signal subspace approach for speech enhancement. IEEE Trans. Speech and Audio Proc., vol. 3, pp. 251-266, July 1995

15. Lev-Ari, H. and Ephraim, Y.: Extension of the signal subspace speech enhancement approach to colored noise. IEEE Sig. Proc. Let., vol. 10, pp. 104-106, April 2003

16. Y. Ephraim: Statistical-model-based speech enhancement systems. Proc. IEEE, 80(10), October 1992

17. Ephraim, Y.: A Bayesian Estimation Approach for Speech Enhancement Using Hidden Markov Models. IEEE Trans. Signal Processing, vol. 40, pp. 725-735, Apr. 1992

18. Lee, K.Y., McLaughlin, S., and Shirai, K.: Speech enhancement based on extended Kalman filter and neural predictive hidden Markov model. IEEE Neural Networks for Signal Processing Workshop, pages 302-10, September 1996

19. Lee, J.; Seo; C., and Lee, K.Y. : A new nonlinear prediction model based on the recurrent neural predictive hidden Markov model for speech enhancement. ICASSP '02. vol. 1, pp.:1037-1040, May 2002

20. Wan, E.A., Nelson, A.T.: Networks for Speech Enhancement. Handbook of Neural Networks for Speech Processing, Edited by Shigeru Katagiri, Boston, USA. 1999

21. Dawson, M.I. and Sridharan, S.: Speech enhancement using time delay neural networks, Proceedings of the Fourth Australian International Conf. on Speech Science and Technology, pages 152-5, December 1992

22. Tamura, S.: An analysis of a noise reduction neural network. ICASSP '87, pp. 2001-4, 1987

23. Tamura, S.: Improvements to the noise reduction neural network, ICASSP '90, vol. 2, pp. 825-8, 1990

24. Knecht, W.G.: Nonlinear Noise Filtering and Beamforming Using the Perceptron and Its Volterra Approximation. IEEE Trans. On Speech and Audio Proc., vol.2, no.1, part 1, 1994

25. Knecht, W, Schenkel, M., Moschytz, G S.,: Neural Network Filters for Speech Enhancement. IEEE Trans. Speech & Audio Proc., 3(6),433-438, 1995

26. X-M. Gao, S.J. Ovaska, and I.O. Hartimo. Speech signal restoration using an optimal neural network structure, IJCNN 96, pages 1841-6, 1996

27. Gannot, S., Burshtein, D. and Weinstein, E.: Iterative and Sequential Kalman Filter-Based Speech Enhancement Algorithms. IEEE Trans. Speech and Audio Proc., vol. 6, pp. 373-385, 1998

28. Wan, E.A., Nelson, A.T.: Neural dual extended Kalman filtering: applications in speech enhancement and monaural blind signal separation. Proceedings Neural Networks for Signal Processing Workshop, 1997

29. Vermaak, J., Andrieu, C., Doucet, A., Godsill, S.J.: Particle Methods for Bayesian Modeling and Enhancement of Speech Signals. IEEE Trans. Speech and Audio Processing, vol. 10, pp. 173 -185, Mar. 2002

30. Fong, W., Godsill, S.J., Doucet, A. and West, M.: Monte Carlo smoothing with application to audio signal enhancement. IEEE Trans. Signal Processing, vol. 50, pp. 438-449, 2002

31. Wan, E. and Van der Merwe, R.: Noise-Regularized Adaptive Filtering for Speech Enhancement. Proceedings of EUROSPEECH'99, Sep 1999

32. Widrow, B., Glover jr., J. R., McCool, J. M., Kaunitz, J., Williams, C. S., Hearn, R. H., Zeidler, J. R., Dong jr., E. and Goodlin, R. C.: Adaptive Noise Cancelling: Principles and Applications. Proceedings of the IEEE, 63 (12): 1692–1716,1975

33. Clarkson, P.M.: Optimal and Adaptive Signal Processing. CRC Press, Boca Raton, 1993.

34. Toner, E.: Speech Enhancement Using Digital Signal Processing, PhD thesis, University of Paisley, UK, 1993

35. Darlington, D.J., Campbell, D.R.: Sub-band Adaptive Filtering Applied to Hearing Aids. Proc.ICSLP'96, pp. 921-924, Philadelphia, USA, 1996
36. 36.Hussain, A., Campbell, D.R.,: Intelligibility improvements using binaural diverse sub-band processing applied to speech corrupted with automobile noise. IEE Proceedings: Vision, Image and Signal Processing, Vol. 148, no.2, pp.127-132, 2001
37. Hussain, A., Campbell, D.R.: A Multi-Microphone Sub-Band Adaptive Speech Enhancement System Employing Diverse Sub-Band Processing. International Journal of Robotics & Automation, vol. 15, no. 2, pp. 78-84, 2000
38. Hussain, A., Squartni, S., Piazza, F.: Novel Subband Adaptive Systems Incorporating Wiener Filtering for Binaural Speech Enhancement. NOLISP05, ITRW on Non-Linear Speech Processing - LNAI 3817, Springer-Verlag, 2005.
39. Cha, I., Kassam, S.A.: Interference Cancellation Using Radial Basis Function Networks, . Signal Processing, vol.47, pp.247-268, 1995
40. Vorobyov, S.A., Cichocki, A.: Hyper Radial Basis Function Neural Networks for Interference Cancellation with Nonlinear Processing of Reference Signal. Digital Signal Processing, Academic Press, July 2001, vol. 11, no. 3, pp. 204-221(18)
41. Giannakis, G.B., Dandawate, A.V.: Linear and Non-Linear Adaptive Noise Cancellers. Proc ICASSP 1990. pp 1373-1376, Albuquerque, 1990
42. Amblard, P., Baudois, D.: Non-linear Noise Cancellation Using Volterra Filters, a Real Case Study. Nonlinear Digital Signal Processing, IEEE Winter Workshop on, Jan. 17-20, 1993
43. Brandstein, M.S. and Ward, D.B.: Microphone Arrays: Signal Processing Techniques and Applications. Springer-Verlag, Berlin, 2001
44. Saruwatari, H., Kajita, S., Takeda, K., Itakura, F.: Speech Enhancement Using Nonlinear Microphone Array Based on Complementary Beamforming, IEICE Trans. Fundamentals, vol.E82-A, no.8, pp.1501-1510, 1999.
45. Saruwatari, H., Kajita, S., Takeda, K., Itakura, F.: Speech Enhancement Based on Noise Adaptive Nonlinear Microphone Array, EUSIPCO 2000, X European Signal Processing Conference, Tampere Finland, 2000
46. Dahl, M. and Claesson, I.: A neural network trained microphone array system for noise reduction. IEEE Neural Networks for Signal Processing VI, pages 311-319, 1996
47. Lotter, T., Benien, C., Vary, P.: Multichannel Direction-Independent Speech Enhancement using Spectral Amplitude Estimation. Eurasip Journal on Applied Signal Processing, 11, pp. 1147-1156, 2003
48. I. Cohen, Berdugo, B.: Noise Estimation by Minima Controlled Recursive Averaging for Robust Speech Enhancement, IEEE Signal Processing Letters, vol.9, no.1 pp. 12-15, 2002
49. Cohen, I. and Berdugo, B.: Speech enhancement based on a microphone array and log-spectral amplitude estimation. Electrical and Electronics Engineers in Israel, the 22nd Convention, pp. 4.:6, Dec. 2002
50. Shinde, T., Takeda, K., Itakura, F.: Multiple regression of log-spectra for in-car speech recognition. ICSLP-2002, pp. 797-800, 2002
51. Li, W., Miyajima, C., Nishino, T., Itou, K., Takeda, K., Itakura, F.: Adaptive Nonlinear Regression using Multiple Distributed Microphones for In-Car Speech Recognition. IEICE Trans. Fundamentals, vol. E88-A, no. 7, pp. 1716-1723, 2005
52. Parveen, S. and Green, P.D.: Speech enhancement with missing data techniques using recurrent neural networks, Proc. IEEE ICASSP 2004, Montreal, 2004
53. Haykin, S. 2002 Adaptive Filter Theory (4th ed) Prentice Hall Information and System Science Series, Thomas Kailath Series Editor

54. Kamath, S. and Loizou, P.: A multi-band spectral subtraction method for enhancing speech corrupted by colored noise, ICASSP 2002
55. Gülzow, T., Ludwig, L. and Heute, U.: Spectral-Substraction Speech Enhancement in Multirate Systems with and without Non-uniform and Adaptive Bandwidths. Signal Processing, vol. 83, pp. 1613-1631, 2003
56. Greenwood, V: A Cochlear Frequency-Position Function for Several Species-29 Years Later. J. Acoustic Soc. Amer., vol. 86, no. 6, pp. 2592-2605, 1990
57. Abutalebi, H. R., Sheikhzadeh, H., Brennan, R. L., Freeman, G.H.: A Hybrid Sub-Band System for Speech Enhancement in Diffuse Noise Fields, IEEE Sig. Process. Letters, 2003
58. Le Bouquin, R., Faucon, G.: Study of a Voice Activity Detector and its Influence on a Noise Reduction System. Speech Communication, vol. 16, pp. 245-254, 1995
59. Bahoura M. and Rouat J., "A new approach for wavelet speech enhancement", Proc. EUROSPEECH, pp. 1937-2001, 2001
60. Bahoura M. and Rouat J., "Wavelet speech enhancement based on the Teager Energy Operator," IEEE Signal Proc. Lett., 8(1), pp. 10-12, 2001
61. Cecchi, S, Bastari, A., Squartini, S. and Piazza, F.: Comparing Performances of Different Multiband Adaptive Architectures for Noise Reduction. Communications, Circuits and Systems (ICCCAS), 2006 International Conference of Guilin-China 2006
62. Wolfe, P.J. and. Godsill, S.J.: "Efficient alternatives to the Ephraim and Malah suppression rule for audio signal enhancement," URASIP Journal on Applied Signal Processing, no. 10, pp. 1043–1051, 2003, special issue: Digital Audio for Multimedia Communications
63. Hussain, A., Campbell, D.R.: "Binaural sub-band adaptive speech enhancement using artificial neural networks," Speech Communication, vol.25, pp.177-186, 1998, Special Issue: Robust Speech Recognition for Unknown Communication Channels

# The Amount of Information on Emotional States Conveyed by the Verbal and Nonverbal Channels: Some Perceptual Data

Anna Esposito[1,2]

[1] Dipartimento di Psicologia, Seconda Università di Napoli
Via Vivaldi 43, 81100 Caserta, Italy
[2] IIASS, Via Pellegrino 19, 84019, Vietri sul Mare, SA, Italy
iiass.annaesp@tin.it, anna.esposito@unina2.it

**Abstract.** In a face-to-face interaction, the addressee exploits both the verbal and nonverbal communication modes to infer the speaker's emotional state. Is such an informational content redundant? Is the amount of information conveyed by each communication mode the same or is it different? How much information about the speaker's emotional state is conveyed by each mode and is there a preferential red communication mode for a given emotional state? This work attempts to give an answer to the above questions evaluating the subjective perception of emotional states in the single (either visual or auditory channel) and the combined channels (visual and auditory). Results show that vocal expressions convey the same amount of information as the combined channels and that the video alone conveys poorer emotional information than the audio and the audio and video together. Interpretations of these results (that seem to not support the data reported in literature proving the dominance of the visual channel in the emotion's perception) are given in terms of cognitive load, language expertise and dynamicity. Also, a mathematical model inspired to the information processing theory is hypothesized to support the suggested interpretations.

## 1 Introduction

It has been and remains difficult to define emotions, and this difficulty continues, even though there have been a lot of attempts to characterize emotional states. The proposed approaches to understand emotions are centered on finding insights on what emotions are, but the question still remains unanswered. James [44] was the first to posit the question and to indicate the bodily approach as a first coherent approach to explain emotions. According to James, emotions are the feeling of <<...*bodily changes that follow directly the perception of the exciting fact...*>>, whereas in Darwin's opinion [16] they are patterns of actions deriving from our evolutionary or individual past and may be <<...*of the least use...*>> in our modern context. Along the past centuries, the social role of emotions has been differently interpreted and they have been either considered as conflicting aspects of soul (Plato, 450 B.C.[60]) or essential in the context of the Ethic (Aristotele, 384 B.C.[5]) as well as disturbing passions (Descartes, 1649 [38]) or as playing a central role in the human behaviour

Y. Stylianou, M. Faundez-Zanuy, A. Esposito (Eds.): WNSP 2005, LNCS 4391, pp. 249–268, 2007.

[64]. Theory of emotions tends to privilege inner and psychological motivations but modern anthropologists conceive emotions as socially embedded responses that <<...*take on behavioural significance within a field of culturally interpreted person-person and person-situations relations...* [80]>>. During the last century, the study of emotions involved different scientific fields and today the effort among psychologists, neurologists, anthropologists, and moral philosophers is to converge towards a holistic theory of emotion. However, there is still the need to define emotions and below a working definition is proposed.

## 1.1  A "Working Definition"

A working definition is not "*the definition*". It is just a way to deal with a phenomenon that is not yet entirely understood to provide an orientation. Such a definition can be changed as soon as new relevant explanations are discovered. On this premise, the central condition of emotions is considered to be the evaluation of an event. A person is consciously or unconsciously evaluating an external or internal event that is relevant to him or to some of his concerns or goals. This is what the psychologists call the appraisal phase. At the core of this evaluation (or concurrently with this evaluation) there is a "readiness to act" and the "prompting of plans" [32-33] that allow the person to handle the evaluated event producing appropriate mental states accompanied by physiological changes, feelings, and expressions. This process can be schematized in the diagram reported in Figure 1 which is a personal interpretation of the feedback loop proposed by Plutchik [61-62].

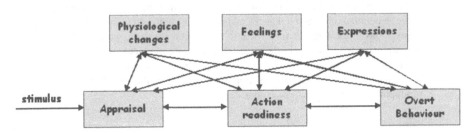

**Fig. 1.** A personal interpretation of the feedback loop proposed by Plutichik [61]

The above interpretation assumes that after the evaluation of an event there are several processes that take place concurrently to the readiness of action. They all affect each other and it is possible that none of them has a primary role. They are all the result of mental processes that take over on the current cognitive state to handle the subject's emotional state. This interpretation is in accord with the largely accepted definition of emotions proposed, among others, by Plutchik [61-62], Frijda [32-33], and Scherer [66, 70], even though it may differ by not assigning a priority to any of them. Our idea is that, being emotions experienced as a comprehensive manifestation of feelings, expressions, physiological changes, action readiness, and prompting of plans, assigning a subsidiary role to any of these signals would produce a restricted interpretation of their essence as a whole.

According to many authors (see also Oatley and Jenkins [58]) emotions have several functional roles, among these the most important in driving social interaction are:

1. They solicit appropriate reactions to events that happen unexpectedly and demand immediate action;

2. They act as signs (exhibited through a variety of comportments) made for the purpose of giving (consciously or unconsciously) notice of a plan of future intents;

3. They play a communicative function.

However, the above functions, do not completely define the role of emotions and why they should exist. At the date, a unique scientific theory of emotions is not yet available. Scientists are debating on divergent opinions ranging from evolutionary vs. socio-cultural theories [12-13, 22, 24, 29-30, 32-33, 40-41, 44, 48-51, 59, 61-62, 70]. It is not in the aims of this work to discuss on them and an interested reader can find very fascinating highlights in the book of Oatley and Jenkins [58]. Our primary aim is on the expressions of emotions, on the perceptual features exploited to recognize them from facial expressions, voice, and body movements, and on trying to establish if there is a preferential channel for perceiving an emotional state. These will be the arguments discussed in the following sections.

## 2 The Expressions of Emotions

We are not sure that the term "expressions" is clearly identifying what we call the "expressions of emotions". This is because, as stated above first, expressions cannot be separated from emotions as secondary processes, and second, in our opinion, also physiological changes and feelings are "expressions" of emotions. However, in this context, the term "expressions" is used to indicate what is perceived on the emotional states in the face-to-face interaction. In this sense, we restricted ourselves to consider the perceptual appearance of emotional states, i.e. the facial, the vocal, and the gestural expressions of emotions. Two of them, the facial, and the vocal, have received a lot of attention by many authors, while gestures have been, at the date, partially neglected. Verbal communication is not considered as an expression of emotions. Firstly, because it seems to involve less immediate and different cognitive processes; and secondly, because the expression of emotions through the verbal channel meets lexical difficulties due to the fact that often subjects can hardly label or recognize their emotional state. We will summarize the main findings about the expressions of emotions in these three domains and we will present some interesting perceptual data on the emotional information conveyed by the visual and the auditory channels.

### 2.1 The Facial Expression of Emotions

Facial expressions as markers of emotions were first suggested by Darwin [16]. Darwin approached the study of facial expressions of emotions from a biological point of view considering them as innate "ancient habits" that can partially be modified by learning and imitation processes. This idea was debated by several authors, among whom the most representatives were Klineberg [48], La Barre [50], and Birdwhistell

[7], and more recently by White and Fridlund [29-30, 80], according to whom any behaviour, and therefore also facial expressions of emotions, are learned.

Darwin's approach was recovered and reinforced about a century later by Tomkins [77-79], which posits the basis for the research on the instrumental role of facial movements and facial feedbacks in experiencing emotions. According to Tomkins, emotions are the driving forces of our primary motivational system acting as amplifiers of what we receive from the environment, and our face is the most important expression of them. This is because facial expressions of emotions are universally shared. People from different cultures can easily recognize a happy or a sad face because of an "innate affective program" for each of what is considered "a primary emotion" that acts on the facial musculature to produce emotional facial expressions. On this research line, Ekman [21-23] and Izard [39-41] identified a small set of emotions (the primary ones) associated with a unique configuration of facial muscle movements and both developed some anatomically based coding systems (the Facial Action Coding System, (FACS) [20, 25-26], the Maximally Discriminative Facial Movement Coding System (MAX) and AFFEX [42-43] for measuring facial behaviours and identifying emotional expressions. The three systems are different both in the primary emotions they include (only six for Ekman - happiness, sadness, anger, fear, surprise, and disgust; nine for Izard) and in the expressions they assign to some of them. Sophisticated instruments, such as facial EMG (Electromyography) were used [12-13, 72-74] to asses the above facial coding systems when emotional information was not visually perceptible in facial actions. Nevertheless, such studies proved that distinction among primary emotions or more generally among negative and positive emotions, was not possible using either visible or EMG information on facial expressions.

At the date, the role of facial expressions of emotions in identifying and recognizing emotions is debated among two theories:

1. The "micro-expression hypothesis" which assumes that emotion-specific facial expressions <u>do exist</u> even when they are not visually perceptible and they emerge as visible expressions as the emotional intensity increases [72-74]. This means that an innate program that controls our facial musculature does exist and it changes our face when we are emotionally involved;

2. The "ethological perspective" that assumes that facial expressions are not directly related to emotional states, being signals associated to the communicative context [29-30]. The essence of this theory is that "we make faces". They are contextual to the moment and the particular situation. Facial expressions may have nothing to do with our emotional states.

## 2.2 The Vocal Expressions of Emotions

Emotions produce changes in respiration, phonation, and articulation which in turn affect vocalizations and the acoustic parameters of the corresponding signal [2, 4, 6, 8, 15, 17-19, 31, 34, 67-69, 71]. Measurements of emotional speech are derived from three perceptual cues such as loudness, pitch, and timing, which in turn are expressed in changes of acoustic variables such as: amplitude (which is the measure of sound pressure), and sound intensity (which is the measure of sound energy at different frequencies) for loudness; the fundamental frequency (F0) of the signal (measured in Hz), and some derived measures on F0 for pitch; and speaking rate, utterance and syllable lengths, empty and filled pauses for timing. The search for acoustic features that describe emotional states in speech is performed through long-term or supra-segmental measurements since emotions are expected to last more than single speech segments and therefore, sophisticated acoustic measurements have been proposed to detect vocal expressions of emotions. Apart from F0 frequency [45, 56], these measurements include the spectral tilting [45], the vocal envelope [71] - defined as the time interval for a signal to reach the maximum amplitude and decay to zero amplitude - the Long Term Average Spectrum (LTAS), the energy in different frequency bands, some inverse filtering measurements [47, 57], the F0 contour, the F0 maximum and minimum excursion, and the F0 jitter - random fluctuations on F0 values [2, 28, 63]. Exploiting this research line, the cited authors identified some acoustic correlates of vocal expressions for some primary emotions (see [63, 67]). However, these studies have shown that the perceptual and acoustic cues to infer emotional states from speech may be complex as much as using physiological variables and facial expressions, and that the acoustic and temporal features that can be used to unequivocally describe emotions have not yet been identified because of the many sources of variability associated with the speech signal.

## 2.3  The Gestural Expressions of Emotions

Gesturing is what people unconsciously do when approaching each other and understanding gestures is crucial to understand social interactions. The Oxford Dictionary of English defines a gesture as "a movement of the body, or any part of it, that is considered as expressive of thought or feeling". This definition incorporates a very large set of body expressions and movements among these facial expressions but also face directions, hand movements, eye contact, posture, proxemics (study on varying patterns of physical proximity), touch, dressing, and so on. Therefore, excluding facial expressions, there is a lot that has been neglected about emotional gestures. Three fundamental questions remain uncovered in this field:

- ❖ What can gestures tell about human emotions?
- ❖ Which gestures are exhibited for a particular emotion?
- ❖ Do humans make use of such non verbal cues to infer a person's emotional state and how?

At present there is limited knowledge about the extent to which body movements and gestures provide reliable cues to emotional states even though several authors have suggested that the use of body motion in interaction is part of the social system and therefore body movements not only have potential meaning in communicative contexts but can also affect the interlocutor's behavior [3, 7, 9-10, 14, 36, 46, 52-55]. However, these studies were often concerned with gestures (in particular hand gestures) used jointly with verbal communication and therefore showing intimate relationships between the speaker's speech and actions and the listener's non-verbal behaviors [36, 46, 52]. These gestures may have nothing to do with emotions since according to Ekman and Friesen [20, 25-27] affective displays are independent from language. However, there is subjective evidence that variations in body movements (e.g. gait, body posture) and gestures (e.g. hand position) convey important information about people's emotions. To this aim, the author performed an informal perceptual experiment showing to about 50 people participating at a conference (Workshop on Nonlinear Speech Processing held in Crete, Greece, September 2005) two silent cartoon characters. One of them displayed a rapid body movement one step back, the other a rapid open hand movement that covered first the eyes and then the face. All the participants attributed to the characters an emotional state of fear and worry respectively, suggesting that they were able to use gestural information to infer emotional states.

At the date, relationships between bodily activity and emotional communicative functions remain a research field to be investigated even though several authors [2, 9-10, 14, 44, 54-55, 65] have drawn attention to the existence of relationships between body posture, head movements, hand gestures (in particular those named *adapters* by [27]) and emotions.

## 3  The Proposed Research Work

Two procedures have been employed to study emotional states:

- ❖ **The coding** procedure that investigates emotional features eliciting emotional states through actor portrayals, induction or clandestine recordings of naturally occurring emotions;
- ❖ **The decoding** procedure that evaluates the listeners' ability to recognize emotional states from speech, gestures and gaze expressions.

Whatever was the exploited procedure, emotions and the related perceptual cues to infer them, have always been investigated, to our knowledge, considering separately the three expressive domains discussed above, even though, some studies have suggested that one of them could be preferential with respect to the others. In particular, some studies sustain that facial expressions are more informative than gestures and vocal expressions [21, 23, 37, 39], whereas others suggest that vocal expressions are more faithful than facial expressions in expressing emotional states since physiological processes, such as respiration and muscle tension, are naturally influenced by emotional responses [4, 11, 66-69]. It should also be noted that while the power of the vocal expressions in expressing emotional states has been tested dynamically along the time dimension because speech is intrinsically a dynamic process, for the facial expressions, a long established tradition attempts to define the facial expression of emotion in terms of qualitative targets - i.e. static positions capable of being displayed in a still photograph. The still image usually captures the apex of the expression, i.e. the instant at which the indicators of emotion are most marked. However, in the daily experience, also emotional states are intrinsically dynamic processes and associated facial expressions are varying along time. Is dynamic visual information still emotionally richer than auditory information? To our knowledge, at the date, there are no data in literature that attempt to answer this question.

At the light of the above considerations, our research proposal is to use the decoding procedure to try to answer the following questions:

- ❖ Which of the two domains is most expressive of emotional states?
- ❖ Does the perception of the speaker's emotional state require both vocal and visual information or is emotional information "redundantly" transmitted both by the visual and the auditory channel?

❖ Is there any preferential channel and can it be culturally specific?

❖ Could a channel be preferential for an emotional state with respect to another in a given culture?

❖ Which channel is preferential for a foreign culture?

Answering these questions will allow to identify emotional features of some basic emotions through a cross-modal evaluation of the visual and auditory channel. The final goal is to identify which modality should be considerably enhanced (reducing computational costs) in the development of embodied conversational agents, i.e. computer interfaces represented by lifelike human or animal characters capable of performing believable actions and naturally reacting to human users.

To answer the above questions we set up a series of perceptual experiments that evaluated the subjective perception of emotional states in the single (either visual or auditory channel) and the combined channels (visual and auditory). We exploited video clips extracted from movies (in our case, Italian movies). This choice allowed to overcome two critiques generally moved to perceptual studies of the kind proposed: 1) the use of video clips avoided the stillness of the pictures in the evaluation of the emotional visual information; 2) even though the emotions expressed in the video clips were still simulations under studio conditions (and may not have reproduced a genuine emotion but an idealization of it) they were able to catch up and engage the emotional feeling of the spectators and therefore we were quite confident of their perceptual emotional contents.

## 3.1 Materials

The collected data are based on extracts from Italian movies whose protagonists were carefully chosen among actors and actresses that are largely acknowledged by the critique and considered capable of giving some very real and careful interpretations. The final database consists of audio and video stimuli representing 6 basic emotional states: *happiness, sarcasm/irony, fear, anger, surprise,* and *sadness*. We introduced sarcasm/irony to substitute the emotional state of disgust, since after one year of movie analysis only 1 video clip was identified for this emotion.

For each of the above listed emotional states, 10 stimuli were identified, 5 expressed by an actor and 5 expressed by an actress, for a total of 60 audio and video stimuli. The actors and actresses were different for each of the 5 stimuli to avoid bias in their ability to portray emotional states. The stimuli were selected short in duration (the average stimulus' length was 3.5s, SD = ± 1s). This was due to two reasons: 1) longer stimuli may produce overlapping of emotional states and confuse the subject's perception; 2) emotional states for definition cannot last more than a few seconds and then other emotional states or moods take place in the interaction [58]. Consequently, longer stimuli do not increase the recognition reliability and in some cases they can create confusion making the identification of emotions difficult, since in a 20 seconds long video clip, the protagonist may be able to express more than one and sometimes very complex emotions.

Care was taken in choosing video clips where the protagonist's face and the upper part of the body were clearly visible. Care was also taken in choosing the stimuli such that the semantic meaning of the sentences expressed by the protagonists was not clearly expressing the portrayed emotional state and its intensity level was moderate.

For example we avoided to include in the data, sadness stimuli were the actress/actor were clearly crying or happiness stimuli where the protagonist was strongly laughing. This was because we wanted the subjects to exploit emotional signs that could be less obvious but that were generally employed in every natural and not extreme emotional interaction. From each complete stimulus - audio and video - we extracted the audio and the video alone coming up with a total of 180 stimuli (60 stimuli only audio, 60 only video, and 60 audio and video).

The emotional labels assigned to the stimuli were given first by two expert judges and then by three naïve judges independently. The expert judges made a decision on the stimuli carefully exploiting emotional information on facial and vocal expressions described in the literature [4, 20-21, 25-26, 42-43, 66-68] and also knowing the contextual situation the protagonist is interpreting. The naïve judges made their decision after watching the stimuli several times. There were no opinion exchanges between the experts and naïve judges however, the final agreement on the labelling between the two groups was 100%. The stimuli in each set were then randomized and proposed to the subjects participating at the experiments.

## 3.2  Participants

A total of 90 subjects participated at the perceptual experiments: 30 were involved in the evaluation of the audio stimuli, 30 in the evaluation of the video stimuli, and 30 in the evaluation of the video and audio stimuli. The assignment of the subjects to the task was randomly. Subjects were required to carefully listen and/or watch the experimental stimuli via headphones in a quite room. They were instructed to pay attention to each presentation and decide as quickly as possible at the end, which of the 6 emotional states was expressed in it.  Responses were recorded on a matrix paper form (60x8) where the rows listed the stimuli's numbers and the columns the 6 possible emotional states plus an option for any other emotion not listed in the form, plus the option that they recognized a *neutral* state in the presentation. Each emotional label given by the participants as an alternative to one of the six listed emotions was included in the emotional classes listed above only if criteria of synonymity and/or analogy were satisfied otherwise it was included in a class labelled "*others*".

For each emotional stimulus, we computed the frequency response distribution among the 8 emotional classes under examination (*happiness, sarcasm/irony, fear, anger, surprise, sadness, others,* and *neutral*) and the percentage of correct recognition.

## 3.3  Results

Table 1 reports the confusion matrix for the audio and video condition. The numbers are percentages computed over the number of the subject's correct answers to each stimulus and averaged over the number of the expected correct answers for each emotional state.

The data displayed in Table 1 show that, in the audio and video condition, the higher percentage of correct answers - 75% - was for **sadness** (in 14% of the cases confused with the *irony*), followed by 64% of correct answers for **irony** (in 12% of the cases confused with *surprise*). **Anger** reached 60% (confusion was made for 11%

**Table 1.** Confusion matrix for the audio and video condition. The numbers are percentages computed considering the number of subject's correct answers over the total number of expected correct answers (300) for each emotional state.

| Audio and Video | Sad | Ironic | Happy | Fear | Anger | Surprise | Others | Neutral |
|---|---|---|---|---|---|---|---|---|
| Sad | **75** | 14 | 0 | 2 | 2 | 0 | 4 | 3 |
| Ironic | 2 | **64** | 5 | 3 | 7 | 12 | 3 | 4 |
| Happy | 1 | 29 | **50** | 3 | 0 | 11 | 0 | 6 |
| Fear | 19 | 2 | 2 | **48** | 4 | 15 | 7 | 3 |
| Anger | 5 | 10 | 1 | 11 | **60** | 0 | 8 | 5 |
| Surprise | 0 | 8 | 5 | 14 | 2 | **59** | 0 | 12 |

**Table 2.** Confusion matrix for the video condition. The numbers are percentages computed considering the number of subject's correct answers over the total number of expected correct answers (300) for each emotional state.

| Video | Sad | Ironic | Happy | Fear | Anger | Surprise | Others | Neutral |
|---|---|---|---|---|---|---|---|---|
| Sad | **49** | 9 | 6 | 9 | 3 | 4 | 7 | 13 |
| Ironic | 8 | **49** | 10 | 2 | 5 | 4 | 8 | 14 |
| Happy | 1 | 24 | **61** | 3 | 1 | 4 | 2 | 4 |
| Fear | 5 | 2 | 3 | **59** | 14 | 8 | 6 | 3 |
| Anger | 3 | 6 | 1 | 9 | **68** | 4 | 3 | 6 |
| Surprise | 4 | 7 | 6 | 11 | 13 | **37** | 4 | 18 |

of the cases with *fear*, and 10% with *irony*), and **surprise** 59% of correct answers (confusion was made for 14% of the cases with *fear*, and 12% with a *neutral* expression). In all cases the percentage of correct recognition was largely above the chance. Surprisingly, **happiness** and **fear** were not very well recognized. **Happiness** had 50% of correct answers but was significantly confused with *irony* in almost 30% of the cases and partially confused with *surprise* in 11% of the cases. The percentage of correct answers for **fear** was 48% and it was confused with *sadness* and *surprise* by almost 20% and 15% of the cases respectively.

Table 2 reports the confusion matrix for the video condition. The numbers are percentages computed over the number of the subject's correct answers to each stimulus and averaged over the number of the expected correct answers for each emotional state.

The data displayed in Table 2 show that, in the video condition, the higher percentage of correct answers - 68% - was for **anger** (the higher confusion, 9%, was with *fear*), followed by 61% of correct answers for **happiness** (significantly confused - 24% - with *irony*). **Fear** reached 59% of correct answers (confusion was made in 14% of the cases with *anger*). **Sadness** and **irony** obtained both the 49% of correct answers. The highest confusion was on *neutral* expressions that had 13% and 14% for sadness and irony respectively. **Surprise** was not well recognized getting only 37% of correct answers. The higher confusion was spread out among *anger* -13%- *fear* -11%- and *neutral* -18%.

**Table 3.** Confusion matrix for the audio condition. The numbers are percentages computed considering the number of subject's correct answers over the total number of expected correct answers (300) for each emotional state.

| Audio | Sad | Ironic | Happy | Fear | Anger | Surprise | Others | Neutral |
|---|---|---|---|---|---|---|---|---|
| Sad | 67 | 7 | 0 | 7 | 1 | 1 | 4 | 13 |
| Ironic | 9 | 75 | 7 | 2 | 2 | 4 | 0 | 1 |
| Happy | 5 | 25 | 48 | 8 | 1 | 5 | 1 | 7 |
| Fear | 12 | 3 | 6 | 63 | 6 | 5 | 2 | 3 |
| Anger | 2 | 9 | 0 | 10 | 77 | 0 | 1 | 1 |
| Surprise | 5 | 21 | 3 | 19 | 4 | 37 | 2 | 9 |

Table 3 reports the confusion matrix for the audio condition. Again, the numbers are percentages computed over the number of the subject's correct answers to each stimulus and averaged over the number of the expected correct answers for each emotional state.

The data displayed in Table 3 show that, in the audio condition, the higher percentage of correct answers - 77% - was for **anger** (the higher confusion, 10%, was with *fear*), followed by 75% of correct answers for **irony** (confused in 9% of the cases with *sadness*). **Sadness** obtained 67% of correct answers and in 13% of the cases was confused with a neutral expression. **Fear** got 63% (confusion was made in 12% of the cases with *sadness*), and **happiness** reached 48% of correct answers. Happiness was significantly confused with irony in 25% of the cases. **Surprise** was not well recognized also in the audio condition getting only 37% of correct answers. It was significantly confused with *irony* and *fear* in 21% and 19% of the cases respectively.

The emotional state better identified in all of the three conditions was anger (60% in the audio and video, 68% in the video, and 77% in the audio). Sadness and irony were easily recognized in the audio and video (75% and 64% respectively) and in the audio (67% and 75% respectively) conditions but hardly recognized in the video alone (49% and 49 % respectively).

Happiness was better identified in the video alone (61%) than in the audio (48%) and in the audio and video (50%) condition. Fear was better perceived in the audio (63%) and video (59%) than in the audio and video condition (49%), whereas, surprise was more easily identified in the audio and video (59%) than in the audio (37%) and video (37%) alone.

A comparative display of the data discussed in Tables 1, 2, and 3 is reported in Figure 2. Figure 2 shows the number of correct answers for each emotional state (sadness in Figure 2a., irony in Figure 2b., happiness in Figure 2c., fear in Figure 2d., anger in Figure 2e., and surprise in Figure 2f.) and for the audio, video and audio and video conditions. On the x-axis are reported the emotional labels and on the y-axis is reported the number of correct answers obtained for each emotional state.

An ANOVA analysis was performed on the above data considering the *condition* (audio alone, video alone, and audio and video) as a between subject variable and the *emotional state* as a six level (a level for each emotional state) within subject variable. The statistic showed that *condition* plays a significant role for the perception of emotional states ($F(2, 12) = 7.701$, $\rho=.007$) and this did not depend on the different

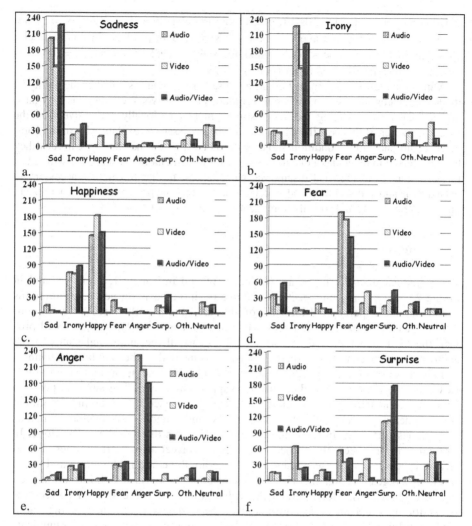

**Fig. 2.** Histograms of the number of correct answers given by the subjects participating to the perceptual experiments for the six emotional states under examination and the three different perceptual conditions (gray for audio, white for video, and black for audio and video – color would be different in a color version of the paper)

emotional states ($F(5, 60) = .938$, $\rho=.46$) since no interaction was found between the two variables ($F(10, 60) = 1.761$, $\rho=.08$). Moreover, female stimuli were more affected ($F(2, 12) = 4.951$, $\rho=.02$) than male stimuli ($F(2, 12) = 1.141$, $\rho=.35$) by condition, even though gender was not significant ($F(1, 12) = .001$, $\rho=.98$) and no interaction was found between condition and gender ($F(2, 12) = .302$, $\rho=.74$). In the details, we found that there was not a significant difference in the perception of the emotional states for the audio alone and the audio and video condition ($F(1, 8) = .004$, $\rho=.95$). Significant differences were found between the video alone and the audio and video condition (F(1, 8) = 10.414, ρ=.01) in particular for sadness (F(1, 8) = 5.548, ρ=.04), and the video and audio alone (F(1, 8) = 13.858, ρ=.005). In this particular case, significant differences were found for sadness (F(1,8) = 8.941, ρ=.01), fear (F(1,8) = 7.342, ρ=.02), and anger (F(1,8) = 9.737, ρ=.01).

A methodological concern that could be raised at this point is whether the ability of the actors and/or actresses in expressing emotions through vocal expressions may have affected the results making the audio stimuli more emotionally expressive than the video. However, if this was the case, it would be necessary to explain why in the combined audio and video condition subjects did not exploited the same vocal cues they have perceived in the audio alone to infer the protagonist emotional state. We will return to this argument in the final discussion. Nonetheless, further research is necessary to evaluate the above possibility, and to determine whether the present results generalize to other geographically and socially homogeneous groups of subjects.

## 4 Discussion

The statistical data discussed above and displayed in Tables 1, 2, and 3, and in Figure 2 show a really unexpected trend and posit the basis for new interpretations of the amount of perceptual information that are caught in the three different conditions. According to common sense it should be expected that subjects will provide the highest percentage of correct answers to all the emotional states in the audio and video condition, since it can be assumed that the combined channels contain more or otherwise redundant information than the audio and video alone. However, the experimental data did not support this trend. The subjects perform similarly, or at least, there is not a significant difference in perceiving emotional states either exploiting only the audio or the audio and video together, whereas they are less effective in recognizing emotional states through the video alone. In particular, in the video alone, the percentage of correct answers for sadness is significantly lower than those obtained in the audio alone and in the audio and video together, suggesting that the visual channel alone conveys less information's on sad perceptual cues. Moreover, in the video alone, the percentage of correct answers for fear and anger is significantly lower than that obtained in the audio alone, attributing to the visual channel also a minor effectiveness in communicating perceptual cues related to these two emotional states. Furthermore, there is not a significant difference between the audio alone and the audio and video together on the subject's perception of the emotional states under consideration. Therefore, it appears that the vocal and the visual communication modes convey a different amount of information about the speaker's emotional state. The vocal or audio channel can be considered as preferential since it conveys the same information as the combined audio and video channels. In some cases it also seems to be able to resolve ambiguities produced by combining information derived from both the channels. For example, for anger, we had a stimulus that was correctly identified by 18 subjects in the audio alone, whereas it was confused with fear by almost all the subjects in the audio and video condition. Even though in a non statistically significant manner, audio beats audio and video for anger, irony and fear, whereas happiness appears to be more effectively transmitted by the video alone than the audio and the audio and video together. Surprise seems to be the only emotional state that to be clearly perceived requires information from both the audio and video channels. We can conclude that the audio channel is preferential for most of the emotional states under examination and that, the combined audio and visual stimuli do not help in improving the perception of emotional states, as it was expected.

## 4.1  The Proposed Explanation

These results first of all suggest a nonlinear processing of emotional cues. In perceiving emotions, expressive information is not added (this is true even in the case of surprise, since the percentage of correct answers in the combined audio and video channels is not the sum of those obtained in the audio and video alone) over the amount of emotional cues provided. Instead, as the number of emotional cues increase (assuming that when combining together the video and the audio, it must increase) the subject's cognitive load increases since she/he should concurrently elaborate gestures, facial and vocal expressions, dynamic information (due to the fact that the video and audio information evolved along the time), and the semantic of the message. These concurrent elaborations deviate the subject's attention from the perceived emotion bringing to a perception that may go beyond the required task since subjects are more inclined to attempt to identify the contextual situation of the protagonist (and the identification of the contextual situation may be harder than the identification of the emotional state due to shortness of the stimuli) than the expressed emotional state. This could be seen from the number of alternative labels given in each task. The fewer contextual cues they have, the fewer alternative labels are given. In fact, in the audio, the total number of alternative labels was 13, against the 64 of the video and the 49 of the video and audio together.

The explanation provided above is not in disaccord with reported data [12-13, 21, 25-26, 37, 39, 42-43, 72-74] demonstrating that facial expressions are more powerful than vocal expressions in eliciting emotional states, since these data are based on still photographs. As we already said in a previous section, still images usually capture the apex of the expression, i.e. the instant at which the indicators of emotions are mostly marked. In this case, the subject's cognitive load is reduced since only static and highly marked emotional information must be processed. These highly marked emotional indicators reproduced in the photos are like emblems universally shared because of the possible existence of an innate motor program [12-13, 72-74] that controls our facial musculature and changes our faces when we are emotionally involved. And their meaning is also universally shared explaining why we make faces also when we are not emotionally but contextually involved in emotional situations.

When dynamic is involved, audio is better. This is because audio is intrinsically dynamic and we are used to processing it dynamically. Moreover, listeners are used to dynamically vocal emotional cues. Therefore, the cognitive load is just reduced and they perform better. Moreover, we must here add a further speculation. Our idea is that audio is better for native speakers of the language, since natives rely on paralinguistic and suprasemental information that is strictly related and unique to their own language. They learned this information by themselves when they were emotionally involved and observed the changes in their vocal expressions. They may have learned how a given word is produced in a particular emotional state, even though the word is not semantically related to the emotional state. Consequently, they may be able to capture very small supra-segmental and paralinguistic cues that are not noticeable to a non native speaker. This is not to say that vocal expressions of emotions are learned. We are not making this point since we do not have data on that. The uncontrolled changes in the vocal motor program when we are emotionally involved may be innate as those in our facial musculature. However, changes in intonation and other paralinguistic information that derive from changes in the vocal motor control may have been learned together with the language. Hence, native speakers may be able to catch up more emotional information in the audio than in the video when the emotions are expressed in their own language. Nonetheless, they may rely more on visual rather than vocal information when they are requested to catch up emotional states in a foreign language. This is because visual cues may share more commonalities being more universal than vocal cues since the visual processing of inputs from the outside world exploits neural processes common to all human beings whereas, languages require a specific expertise or training to be processed.

At the light of the above considerations, we may expect that using a foreign language, we will find that the percentage of correct answers will not vary significantly between the video alone and the combined audio and video channels and that significant differences will be reported for the audio alone. We are actually testing this hypothesis (and we have already some preliminary results) through a set of perceptual experiments similar to those reported above, with the differences that in this case the protagonists of our clips speak a foreign language and therefore in the audio alone condition the participants cannot rely on their language expertise. To this aim, we checked that the subjects participating at the experiments did not know the language.

Dynamicity and language expertise is also able to explain why subjects performed poorer in the audio and video alone than in the combined channels for surprise. Surprise is an almost instantaneous state, is like a still image. The short duration of this emotional state allow the listener to exploit both the visual and auditory information without increasing the cognitive load and avoid to diverge her/his attention from the perceived emotion.

The discussion on the language expertise however, rises a more fundamental question on how much of the expressions of emotions are universally shared. Data reported in literature support a universal interpretation of emotional facial expressions [12-13, 21-23, 39, 72-74] but these data were based, as we already pointed out, on still images. In our case the question is how much of the dynamic features of emotional faces are universal? We have already speculated that the perception of emotional vocal expressions can strictly depend on the language expertise and that, in such a case, visual cues are more universally recognized than vocal cues. However, we have not considered that dynamic emotional visual stimuli can also be culture specific. This means that we may expect subjects to perform better on culturally close visual emotional cues than on culturally distant ones. The above proposed experiments could be able to answer also to this question, and quantify how much dynamical emotional information we are able to capture in a foreign face-to-face interaction. They should also be able to identify how much is universally and how much is culture specific in the expressions of emotions.

## 4.2 A Mathematical Model Fitting the Experimental Data

The above results are also interesting from an information processing point of view. Information processing theory is a research branch of communication theory that attempts to quantify how well signals encode meaningful information and how well systems process the received information. In this context, *entropy* is defined as a measure of "self-information" or "uncertainty" transmitted by a given signal source as it can be considered in our case, both the audio and video channels. Mathematically the entropy is described by the equation:

$$H(X) = -\sum_{n=1}^{N} p(X_n) \log p(X_n) \tag{1}$$

Where $X_n$, $n=1, ..., N$ are the symbols that can be emitted by the source and $p(X_n)$ the probability for a given symbol to be emitted. In the Shannon view, the entropy is a measure of the complexity or the information contained in the set of symbols and its value is highly affected by the symbol's probability distribution. The entropy model can be extended to more than one source defining what is called the *joint entropy*, which, for two sources is mathematically described by the equation:

$$H(X,Y) = -\sum_{n=1}^{N}\sum_{m=1}^{M} p(X_n, Y_m) \log p(X_n, Y_m) \tag{2}$$

Where $X_n$, $n=1, ..., N$, and $Y_m$, $m=1, ..., M$ are the symbols that can be emitted by the sources $X$ and $Y$, and $p(X_n, Y_m)$ the joint probability distribution.

Theoretically, it can be proved that the joint entropy of two different sources is greater than that of a single source, and therefore, it can be expected that increasing the number of sources the amount of information transmitted over a communication channel will consequently increases [75]. The theoretical definition of entropy does not take into account the informative value of the source, i.e. the meaning the signal can convey and what the receiver assumes to be informative about the received signal. Consequently, entropy measure does not consider cases where the source can be only noise, and/or cases where extraneous information can be exploited by the receiver. In our context entropy cannot be considered an objective measure of the information transmitted by the audio and video channels. A more adequate measure could be the mutual information that takes into account the effects of the transmission channel on the received signal. Mutual information is a measure of the dependence between the source and/or the receiver and it produces a reduction of the "uncertainty" or the amount of information transmitted by the source. Mutual information is mathematically expressed by the equation:

$$I(X,Z) = -\sum_{n=1}^{N}\sum_{k=1}^{K} p(X_n, Z_k) \log \frac{p(X_n, Z_k)}{p(X_n)p(Z_k)} \tag{3}$$

Mutual information could be an appropriate mathematical model to describe our results, since being always less greater or equal to the entropy of the source it can explain why by combining audio and video channels the information about the emotional states does not increases. However, mutual information requires a complete knowledge on how the receiver filters (or transforms) the information emitted by the source. In our case this information is completely unknown, since we do not have at the date a clear idea on how our brain process information received by visual and auditory channels. Moreover, mutual information cannot explain our hypothesized differences in perception between native and non native speakers and between close and distant cultural backgrounds.

A more adequate model could be the *information transfer ratio* proposed by Sinanović and Johnson [76] that quantifies how the receiver affects the received information by measuring the distance between (the probability distributions of) the actions performed by the receiver for given received inputs and (the probability distributions of) the received inputs. Assuming that emotional information encoded through the audio and the video represents the input to a processing system, the information transfer ratio value can be quantified as the ratio of the distances between the information transmitted by the sources and the distances between the outputs (for those sources) of the processing system. Information transfer ratio is described by the following equation:

$$\gamma_{XY,Z}(\alpha_0,\alpha_1) \equiv \frac{d_Z(\alpha_0,\alpha_1)}{d_X(\alpha_0,\alpha_1)} + \frac{d_Z(\alpha_0,\alpha_1)}{d_Y(\alpha_0,\alpha_1)} \tag{4}$$

Where $\alpha_1$ indicates the changes in the emotional contents of the sources with respect to a reference point $\alpha_0$, which depends not on the signals itself but on their probability functions $p_X(x; \alpha_0)$, $p_X(x; \alpha_1)$, $p_Y(y; \alpha_0)$, $p_Y(y; \alpha_1)$, and $p_Z(z; \alpha_0)$, $p_Z(z; \alpha_1)$. $X$ and $Y$ are the sources (audio and video), $Z$ the processing systems, and $d(...)$ indicate an information theoretic distance (for example, the Kullback-Leibler distance [1]) that obeys to the Data Processing Theorem [35], which roughly states that the output of any processing system cannot contain more information than the processed signal.

The information transfer ratio quantifies the ability of the receiver to process the received information and predicts in the case of multiple sources that the overall information transfer ratio may be smaller than the individual ratios for each input signal. This is due to the arbitrary filtering action performed by the receiver (the human being) whose transfer function is in our case unknown, even though its ability to catch emotional information can be derived by the number of the subject's correct answers. In simple words, in the complex world of emotion's perception the whole, in some cases, seems not to be more than the sum of its parts.

## 5  Conclusions

The present paper reports on perceptual data showing that native speakers rely more on the auditory than on the visual channel to infer information on emotional states, and that the amount of emotional information conveyed does not increases combining auditory and visual information. An attempt is made to explain this phenomenon in terms of the subject's cognitive load and information processing theory.

# Acknowledgements

This research has been partially supported by the project *i-LEARN: IT's Enabled Intelligent and Ubiquitous Access to Educational Opportunities for Blind Student,* at Wright State University, Dayton, Ohio, USA. Acknowledgment goes to Tina Marcella Nappi for her editorial help. Acknowledgement also goes to Professors Maria Marinaro and Olimpia Matarazzo for their useful comments and suggestions. In particular, Olimpia has greatly helped in the selection of stimuli. The students Gianluca Baldi, Eliana La Francesca, and Daniela Meluccio are greatly acknowledged for running the perceptual tests.

# References

1. Ali, S.M., Silvey, S.D.: A general class of coefficients of divergence of one distribution from another. Journal of Royal Statistic Society, 28, 131-142 (1966)
2. Apple, W., Hecht, K.: Speaking emotionally: The relation between verbal and vocal communication of affect. Journal of Personality and Social Psychology, 42, 864–875 (1982)
3. Argyle, M.: Bodily Communication. New York: Methuen & Co (1988)
4. Banse, R., Scherer, K.: Acoustic profiles in vocal emotion expression. Journal of Personality & Social Psychology 70(3), 614-636 (1996)
5. Barnes, J.: Aristotele complete work. Revised Oxford translation in 2 volumes, Princeton University press (1984)
6. Bachorowski, J.A. (1999). Vocal expression and perception of emotion. Current Directions in Psychological Science, 8, 53–57.
7. Birdwhistell, R.: Kinesies and context. Philadelphia,  University of Pennsylvania Press (1970)
8. Breitenstein, C., Van Lancker, D., & Daum, I. The contribution of speech rate and pitch variation to the perception of vocal emotions in a German and an American sample. Cognition & Emotion, 15, 57–79 (2001)
9. Burgoon, J.K.: Nonverbal signals. In Knapp, J. L., Miller, G. R. (eds.). Handbook of interpersonal communication, Thousand Oaks, CA: Sage, 229-285 (1994)
10. Burleson, B.R.: Comforting messages: Features, functions, and outcomes. In Daly, J.A., Wiemann, J.M. (eds.), Strategic interpersonal communication, Hillsdale, NJ: Erlbaum, 135-161 (1994)
11. Burns, K. L., Beier, E. G.: Significance of vocal and visual channels in the decoding of emotional meaning. Journal of Communication, 23, 118–130 (1973)
12. Caccioppo, J. T., Klein, D. J: Bernston, G.C., Hatfield, E.: The psychophysiology of emotion. In Haviland, M., Lewis, J. M. (eds) Handbook of Emotion, New York: Guilford Press, 119-142 (1993)
13. Caccioppo, J. T., Bush, L.K., Tassinary, L.G.: Microexpressive facial actions as a functions of affective stimuli: Replication and extension. Personality and Social Psychology Bullettin, 18, 515-526 (1992)
14. Corraze, G.: Les communications nonverbales. Presses Universitaires de France, Paris (1980)
15. Cosmides, L.: Invariances in the acoustic expressions of emotions during speech..Journal of Experimental Psycology, Human Perception Performance, 9, 864-881 (1983)
16. Darwin, C.: The expression of the emotions in man and the animals (1872). Reproduced by the University of Chicago, Chicago press (1965)

17. Davitz, J. R.: Auditory correlates of vocal expression of emotional feeling. In Davitz J. R. (ed.), The communication of emotional meaning, New York: McGraw Hill, 101-112 (1964)
18. Davitz, J.: The communication of emotional meaning. McGraw-Hill (1964)
19. Davitz, J. R.: Auditory correlates of vocal expression of emotional feeling. In Davitz J. R. (ed.), The communication of emotional meaning, New York: McGraw Hill, 101-112 (1964)
20. Ekman, P., Friesen, W.V., Hager, J.C.: The facial action coding system. Second edition. Salt Lake City: Research Nexus eBook.London: Weidenfeld & Nicolson(2002)
21. Ekman, P. Facial expression of emotion: New findings, new questions. Psychological Science, 3, 34-38 (1992)
22. Ekman, P.: An argument for basic emotions. Cognition and Emotion, 6, 169-200 (1992)
23. Ekman, P.: The argument and evidence about universals in facial expressions of emotion. In H. Wagner, H., Manstead, A. (eds.). Handbook of social psychophysiology, Chichester: Wiley, 143-164 (1989)
24. Ekman, P.: Expression and the nature of emotion. In Scherer, K., Ekman, P. (eds), Approaches to emotion, Hillsdale, N.J.: Lawrence Erlbaum, 319-343 (1984)
25. Ekman, P. Friesen, W. V.: Facial action coding system: A technique for the measurement of facial movement. Palo Alto, Calif.: Consulting Psychologists Press (1978)
26. Ekman, P., Friesen, W.V.: Manual for the Facial Action Coding System, Palo Alto: Consulting Psychologists Press (1977)
27. Ekman, P., Friesen, W.V.: Head and body cues in the judgement of emotion: A reformulation. Perceptual Motor Skills 24: 711-724 (1967)
28. Frick, R.: Communicating emotions: the role of prosodic features. Psychological Bullettin, 93, 412-429 (1985)
29. Fridlund, A.J.: The new ethology of human facial expressions. In Russell J.A., Fernandez-Dols J. (eds.), The psychology of facial expression Cambridge: Cambridge University Press, 103-129 (1997).
30. Fridlund, A.J.: Human facial expressions: An evolutionary view. San Diego: CA Academic press (1994)
31. Friend, M.: Developmental changes in sensitivity to vocal paralanguage. Developmental Science, 3, 148–162 (2000)
32. Frijda, N.H.: Moods, emotion episodes, and emotions. In Haviland, M., Lewis, J. M. (eds) Handbook of Emotion, New York: Guilford Press, 381-402 (1993)
33. Frijda, N.H.: The emotions, Cambridge University press (1986)
34. Fulcher, J.A.: Vocal affect expression as an indicator of affective response. Behavior Research Methods, Instruments, & Computers, 23, 306–313 (1991)
35. Gallager, R.G.: Information theory and reliable communication. John Wiley & Son (1968)
36. Goldin-Meadow, S.: Hearing gesture: How our hands help us think. The Belknap Press at Harvard University Press (2003)
37. Graham, J., Ricci-Bitti, P.E., Argyle, M.: A cross-cultural study of the communication of emotion by facial and gestural cues. Journal of Human Movement Studies, 1, 68-77 (1975)
38. Haldane, E.L., Ross, G.R.: The philosophical work of Descartes. New York: Dover, current edition (1911)
39. Izard, C.E.: Innate and universal facial expressions: Evidence from developmental and cross-cultural research. Psychological Bulletin, 115, 288–299 (1994)
40. Izard, C.E.: Organizational and motivational functions of discrete emotions. In Lewis M., Haviland J. M (eds.), Handbook of emotions New York: Guilford Press, 631–641 (1993)

41. Izard, C.E.: Basic emotions, relations among emotions, and emotion–cognition relations. Psychological Review, 99, 561–565 (1992)
42. Izard, C.E., Dougherty, L.M., Hembree, E.A.: A system for identifying affect expressions by holistic judgments. Unpublished manuscript. Available from Instructional Resource Center, University of Delaware (1983)
43. Izard, C.E.: The maximally discriminative facial movement coding system (MAX). Unpublished manuscript. Available from Instructional Resource Center, University of Delaware (1979)
44. James W.: What is an Emotion? First published in Mind, 9, 188-205 (1884). See http://psychclassics.asu.edu/James/emotion.htm
45. Junqua, J.C.: The Lombard reflex and its role on human listeners and automatic speech recognizers. JASA, 93(1), 510-524 (1993)
46. Kendon, A.: Gesture : Visible action as utterance. Cambridge University Press (2004)
47. Klasmeyer, G., Sendlmeier W. F.: Objective voice parameters to characterize the emotional content in speech. In Proceedings of ICPhS 1995, Elenius, K., Branderudf, P. (eds), 1,182-185, Arne Strömbergs Grafiska (1995)
48. Klinerberg, O.: Emotional expression in chinese literature. Journal of Abnormal and Social Psychology, 33, 517-520 (1938)
49. Klinnert M.D., Campos J.J., Sorce J.F., Emde R.N., Svejda M.: Emotions as behaviour regulators: Social referencing in infancy. In Plutchik R,. Kellerman H.' (eds), Emotions,: Theory, research, and experience, 57-86, New York, Academic Press (1983)
50. La Barre, W.: The cultural basis of emotions and gestures. Journal of Personality, 16, 49-68 (1947)
51. Lumsden, C.J., Wilson E.O.: Genes mind and culture: The co-evolutionary process. Harvard University Press (1981)
52. McNeill, D.: Gesture and thought. Chicago: University of Chicago Press (2005)
53. Mehrabian, A.: Orientation behaviors and non verbal attitude communication. Journal of Communication, 17(4), 324-332 (1967)
54. Millar, F.E., Rogers, L.E.: A relational approach to interpersonal communication. In Miller, G.R. (ed.), Explorations in interpersonal communication Beverly Hills, CA: Sage, 87-105 (1976)
55. Miller: Explorations in interpersonal communication. London: Sage, (1976)
56. Mozziconacci, S.: Pitch variations and emotions in speech. In Proceedings of ICPhS 1995, Elenius, K., Branderudf, P. (eds), 1, 178-181, Arne Strömbergs Grafiska (1995)
57. Nushikyan, E. A.: Intonational universals in texual context. In Proceedings of ICPhS 1995, Elenius, K., Branderudf, P. (eds),1, 258-261, Arne Strömbergs Grafiska (1995)
58. Oatley, K., Jenkins, J. M.: Understanding emotions. Oxford, England: Blackwell (1996)
59. Panksepp, J.: Affective neuroscience: A conceptual framework for the neurobiological study of emotions. In Strongman K (ed.) International Review of Studies of Emotions, Chichester, England: Wiley, 1, 59-99 (1991)
60. Plato: The Republic. (375 BC). Harmondworth, Middlesex: Penguin, current edition (1955)
61. Plutchik, R.:Emotion and their vicissitudes: Emotions and Psychopathology. In Haviland, M., Lewis, J. M. (eds) Handbook of Emotion, New York: Guilford Press, 53-66 (1993)
62. Plutchik, R.: The emotions. Lanham, MD: University Press of America (1991)
63. Pittam, J., Scherer, K.R.: Vocal expression and communication of emotion. In Haviland, M., Lewis, J.M. (eds) Handbook of Emotion, New York: Guilford Press, 185-197 (1993)
64. Ricouer, P.: The voluntary and the involuntary. Translation of Kohak K. Original work 1950, Northwestern University Press (1966)

65. Rosenberg, B.G., Langer, J.: A study of postural-gestural communication. Journal of Personality and Social Psychology 2(4), 593-597 (1965)
66. Scherer, K: Vocal communication of emotion: A review of research paradigms. Speech Communication 40, 227-256 (2003)
67. Scherer, K.R., Banse, R., Wallbott, H.G.: Emotion inferences from vocal expression correlate across languages and cultures. Journal of Cross-Cultural Psychology, 32, 76–92 (2001)
68. Scherer, K.R., Banse, R., Wallbott, H.G., Goldbeck, T.: Vocal cues in emotion encoding and decoding. Motivation and Emotion, 15, 123–148 (1991)
69. Scherer, K.R: Vocal correlates of emotional arousal and affective disturbance. In Wagner, H., Manstead, A. (eds.) Handbook of social Psychophysiology New York: Wiley, 165–197 (1989)
70. Scherer, K.R.: Experiencing Emotion: A Cross-cultural Study, Cambridge University Press, Cambridge (1982)
71. Scherer, K.R., Oshinsky, J.S.: Cue utilization in emotion attribution from auditory stimuli. Motivation and Emotion, 1, 331–346 (1977)
72. Schwartz, G.E., Weinberger, D.A., Singer, J.A.: Cardiovascular differentiation of happiness, sadness, anger, and fear following imagery and exercise. Psychosomatic Medicine, 43, 343–364 (1981)
73. Schwartz, G.E., Ahern, G.L., Brown, S.: Lateralized facial muscle response to positive and negative emotional stimuli. Psychophysiology, 16, 561-571 (1979)
74. Schwartz, G.E., Fair, P.L., Salt, P., Mandel, M.R., Klerman, G.L.: Facial muscle patterning to affective imagery in depressed and non-depressed subjects. Science, 192, 489- 491 (1976)
75. Shannon, C.E., Weaver, W.: Mathematical Theory of Communication. US: University of Illinois Press (1949)
76. Sinanović, S., Johnson, D.H.: Toward a theory of information processing. Submitted to Signal Processing. http://www-ece.rice.edu/~dhj/cv.html#publications (2006)
77. Tomkins, S.S.: Affect, imagery, consciousness. The positive affects. New York: Springer, 1 (1962)
78. Tomkins, S.S.: Affect, imagery, consciousness. The negative affects. New York: Springer, 2 (1963)
79. Tomkins, S.S.: Affect theory. In Scherer, K.R., Ekman, P.(eds.), Approaches to emotion, Hillsdale, N.J.: Erlbaum, 163-196 (1984)
80. White, G.M.: Emotion inside out The anthropology of affect. In Haviland, M., Lewis, J. M. (eds) Handbook of Emotion, New York: Guilford Press, 29-40 (1993)

# Author Index

# Lecture Notes in Computer Science

For information about Vols. 1–4326

please contact your bookseller or Springer

Vol. 4373: K. Langendoen, T. Voigt (Eds.), Wireless Sensor Networks. XIII, 358 pages. 2007.

Vol. 4372: M. Kaufmann, D. Wagner (Eds.), Graph Drawing. XIV, 454 pages. 2007.

Vol. 4371: K. Inoue, K. Satoh, F. Toni (Eds.), Computational Logic in Multi-Agent Systems. X, 315 pages. 2007. (Sublibrary LNAI).

Vol. 4370: P.P Lévy, B. Le Grand, F. Poulet, M. Soto, L. Darago, L. Toubiana, J.-F. Vibert (Eds.), Pixelization Paradigm. XV, 279 pages. 2007.

Vol. 4369: M. Umeda, A. Wolf, O. Bartenstein, U. Geske, D. Seipel, O. Takata (Eds.), Declarative Programming for Knowledge Management. X, 229 pages. 2006. (Sublibrary LNAI).

Vol. 4368: T. Erlebach, C. Kaklamanis (Eds.), Approximation and Online Algorithms. X, 345 pages. 2007.

Vol. 4367: K. De Bosschere, D. Kaeli, P. Stenström, D. Whalley, T. Ungerer (Eds.), High Performance Embedded Architectures and Compilers. XI, 307 pages. 2007.

Vol. 4366: K. Tuyls, R. Westra, Y. Saeys, A. Nowé (Eds.), Knowledge Discovery and Emergent Complexity in Bioinformatics. IX, 183 pages. 2007. (Sublibrary LNBI).

Vol. 4364: T. Kühne (Ed.), Models in Software Engineering. XI, 332 pages. 2007.

Vol. 4362: J. van Leeuwen, G.F. Italiano, W. van der Hoek, C. Meinel, H. Sack, F. Plášil (Eds.), SOFSEM 2007: Theory and Practice of Computer Science. XXI, 937 pages. 2007.

Vol. 4361: H.J. Hoogeboom, G. Păun, G. Rozenberg, A. Salomaa (Eds.), Membrane Computing. IX, 555 pages. 2006.

Vol. 4360: W. Dubitzky, A. Schuster, P.M.A. Sloot, M. Schroeder, M. Romberg (Eds.), Distributed, High-Performance and Grid Computing in Computational Biology. X, 192 pages. 2007. (Sublibrary LNBI).

Vol. 4358: R. Vidal, A. Heyden, Y. Ma (Eds.), Dynamical Vision. IX, 329 pages. 2007.

Vol. 4357: L. Buttyán, V. Gligor, D. Westhoff (Eds.), Security and Privacy in Ad-Hoc and Sensor Networks. X, 193 pages. 2006.

Vol. 4355: J. Julliand, O. Kouchnarenko (Eds.), B 2007: Formal Specification and Development in B. XIII, 293 pages. 2006.

Vol. 4354: M. Hanus (Ed.), Practical Aspects of Declarative Languages. X, 335 pages. 2006.

Vol. 4353: T. Schwentick, D. Suciu (Eds.), Database Theory – ICDT 2007. XI, 419 pages. 2006.

Vol. 4352: T.-J. Cham, J. Cai, C. Dorai, D. Rajan, T.-S. Chua, L.-T. Chia (Eds.), Advances in Multimedia Modeling, Part II. XVIII, 743 pages. 2006.

Vol. 4351: T.-J. Cham, J. Cai, C. Dorai, D. Rajan, T.-S. Chua, L.-T. Chia (Eds.), Advances in Multimedia Modeling, Part I. XIX, 797 pages. 2006.

Vol. 4349: B. Cook, A. Podelski (Eds.), Verification, Model Checking, and Abstract Interpretation. XI, 395 pages. 2007.

Vol. 4348: S.T. Taft, R.A. Duff, R.L. Brukardt, E. Ploedereder, P. Leroy (Eds.), Ada 2005 Reference Manual. XXII, 765 pages. 2006.

Vol. 4347: J. Lopez (Ed.), Critical Information Infrastructures Security. X, 286 pages. 2006.

Vol. 4346: L. Brim, B. Haverkort, M. Leucker, J. van de Pol (Eds.), Formal Methods: Applications and Technology. X, 363 pages. 2007.

Vol. 4345: N. Maglaveras, I. Chouvarda, V. Koutkias, R. Brause (Eds.), Biological and Medical Data Analysis. XIII, 496 pages. 2006. (Sublibrary LNBI).

Vol. 4344: V. Gruhn, F. Oquendo (Eds.), Software Architecture. X, 245 pages. 2006.

Vol. 4342: H. de Swart, E. Orłowska, G. Schmidt, M. Roubens (Eds.), Theory and Applications of Relational Structures as Knowledge Instruments II. X, 373 pages. 2006. (Sublibrary LNAI).

Vol. 4341: P.Q. Nguyen (Ed.), Progress in Cryptology - VIETCRYPT 2006. XI, 385 pages. 2006.

Vol. 4340: R. Prodan, T. Fahringer, Grid Computing. XXIII, 317 pages. 2007.

Vol. 4339: E. Ayguadé, G. Baumgartner, J. Ramanujam, P. Sadayappan (Eds.), Languages and Compilers for Parallel Computing. XI, 476 pages. 2006.

Vol. 4338: P. Kalra, S. Peleg (Eds.), Computer Vision, Graphics and Image Processing. XV, 965 pages. 2006.

Vol. 4337: S. Arun-Kumar, N. Garg (Eds.), FSTTCS 2006: Foundations of Software Technology and Theoretical Computer Science. XIII, 430 pages. 2006.

Vol. 4336: V.R. Basili, D. Rombach, K. Schneider, B. Kitchenham, D. Pfahl, R.W. Selby, Empirical Software Engineering Issues. XVII, 193 pages. 2007.

Vol. 4335: S.A. Brueckner, S. Hassas, M. Jelasity, D. Yamins (Eds.), Engineering Self-Organising Systems. XII, 212 pages. 2007. (Sublibrary LNAI).

Vol. 4334: B. Beckert, R. Hähnle, P.H. Schmitt (Eds.), Verification of Object-Oriented Software. XXIX, 658 pages. 2007. (Sublibrary LNAI).

Vol. 4333: U. Reimer, D. Karagiannis (Eds.), Practical Aspects of Knowledge Management. XII, 338 pages. 2006. (Sublibrary LNAI).

Vol. 4332: A. Bagchi, V. Atluri (Eds.), Information Systems Security. XV, 382 pages. 2006.

Vol. 4331: G. Min, B. Di Martino, L.T. Yang, M. Guo, G. Ruenger (Eds.), Frontiers of High Performance Computing and Networking – ISPA 2006 Workshops. XXXVII, 1141 pages. 2006.

Vol. 4330: M. Guo, L.T. Yang, B. Di Martino, H.P. Zima, J. Dongarra, F. Tang (Eds.), Parallel and Distributed Processing and Applications. XVIII, 953 pages. 2006.

Vol. 4329: R. Barua, T. Lange (Eds.), Progress in Cryptology - INDOCRYPT 2006. X, 454 pages. 2006.

Vol. 4328: D. Penkler, M. Reitenspiess, F. Tam (Eds.), Service Availability. X, 289 pages. 2006.

Vol. 4327: M. Baldoni, U. Endriss (Eds.), Declarative Agent Languages and Technologies IV. VIII, 257 pages. 2006. (Sublibrary LNAI).